The New York Times

DESSERT
COOKBOOK

Also by Florence Fabricant

The New York Restaurant Cookbook
The Great Potato Book
Elizabeth Berry's Great Bean Book
Venetian Taste
New Home Cooking: Feeding Family, Feasting Friends
Florence Fabricant's Pleasures of the Table

Edited by Florence Fabricant

The New York Times Seafood Cookbook

The New York Times

DESSERT COOKBOOK

Edited by Florence Fabricant

ST. MARTIN'S PRESS

New York

www.stmartins.com

Design by Kathryn Parise

Photographs are courtesy of *The New York Times* and the following photographers:

Jim Wilson: Intense Chocolate Mousse Cake

Andrew Scrivani: Berries with Lemon Soufflé Topping, Quick Classic Berry Tart, Cardamom Ice Cream, Big Apple Pie, Mary Louise's Rice Pudding, Double Dip of Chocolate Pudding, Vanilla Cheesecake, Tropical Fruit Trifle, Chocolate Black Pepper Cake, Baked Chocolate Pudding for Two, Goat's Milk Ice Cream, Magie Noire, Warm Vanilla Cakes, Spicy Gingerbread, and Crêpes Belle Hélène

Chester Higgins, Jr.: Ricotta Tart

Tony Cenicola: Madeleines with Orange Confit and Honey, Mango Cheesecake, Lemon Coconut Cake, Vietnamese Coffee Tapioca Affogato with Condensed Milk Ice Cream, and Cherry Sauce

Jonathan Player: One-Pan Christmas Cake, Strawberry Pavlova, Blueberry Kuchen

David van Ackere: Strawberries with Pink Peppercorn Sauce and Hot Fudge Sauce

Annie Marie Musselman: Chocolate Caramel Mousse

Michelle V. Agins: Limoncello Babas with Lemon Cream

Paul O. Boisvert: Plum Crumble

Don Hogan Charles: Baked Butterscotch Pudding

Travis Bell: Ginger Buttermilk Pie

LIBRARY OF CONGRESS CATALOGING-IN-PUBLICATION DATA

The New York Times dessert cookbook / edited by Florence Fabricant.
    p. cm.
  ISBN-13: 978-0-312-34060-5
  ISBN-10: 0-312-34060-5
    1. Desserts. I. Fabricant, Florence.

TX773.N46 2006
641.8'6—dc22

2006043586

First Edition: October 2006

10   9   8   7   6   5   4   3   2   1

CONTENTS

INTRODUCTION

Instinctively, humans enjoy sweets. Our hunter-gatherer ancestors knew that what was sweet on the bush was probably safe to eat. And good to eat, besides.

Nothing has changed. The genetic sweet tooth prevails more than ever. A well-balanced meal, one that does not overdo the sweet flavors in the early courses, is rewarded with a dulcet finale.

At home all it might take is a cookie, a slice of cake, some fresh berries or a scoop of ice cream. In restaurants far more elaborate creations are paraded out to tempt the customer. And, increasingly, sophisticated home cooks are up to the challenge of the pastry chef's most dizzying follies. How else can one explain the sales of home blowtorches for sealing the surface of a crème brûlée?

Over the past few decades, the food pages of *The New York Times*, in the Living Section and then in the Dining Section, walked a tightrope between homestyle baking and dessert-making, and restaurant creations. Chocolate layer cake meets molten flourless chocolate cake. Apple pie beckons the cook who may also be tempted by an authentic French tarte Tatin. And though you can buy a pint of good vanilla ice cream, consider the pride of having churned it in your kitchen.

Exploring the food sections over the past ten years or so indicated several trends at work. First, despite some naysayers, old-fashioned home baking is alive and well. For some cooks, especially those who might be daunted by custard or pie crust, it remains a challenge, leading to the purchase of pastries to culminate a dinner that may otherwise have been a showcase for several courses of home cooking. And it happens in reverse, too. Chefs are tapping into their mother's upside-down cakes and cobblers and serving them with pride and giving new recognition to desserts that do not require teams of famous pastry chefs.

At the same time, there are other home cooks who might be capable of whipping up a layer cake with accomplished ease, but who welcome more challenging recipes, for soufflés, cream puffs and other elaborate confections presented with complicated garnishes, following recipes that come straight from the kitchens of chefs.

Recipes that fit both these categories have been assembled in this book. Indeed, the interest in restaurant desserts at home represents the most significant trend reflected here.

Important changes in the ingredients and equipment that have become available for home cooks during this time have improved home baking and dessert-making, and have made those restaurant-style confections possible.

Better-quality chocolate, cocoa, butter and flavoring ingredients like vanilla beans are widely sold, even in supermarkets. Though desserts are not a significant part of most Asian cuisines, ingredients like ginger, lemongrass, mango, green tea and sticky rice are giving new tastes to old desserts. Homely tapioca has even become trendy.

Gear that pastry chefs have long taken for granted like heavy-duty baking pans with or without convenient nonstick finishes, generous spatulas, sieves, efficient zesters, powerful standing mixers and rolls of parchment paper are also easy to find. Flexible silicone mats, molds and even basting brushes have simplified many baking jobs. Even the quality of home ice cream makers has improved, as the prices have dropped. And stainless steel wire whisks in assorted sizes now come with a choice of handles, including cushioned rubber. These improvements have made baking easier.

With them, some desserts come out of the oven and produce the proper "wow" effect around the table. But there are subtler successes to be had. Recipes in this book also suggest desserts made with delicious seasonal fruit that has been handled with care, simple crêpes given a buttery finish and a splash of liqueur, or a classic soufflé, always an impressive presentation, but one that is far sturdier than generally assumed, as you will see.

But unlike baking a potato or grilling a steak, preparing dessert often requires a certain degree of technical expertise and careful attention to the details of measuring and weighing, of texture and temperature. Once learned, they become second nature. The cake-baker automatically takes the butter out of the refrigerator so it can soften for proper creaming, chills the bowl and beaters for whipping cream and is careful how the chocolate has been stored. Specialized equipment may be necessary.

A degree of precision is frequently required. You cannot tweak a cake batter as you would a simmering stew. By and large, you cannot taste as you go and make adjustments. Once a cake is done, it is done. If it falls on the floor, you can Julia-Child it with a slather of good icing. But if the flavor and texture are wrong, best run out for ice cream.

For entertaining, the beauty of the dessert course is that most sweets can be prepared in advance, with minimal fuss just before serving. In restaurants, the pastry chefs routinely work in the morning, doing all the baking, ice-cream-making and other necessary preparation long before the dinner hour, leaving any last-minute assembly before serving to other chefs.

Your mother might have insisted that the dessert be eaten last. But a good cook knows to make the dessert first.

UNDERSTANDING DESSERT RECIPES

Though many of the tasks and techniques, like zesting citrus, dicing, pulsing in a food processor, sautéing and simmering, are techniques that apply to cooking in general, some specialized techniques are required, especially for baking. Melting chocolate, an especially fragile, heat-sensitive ingredient, is one. Creaming butter—that is, whipping soft butter with sugar to make the base of a cake—is another. Making pastry dough, rolling and shaping it, is one that sends many cooks to the nearest bakery.

Because dessert recipes do not offer much wiggle room, or opportunities for improvisation, once you have selected a recipe, it is essential to read it through, to make sure you have enough time to prepare it, since some require extra chilling or freezing before, during or after the actual preparation.

Once you have decided on a recipe, the best approach is to devote the necessary time to it. Other kitchen tasks are possible if ingredients have to chill or rest, or bake for more than a few minutes. But it pays to concentrate on the recipe at hand. Set out the equipment you need. Assemble all the ingredients, making sure they are the proper temperature.

Measuring for dessert recipes must often be very precise, especially if baking is involved. Baking often involves chemical and physical reactions, of leavenings with liquid, of sugar with heat, that the cook who sautés potatoes or roasts a leg of lamb never encounters. And the quantities of the ingredients can affect these reactions.

Though weighing ingredients is the most accurate measurement, and the one that is used by chefs, Americans measure by cups and spoonfuls. These recipes have been edited with that in mind.

The temperature of ingredients is often critical. Butter at room temperature for a cake or chilled for a pie crust are two common examples. If an ice cream or sorbet base is insufficiently chilled, the end result will not have a good consistency. Sometimes a thermometer is necessary to be sure that boiling sugar has reached the correct temperature so it will react properly with the other ingredients. Before starting your preparation, be sure your ingredients are warm or cold enough. Even the ambient temperature of the kitchen can make a difference in how easy it is to roll dough.

But dessert-making does share one requirement with cooking in general. The freshness and quality of your ingredients must not be compromised.

INGREDIENTS

As with cooking in general, the quality of the ingredients you use will affect the outcome. But for desserts, and especially in baking, which often involves chemical reactions, the ingredients should comply with the requirements of the recipe. Not all flours are alike, sugar can vary according to texture, chocolate comes in a range of sweetness and oil can rarely be substituted for butter since it affects the amount of liquid. Even the size of eggs is important.

With the particular ingredients, quality may not change the composition of a recipe but it will affect the flavor. Unblemished fruits in peak season are easy to understand. Nuts must also be fresh, so they do not have an off taste, flavorings like citrus juices must also be fresh, and even dry ingredients, like grains and flours, must not have languished too long in the pantry. The best chocolate will provide a depth of flavor that most run-of-the-mill supermarket brands cannot match. The Internet has made shopping easier.

SWEETENERS

Sweetness is the essence of most desserts. Some ingredients, like fruits, are naturally sweet. But added sweeteners are usually required. There are many types of sugar, the most common being white, refined, granulated sugar. Granulated is the default sugar, and only specified when the recipe contains other kinds of sugar as well. Superfine sugar has a finer texture and dissolves faster. Some cooks, notably Nigella Lawson, prefer it. Confectioners' sugar is sometimes called powdered sugar. It is treated with cornstarch to keep it from clumping. Still, it should be sifted through a fine sieve before using. Brown sugars come in several variations, the most usual being light, which is what more recipes require, and dark. Turbinado, muscovado and demerara are other types of brown sugars. Brown sugar is always measured by packing it into a cup or spoon. Anyone who bakes regularly should have confectioners' sugar and light brown sugar on hand. Keep brown sugar tightly sealed so it does not dry out and harden. I store mine in the vegetable drawer of the refrigerator. And when you buy it, give the box a squeeze to make sure it is soft.

Some recipes call for liquid sweeteners, including honey, light or dark corn syrup, maple syrup and molasses. When a recipe calls for maple syrup, always use pure maple syrup, not a blend. But it does not have to be Grade A. Grade B, sometimes called "cooking grade," actually has more flavor. It is a good idea to have honey in the pantry, and light corn syrup, which should be kept in the refrigerator to prevent it from spoiling. It is easiest to measure and pour liquid sweeteners from a cup or spoon that has been lightly greased.

Many recipes call for caramel, giving instructions for making it. Basically it involves melting sugar, usually mixed with some water, in a pan, then cooking it until the water evaporates and the melted sugar reaches a temperature of more than 300 degrees and turns amber. It is important to remove it from the heat as soon as it reaches the proper color because it can easily become too dark and turn acrid. Liquid caramel is extremely hot and must be handled with care. Never taste it. It will harden as it cools.

In some recipes other ingredients are added to the hot caramel, a step that must be done with care because the caramel is likely to spatter. Wear oven mitts to protect your hands and stand as far from the pan as you can when adding the other ingredients.

After you have used the caramel, you can easily wash your pot, pan spoon or other utensils by first soaking them in warm water.

There are also some milk caramels in a few recipes: *cajeta,* a Mexican caramel made with goat's milk, and *dulce de leche,* a South American caramel made with cow's milk. There is a recipe for *dulce de leche* on page 536, and both *dulce de leche* and *cajeta* are sold in jars in specialty food shops and online.

FATS

Most baking depends on some kind of fat. Butter is the most common, and most of the recipes in this book call for unsalted butter. American supermarket butters are usually 80 percent butterfat, the minimum by law. But for baking, and especially for pastry, it pays to look for European-style butters, which can range from 82 to 86 percent. The difference may not sound significant, but the lower moisture content can contribute to flakier pastry (see essay on page 135).

There are several ways to measure butter. In this book, the butter is given in ounces or tablespoons, and also sticks, which is how butter is packaged and sold. To me, cups of butter (a cup of butter is ½ pound or 2 sticks) is a meaningless measurement. Pay careful attention to the temperature of your butter. A quick way to soften butter is to whirl it in the food processor. Placing a stick of cold butter in a microwave oven for 15 seconds will also soften it, but watch it closely, because it must not melt.

Vegetable shortening, which should be kept refrigerated, is called for in some pastry, as is lard, an old-fashioned ingredient that is coming back into favor.

A few desserts in this book call for olive oil. Always use extra-virgin, even in a cake.

Fats also play a role in preparing baking pans to keep the finished product from sticking. Butter adds flavor, and butter, with a dusting of flour, is a common pan lining. Some cooks whose recipes have appeared in the *Times* specify cooking sprays, which may have a chemical flavor. Softened butter can be substituted, which is what I do. Avoid cooking sprays that contain flour because they tend to apply more unevenly than regular cooking sprays.

Some recipes call for oil for greasing a pan, but if there is butter in the cake, I'd grease the pan with it, not oil.

FLOURS AND GRAINS

Most of the baking in this cookbook is done with all-purpose flour. What differentiates various flours is the amount of protein in the grain: the harder the wheat, the more protein or structure in the flour. All-purpose flour is a blend of hard- and soft-wheat flours, making it, as its name suggests, good for most jobs, with a protein content of 10 to 11 percent. Cake flour is made from softer wheat, is about 9 percent protein, and will produce a more tender result. Bread flour, best used for yeast baking, but also used in one cake in this book (page 76) is harder, stronger and has a higher protein or gluten content than all-purpose flour, 12 to 13 percent. Whole wheat flour is also high in protein and has a stronger flavor.

The all-purpose flour you use should be unbleached unless a recipe calls for bleached flour, which has a slightly lower protein content than unbleached. And the cake flour should not be self-rising, unless specified. Some chefs use Wondra, which is granulated and has less gluten.

Cornmeal, which some recipes require, is best when stone-ground. Some recipes specify white or yellow. They are interchangeable, with color the only consideration.

Flours and grains should be kept in canisters with a tight seal.

EGGS

All the recipes in this book call for large eggs. Organic eggs are less likely to cause problems with salmonella when raw, a worthwhile tip for those who like to lick the batter bowl. For most baking jobs, eggs should be at room temperature. A quick method for warming ice-cold eggs is to put them, in the shell, in a bowl of warm water for 10 minutes. Eggs come to the market very fresh these days, so you can keep eggs in the refrigerator for a couple of weeks without fear of spoilage.

LEAVENINGS

Eggs are a common leavening, the whipped whites giving loft to a sponge cake, a meringue and a soufflé. Chemical leavenings are often used in cakes and cookies. Baking powder and baking soda are the usual ones and they react with liquid, heat and acid. Baking powder contains some baking soda, but does not require the amount of acidity that plain baking soda needs to do its work. Be sure your leavenings are fresh. Yeasts can be either dry, often instant, or the soft cake variety. Keep yeast refrigerated and use the kind that the recipe specifies. If you need to substitute, use half as much dry yeast as fresh.

CHOCOLATE

The variety of chocolates that have come on the market in recent years is astonishing. Home cooks can easily obtain brands that were once available only to chefs. And there is merit in trying to find these brands, even though they are more expensive, because they have smoother textures and richer, more complex flavors, even with the unsweetened kind. Many brands of chocolate are now sold with the percentage of cacao, or chocolate solids, in the mixture.

The recipes may call for unsweetened, which is usually 99 percent cacao, bittersweet and semisweet, which range from about 60 to 72 percent, and milk chocolate, usually less than 50 percent. White chocolate is not chocolate, but the best does contain cocoa butter.

For more about chocolate and cocoa, see the essays on pages 289 and 510.

OTHER FLAVORINGS

Though the recipes do not specify "fresh" lemon juice, it should be understood that flavorings are to be fresh. Similarly, any extracts should be pure. If whole vanilla beans are not available, pure vanilla extract can usually be substituted. You can assume that the scraped seeds from a whole split vanilla bean are the equivalent of a teaspoon of extract.

Spices, such as cinnamon, mace and ground ginger, should also be as fresh as possible for maximum flavor impact. Store spices in opaque containers to prevent damage from light. You can use ground nutmeg, but the freshly grated spice from whole nutmegs will be more intense.

A number of recipes call for spirits, like brandy, liqueurs, port and wine. It is not necessary to use the most expensive, but look for drinkable, good-quality examples. And when a particular spirit of liqueur is not something you might want to use very frequently, you can buy a small bottle just for the recipe.

The recipes from chefs often require particular kinds of salt, sea salt, for example. It is a good idea to use sea salt on an everyday basis, both fine and coarse, but for the most part, kosher salt will be acceptable in most of the recipes.

FRUITS AND VEGETABLES

As with savory cooking, seasonality is a primary consideration when deciding on a dessert that involves fruits and, in a few instances, vegetables like pumpkin or squash. Select ripe fresh fruits in good condition and, for best flavor, at seasonal peak. And also bear in mind that some, like pears and peaches, might need an extra day or two for ripening on your kitchen counter, so instead of last-minute shopping, plan ahead, or be prepared to substitute nectarines for peaches, for example, if they are in better condition. Some of the recipes call for particular types of apples, which may not be available in your market. As a rule of thumb, the best apples for cooking and baking are on the tart side, and fairly dry in texture. French chefs prefer Golden Delicious; Americans like Granny Smith and Cortland. For stone fruits like peaches and nectarines, always look for the freestone variety.

Try to buy fruits that are uniform in size so your dessert will have more eye appeal.

When buying dried and candied fruits, select those that appear to be in good condition, not overly dried out, and store them in airtight containers.

DAIRY PRODUCTS

Aside from butter and eggs, many dessert recipes require milk, cream, sour cream, yogurt, crème fraîche, buttermilk and some cheeses. Pay attention to the "sell by" dates when you buy these products.

Unless a recipe specifies whole milk, when milk is among the ingredients, you can use any type except skim. Most cream in dessert recipes is heavy cream, which now is invariably ultra-pasteurized. When ultra-pasteurization was first introduced, the cream did not whip as well as regular pasteurized cream, but now that is no longer a concern. Just be sure your cream is very cold when you take it out for whipping. Half-and-half has about 10 percent butterfat, or around a third that of heavy cream. It cannot be whipped. Light cream has about half the butterfat of heavy cream. Other dairy staples for dessert-making, including crème fraîche and *fromage blanc,* are widely sold these days. Cultured buttermilk is increasingly difficult to find in supermarkets, but non-fat plain yogurt, well stirred to thin it, can be substituted.

NUTS

Store all nuts in your freezer to keep them fresh. When in doubt, a light toasting always improves them. Some recipes require that hazelnuts or almonds be skinned or blanched. They can also be purchased that way. Grated coconut is sold both sweetened, the supermarket variety, and unsweetened, in Asian and other specialty food stores. Unsweetened coconut must be stored air-tight.

THICKENERS

In pies, custards and many fruit desserts, various thickeners may be required. Cornstarch tossed with fruit for a pie or dissolved in cold water, then heated, can thicken all sorts of juices and sauces, and the result will be clearer than with flour. Tapioca can also be used to thicken the filling of a fruit pie. Arrowroot works like cornstarch.

Gelatin is the opposite of cornstarch or flour in that it thickens as it cools, not as it is heated. Most of the time, the gelatin in these recipes is powdered, unflavored. Some chefs' recipes call for sheet gelatin, which specialty baker's supply companies and Web sites sell. Gelatin has to be softened by soaking in cold water before it is used, then gently heated. To substitute powdered gelatin for sheet gelatin, use the same amount, by weight (usually given in grams). Though sheets of gelatin vary in weight, a good rule of thumb is that three sheets are about the equivalent of a package (¼ ounce) of granulated gelatin.

PACKAGED PASTRY DOUGHS

A cook who has mastered making pie and tart pastry will not resort to the commercially packaged kind. And for those who have not acquired the skill, there are many recipes for pies and tarts made with nut and crumb crusts that do not require making and rolling dough.

This book does not give a recipe for making classic puff pastry. A convenient, shortened recipe has been included. Several recipes do call for frozen puff pastry. Check the ingredient list on the kind you buy and be sure butter is on it. The most popular brand is not made with butter and therefore does not contribute the flavor of a good French puff pastry. Some chefs' recipes use sheets of phyllo in place of puff pastry, a reasonable shortcut.

WATER

Water is not listed among the ingredients, but when needed in a recipe, the quantity is given in the instructions.

EQUIPMENT

A heavy saucepan, a skillet, a casserole and a good knife kept sharp are all it takes to accomplish the majority of cooking tasks. For dessert-making, you also need most of these utensils. The saucepan, skillet and knives, to be sure, but also wooden spoons, rubber and metal spatulas, measuring cups and spoons, mixing bowls, a swivel peeler and baking dishes—all of which are standard in a well-equipped kitchen—are dessert and baking essentials.

But, in addition, for making desserts and especially for baking, some specialized equipment is necessary.

Consider your oven. Any oven, either electric or gas, can be used for baking. But it is important that the temperature is accurate. Use an oven thermometer to check it. And if it is off by 25 degrees or more, which is not uncommon, have the company that services the appliance recalibrate it. When baking, pay attention to where the racks are placed. The middle of the oven is usually best, but some recipes call for higher or lower placement. Convection ovens bake faster and also more evenly. If you use one, watch your baking time carefully.

A microwave oven is of limited use, but comes in handy as a reliable way to melt chocolate and butter. A toaster oven, if you have one, is useful for toasting nuts and even for quick surface browning for a cake or dessert in a small baking pan.

For electric appliances, anyone considering serious baking should own a heavy-duty standing electric mixer, one that comes with a paddle attachment and a whisk and has bowls that hold at least 4 quarts. A dough hook may be included, though some bakers enjoy kneading yeast doughs by hand.

There are many tasks that a food processor can handle with ease, including chopping nuts, mixing pie dough, creaming butter, pureeing fruit and making batters. A blender is of more limited use, but will produce the smoothest fruit purees.

THE COMPLETE KITCHEN
By Amanda Hesser

In the past decade, some lofty designs have made their way into the mainstream home kitchen. The Sub-Zero refrigerator, for instance. The Viking stove. A powder-blue Kitchen-Aid mixer, and don't forget the juice extractor.

And while they are all quite handsome to look at, they haven't made cooks any better or less harried. None quite measure up to the Cuisinart food processor, which seduced the nation in the late 1970s and the 1980s, became a life necessity after the microwave oven and toaster and provided cooks with pureed soups and nuts chopped to fine powder at the flick of a switch.

As the business of the vanity kitchen boomed, though, small new tools—two tools and a mat, actually—were picked up by cooks. You may own one or all of them: the Microplane grater, the OXO vegetable peeler and the Silpat mat. None is particularly attractive. All are simple yet exceptional workhorses, and deserve to be regarded as new classics of the modern kitchen—less flashy than the Cuisinart, perhaps, but just as impossible to live without. Each has not only subtly and stealthily improved many cooks' lives, but changed what people cook as well.

Silpat is not yet a household name. And its mat is the only one of the three to have descended through restaurant kitchens, first in Europe (it is widely used in French pastry shops), and then in this country. The mat was developed in France in 1982 by Guy Demarle. By the time it started showing up in the United States in 1990, parchment paper was finally making it into conventional supermarkets.

The mat, which is essentially silicone-coated fiberglass mesh, feels like something you would put down in your car to protect the rugs. It is meant for laying over baking sheets, to eliminate the need to measure and cut parchment paper or to grease and flour the sheets. Nothing sticks to the mat, so you can bake cookies on it, roll out pie dough, bake a loosely wrapped tart, pour out caramel or even make tuiles, which are nearly impossible at home, even with parchment. The mat is pliable, so you can peel things like caramel away from it. And since nothing sticks, you can use it again immediately.

Although Silpat mats do not melt, the company recommends not using them at temperatures above 500 degrees. (Very few baking recipes would require such heat.)

Heavy saucepans, both small and large, are useful. So is a heavy-duty 10-inch skillet. Nonstick has become controversial, and should not be used over high heat.

Mixing bowls are best when stainless steel, which permits multiple uses, like mixing dough and batter, whisking egg whites or cream and general stirring and combining jobs. Metal bowls will chill ingredients faster than pottery or glass, and a metal bowl can also be placed over a pan of simmering water to heat ingredients or melt chocolate. It is always better to use a bowl that is too big than one that is too small.

Baking pans come in hundreds of shapes and sizes. A 9- or 10-inch pie pan with a rim that is generous enough to hold a fluted crust, a 9- or 10-inch fluted straight-sided tart pan with a loose bottom, a pair of 8- or 9-inch round baking pans, a 9-inch springform, a 9-inch square pan, a loaf pan that holds 6 cups and an oblong, 9-by-13-inch baking pan are some of the basics. Muffin tins in several sizes, tartlet pans, madeleine pans, Bundt pans, tube or angel food pans, cannelet molds and 4-ounce ceramic ramekins are some specialized pans that a well-equipped kitchen may require.

Flat baking sheets and baking sheets with low sides are essential. They should be heavy so they do not warp in the oven, but they do not have to be nonstick because they will probably be covered with parchment paper or a nonstick liner.

Reusable nonstick lining sheets and flexible silicone baking molds are the latest useful additions to the baker's arsenal.

No baker's kitchen should be without wire racks to use for cooling.

Small cooking and baking utensils that are indispensable include wooden spoons, rubber spatulas, metal spatulas and especially offset spatulas for lifting cakes and cookies and applying icing (the handle is not on the same plane as the blade), and dough scrapers. A dough scraper is a thin square of metal or plastic, useful for lifting dough off a work surface and cleaning it.

You can roll pastry with a wine bottle, but a rolling pin is far better. Some bakers prefer a narrow, tapered French-style pin, others like a heavy American-style pin with ball bearings. There is no definite answer. But avoid rolling pins that are made of marble or that can be filled with ice. One that is wrapped with silicone, so dough does not stick, is useful. A pastry cloth or a cloth sleeve for a rolling pin can facilitate pie-making.

The best surface for rolling dough is marble or stone because it stays cool and will not cause the butter in the pastry to become too warm. There are plastic pastry boards that can be fitted with frozen gel packs to keep them cool.

Anyone who expects to bake pies and tarts should keep a supply of baker's weights—either metal or ceramic—on hand. Unlike dried beans or rice, which can be used to weight down pastry that is being baked "blind," without a filling, these can be reused. And they conduct heat, speeding up the baking.

A professional pastry docker, to stud the surface of pastry with tiny holes, is more efficient than using a fork. A pastry crimper is another piece of specialized equipment that some bakers want to have on hand. There are also special forms for creating a lattice crust. And a ravioli cutter will give a nice pinked edge to pastry strips. For cookie-baking, round and heart-shaped cutters will come in handy.

For pastry and cakes, a few good brushes are necessary. Cake-decorating requires a pastry bag and various tips. These days, inexpensive disposable ones are sold. In a pinch, a zip-lock plastic bag with one corner cut off can be used for piping whipped cream or icing.

A set of sturdy stainless steel measuring cups for dry ingredients, and glass measuring cups that hold 1 and 2 cups, are essential, as are metal measuring spoons. A scale is of secondary use, but any well-equipped kitchen should have one because some ingredients are given by weight.

A small 6-inch whisk and a larger balloon whisk are also necessary. A sifter is less essential because a whisk or a whirl in a food processor can accomplish the task. But a small, fine sieve for confectioners' sugar and cornstarch is a must.

A swivel peeler, especially one of the new ones with serrated edges that can be used to peel soft fruit like plums, is essential, as are a good grater, especially Microplane, and an efficient zester.

There are some other gadgets, like cherry pitters, that can be useful, strawberry hullers that are less so; spice grinders or mortars and pestles, scissors, rulers, candy thermometers and on and on, can facilitate preparation.

How many of these items you have on hand will be determined by the amount of serious cooking and baking you are likely to do. But it pays to invest in good quality, no matter the piece of equipment. It will be an investment that will contribute to the end result. And now, it's time to light the oven.

GADGETS WORTH KEEPING:
Microplane Graters and More
By Amanda Hesser

The depth of the teeth is particularly important when grating the zest of citrus. More primitive graters have star-shaped obtrusions that are meant to scrape at the surface of the citrus and collect the zest—a miserable design. The grater savages the surface of the fruit, and whatever zest it removes sticks fast to the grater and inside all its crevices. I once learned a trick to avoid this: wrapping plastic wrap around the grater, so that, supposedly, the zest would catch in the plastic rather than in the grater. It is a telling sign that a design is bad when you have to turn a simple kitchen gadget into a Rube Goldberg contraption.

The original Microplane, on the other hand, is a long, thin strip, like a ruler. The flat, square teeth are all angled in the same direction, and because they are straight and shallow, all the zest collects behind them. To remove it, you simply slide your finger down the smooth side.

The shallowness of the teeth means that they also cut across many oily pockets in the skin (but not into the pith), which leaves a moister zest, and, as I discovered, more of it. Grating with both a box grater and a Microplane, I got a third more orange zest from the Microplane. This means that recipes calling for the zest of two lemons will no longer elicit a groan. And you may end up adding more than you used to.

The OXO vegetable peeler was unveiled at the Gourmet Products Show in San Francisco in 1990. It has a now much-copied black-cushioned handle.

That is why the OXO style is the only peeler that lets you peel butternut squash and hard vegetables like celery root. More than that, the blade angle is perfect for shaving. You can shave chocolate without breaking off any pieces. But even a gadget as standard as the best vegetable peeler can be improved. A new type, with finely serrated blades, can peel soft fruit like peaches, plums and even grapes. It's a must-have.

The lemon zester has a handy, if a bit esoteric, function. When its head is pressed against the skin of a lemon or other citrus fruit and dragged along the contours, it strips fine curly strands of rind. It's not the same as grating.

Lemon zest is filled with essential flavoring oils that infuse dishes with the fruit's evocative essence. It can be added either whole or finely chopped to everything from marinades to cake batter.

A sharp, precise zester—a straight-handled tool with a flat metal head rimmed with five holes—will produce strips about an inch or two long and a millimeter or so wide. The strips should be neither so deep that they cut into the pith, which is bitter, nor so shallow that they merely skim off the top layer of skin.

Most zesters work, but few shine. Until OXO came along, it seems little attention was paid to comfort. The company, whose kitchen equipment is known for its black-rubber, ergonomically correct handles, has two zester models, which outshone nine others I tested. They not only worked superbly but were also comfortable enough that if you had to zest a bucket of lemons, you could.

Many zesters are equipped with a stripper, which removes a single, wider strip of peel. If you drink martinis with a twist, you know the dimensions well. (It is, in fact, the only good use I know of for a stripper.) The strip is about two inches long and one-eighth inch wide. A stripper is either a thin circle, like an eyelet, on the side of the zester head, or a pointed wedge pressed into the center of the zester head. Unfortunately, both designs are often positioned so that only right-handed people can use them; for everyone, eyelet strippers generally work more easily.

There is an alternative to buying a zester: wide, flat strips of peel can be removed with a vegetable peeler and then cut into thinner strips. But it takes longer and fails to open up as many of the oily cells as a good-quality zester does.

FREEZING DESSERTS

Many kinds of pastry desserts, including cakes, pies, bars, cookies and so forth, can be frozen for later use. But limit their time in the freezer to no more than four to six weeks. After that, the quality is likely to deteriorate. Always wrap them well for freezing. And with cakes or pies that have fragile toppings, like icings, the best way to freeze them is to first put them in the freezer completely uncovered until they become frozen hard, about four hours or overnight. Then take them out and wrap them well and return them to the freezer. Though many kinds of pastry can go directly from the freezer to a warm oven, in general it is best to thaw frozen desserts slowly, first in the refrigerator, then at room temperature.

WINE AND DESSERT

Sweet wines are often referred to as dessert wines, a term that I find limiting. Sauternes, after all, is a classic accompaniment to foie gras, and I'd guess rich rieslings would do the trick, too. And the one thing I hesitate to pair with a sweet wine is dessert. Somehow, I've always found matching sweet with sweet to be redundant. Besides, at their best, these wines are desserts themselves.

WINES OF THE TIMES:
After Dinner, the Sweetest Note
By Eric Asimov

Sweet wines are sometimes considered an acquired taste. If so, I acquired it long ago. Few things are as pleasing after a meal as a good sweet wine, one that balances sugar with a bracing acidity that leaves you with a clean, refreshed feeling in your mouth. I'm especially drawn to sweet wines in the holiday season, when a glass poured after a meal with some good cheese can add just the right festive touch.

Sauternes, from the Bordeaux region, is probably the most famous example. The wines are no doubt voluptuous, but I rarely find a Sauternes that is as refreshing as it is sweet. For that, I look elsewhere, sometimes to the Loire for Coteaux de Layon, made from the chenin blanc grape, or to Hungary, where Tokaji Aszu is one of the greatest little-known wines in the world. But above all, I look to the sweet rieslings of Germany, which year in and year out offer that combination of lusciousness and razor-sharp freshness that keeps me coming back for more.

Not everybody feels the way I do.

My enthusiasm is more than matched by the high prices for these wines, a reflection of both the intensive labor required to make them and the randomness of nature, which makes their annual production a dicey venture.

Most sweet wines are produced by halting the fermentation of grape juice before all the sugar in the juice is converted to alcohol. The residual sugar is, naturally, what makes the wine sweet. In wines like these rieslings, the best grapes are left to ripen on the vines for an extra-long time until they are practically bursting with sugar. Sometimes these late-harvest grapes are left on the vine so long that the water content freezes, leaving a very sweet, very concentrated juice used to produce ice wine, or eiswein, as the Germans say.

As both an added bonus and a complication, ripe grapes left on the vine are sometimes attacked by the botrytis cinerea mold, famously called the noble rot. Under the wrong weather conditions or if not carefully managed, the mold can ruin grapes. But if mornings are foggy and middays sunny, and the growers carefully tend each vine, botrytis can intensify the grape's sweetness and flavors while allowing acidity to remain high, which keeps the wine from becoming cloying.

Many believe that Germany's late-harvest rieslings are the best in the world. While North American wineries have adopted the German-derived term ice wine, they have thankfully steered clear of other, more brain-numbing Germanic words, like auslese, beerenauslese and trockenbeerenauslese. These terms indicate the sugar content in grapes at harvest. Ausleses can range from lightly sweet and graceful to very sweet, depending on whether they have been infected with botrytis, but beerenausleses and trockenbeerenausleses are wines of rare intensity and for the most part surpass $100 for a half bottle.

PORT

What will the lovebirds be drinking with that soft, warm, heart-shaped chocolate cake they are sharing on Valentine's Day? There's a better chance than ever that instead of flutes of rosé Champagne or sweet love potion cocktails they will be sipping glasses of port.

With chocolate, when port pops the question, the answer is a resounding yes. And in America today, the popularity of chocolate desserts, not just on Valentine's Day, has more than a little to do with the growing taste for port because port is a wine that has an affinity for chocolate. The growing American taste for port is evolving on its own freewheeling terms. The wine is shedding its image as a rare, stuffy after-dinner men's club drink, English-style, with a host of sacrosanct conventions.

In 2002 the United States overtook England as the number one importer of vintage port. Though some American wine connoisseurs buy vintage ports to put away in their cellars until they are fully matured, others, especially affluent young wine buffs, have less patience.

Bartholomew Broadbent, a California-based importer of ports, also pointed out that port fits the American taste in wine. "In America you're drinking expensive, highly concentrated California cabernets very young," he said. "To go from a big young table wine to young vintage port is a natural progression." He said that recently, at tastings, Americans preferred young vintage ports to mature ones. "To admit something like that would be frowned upon in England," he said. To some extent, Americans are drinking port more the way the Portuguese do these days, often in restaurants and without enshrining it.

All ports can be divided into two broad categories: vintage or vintage-style, and wood-aged, all sweet. Most ports can be paired with chocolate, though wood-aged ports are more versatile than plummy vintage-style ports, and are delicious with caramel desserts, crème brûlée and tarte Tatin, and complement cheese, especially strong cheeses like Stilton.

AFTER DINNER DOWN UNDER,
Chances Are It'll Be a "Sticky"
By R. W. Apple, Jr.

The Australians call them "stickies" and treasure them. So do many others lucky enough to have tasted these fortified dessert wines, properly named muscat and tokay, a pair of uncommon elixirs made only near Rutherglen, Australia, a dozy old town northeast of Melbourne and southwest of Sydney.

Muscat comes from the grape of the same name used in the sweet wines of southern France. Tokay, unrelated to the famous Hungarian wine, comes from muscadelle, a grape that lends fragrance to Sauternes. The best of both, dark and viscous after aging for years in old oak casks, through torrid summers under hot tin roofs, achieve what the English wine writer Jancis Robinson calls "an astonishingly silky richness."

Imagine fruitcake in liquid form, and lay in a bottle or two for the Christmas and New Year's festivities—or for any gala occasion, for that matter. Pair them with chocolate desserts, which are notoriously hard to match, or—a union surely blessed by the gods—with plum pudding. Best of all, sip a soothing glass slowly at day's end, preferably while relaxing in a comfortable chair in front of a blazing fire. Remarkably, the flavor lingers in the mouth with magnificent intensity for five or six or even ten minutes after the glass has been emptied.

These luscious wines have been made since Victorian times, and methods have changed very little in more than a century.

The ripening season here lasts deep into the autumn, which is typically dry. As the grapes hang on the vine past maturity, gradually shriveling, their richness, their sugars and their structure-building acidity are intensified. No botrytis, or noble rot, is involved, as in many sweet wines, but concentration is achieved all the same.

In the winery, fermentation is permitted to continue only briefly before being cut short by the addition of grape spirit, which kills the yeast. The 18 percent alcohol typical of stickies comes mostly from this dosage rather than fermentation, which makes for unparalleled richness.

To achieve the finished products, younger wines, still full of vim, vigor and fruity aromas, are blended with older ones, including minute quantities of dark olive-brown stuff from before 1898, when the phylloxera louse devastated the region. It has the syrupy consistency of molasses.

ABOUT THE RECIPES AND TEXT

The recipes in this book have all been attributed to writers and contributors to *The New York Times*, to cookbook authors and to chefs. For chef's recipes, the chefs are often identified with the restaurants at which they were cooking when the recipes were first published—and not necessarily the restaurants where they are working now. Indeed, some of the restaurants cited are no longer in business.

The essays have been adapted from articles that were published in *The New York Times*, and include the byline of the writer.

CAKES

Of all the categories in the dessert repertory, cake-baking is the most exacting and the least forgiving. It allows little room for improvisation or adjustment along the way. Even a soufflé, for all its magic, is less demanding. And though some bakers might find that a pie crust is more difficult to make successfully, pastry recipes are rarely as precise as those for cakes, and can often be adjusted on the spot.

Once the cake is baked, it's a different story, of course, as it offers a blank slate that will welcome adornment, from a simple dusting of powdered sugar to elaborate filling, icing and decoration.

The recipes in this chapter run the gamut from classics, like chocolate layer cake and pound cake, to more inventive cakes studded with fruit, made with chestnuts and wine, or suited to the holiday table.

A cake is a formula, a chemical one, and when properly devised and followed, a few basic ingredients in contact with heat will become tender, moist and often buttery-rich. It is important to read the recipe, then assemble the ingredients before beginning. Most cake recipes require flour, sweetening and flavoring, fat and eggs. Though the eggs can leaven the mixture, a chemical leavening is often used in small amounts. A liquid, like milk or melted chocolate, may also be in the recipe. The quantities of the ingredients must be in balance or the result can be leaden, badly textured or poorly flavored, or the batter may not bake properly. The baker must measure the ingredients with care, and be sure they are the correct temperature.

Even the size and the shape of the pan is critical. A cake designed for a loaf pan may not turn out well if baked in a round layer-cake pan, even if both have the same capacity. The pan must also be prepared by greasing, flouring or lining so the baked cake can easily be removed. Some cakes must exit the baking pan the minute they come out of the oven. Others must cool completely before unmolding. If you intend to frost the cake, be sure to allow ample time for it to be thoroughly cooled.

Many cake recipes are designed with several dry ingredients like flour, salt, cocoa, baking powder or baking soda and perhaps sugar, which may be mixed together and added after the moist ingredients in the batter have been prepared. Though recipes often call for sifting the dry ingredients together, they can be effectively blended together with a sturdy whisk. I find I use my sifter less and less; even when a recipe calls for a certain amount of sifted flour, a fine sieve will do.

Creaming butter means beating it to lighten it, often with sugar. Do not shortchange this step. Other recipes may require beating eggs and sugar until the mixture turns thick and light, another step that must be thoroughly completed. Always use generous bowls for mixing. Big spatulas make folding delicate ingredients, like egg whites, easier. Fold from the middle of the bowl to the outside, turning the bowl as you go.

A standing electric mixer is a great time- and labor-saver for cakes. Even a handheld mixer is useful, and some cake batters can be assembled in a food processor. As a general rule, once a batter has been made, it should be baked immediately. But there are some chef's recipes that call for chilling the batter several hours or overnight before baking, which enables the dessert to be popped in the oven and baked just before serving, and presented warm.

The baking times given for these recipes are accurate up to a point, because every oven bakes somewhat differently. A common test for doneness is to slip a toothpick into the center of the cake and if it emerges with no batter clinging to it, the cake should be done. Lightly touch the top of the cake: it should spring back, another indication the cake is done. And simply look at it, because it is probably done if it shrinks from the sides of the pan. It's a good idea to begin checking on the cake about 10 minutes before the suggested end of the baking time, and do not be concerned if the cake takes as much as 10 minutes beyond the baking time to finish.

For this part of cake-baking, formulas give way to judgment.

CHOCOLATE CAKES

Why did I decide that the first group of recipes in this book would be for chocolate cakes? For many people, dessert amounts to chocolate cake, pure and simple. But it's really not so simple. Chocolate cake can be anything from an old-fashioned layer cake, which has been included among these recipes; to dense, flourless, truffle-like confections; to cakes that play chocolate off against other flavors, including halvah and black pepper. Some are layered and frosted; others are one-pan affairs; and still others are elaborately garnished and sauced, appropriate for breathtaking dinner party finales. The skills necessary for baking chocolate cake are no different than those required for other cakes. It's the quality of the chocolate that will make the difference. (See essays on pages 289 and 510 for more about chocolate and cocoa.)

Granny's Chocolate Cake

Larry
Forgione,
An American
Place,
New York

This cake is an American classic, a grand, triple-layer chocolate cake with a creamy chocolate icing. It would provide the perfect finale for a comfort-food supper, and could easily be a celebration cake for a birthday or anniversary. Larry Forgione, whose restaurant, An American Place, is now in a Fifth Avenue department store, is one of the first generation of great American chefs who rose to prominence beginning in the late 1970s.

TIME: 1½ hours, plus cooling   YIELD: 8 to 10 servings

12 tablespoons unsalted butter, softened, plus 1½ tablespoons for pans
2½ cups all-purpose flour, plus flour for dusting pans
1 teaspoon baking soda
½ teaspoon baking powder
½ teaspoon salt
1¼ cups buttermilk
1 teaspoon vanilla extract
1½ cups sugar
2 large eggs
4 ounces unsweetened chocolate, melted
Chocolate frosting (page 530)

1. Preheat oven to 350 degrees. Use about 1 tablespoon of butter to grease 3 9-inch round cake pans, and line the bottoms with waxed or parchment paper. Lightly butter the paper with another ½ tablespoon butter. Dust pans with flour, and shake out excess.

2. Sift together the flour, baking soda, baking powder and salt. In a small bowl, combine buttermilk and vanilla.

3. In a large bowl, using an electric mixer set at medium-high speed, cream the remaining butter. Slowly add the sugar, and continue beating until well blended and light colored. Add eggs one at a time, beating well after each addition. Add dry ingredients alternately with the buttermilk mixture in two or three additions, beating well after each addition. Mix in the melted chocolate until well blended. Spoon batter into prepared pans, and smooth tops with a rubber spatula.

4. Bake for 30 to 35 minutes, or until a toothpick inserted in the center of a cake layer comes out clean. Let cake layers cool in the pans on wire racks for 10 minutes, then invert onto other racks and peel off the paper. Invert again, and let cool completely on the racks. Frost with chocolate frosting.

Chocolate-Hazelnut Cake

The affinity for chocolate and hazelnuts is so strong that the Italians even have a word for the combination: *gianduja.* And the commercial product that is the peanut butter of Italy is a mixture of hazelnut puree and chocolate called Nutella. I love the way the slightly bitter, earthy toastiness of the nuts plays off against the richness of the chocolate.

Florence
Fabricant

TIME: 1½ hours   YIELD: 6 servings

5½ tablespoons unsalted butter, softened, plus more for pan

1 cup all-purpose flour, plus more for pan

1 cup very finely chopped skinned hazelnuts

1 teaspoon baking powder

Pinch of salt

1 cup sugar

2 large eggs

2 ounces semisweet chocolate

2 tablespoons brewed coffee

1 tablespoon Frangelico liqueur

½ cup hazelnut halves

1. Preheat oven to 350 degrees. Butter and flour an 8-inch round cake pan.

2. In a small bowl, mix remaining flour with hazelnuts, baking powder and salt. Set aside.

3. In a larger bowl, cream 4 tablespoons butter. Add sugar, beating until mixture is light and fluffy. Beat in eggs one at a time. Fold in flour mixture. Spread batter in pan and bake 40 minutes, or until cake tester comes out clean. Cool on rack, then remove from pan.

4. When cake has cooled, prepare icing. In the top of a double boiler, melt chocolate over hot water, stir in remaining butter and allow to cool to room temperature. Beat until smooth.

5. Stir in coffee and Frangelico, beating until mixture is spreadable. Spread on cake and stud top with hazelnut halves in an attractive pattern.

All-in-One Chocolate Cake

Nigella
Lawson

Here is a two-layer chocolate cake. The layers can also be split horizontally to make four layers. But, then, if you do split them, you will have to double the amount of frosting. Nigella Lawson is an English cookbook author and television personality.

TIME: 1 hour 15 minutes, plus cooling   YIELD: 10 to 12 servings

18 tablespoons unsalted butter, softened, plus 1 tablespoon for pans
1½ cups all-purpose flour
1 cup sugar
1 teaspoon baking powder
½ teaspoon baking soda
⅓ cup Dutch-process cocoa
2 large eggs, at room temperature

3 teaspoons vanilla
1¼ cups sour cream, at room temperature
6 ounces good-quality semisweet chocolate, broken into small pieces
1 tablespoon light corn syrup
2½ cups confectioners' sugar, sifted

1. Preheat oven to 350 degrees. Butter sides of 2 8-inch round cake pans, and line bottoms with parchment paper. In the bowl of a food processor, combine flour, sugar, baking powder, baking soda, cocoa powder, 12 tablespoons butter, eggs, 2 teaspoons vanilla and ¾ cup sour cream. Process to make a smooth, thick batter. Batter can also be made in an electric mixer.

2. Divide batter between pans, and smooth tops. Bake until a cake tester inserted in center comes out clean, 25 to 35 minutes. Transfer to a wire rack to cool for 10 minutes before removing from cake pans. Allow to cool completely.

3. While cake is cooling, combine chocolate and remaining 6 tablespoons butter in a large heatproof bowl. Place over a pan of simmering water to melt, or, using a microwave-safe container, melt in a microwave oven. Remove from heat, and allow to cool for 5 minutes. Stir in corn syrup, remaining sour cream and remaining vanilla. Whisk in confectioners' sugar until very smooth. Frosting should be thick and spreadable. If necessary, add a teaspoon or two of boiling water to thin it, or additional sifted confectioners' sugar to thicken.

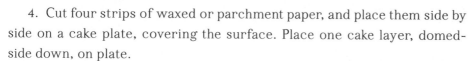

4. Cut four strips of waxed or parchment paper, and place them side by side on a cake plate, covering the surface. Place one cake layer, domed-side down, on plate.

5. Spoon about a third of the frosting onto center of cake, and spread it evenly. Place the other layer on top, domed side up. Spoon another third of frosting on top of cake and spread. Cover sides of cake with remaining frosting, and allow to sit for a few minutes until set. Carefully slip out paper strips.

Intense Chocolate Mousse Cake

Nigella
Lawson

This is a classic flourless chocolate cake, which relies only on egg whites for leavening. It is halfway between a cake and a soufflé. It can be used as a Passover cake, but you will have to omit regular confectioners' sugar, which contains cornstarch, and sprinkle the cake with superfine sugar or Passover confectioners' sugar (without cornstarch) once it has cooled. It is a rich cake that can serve as many as 12 in small slivers. Nigella Lawson is an English cookbook author and television personality.

TIME: 65 minutes   YIELD: One 9-inch cake

10 ounces bittersweet chocolate
9 tablespoons unsalted butter
6 large eggs, separated
Pinch of salt

¾ cup sugar
2 tablespoons brandy
1 teaspoon confectioners' sugar

1. Preheat oven to 350 degrees. Cover the outside of a 9-inch spring-form pan with a double layer of foil. Using a microwave oven or double boiler, melt together chocolate and butter. Set aside to cool.

2. Using an electric mixer, whisk egg whites and salt until thick. Add ¼ cup granulated sugar, and continue to whisk until stiff and shiny but not dry. In another bowl, whisk together egg yolks and remaining ½ cup sugar until pale and thick. Whisk in brandy, then fold in cooled chocolate mixture.

3. Place a kettle of water over heat, and bring it to a boil. Fold about ½ cup whisked egg whites into the chocolate mixture to lighten it. Gently fold in remaining whites, being careful not to let the mixture deflate. Pour mixture into prepared springform pan, and place pan in a roasting pan. Add boiling water to roasting pan to come halfway up side of springform pan. Bake for 45 minutes; top of cake will be hard and inside will be gooey.

4. Remove cake pan from water, and place on a rack to cool completely. Unwrap foil and remove side of springform pan. Place cake on a serving platter. Just before serving, dust top with sifted confectioners' sugar.

Magie Noire (Black Magic Cake)

Another flourless chocolate cake, this one does get some help from ground almonds. It has a silken chocolate glaze. It can be used for Passover if you dust the pan with cake meal instead of flour. Carol Germain-Robin's husband, Hubert, is one of the founders and owners of Craft Distillers, in Ukiah, California, which makes high-end artisanal brandies and other spirits.

Carole
Germain-
Robin

TIME: 1 hour 15 minutes, plus 1 hour chilling and resting   YIELD: 8 to 10 servings

15½ tablespoons unsalted butter	8 large eggs, separated
Flour for pan	1 cup sugar
¼ cup blanched slivered almonds	2½ tablespoons brandy
12 ounces semisweet chocolate	2 tablespoons heavy cream

1. Grease a 9-inch springform pan with ½ tablespoon butter, dust with flour and tap out the excess. Preheat oven to 400 degrees.

2. Using a food processor or blender, chop the almonds very fine; set aside. In a microwave-safe bowl or the top of a double boiler, combine 8 ounces of the chocolate and 10 tablespoons of the remaining butter. Melt the chocolate mixture and set aside.

3. In the bowl of an electric mixer, combine the egg yolks and sugar. Mix well until very smooth. Add the melted chocolate mixture, and mix to blend. Add the ground almonds and brandy.

4. In a clean bowl, whisk the egg whites until stiff but not dry. Add about ½ cup of the beaten whites to the chocolate batter, and stir to thin and loosen it. Carefully fold in the remaining whites until smooth. Pour the batter into the prepared pan.

5. Bake until a toothpick inserted into the center of the cake comes out clean, 35 to 40 minutes. Transfer to a rack, and allow to cool in the pan; the center of the cake will sink slightly when cooled.

6. When the cake is cool, remove from pan and transfer to a serving plate. In a small pan over low heat, combine the remaining 4 ounces chocolate, 5 tablespoons butter and the cream. Stir until smooth and glossy. Slowly pour over the cake, starting in the center and letting it run down the sides. Allow to cool, then refrigerate for one-half hour. Bring to room temperature for 20 to 30 minutes before serving.

Flourless Chocolate Cake with Halvah Honey Sauce

Melissa
Clark

Halvah in the sauce provides a whiff of the exotic for this cake. And if the notion of combining halvah, which is made essentially from ground sesame seeds, with chocolate seems odd, as it might to someone from the Middle East, where the confection originated, consider the chocolate-covered blocks of halvah and the chocolate-marble halvah that are sold in various American shops. Though the recipe specifies plain halvah, the chocolate profile can be intensified by using marble or chocolate halvah. Tahini is sesame paste, sold in jars. Melissa Clark is a writer who specializes in baking.

TIME: 45 minutes, plus 3 hours or overnight chilling   YIELD: 10 to 12 servings

4 ounces (1 stick) unsalted butter, plus more for pan

All-purpose flour for pan

8 ounces bittersweet chocolate, chopped

1 tablespoon brandy or rum

6 large eggs, separated

½ cup plus 2 tablespoons sugar

1 teaspoon salt

1 cup heavy cream

3 tablespoons tahini

1½ tablespoons honey, or to taste

2 tablespoons plain halvah, firmly packed

1. Preheat oven to 350 degrees. Butter and flour a 9-inch springform pan, line it with parchment paper, and grease and flour parchment.

2. In a saucepan over medium-low heat, melt butter, then add chocolate. Melt, stirring frequently, until just smooth. Remove from heat, whisk in brandy or rum, and let cool.

3. In a large bowl, whisk egg yolks with ½ cup sugar and ½ teaspoon of the salt, then whisk in cooled chocolate mixture.

4. In an electric mixer on medium speed, beat egg whites to soft peaks. Gradually add remaining 2 tablespoons sugar, and beat to stiff peaks.

5. Stir a little of the whites into chocolate mixture to lighten it, then gently fold all the whites into chocolate. Scrape batter into prepared pan, and bake until cake springs back when gently touched in center and a toothpick inserted in center comes out with some crumbs attached, about 35 minutes. Transfer to a wire rack, and let cool for 20 minutes, then turn

cake out onto rack, and cool completely. Wrap well, and refrigerate for at least 3 hours or overnight to firm texture.

6. In a saucepan, bring cream to a simmer. Whisk in the tahini, honey and remaining salt. Simmer the mixture, whisking, until it thickens to a custardlike consistency, about 2 minutes. Let mixture cool, then crumble in the halvah. Serve with chocolate cake.

Chocolate Black Pepper Cake

Amanda
Hesser

Chocolate takes beautifully to spices, as this recipe proves. Indeed, the Aztecs, who used chocolate for centuries and from whom the Spaniards learned about it, often seasoned their chocolate drinks with chili. Amanda Hesser is food editor of *The New York Times Magazine*.

TIME: 1 hour, plus cooling   YIELD: 8 servings

6 tablespoons unsalted butter, plus more for pan

10 ounces bittersweet chocolate, chopped

¼ cup granulated sugar

¼ cup honey

½ teaspoon kosher salt

5 large eggs, separated

½ cup ground almonds

⅓ cup all-purpose flour

2 teaspoons coarse-ground black pepper

½ teaspoon ground allspice

¼ teaspoon ground cinnamon

Pinch of cayenne pepper

Pinch of salt

Confectioners' sugar, for dusting

Unsweetened whipped cream, for garnish

1. Preheat oven to 375 degrees. Butter a 9-inch springform pan. In top of a double boiler, melt butter and chocolate, stirring constantly, just until chocolate is melted. Remove from heat. Stir in granulated sugar, honey and salt, then egg yolks. Transfer to a large mixing bowl. Whisk in the ground almonds, flour, black pepper, allspice, cinnamon and cayenne, just until combined. Do not overmix.

2. In a large bowl, beat egg whites with a pinch of salt by hand or with an electric mixer until they are stiff but still creamy. Fold three-quarters of the egg whites into chocolate mixture. Pour chocolate mixture into remaining egg whites and fold gently, just until there are no clumps of egg white. Spread in prepared pan. Bake until firm and springy, 30 to 35 minutes.

3. Remove cake from oven and let cool completely on a rack. Remove sides of pan, sprinkle cake lightly with confectioners' sugar and serve with whipped cream.

Molten Chocolate Cakes ✳

Here you have the wildly popular little molten chocolate cakes. They are best when served warm. The soufflé dishes can be filled and refrigerated several hours before serving, brought to room temperature, then baked at the last minute. Petrossian, the caviar company based in Paris, has a restaurant and café in New York.

Petrossian
Boutique
and Café,
New York

TIME: 30 minutes   YIELD: 4 servings

6 tablespoons unsalted butter, softened, plus more for pans or soufflé dishes	2¾ ounces bittersweet chocolate
⅓ cup all-purpose flour, plus more for pans or soufflé dishes	⅓ cup sugar
	3 large eggs
	4 pinches fleur de sel

1. Preheat oven to 475 degrees. Butter and flour 4 half-cup soufflé dishes or muffin tins.

2. Using a double boiler, melt chocolate and 6 tablespoons butter. Add sugar, and stir until melted. Remove from heat, and set aside to cool.

3. In a bowl, beat eggs until whites and yolks are blended. Stir in ⅓ cup flour until smooth. Gradually whisk in chocolate mixture until well blended. Divide among soufflé dishes.

4. Bake cakes until puffed and dry on surface but still soft in center, about 6 minutes. Unmold cakes from dishes or pans, and place on serving plates. Sprinkle with fleur de sel, and serve hot or cool.

ONCE JUST A CUPCAKE, THESE DAYS A SWELL
By Julia Moskin

What is it about a cupcake? Some fans cite the high frosting-to-cake ratio as the source of the appeal; others, its portability. (Unlike a slice of cake, a cupcake can be eaten on the street, like a hot dog.) But a cupcake is just cake, some batter, some frosting, some sprinkles. Or is it?

Bakers agree that the swelling trade in cupcakes is all about a combination of childhood and chic.

Like skimpy Petit Bateau T-shirts and Hello Kitty knapsacks, cupcakes are supposedly designed for children, but they have also become fashionable accessories for knowing grown-ups. Seizing on the back-to-childhood trend, bakeries have engineered copies of the packaged Hostess cupcake, right down to the squiggle of white icing on the top, the chocolate frosting that peels off in one piece and the cream filling. It happens to be a delicious combination; it's also a visual joke. So the connection of cupcakes and chic is inescapable.

But the showiest cupcakes are not necessarily the tastiest. And freshness is crucial. Because cupcakes, unlike cakes, are not sealed all over with frosting, they go stale more quickly. And, unlike some cakes, they are easy to bake at home.

Chocolate Cupcakes with Vanilla Icing ✳

These days, lard is not the fat of choice in baking. But this old-fashioned recipe calls for it. You can always substitute unsalted butter. Matt Lee and Ted Lee are brothers who write about food together.

Matt Lee
and
Ted Lee

TIME: 30 minutes, plus cooling   YIELD: 12 cupcakes

1½ cups all-purpose flour

¾ teaspoon baking soda

¾ teaspoon baking powder

½ teaspoon salt

6 tablespoons lard or unsalted butter

1 cup brown sugar

2 large egg yolks

4 ounces unsweetened chocolate, melted and cooled 10 minutes

1 large egg white

1¼ cups milk

2 teaspoons vanilla

4 ounces (1 stick) unsalted butter, softened

3 cups confectioners' sugar, approximately

1. Preheat oven to 350 degrees. Line a muffin tin designed for 12 medium-size cupcakes (4 ounces) with cupcake liners. In a bowl, whisk together flour, baking soda, baking powder and salt and set aside.

2. In a large bowl, cream lard with brown sugar. Beat yolks and add, beating until smooth. Stir in chocolate. Beat egg white until frothy and fold into batter. Add half the dry ingredients to batter, and beat gently while adding ½ cup of milk and 1 teaspoon vanilla. Repeat with remaining dry ingredients, then another ½ cup milk.

3. Pour batter into pan, nearly filling each mold. Bake 18 to 20 minutes, or until a toothpick inserted into center comes out clean. Remove from oven, and let cool in pan for 5 minutes. Remove cupcakes and place on a cooling rack until cupcakes are completely cool.

4. In a bowl, beat remaining butter, confectioners' sugar, remaining milk and vanilla until creamy. For stiffer consistency, beat in more confectioners' sugar. Spread over cooled cupcakes.

FILLED CAKES, LAYER CAKES AND LAYERED CAKES

Filled cakes are often one-pan jobs, made with fruit, that need no additional embellishment. Layer cakes presuppose baking in two or more pans or baking a single layer that is then split and filled. Sometimes, the filling, like fruit, is part of the cake, but often, it involves a separate icing. Just be sure to give your cake time to cool completely before icing it. Otherwise, if a few hours are not an option, select a recipe that does not require cooling. For chocolate layer cakes, consider Granny's Chocolate Cake, page 26, and All-in-One Chocolate Cake, page 28.

Original Plum Torte

This plum torte, a delicious late-summer dessert, is the most frequently requested recipe that has been published in the *Times.* Starting in the late 1980s, it would run year after year. It is extremely easy to make, and can be varied, for example, by quartering the plums and arranging them skin-side down; by using other fruits in season, like peaches, nectarines, blueberries, blackberries or even chunks of poached quince. The springform pan in which it bakes does not require greasing. It freezes well, so it pays to make more than one torte when the plums are in season, to serve several months later. Another version of this dessert is the Plum and Ginger Crumble on page 216. Marian Burros is a food reporter for *The New York Times.*

Marian
Burros

TIME: 1 hour 15 minutes   YIELD: 8 servings

½ cup unsalted butter, softened
¾ cup sugar, plus more for
   topping
1 cup all-purpose flour,
   sifted
1 teaspoon baking powder

Pinch of salt
2 large eggs, lightly beaten
12 Italian prune plums, halved and
   pitted
1 teaspoon ground cinnamon, or
   more to taste

1. Preheat oven to 350 degrees.

2. Cream butter and sugar in a bowl. Whisk together flour, baking powder and salt. Add to creamed mixture. Add eggs, and beat well.

3. Spoon the batter into an 8, 9 or 10-inch springform pan. Place the plum halves skin side up on top of the batter. Sprinkle lightly with sugar, depending on the sweetness of the fruit. Sprinkle with 1 teaspoon cinnamon, or to taste.

4. Bake for 40 to 50 minutes. Remove and cool to lukewarm, remove sides of pan, and serve. Or refrigerate or freeze if desired—first double-wrap in foil, then place in a plastic bag and seal. To serve a torte that has been frozen, defrost and reheat it briefly at 300 degrees.

Bolzano Apple Cake

Scott
Carsberg,
Lampreia,
Seattle,
Washington

Apple slices permeate this buttery cake, and they are guaranteed to show up on every forkful. It's an excellent autumn dessert from a chef based in apple country, in Seattle, Washington.

TIME: 1¼ hours   YIELD: 6 to 8 servings

4 ounces (1 stick) unsalted butter,
  plus more for pan
½ cup all-purpose flour, plus
  more for pan
2 large eggs
1 cup granulated sugar

1 vanilla bean
5 Granny Smith apples
2 teaspoons baking powder
½ cup milk, at room temperature
Confectioners' sugar

1. Preheat oven to 375 degrees. Line an 8-inch-square pan with foil, then grease with thick layer of butter. Dust with flour and tap lightly to remove excess.

2. Melt butter in a small saucepan. Set aside. Beat together eggs and half the granulated sugar to blend. Continue to beat while slowly adding remaining sugar until the mixture is thick and light and forms a ribbon when dropped from a spoon.

3. Split vanilla bean in two lengthwise. Scrape seeds into the egg-sugar mixture and add pod to melted butter.

4. Peel, quarter and core the apples, then trim ends and slice thin.

5. Remove vanilla pod from butter and stir butter into egg-sugar mixture. Whisk together ½ cup flour and the baking powder, then stir it into the batter alternately with milk. Fold in apples, making sure they are well-coated with batter. Pour batter into pan and smooth top.

6. Bake for 25 minutes, then rotate the pan; bake for about 25 minutes more, until cake pulls away from pan and is brown on top. A thin-bladed knife inserted into the center will come out clean. Cool 30 minutes. Unmold. Dust with sifted confectioners' sugar before serving.

Almond, Apple and Vin Cotto Cake

I Trulli,
New York

Layers of apples alternate with a fine, almond-scented cake. Almond flour is sold in fancy food shops, and from bakers' supply companies. Other nut flours can be substituted, and blanched almonds ground until fine with a tablespoon of the sugar can also be used, but the end result will be a little more crumbly. Vin cotto is unfermented grape juice (must) that has been boiled down until it is syrupy, like honey. It is often sold as saba. Apple cider, boiled until it has been reduced by two thirds, can be substituted. I Trulli is an Italian restaurant and wine bar in New York.

TIME: 1 hour, plus cooling   YIELD: 8 to 10 servings

4 tablespoons melted unsalted
  butter, plus more for pan
¼ cup cake flour, plus more for
  pan
6 tart apples, peeled, cored and
  each cut in 16 slices
1 cup plus 3 tablespoons
  granulated sugar

1 teaspoon vanilla extract
8 large egg yolks
½ cup vin cotto or saba
4 large egg whites
2½ cups almond flour
1 tablespoon confectioners' sugar

1. Heat oven to 350 degrees. Butter and flour a 10-inch springform pan.

2. Place 1 tablespoon butter in large skillet over medium heat. Add apples, and sprinkle with 3 tablespoons granulated sugar and ½ teaspoon vanilla. Sauté 4 to 5 minutes, until fruit starts to soften. Spread on baking sheet to cool.

3. Beat yolks with ½ cup granulated sugar in large bowl until very light. Fold in remaining butter and vanilla, ¼ cup vin cotto and cake flour.

4. Whip egg whites until firmly peaked. Gradually beat in remaining granulated sugar until glossy. Fold egg-white mixture into egg-yolk mixture. Fold in almond flour.

5. Spread half the apples in pan. Add half the batter. Repeat layers. Sift confectioners' sugar over top. Bake 40 to 45 minutes, until browned. Cool, remove from pan and serve with vin cotto drizzled on each portion.

Chestnut Cake with Chocolate Ganache and Single-Malt Scotch Syrup

Bill
Yosses

This is a grand, special-occasion cake, suitable for a fall or winter dinner. Chestnut flour is sold by baking supply houses. Other fine-textured nut flours can be substituted, or the almond flour can be increased to 1½ cups. Marrons glacés are big candied chestnuts that are sold only around Christmas. They would add real luxury to the top of this cake. Though single-malt Scotch is called for, mainly because it has cachet on a menu, other kinds of Scotch whisky, and even bourbon, brandy or dark rum, can be used. Bill Yosses, a pastry chef who first became prominent at Bouley, was the chef for Citarella stores and restaurants.

TIME: 2½ hours, plus overnight chilling   YIELD: 8 servings

14 ounces milk chocolate, chopped

3 cups heavy cream

1 tablespoon unsalted butter, softened, for pans

½ cup all-purpose flour, plus more for pans

1 cup almond flour

½ cup chestnut flour

1 cup confectioners' sugar, plus more for serving

8 large egg whites, at room temperature

Pinch of cream of tartar

1 cup lightly packed light brown sugar, sifted

½ cup granulated sugar

¼ cup single-malt Scotch whisky, or other Scotch whisky

1 cup walnut halves

1 15-ounce jar chestnuts in syrup, drained, or 8 marrons glacés

1. Place chocolate in a 2-quart heatproof bowl. In a small saucepan, bring cream to a boil. Pour hot cream over chocolate, and let sit for 3 minutes. Whisk until thoroughly combined and slightly cooled, then cover and refrigerate this ganache overnight.

2. Preheat oven to 375 degrees. Butter and flour 3 8-inch round cake pans, and line with parchment paper. Sift all-purpose flour, almond flour, chestnut flour and confectioners' sugar into a bowl.

3. In the bowl of a mixer fitted with a whisk attachment, whip egg whites until foamy. Add cream of tartar and 1 tablespoon brown sugar, and

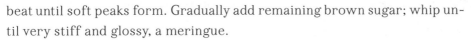

beat until soft peaks form. Gradually add remaining brown sugar; whip until very stiff and glossy, a meringue.

4. Gently fold sifted dry ingredients into meringue in three stages. Divide batter among pans, and smooth tops. Bake for 17 to 20 minutes, until tops are brown and spring back when lightly pressed. Transfer cakes in pans to a wire rack, and let cool.

5. Reduce oven temperature to 325 degrees. Line a rimmed baking sheet with parchment or a nonstick liner. In a small saucepan, combine granulated sugar with ½ cup water. Bring to a boil, stirring until sugar dissolves. Let cool.

6. Stir whisky into sugar syrup. Place walnuts in a bowl, and toss them with ¼ cup syrup. Pour nuts out onto baking sheet in a single layer. Bake for 15 minutes, stirring every 5 minutes. Transfer to a wire rack to cool. Meanwhile, chop all but four of the candied chestnuts, and set aside.

7. Transfer ganache to the bowl of an electric mixer and whip on medium-low speed, just until it holds soft peaks. Do not overwhip.

8. To assemble cake, cut a piece of cardboard into an 8-inch round or use removable bottom of a springform pan. Place a cake layer upside down on this base. Brush cake with a generous amount of the whisky syrup. Spread about ¾ cup ganache on top, and sprinkle with half the chopped chestnuts. Lay another upside-down cake layer on top, and brush with more syrup. Spread on another layer of ganache, and sprinkle with remaining chopped chestnuts. Repeat with final layer of cake, more syrup and more ganache. Using a metal spatula, spread a thin layer of ganache onto sides of cake. Refrigerate for 1 hour. Spread another coat of ganache onto top and sides of cake, smoothing it well. Press candied walnut halves onto sides, and arrange candied chestnuts on top. Refrigerate until ready to serve, and sprinkle with sifted confectioners' sugar before serving.

Vanilla Cake with Roasted Peaches and Blueberries

Beacon
Restaurant,
New York

This cake, filled with roasted fruit, is a summer confection that should only be attempted when ripe, juicy peaches and fresh blueberries are in the market. It begs to be made early in the day to allow for proper chilling. Beacon Restaurant in New York is known for using a wood-fired oven for many of its dishes.

TIME: 1½ hours, plus 8 hours' chilling   YIELD: 10 to 12 servings

6 large ripe peaches, pitted and
    sliced
6 cups blueberries
1½ cups sugar
Juice of 1 lemon
¼ vanilla bean
4 ounces (1 stick) unsalted butter,
    plus more for pan
1 cup all-purpose flour, plus more
    for pan
2 large eggs

1 teaspoon vanilla extract
1½ teaspoons baking powder
½ teaspoon salt
½ cup milk
Whipped heavy cream or crème
    fraîche for garnish
Mint sprigs, for garnish

1. Preheat oven to 500 degrees. In a bowl, place peaches, blueberries, 1 cup of the sugar and the lemon juice; toss to coat well. Pour all but 2 cups of the fruit into a 9-by-13-inch baking dish. Cover reserved fruit, and re-frigerate.

2. Scrape seeds from vanilla bean, and reserve. Bury the vanilla pod in the fruit in the baking dish, and arrange 4 tablespoons of the butter, in pieces, on top. Bake for 30 minutes, stirring after about 15 minutes. Let cool on a rack; discard vanilla pod.

3. Lower oven temperature to 350 degrees. Butter and flour a 9-inch round cake pan. In the bowl of an electric mixer fitted with the paddle at-tachment, cream remaining sugar and butter until very smooth. Beat in the eggs, vanilla extract and vanilla seeds. In a small bowl, combine flour, bak-ing powder and salt. On low speed, add flour mixture to the batter in three stages, alternating with the milk. Pour batter into the prepared pan, and

bake for 25 minutes, until a tester inserted into middle comes out clean. Let cool, then unmold cake.

4. With a long serrated knife, carefully slice cake horizontally into three layers. Line a clean 9-inch springform cake pan with plastic wrap, leaving plenty of wrap overhanging. Place bottom layer of cake in pan, cut side up. Using a slotted spoon, layer half of the cooled fruit, drained of juices, over cake. Top with middle layer of cake, and spoon on remaining fruit; reserve fruit juices. Cover with the top cake layer, cut side down. Press down gently on cake, and cover with the overhanging plastic wrap. Chill cake for at least 8 hours, preferably overnight.

5. When ready to serve, unmold cake. To serve, garnish each slice with a generous drizzle of the reserved fruit juices, the reserved raw fruit and a dollop of whipped cream. Top with mint sprigs.

Pear and Rosemary Cake

Florence
Fabricant

I love the way the rosemary gives this cake a haunting, almost piney fragrance and a lovely hint of the herb in the flavor. The cake's sweetness is extremely restrained, making it an excellent choice to accompany a dessert wine.

TIME: 1 hour 15 minutes   YIELD: 8 servings

2½ tablespoons unsalted butter, melted and cooled
¾ cup plus 1 tablespoon sugar
1 cup sifted all-purpose flour
½ teaspoon baking powder
1½ cups finely diced ripe peeled pears (about 2)

Juice of ½ lemon
4 large eggs, at room temperature
½ teaspoon almond extract
1 teaspoon minced fresh rosemary leaves
1 sprig fresh rosemary

1. Preheat oven to 350 degrees. Brush ½ tablespoon butter in a 6-cup loaf pan. Dust with 1 tablespoon sugar.

2. Whisk flour and baking powder together and set aside. Mix pears with lemon juice and set aside in a separate bowl.

3. Place eggs in bowl of an electric mixer. Add remaining sugar, beat to combine, then beat at high speed about 5 minutes with whisk attachment if possible, until mixture is very light and thick, like softly whipped cream. Fold in flour mixture, pears, almond extract and minced rosemary. Fold in remaining melted butter.

4. Pour into pan, smooth top and place rosemary sprig on top. Bake 40 to 45 minutes until cake is browned and cake tester comes out clean. Cool briefly on rack, then unmold to finish cooling.

Strawberry Sour Cream Streusel Cake ✳

This buttery cake contains a layer of strawberry puree. Bake it when seasonal strawberries are at their peak and garnish it with sliced strawberries and whipped cream or ice cream. Demerara or turbinado is what light brown sugar is called in England, and can be used in this recipe. Sugars called demerara or turbinado are also sold here. Nigella Lawson wrote a recipe column for the Dining In/Dining Out section of the *Times*.

Nigella
Lawson
∼

TIME: 1 hour, plus cooling   YIELD: 8 servings

1 cup hulled, sliced strawberries
3 tablespoons strawberry
    preserves
2 teaspoons cornstarch
2 teaspoons vanilla extract
Vegetable oil or butter for
    pan
¾ cup granulated sugar
2 cups plus 2 tablespoons all-
    purpose flour

1 teaspoon baking powder
½ teaspoon baking soda
6 ounces (1½ sticks) cold butter,
    in ½-inch cubes
1 cup sour cream
1 large egg
1 tablespoon vanilla extract
2 teaspoons demerara or
    turbinado sugar, or light brown
    sugar

1. In a blender, combine strawberries and preserves. Make a paste by mixing cornstarch and vanilla, and add. Puree and set aside.

2. Preheat oven to 375 degrees. Oil a 9-inch springform pan and set aside. In a large bowl, whisk together granulated sugar, flour, baking powder and baking soda. Sprinkle in butter cubes and, using your fingertips, rub them in until mixture resembles large coarse crumbs. Remove ½ cup and set aside. Add sour cream, egg and vanilla to crumbs in large bowl. Mix well.

3. Drop dollops of half the batter into the prepared pan. Pat batter across bottom of pan and about 1 inch up sides; mixture will be very sticky and somewhat uneven. Add strawberry puree, making an even layer across the layer of batter and leaving a ½-inch border. Cover with remaining batter.

4. In a medium bowl, combine reserved ½ cup crumbs and demerara sugar. Stir lightly with a fork to mix. Sprinkle evenly over cake.

5. Bake cake until lightly golden, about 45 minutes. Cool on a rack completely before removing sides of pan and serving.

Strawberry Cream Sponge Roulade

Florence
Fabricant

There are two styles of strawberry shortcake: made with biscuit and made with cake, the kind I usually make because my husband prefers it. Personally, I'll take the biscuit kind. Indeed, I believe the world of dessert-eating can be divided into pastry-lovers like me and cake-lovers like my mate. This dessert, which I usually bake in early summer when the lush, locally grown strawberry crop is at its peak, is like a strawberry shortcake made with sponge cake, only it is shaped into a roulade instead of a layered cake. (For biscuit-style shortcake, see pages 225 and 226.)

TIME: 1 hour, plus cooling and chilling   YIELD: 8 servings

Unsalted butter for greasing pan
¾ cup cake flour
¾ teaspoon baking powder
Pinch of salt
4 eggs, at room temperature
½ cup granulated sugar

Confectioners' sugar
1½ cups heavy cream, whipped
1 pint ripe strawberries, hulled
   and halved, plus whole berries
   for garnish
Superfine sugar to taste

1. Preheat oven to 350 degrees. Butter a 10-by-15-inch jelly roll pan. Line it with a sheet of waxed or parchment paper cut to fit the width but extending a few inches at either end. Butter the paper.

2. Sift the flour, baking powder and salt together and set aside.

3. Beat the eggs at high speed for 5 minutes, until very thick and light. Gradually beat in the granulated sugar; then at low speed fold in the flour.

4. Spread batter in the pan and bake 20 minutes, until puffed and golden. Run a knife around the edges.

5. Heavily dust a clean linen towel with sifted confectioners' sugar and invert the cake, pan and all, onto the towel. Lift off the pan and peel off the paper. Roll the cake in the towel and set aside to cool.

6. When the cake is cool, gently unroll it and spread it with the whipped cream. Sweeten the berries to taste and spread them over the cream. Reroll the cake. Wrap the cake in foil and refrigerate. To serve, unwrap, transfer to a platter and dust with sifted confectioners' sugar and garnish with berries.

Boston Cream Pie

Despite its name, Boston cream pie is a layer cake, filled with pastry cream and iced with chocolate. It is said to have originated in 1855 and was not always made with chocolate icing. And when it was, it was sometimes called Parker House Chocolate Pie after the historic hotel in Boston where the chocolate embellishment was first added.

Omni
Parker House,
Boston,
Massachusetts

TIME: 90 minutes, plus cooling   YIELD: 10 servings

2 tablespoons unsalted butter,
   melted, plus more for pan
7 large eggs, separated
1 cup granulated sugar
1 cup all-purpose flour, sifted

6 ounces semisweet chocolate
4 cups pastry cream (page 532)
1 cup confectioners' sugar
1 teaspoon light corn syrup
½ cup sliced almonds, toasted

1. Preheat oven to 350 degrees. Butter a 10-inch springform pan.

2. Place whites and yolks in separate mixing bowls. Add ½ cup granulated sugar to each bowl. Beat the egg whites until moderately stiff, but not dry. Beat the yolks at high speed until light yellow and thick, about 3 minutes. Fold one-third of the egg whites into the yolks, then fold in the remaining whites. Gradually add the flour, folding in with a spatula. Fold in the melted butter.

3. Spread the batter in the springform pan. Bake for about 25 minutes, or until the surface is golden and a cake tester comes out clean. Remove from the oven and cool thoroughly. Remove sides of pan.

4. Combine the chocolate with 2 tablespoons water, and melt in a microwave oven or double boiler. Reserve.

5. Using a long serrated knife, level the top of the cake and slice into two layers of equal thickness. Reserve 1½ cups of the pastry cream. Spread the remaining cream on one layer. Top with the second layer.

6. Spread the cake with the chocolate mixture. Combine confectioners' sugar, corn syrup and 1 tablespoon water. Mix well. Place in a piping bag with a ⅛-inch tip. Pipe a spiral line starting from the center of the cake. Score lines with the point of a paring knife, starting at the center and pulling outward to the edge. Spread the sides of the cake with a thin layer of pastry cream, and press toasted almonds into the cream.

Coffee Walnut Layer Cake

Nigella
Lawson

This cake is a pretty one, suitable for a dinner party. Pecans can be used in place of walnuts. Nigella Lawson is an English cookbook author and television personality.

TIME: About 1 hour   YIELD: 8 to 10 servings

14 ounces (3½ sticks) unsalted
  butter, softened
½ cup walnut pieces
1 cup plus 2 tablespoons
  granulated sugar
1⅔ cups all-purpose flour
1 tablespoon baking powder
4 large eggs

2 tablespoons milk, at room
  temperature, approximately
2 tablespoons instant coffee
  dissolved in 2 tablespoons
  boiling water
2½ cups confectioners' sugar
¼ cup walnut halves, for
  decoration

1. Preheat oven to 350 degrees. Use a little of the butter to grease 2 8-inch cake pans. Line the bottom of each with parchment paper.

2. In a food processor, combine walnut pieces and granulated sugar. Process to a fine powder. Add 8 ounces (2 sticks) butter, the flour, baking powder and eggs. Process to a smooth batter. Add milk to half the coffee mixture. With the processor running, pour the milk and coffee mixture down feed tube. Mixture should be just soft enough to drop from a spoon; if not, add a little more milk.

3. Divide cake batter between two pans. Bake until risen and springy to touch, about 25 minutes. Cool on a rack for 10 minutes, then remove from pan and place on rack. Remove parchment paper. Cool completely.

4. To make frosting, place confectioners' sugar in a food processor and pulse until lump-free. Add remaining butter and process until smooth. Add remaining coffee mixture down the feed tube and pulse until well blended.

5. Place one cake layer upside down on a plate or cake stand. Spread with about one-third of the frosting. Top with second layer right side up, and cover top and sides with remaining frosting in a swirly pattern. Place a walnut half in center of cake, and gently press remaining halves into top of cake, around the edge.

ENDANGERED:
The Beloved American Layer Cake
By Melissa Clark

The layer cake, an American icon, is in dire straits.

Decades of supermarket cake mixes have inflicted some real harm at home, of course. Most bakeries, with their airy cakes frosted in sugared shortening, have simply failed to hold up their end of the bargain. And high-end restaurants, where the layer cake once played such a proud role, have left it for dead, a casualty of the war among today's dueling pastry chefs. Even the wave of heartwarming comfort food that carried mashed potatoes and roast chicken back into the restaurant mainstream rolled right by the layer cake.

The neglect in restaurants, at least, isn't completely irrational. A whole cake, resplendent on its pedestal, concealing the pastry and filling within, radiates potential and drama. But that's not how it's presented in a restaurant.

"I think the whole movement against serving just a slice of cake on a plate started quietly in Europe," said Timothy Moriarty, a coauthor of *Grand Finales: The Art of the Plated Dessert* (John Wiley & Sons, 1996). "It used to be that desserts were served from a cart, and the presentation was up to the waiter. Pastry chefs wanted more control, and assembling desserts at the last minute allowed them to serve fresher creations that also looked great. Now, individually plated desserts are the norm. It's what people expect."

The wedge of layer cake—with its precisely contrasted flavors and textures, its perfect proportion of crumb to buttercream—is a stellar representative of confectionery harmony. But it's just no dazzler.

The way things are going, if the genuine layer cake is going to survive, a few professional mavericks aren't likely to be its saviors. It's time for the home cook to go back to the first principles—and start from scratch.

No one knows for certain just how the layer cake originated, but it's easy to trace its rise and its decline. Layer cakes as we know them first appeared around the latter half of the 1800s in the United States. What truly spawned the layer cake, later in the century, was the cast-iron stove, which gradually replaced less reliable brick hearths in American kitchens, said the culinary historian Karen Hess. The availability of baking powder, starting in the mid-1800s, also made cakes easier to tackle, she continued, adding, "The oven and the use of chemical leaveners went hand and hand."

Hess said that some of the earliest recipes for layer cakes were published in 1871 in *Mrs.*

Porter's New Southern Cookery Book, one of the first cookbooks written for people who had those newfangled iron stoves. One recipe, for White Mountain cake, filled and frosted with meringue, may offer a clue to the popularity of layer cakes for birthdays. The text accompanying it says that it "is very nice indeed, particularly for weddings and parties." Birthday parties, say.

By the 1890s there were numerous recipes for fancy layer cakes filled with sherry-macerated dried fruits, preserves and whisky- or fruit-flavored curd. In well-off households on special occasions, the entire dining room sideboard would be filled with different layer cakes, their icings tinted pink, green or chocolate brown and festooned with rosettes, swags, nuts and glacéed cherries.

The beginning of the end of the layer cake as extravaganza came in the 1940s. Soon after the end of World War II, the first commercial cake mixes were introduced. In *Paradox of Plenty: A Social History of Eating in Modern America* (Oxford University Press, 1993), Harvey Levenstein wrote that by 1957 more than half of the cakes baked in America were made from mixes.

The lockout was complete by the 1990s, as trends turned away from anything simply sliced and served on a plate.

Lane Cake

A thoroughly Southern creation, the cake was named after Emma Rylander Lane of Clayton, Alabama, who called it "Prize cake" when she published the recipe in 1898. It is a prizewinning white layer cake with a bourbon-flavored custard filling, and is said to be better the day after it has been made. Refrigerate it, well wrapped, if you wish to wait before serving it, and see page 16 for a tip. Craig Claiborne was the former food editor of *The New York Times*.

Craig
Claiborne

TIME: 1½ hours   YIELD: 10 servings

½ pound plus 4 tablespoons unsalted butter, softened, plus more for pan
3½ cups all-purpose flour, plus more for pan
4 teaspoons baking powder
1 teaspoon salt
4¼ cups sugar
3¼ teaspoons vanilla extract
1¼ cups milk
10 large egg whites

9 large egg yolks
1 teaspoon grated orange zest
⅓ cup bourbon
½ teaspoon ground mace
1 cup chopped pecans
1 cup shredded unsweetened coconut
1 cup candied cherries, quartered
1 cup raisins
⅛ teaspoon cream of tartar

1. Preheat oven to 375 degrees. Butter and flour 3 9-inch layer cake pans.

2. Sift together the flour, baking powder and salt. Sift a second time.

3. Beat 2 cups sugar with remaining butter until light and fluffy. Add 1½ teaspoons vanilla. Add flour mixture alternately with milk.

4. Beat 8 egg whites until stiff but not dry. Fold one-fourth of the egg whites into the batter. Fold in remaining beaten egg whites. Divide batter among the pans. Bake 20 to 25 minutes, until a cake tester comes out clean.

5. Place pans on cooling racks for 10 minutes, then remove cakes from pans and allow to cool completely.

6. For the filling, combine the egg yolks with 1¼ cups sugar and orange zest in the top of a double boiler set just touching a pan of simmering water. Cook, stirring, until mixture thickens enough to coat a wooden spoon.

Remove from heat and beat in bourbon, ¾ teaspoon vanilla, the mace, pecans, coconut, cherries and raisins. Allow to cool to room temperature, then spread between the cake layers.

7. Beat remaining 2 egg whites until stiff and leave in mixer. In a small saucepan, combine remaining cup of sugar with ½ cup water, the cream of tartar and remaining teaspoon vanilla. Bring to a boil, stirring. Cook for 5 minutes over medium heat. Gradually pour this mixture over the beaten egg whites, beating constantly until cooled. Use to frost top and sides of the cake.

Lemon Coconut Cakes ✳

These tender little cakes with their surprise filling can be baked and filled well in advance and refrigerated, making them convenient to serve when entertaining. Pichet Ong is a pastry chef who has worked at a number of Southeast Asian restaurants, where his specialty has been French-style desserts with Asian touches. The lemon and coconut, with a mint garnish, fill that requirement.

Pichet Ong

TIME: 45 minutes, plus cooling   YIELD: 12 cakes

1 tablespoon melted unsalted
   butter
½ cup granulated sugar, plus
   more for pans
3 large egg whites
4 large egg yolks
Grated zest of 1 lemon
1 teaspoon vanilla extract
Pinch of salt

½ cup all-purpose flour
½ cup shredded unsweetened
   coconut
Lemon cream (page 535), for
   serving
Confectioners' sugar, for serving
Raspberry coulis (page 536), for
   serving
Mint sprigs, for serving

1. Preheat oven to 350 degrees. Brush a tin to hold 12 half-cup muffins with melted butter, then sprinkle cups with sugar to coat. Place muffin tin in refrigerator.

2. In bowl of an electric mixer fitted with whisk attachment, beat egg whites on high speed until frothy. With mixer running, gradually add ¼ cup sugar. Continue to beat until the egg whites form stiff peaks.

3. In another mixing bowl, combine egg yolks, lemon zest, vanilla and salt with remaining ¼ cup sugar. Beat with whisk attachment at medium speed until very light and fluffy, about 2 minutes.

4. Using a rubber spatula, fold about a third of egg whites into yolks. Fold remaining whites into yolks.

5. Sift flour over batter and fold it in. Fold in coconut. Divide batter among chilled muffin tins.

6. Bake cakes until a toothpick inserted into center of one comes out clean, about 10 minutes. Let cool in pans; cakes will sink a little as they cool.

7. To fill cooled lemon coconut cakes, insert a paring knife into bottom center of each cake and rotate it to form a hole that comes about three-quarters of the way up toward top of cake. (Don't cut through top of cake.) Insert pastry tip into this hole, and pipe in lemon cream until bottom of cake begins to swell slightly. Serve each cake sprinkled with confectioners' sugar, then garnished with a dollop of raspberry coulis on the side, and a mint sprig.

POUND CAKES AND PLAIN CAKES

For some cake-lovers, a slice of butter-rich pound cake is all the satisfaction they need. A few of the cakes in this chapter are plain pound cakes intensified with just enough lemon, or those meant to be garnished with fruit. Some have a fruit component in the batter or as part of the recipe. The term pound cake, by the way, refers to the way the cakes were originally made, before recipes became as exacting as they often are today. A pound each of butter, flour, sugar and eggs were all it took. And of these ingredients, the quality of the butter is the one element that can determine just how delicious the end result will be. Try to use top-quality high-butterfat butter, or even a European-style cultured butter. For more about what that means, there is an essay on page 135.

Lemon Pound Cake ✳

Lemon is the quintessential flavoring for pound cake. It is used liberally here, in the batter and as an added finish to be absorbed by the warm cake, fresh from the oven. The recipe calls for mint ice, but other ices, sorbets, sherbets or ice creams can be used. Bill Yosses is the former pastry chef at Bouley.

Bill
Yosses

∽

TIME: 2½ hours, plus cooling   YIELD: 8 servings

12 tablespoons (1½ sticks)
   unsalted butter, melted
9 lemons
2¾ cups all-purpose flour
1½ cups superfine sugar
1½ teaspoons baking powder
¾ cup crème fraîche or heavy
   cream

6 large eggs
1½ cups granulated sugar
½ cup confectioners' sugar
Raspberry coulis (page 536)
Mint ice, optional (page 476), or
   other ice or ice cream

1. Preheat oven to 350 degrees. Use ½ tablespoon butter to grease a 9-by-5-inch loaf pan. Line with parchment or waxed paper. Use ½ table-spoon butter to grease paper.

2. Grate zest of 4 lemons; slice tops and bottoms off 3 of them. Stand lemons on end on a cutting board, and cut away white pith until the flesh is exposed. Over a bowl, cut segments from membranes, letting fruit and juice fall into bowl. Remove seeds. With fork, break segments into 1-inch pieces.

3. Sift flour, superfine sugar and baking powder into the bowl of an electric mixer. Begin mixing on low speed, then add crème fraîche or cream. Increase speed to medium, and beat in eggs, one at a time, then melted butter. Gently fold lemon segments and juices and 3 tablespoons zest into batter. Spread in pan, and bake 15 minutes. Use a sharp knife to cut an incision lengthwise down middle of cake, and bake 30 minutes longer. Reduce temperature to 325 degrees, and bake 40 to 45 minutes longer, or until a tester comes out clean.

4. Meanwhile, juice the remaining 6 lemons. Put granulated and confectioners' sugars in a pot, and add 1½ cups water. Bring to a simmer, and cook, stirring, until sugar dissolves. Stir in lemon juice and remaining zest, and let cool.

5. When cake is done, cool in pan on a wire rack for 30 minutes. Increase oven temperature to 350 degrees. Prick cake all over with a thin skewer, penetrating to the bottom of the cake. Slowly pour lemon syrup over cake, so it absorbs syrup. Return cake to oven for 10 minutes. Cool on a rack, then unmold.

6. To serve, lightly toast ½-inch-thick slices of the cake on both sides under a broiler or in a toaster oven. Put raspberry coulis on each serving plate. Place two slices of cake slightly overlapping on top and, if using, a scoop of mint ice on top of cake.

Brittany Butter Cake (Gâteau Breton)

Good dark rum adds personality to this dense butter cake. European-style butter has a higher fat content, 82 to 86 percent, than the commercial standard, which is 80 percent, and thus has less moisture. Using it in a cake makes for a richer end result; and it makes pastry crisper. Kay Rentschler is a cook and food writer who contributed recipes to *The New York Times* when she lived in New York.

Kay
Rentschler

TIME: 20 minutes, plus cooling   YIELD: 8 to 10 servings

16 tablespoons (2 sticks)
   European-style (high butterfat)
   unsalted butter, softened, plus
   more for pan
2 cups all-purpose flour, plus
   more for pan
1 cup superfine sugar

4 large egg yolks
1 tablespoon dark rum or
   2 teaspoons orange flower
   water
½ teaspoon fine sea salt
1 large egg white

1. Butter and flour a 9-inch cake or tart pan 2¼ inches deep with a removable bottom. Adjust rack to middle position and preheat oven to 325 degrees. Using a mixer with a paddle, beat butter in a medium bowl on medium speed until light and fluffy, 1 minute. Add sugar and beat until smooth. Add egg yolks one at a time, beating between additions. Scrape down bowl, add rum and beat 15 seconds.

2. Whisk flour and salt together in a medium bowl. With mixer on low speed, add flour mixture to butter mixture a little at a time, beating until dry ingredients are incorporated and a soft doughlike batter has formed.

3. Turn batter into cake pan. In a small bowl, beat egg white and brush over surface of cake. Press a lattice design across top of cake with tines of a fork. Bake until cake is deep golden brown and a toothpick inserted in the center comes out clean, 40 to 45 minutes.

4. Remove cake from oven, cool in pan on a wire rack 5 minutes. Remove sides of pan. Continue cooling. Cake is best eaten the first day.

Papa's Apple Pound Cake

Payard
Pâtisserie
and Bistro,
New York

François Payard, whose family owned a pastry shop on the French Riviera, and now has his own pastry shop and restaurant in New York, kept many of the recipes he grew up with in his repertory. This one is for an unfancy home-style cake. Like most pound cakes, rich in butter, it keeps well, and in this case, because of the glaze, especially well.

TIME: 1 hour 45 minutes, plus cooling   YIELD: 6 to 8 servings

4 ounces (1 stick) unsalted butter, softened, plus more for pan

1 cup plus 3 tablespoons all-purpose flour, plus more for pan

1⅓ cup raisins

1 tablespoon plus 2½ teaspoons dark rum

2 apples, peeled and cored, preferably Fuji apples

¼ teaspoon baking powder

1⅓ cups confectioners' sugar

3 large eggs, at room temperature

4 tablespoons strained apricot preserves, melted and kept warm

1. Preheat oven to 350 degrees. Butter and flour an 8-by-4-by-2½-inch loaf pan. Line pan with parchment paper, allowing an extra inch or two to drape over the opposite ends.

2. Bring a small pan of water to a boil, add the raisins and boil 1 minute to soften them. Drain and repeat the process. Drain raisins well a second time, and place in a small bowl with 1 tablespoon of the rum; stir and set aside. Cut 1 apple into 12 wedges. Cut the other into 8 wedges, and each of these wedges in half crosswise. Set apples aside. In a medium mixing bowl, sift the remaining flour and baking powder together; set aside.

3. Working in a mixer with a paddle, or by hand with a wooden spoon, beat 4 ounces butter until it is smooth. Slowly add 1 cup of the confectioners' sugar, and beat until creamy. Add eggs, one at a time, beating until mixture is well blended.

4. Fold sifted flour mixture into egg mixture just until blended. Fold the raisins into the batter. Spoon half the batter into the prepared pan, and smooth the top. Lay the 12 apple wedges down the center of the pan, so their sides touch and the domed side of each wedge is on top. There will be a thin strip of exposed batter on either side of the row. Spoon the rest of

the batter over and around the apples, and again smooth the top. Arrange halved apple slices in a single row along each long side of the pan, pressing center-cut sides of the apples against the sides of the pan. There will now be two rows of apple slices, with their points toward the center of the pan, and exposed batter in the center. Gently push apples into batter, leaving the tops of the apples exposed. Mixture in center of pan will be slightly shallower than the sides. Let rest for 10 minutes.

5. Place pan on rack in center of the oven, and bake for 10 minutes. Using a sharp knife, cut a slit down the center of the batter to help it rise evenly. Continue to bake until a knife inserted into cake comes out clean, another 40 to 50 minutes. Remove pan from oven, and turn off heat. Gently brush warm apricot preserves over the hot cake. Allow glaze to dry for 5 minutes.

6. In a small saucepan, combine the remaining 2½ teaspoons rum and ⅓ cup confectioners' sugar. Stir well, and warm the icing over low heat for a minute. Brush it over the dried apricot glaze, and return the pan to the turned-off oven just until the rum icing is dry, about 2 minutes. Place cake on a cooling rack still in its pan, and cool to room temperature. To keep the cake moist, keep it in its pan until serving time. To remove cake from pan, lift it by the edges of the parchment paper, carefully remove paper, and transfer to a platter. Cut into slices, and serve.

Somerset Cider Cake

Elizabeth
Ryan,
Breezy Hill
Orchard,
Staatsburg,
New York

In this recipe, the nuts and fruit are dusted with flour to keep them from falling to the bottom of the pan as the cake bakes. The fragrant, spicy cake suggests autumn holidays. Breezy Hill Orchard, which is owned by Elizabeth Ryan, is one of the premier orchards in New York's Hudson Valley, known for heirloom apples.

TIME: 1½ hours, plus cooling   YIELD: 12 servings

4 ounces (1 stick) unsalted butter, plus more for pan

3 cups fresh apple or pear cider, or hard cider

1½ cups dried fruit, one variety like apples, or a mixture including apricots and figs

2½ cups all-purpose flour, plus more for dusting fruit

2 teaspoons ground ginger

1 teaspoon ground nutmeg

1 teaspoon baking soda

1 cup packed dark brown sugar

4 large eggs, at room temperature

1 cup chopped walnuts

1. Preheat oven to 325 degrees. Butter a 5-cup loaf pan, and set aside. Heat 2 cups cider in a small saucepan just until it simmers. Stir in dried fruit, turn off heat and set aside for 10 minutes. Pour into a colander, and allow to drain well over a bowl. Reserve juice for another use.

2. Whisk flour, ginger, nutmeg and baking soda together in a small bowl. Cream butter and sugar together with an electric mixer or by hand. Whisk eggs and remaining 1 cup cider together until well combined. Add a third of egg mixture to creamed butter, and mix. Add a third of flour mixture, and mix. Repeat with remaining egg and flour mixtures, and mix just until combined.

3. Toss walnuts and drained fruit in a bowl. Working quickly, sprinkle with 1 tablespoon flour, and toss to coat very lightly. If needed, continue adding flour a little at a time. Fold fruit and nuts into batter, and spread in loaf pan. Bake until a tester inserted into center of cake comes out clean (a few crumbs are all right), about 1 hour. Let cool in pan. Turn cake out, and wrap tightly in foil until ready to serve. Cake will keep for at least a week.

Vanilla Bean Pound Cake with Muscat-Macerated Fruit

Morrell
Wine Bar
& Café,
New York

The muscat-macerated fruit served alongside this pound cake soaks into the cake and flavors it. But fresh berries, sliced peaches or nectarines, lightly poached clementine segments and even pineapple can be used, with or without a splash of liqueur. Morrell Wine Bar & Café is owned by the same Morrell family as the New York wine merchants.

TIME: 90 minutes, plus cooling   YIELD: 8 to 10 servings

4 ounces (1 stick) unsalted butter, softened, plus more for pan

1¾ cups all-purpose flour, plus more for pan

½ cup vegetable shortening, at room temperature

1 cup sugar

4 large eggs

¼ teaspoon vanilla extract

½ vanilla bean, split lengthwise and center scraped with tip of a knife, bean reserved

¾ teaspoon salt

Muscat-macerated fruit (page 361)

1. Preheat oven to 350 degrees. Butter and flour a 9-by-5-by-3-inch loaf pan.

2. Using an electric mixer, cream butter, shortening and sugar until very fluffy, about 3 to 4 minutes. Whisk together eggs, vanilla extract and vanilla bean scrapings. Gradually add egg mixture to butter mixture, beating well.

3. Sift together flour and salt. Add half the flour mixture to batter, and beat to combine. Add remaining flour, gently folding it in with a spatula. Spread batter in prepared pan, and smooth the top.

4. Bake cake until a tester inserted into middle comes out clean, about 1 hour and 10 minutes. If top of cake seems to be getting overly browned before center is set, cover with foil, and continue baking. Let cool on a rack. Remove from pan.

5. Serve slices of cake with fruit.

Toasted-Almond Pound Cake with Pan-Roasted Strawberries and Strawberry-Rhubarb Compote

Gotham Bar
and Grill,
New York

Strawberries and rhubarb marry in a traditional tart-sweet springtime partnership, but usually in pie or cobbler. Here they adorn a toasted almond pound cake. Gotham Bar and Grill in New York is known for its contemporary take on American cuisine, and especially the towering, vertical food constructions created by its chef, Alfred Portale.

TIME: 1 hour 20 minutes, plus cooling   YIELD: 8 servings

8 ounces (2 sticks) plus
   2 tablespoons unsalted butter,
   melted and cooled
All-purpose flour for pan
5 large eggs
1¾ cups sugar, plus more to taste
1⅓ cups almond flour

1¼ cups cake flour
1 teaspoon grated tangerine or
   orange zest
2 tablespoons sliced almonds
3 pints strawberries, hulled
4 cups trimmed rhubarb in
   1-inch slices

1. Preheat oven to 350 degrees. Use 1 tablespoon butter to grease a 9-by-5-by-3-inch loaf pan. Dust with flour.

2. Using an electric mixer fitted with whisk attachment, beat eggs and 1 cup sugar until thick and light, about 3 minutes.

3. In a bowl, whisk together almond flour, cake flour and zest. Fold ⅓ of the flour mixture into eggs until thoroughly combined. Fold in rest of flour in 2 batches. Fold in all but 2 tablespoons of the melted butter. Scrape batter into pan, and sprinkle almonds on top. Lightly brush remaining butter over almonds.

4. Bake cake until a tester inserted into the middle comes out clean, 40 to 45 minutes. If the top of the cake seems to be getting overly browned before the center is set, cover with foil and continue baking. Let cool on a rack before unmolding.

5. In a medium saucepan, combine 1 pint of the strawberries, the rhubarb, ¾ cup sugar and ¼ cup water. Bring mixture to a simmer and cook, stirring occasionally, until fruit breaks down into a puree, about 30 minutes. Let mixture cool, then taste and add more sugar if desired.

6. Just before serving, place remaining strawberries in a large skillet, and sprinkle with sugar to taste. Cook strawberries over high heat until they release their juices and sugar dissolves. Serve slices of the pound cake surrounded by strawberry-rhubarb compote and topped with sautéed strawberries.

Orange Sour Cream Cake with Blueberry Compote

March
Restaurant,
New York

The cake in this recipe is a fairly standard sour cream pound cake. The blueberries alongside give it character. The recipe comes from March, a townhouse restaurant on New York's East Side.

TIME: 45 minutes, plus cooling   YIELD: 6 to 8 servings

4½ ounces (9 tablespoons) unsalted butter, softened, plus more for pan
1½ cups sifted cake flour
1¼ cups sugar
¾ teaspoon baking powder
¼ teaspoon baking soda
Grated zest of 1 orange
Salt
½ cup sour cream

3 large egg yolks
½ teaspoon orange extract
1½ teaspoons vanilla extract
¼ cup lemon juice
1 tablespoon cornstarch
2 pints (about 5 cups) fresh blueberries, washed and dried
1 teaspoon elderberry or lingonberry syrup, optional (sold in fancy food shops)

1. Preheat oven to 350 degrees. Butter bottom and sides of an 8-inch round cake pan.

2. In bowl of a mixer with a paddle attachment, combine flour, ¾ cup of the sugar, baking powder, baking soda, orange zest and a pinch of salt. Cut butter into small pieces and add to bowl. Mix at low speed until crumbly.

3. Add ¼ cup of the sour cream. Mix at medium speed until smooth and pastelike. Scrape bowl, and add remaining ¼ cup sour cream and egg yolks. Beat at high speed for 1 minute. Scrape bowl, and add orange extract and ½ teaspoon of the vanilla extract. Beat at high speed until light and fluffy, about 1 more minute.

4. Scrape batter into pan, and smooth with a spatula. Bake until top is golden brown and a toothpick inserted in center of cake comes out clean, about 30 minutes. Remove from oven. Cool.

5. In a medium nonreactive saucepan, whisk lemon juice, cornstarch and remaining ½ cup sugar together. Mix until smooth. Add blueberries,

remaining vanilla extract, elderberry syrup and a pinch of salt. Stir gently
to mix. Place over medium-low heat, and simmer just until liquid thickens
and blueberries darken in color. Remove from heat, and transfer to a bowl.

6. To serve, remove cake from pan. Slice, and serve topped with blueberry compote.

Prune-Orange Pound Cake

Florence
Fabricant

Though this cake is not quite as dense as the typical pound cake, it is just as buttery. As for the prunes, these days the term to use is "dried plums," but to me they will always be prunes. Try to find moist, good-quality fruit. And there are even some that are made with orange flavoring, which would be delicious in this recipe.

TIME: 1½ hours, plus cooling   YIELD: 8 servings

12 ounces pitted prunes
⅔ cup orange juice
3 tablespoons Grand Marnier
1 cup plus 2 tablespoons
   granulated sugar
½ pound unsalted butter (2
   sticks), at room temperature,
   plus more for pan

6 large eggs, at room temperature
1 teaspoon vanilla extract
1½ tablespoons grated orange zest
Pinch of salt
2 cups all-purpose flour
1 tablespoon baking powder
Sifted confectioners' sugar

1. Place the prunes in a saucepan with the orange juice and Grand Marnier. Bring to a boil, lower heat and simmer 6 to 8 minutes, until the prunes are soft. Stir in 2 tablespoons sugar and set aside.

2. Preheat oven to 350 degrees. Butter a 9-inch square baking pan or a 9-inch round springform pan.

3. Cream the butter and remaining sugar in an electric mixer. Add 3 whole eggs and 3 egg yolks, reserving the 3 egg whites. Increase the speed to high and beat about 10 minutes, until the batter has become thick, pale yellow and very smooth. Stop the mixer and scrape down the sides of the bowl once or twice.

4. Fold in the vanilla and orange zest.

5. Beat the 3 egg whites with the salt until stiff but not dry. Fold them into the batter.

6. Sift the flour and baking powder together and fold it in. Spread the batter in the baking pan. Cover the top with the prunes. Drizzle any left-over juice from the prunes over the top.

7. Place in the oven and bake about 45 minutes, until a cake tester comes out clean. Allow to cool, then dust with confectioners' sugar before serving.

Orange and Olive Oil Cake

Olive oil is an unusual ingredient in a cake everywhere but in areas that border the Mediterranean. And for the best results, this one demands a fine, fragrant extra-virgin oil. The result is a cake that's as dense and rich as a pound cake, but made without the butter. I like to substitute finely ground almonds for half the flour.

Florence
Fabricant

TIME: 1½ hours   YIELD: 8 servings

⅔ cup extra-virgin olive oil, plus
   more for pan
1½ cups all-purpose flour, plus
   more for pan
½ cup baking powder
¼ cup baking soda
Pinch of salt

2 large eggs
1¾ cups granulated sugar
Grated zest and juice of 2 oranges
   (⅔ cup juice)
Confectioners' sugar
Orange sorbet, optional, for
   serving

1. Preheat oven to 375 degrees. Oil and flour a 10-inch springform pan.

2. Whisk flour with baking powder, baking soda and salt and set aside. Beat eggs, then gradually beat in granulated sugar and continue beating until thick. Mix orange zest, juice and olive oil together. Add to egg mixture in thirds, alternating and ending with flour mixture.

3. Spread batter in pan and bake about 50 minutes, until cake tester comes out clean. Cool on rack 15 minutes and remove sides of pan. Continue cooling, then dust with confectioners' sugar and serve with orange sorbet.

Poppy Seed Cake

Wallsé,
New York

A batter richly strewn with poppy seeds is traditional in Austria, the source of this recipe. The cake has a unique fragrance and flavor, with a hint of lemon. The large amount of poppy seeds needed for the cake are best purchased from a baking or spice supply company. Small jars of poppy seeds sold in supermarkets will not provide enough and wind up being much too costly. The recipe comes from Wallsé, an Austrian restaurant in New York.

TIME: 1¾ hours, plus cooling   YIELD: 8 to 12 servings

8 ounces (2 sticks) unsalted butter, softened, plus more for pan

½ cup all-purpose flour, plus more for pan

¾ cup finely ground blanched almonds

¾ cup dry bread crumbs

1¾ cups (½ pound) poppy seeds

9 large eggs, separated and at room temperature

1⅓ cups granulated sugar

1 teaspoon grated lemon zest

2 tablespoons confectioners' sugar

1. Preheat oven to 350 degrees. Butter and flour a 10-inch springform pan. In large bowl, mix ½ cup flour with almonds, bread crumbs and poppy seeds. Set aside.

2. Place ½ pound butter in bowl of electric mixer, and beat at medium-low speed until creamy. Add egg yolks one at a time, beating after each addition. Scrape sides of bowl from time to time. When all yolks have been added, mixture may look slightly curdled. Increase speed to high and beat 2 minutes, or until butter and yolk mixture is very smooth. Set aside.

3. In clean bowl, beat whites on medium speed until softly peaked. Gradually add granulated sugar. When all sugar has been added, continue beating at high speed until whites hold peaks but are still creamy.

4. Fold whites into poppy-seed mixture. Fold in yolk mixture. Fold in lemon zest. Transfer batter to pan, smooth top and bake 50 minutes to 1 hour, until cake is golden brown and a cake tester comes out clean. Cool in pan 10 minutes, remove sides of pan and continue cooling.

5. To serve, dust top of cake with sifted confectioners' sugar.

Coconut Marzipan Cake

Marzipan and coconut enrich this pound cake baked in a tube pan. Though many coconut desserts are made with unsweetened coconut, this one calls for the sweetened kind, sold in cans. With the coconut, consider filling the center of the cake with tropical fruit like mango or pineapple. Nigella Lawson is the host of an English television cooking show, *Nigella Bites*.

Nigella Lawson

TIME: 1 hour 15 minutes   YIELD: 8 to 10 servings

8 ounces (2 sticks) unsalted butter, softened, plus more for pan
¼ cup sweetened flaked coconut
8 ounces marzipan
1 cup cake flour
½ teaspoon baking powder
½ teaspoon baking soda

¼ teaspoon salt
½ cup granulated sugar
½ teaspoon coconut or almond extract
6 large eggs
2 to 3 cups fresh raspberries or other fruit
1 teaspoon confectioners' sugar

1. Preheat oven to 350 degrees. Butter a 10-inch springform ring mold, and sprinkle flaked coconut around its bottom and sides. Soften marzipan by heating it in a microwave oven, 10 to 15 seconds. Whisk flour, baking powder, baking soda and salt together and set aside.

2. In a food processor, combine marzipan, butter, granulated sugar and extract. Process until mixture is very smooth. With processor running, add eggs one at a time through the feed tube. Stop processor and sprinkle dry ingredients evenly over batter. Process again until mixture is smooth, making sure there are no lumps in the batter.

3. Pour mixture into prepared pan. Bake until surface is golden brown and a toothpick inserted in center comes out clean, 40 to 50 minutes. Remove from oven, and allow to cool in pan until slightly warm.

4. To release cake from pan, remove springform sides. Holding a cake plate over the center tube of pan, invert cake so that it falls onto plate. Fill center of cake with berries and scatter remainder around perimeter of cake. Pass confectioners' sugar through a small sieve and sprinkle over cake and fruit. Serve immediately.

Carrot Cake

Craig
Claiborne

This cake is a staple and a perennial favorite. Craig Claiborne, who was the food editor of *The New York Times*, understood the value of classic recipes as well as he did the most modern, cutting-edge attempts.

TIME: 1 hour 15 minutes, plus cooling   YIELD: 8 to 10 servings

1½ cups corn or peanut oil, plus
   more for pans
1 pound carrots, approximately
2 cups sugar
4 large eggs
2 cups all-purpose flour

2 teaspoons baking powder
2 teaspoons baking soda
1 teaspoon salt
½ cup coarsely chopped pecans
Cream cheese frosting (page 530)

1. Preheat oven to 325 degrees. Oil 3 9-inch cake pans. Line bottoms with parchment paper and oil the paper.

2. Trim, peel and grate the carrots. You should have 3 cups. Set aside.

3. Combine sugar and 1½ cups oil in the bowl of an electric mixer and start beating. Add eggs one at a time, beating well after each addition.

4. Sift together the flour, baking powder, baking soda and salt. Add to batter, beating on medium speed. Stir in grated carrots and pecans.

5. Spread batter in pans and bake 45 minutes. Allow cakes to cool on racks, remove from pans, peel off paper and ice with cream cheese frosting.

Tropical Oatmeal-Mango Cake

The diced mango adds a grace note of tangy sweetness to the cake. Dried mango that has been soaked in hot water, then well drained, can be used in place of fresh. And note that unlike the recipe on page 71, the coconut is unsweetened. This variety is usually sold in health food stores and baking supply specialists. Las Olas in Fort Lauderdale, Florida, is the flagship restaurant for chef Mark Militello.

Mark's
Las Olas,
Ft. Lauderdale,
Florida

TIME: 1½ hours, plus cooling   YIELD: 8 servings

9 tablespoons unsalted butter,
   softened
1 cup plus 2 tablespoons
   granulated sugar
1 cup rolled oats (not instant)
1½ cups all-purpose flour
1 teaspoon ground cinnamon
¼ teaspoon ground nutmeg
1 teaspoon baking soda

Pinch of salt
1⅔ cups dark brown sugar
2 large eggs
1 teaspoon vanilla extract
1 cup finely diced mango
⅔ cup chopped pecans
¼ cup heavy cream
1 cup shredded unsweetened
   coconut

1. Use about ½ tablespoon butter to grease a 10- to 11-inch springform pan. Dust with 2 tablespoons sugar. Preheat oven to 350 degrees.

2. Place oats in a dry skillet, and toast until light brown. Transfer to a bowl, and add 1¼ cups hot water. Set aside. Sift flour with cinnamon, nutmeg, baking soda and salt.

3. Mix 1 cup granulated sugar and 1 cup brown sugar in the bowl of an electric mixer. Beat in eggs until smooth and mixture falls in a ribbon when beater is lifted. Fold in vanilla, softened oats and mango, then flour mixture.

4. Transfer batter to pan, place in oven and bake for 45 minutes, until cake tester comes out clean and surface is lightly browned. Remove from oven. Turn on broiler.

5. Mix pecans with remaining butter and remaining brown sugar. Stir in cream, and fold in coconut. Gently spread this mixture on top of cake.

6. Place cake under broiler, and broil until surface is bubbly and lightly browned. Watch carefully so topping does not burn. Transfer cake to rack, and allow to cool before removing sides of pan.

Castagnaccio

Babbo,
New York

The mixture of fruits, nuts and honey makes this almost a fruitcake. And it would certainly suit a Christmas dinner. The chestnut flour is sold by baking suppliers, in catalogs and online. For the sour cherries, dried tart cherries or even dried cranberries can be used. This recipe, from *The Babbo Cookbook* by Mario Batali (2002), is included by permission of Clarkson Potter, a division of Random House.

TIME: 55 minutes, plus cooling   YIELD: 8 servings

Oil or nonstick cooking spray for pan
1½ cups chestnut flour
¼ cup granulated sugar
1 tablespoon baking powder
1 tablespoon unsweetened Dutch-process cocoa, plus more for dusting
½ teaspoon salt
2 large eggs

½ cup extra-virgin olive oil
4 tablespoons honey, preferably chestnut
1½ cups roughly chopped toasted walnuts
¾ cup dried sour cherries
¾ cup golden raisins
⅔ cup toasted pine nuts
Confectioners' sugar

1. Preheat oven to 350 degrees. Lightly grease a 9-inch springform pan with oil or nonstick cooking spray.

2. In large mixing bowl, combine chestnut flour, granulated sugar, baking powder, cocoa and salt. In another bowl, whisk together eggs, olive oil and 2 tablespoons honey, and add to dry mixture, mixing well to combine. Stir in walnuts, cherries, raisins and pine nuts, and mix until evenly distributed. Spread batter in pan, smoothing the surface.

3. Bake for 35 minutes, or until cake begins to puff slightly and is lightly golden brown and the middle is set. Cool completely on wire rack before removing from pan.

4. To serve, heat remaining honey gently in microwave or in small saucepan over low heat, just to melt it slightly. Brush top of cake with honey, and dust lightly with confectioners' sugar and cocoa.

Angel Food Cake

Craig
Claiborne

Craig Claiborne, who was the food editor of *The New York Times*, said that this was his absolutely favorite dessert. "To me it was divine, celestial, manna from heaven," he said. Angel food cake is a feat of culinary magic helped by technical requirements. It is absolutely essential that great care be taken in beating the egg whites so they remain creamy and do not weep or break from overbeating and prevent the cake from rising so magnificently. It's best to underbeat them slightly. And they will beat best if they are not ice-cold. The pan is not greased so the batter easily "climbs" up the sides as it bakes, increasing the loftiness of the cake. Tracing a square in the top of the unbaked batter with a knife also encourages rising. And keeping the cake upside down until it cools is essential to prevent it from falling.

TIME: 1 hour 15 minutes, plus cooling   YIELD: About 10 servings

1⅓ cups superfine sugar
1 cup sifted cake flour
¼ teaspoon salt
12 large egg whites, at room
    temperature

1¼ teaspoons cream of tartar
1 teaspoon vanilla extract
½ teaspoon almond extract

1. Preheat oven to 350 degrees.

2. Combine ⅓ cup sugar, the cake flour and salt in a sifter. Sift the mixture three times.

3. Place the egg whites in the bowl of an electric mixer and beat until foamy. Add cream of tartar. Continue beating until whites hold soft peaks.

4. Continue beating, gradually adding the remaining cup of sugar, about a tablespoon at a time. Fold in vanilla and almond extracts. Sift about a quarter of the flour mixture over the egg whites and fold in. Repeat until remaining flour mixture is folded in.

5. Pour batter into an ungreased deep 9-inch tube pan. Using a knife or spatula, trace a square about 2 inches deep in the top of the batter. Bake 45 minutes or until cake has risen, is lightly browned and springy.

6. Immediately invert cake on a rack or suspend the pan upside down over the neck of a sturdy bottle. Allow to cool completely, about 1½ hours. Run a knife or metal spatula around sides of pan to release cake.

Warm Vanilla Cakes

Bill
Yosses

To make these cakes more convenient to bake at the last minute and serve while still warm, the molds can be filled and then refrigerated for at least 8 hours, then baked. Bill Yosses is a pastry chef who first became well-known in the early 1990s at Bouley.

TIME: 1 hour, plus 8 hours' resting time for batter   YIELD: 12 cakes

7 tablespoons unsalted butter, plus
    more for molds
10 ounces white chocolate
5 large eggs at room temperature,
    separated
3 vanilla beans, split in half
    lengthwise, seeds scraped out

¼ cup plus 2 tablespoons bread
    flour, sifted
Pinch of cream of tartar
¼ cup plus 2 tablespoons sugar
Vanilla ice cream for serving
    (page 446)

1. Melt butter and 7 ounces white chocolate in a double boiler over hot, not boiling, water. When mixture is melted, remove from heat and stir until smooth. Whisk in egg yolks and half the vanilla-bean seeds. Sift flour over mixture. Whisk until smooth.

2. In an electric mixer fitted with a whisk, combine egg whites and cream of tartar. Whisk until fluffy. Slowly add sugar a little at a time, until meringue is shiny and stiff. Fold a little of the chocolate mixture into meringue; then fold meringue into remaining chocolate mixture, until mixture is smooth. Cover with plastic wrap, and refrigerate about 8 hours.

3. Preheat oven to 375 degrees. Line a baking sheet with parchment paper. Butter 12 metal rings 2½ inches in diameter and 1¼ inches high and place them on parchment paper. Or use 12 2-ounce muffin or other molds. Using a spatula, spoon cool batter into a pastry bag with a tip opening of about ½ inch or use teaspoons to fill molds one-third full. Break remaining chocolate into pieces about 1 inch square and ⅛ inch thick. Drop a piece in each mold. Sprinkle a little cluster of vanilla seeds from remaining beans on top. Cover chocolate with more batter so molds are barely two-thirds full.

4. Bake 12 to 14 minutes, until risen and still a bit jiggly in center. Remove from oven. Have 12 plates ready. Slip tip of a knife under cake, and

lift it a little. Then slide a spatula underneath, and transfer to a serving plate, and, holding mold in place with tongs, run a sharp knife around top edge of mold, then lift mold off cake with tongs. Repeat with other cakes. If using muffin tins or other molds in a single form, run a knife around the edges, place a baking sheet on top of the pan, invert, and tap bottoms of molds so cakes come out. Serve immediately with ice cream.

UPSIDE-DOWN CAKES

The allure of upside-down cakes is that they come to the table glistening with caramel glaze and need no icing or even a finishing drift of confectioners' sugar. The classic, of course, is pineapple, made with rings of canned fruit. Fresh pineapple actually works well, too. The following recipes offer other variations, with pears, mango, cranberries and blueberries.

Apple Upside-Down Cake

Upside-down caramelized apples can be done as a cake, as it is here, or as a tart, the famous tarte Tatin (page 269).

Florence
Fabricant

TIME: 1 hour 15 minutes   YIELD: 6 to 8 servings

6 tablespoons unsalted butter	2 large eggs
4 medium-size apples, peeled, cored and cut into slices ½ inch thick	¾ cup granulated sugar
	1 tablespoon apple cider, applejack or Calvados
¾ cup dark brown sugar	¾ cup sifted cake flour
½ teaspoon ground cinnamon	¾ teaspoon baking powder

1. Melt 4 tablespoons of the butter in a heavy skillet. Add the apple slices and sauté over high heat about 5 minutes, until the apples are tender, beginning to brown but still holding their shape. Remove the skillet from the heat.

2. Preheat oven to 350 degrees. Place a 9-inch pie pan in the oven, add the remaining butter and allow it to melt. Remove the pie pan from the oven.

3. Tip the pan so it is completely coated with butter. Mix the brown sugar and cinnamon together and spread in the pan. Return the pan to the oven just until the sugar has melted. Remove from the oven and spread the sugar mixture evenly over the bottom of the pan.

4. Arrange the apple slices in a pattern over the brown sugar in the bottom of the pan. Any slices that do not fit in the pattern can be scattered over the rest—they will not show.

5. Beat eggs until thick, gradually adding the granulated sugar, beating until light and lemon-colored. Stir in cider or spirits.

6. Sift the flour with the baking powder and fold into the batter. Spread the batter over the apples in the pan. Bake 30 minutes. Allow to cool at least 30 minutes, then unmold the cake onto a large platter and serve while still warm.

Pear Upside-Down Cake

Old Chatham
Sheepherding
Company
Inn, Old
Chatham,
New York

This is a fragrant, spicy upside-down cake. Instead of pears, consider ripe peaches or nectarines in summer, or apples in winter. The Old Chatham Sheepherding Company Inn was a lovely, historic property in New York's Hudson Valley. The inn has closed, alas, but the Old Chatham Sheepherding Company, with its large herd of dairy sheep, is still in business, and makes sheep milk cheeses and yogurt. Some of that yogurt, lightly sweetened, would be excellent alongside this cake.

TIME: 1 hour 15 minutes, plus cooling   YIELD: 10 servings

11 tablespoons unsalted butter
5 large ripe Bartlett pears, peeled,
   cored and quartered
2 tablespoons lemon juice
4 tablespoons granulated sugar
8 tablespoons Poire Williams
   (pear eau de vie)
1 cup all-purpose flour
1 tablespoon ground ginger
1 teaspoon ground cinnamon

¼ teaspoon ground cloves
¼ teaspoon ground nutmeg
¼ teaspoon salt
¼ cup dark brown sugar, packed
3 large eggs
½ cup molasses
2 tablespoons grated fresh ginger
1 teaspoon baking soda
¾ cup heavy cream, whipped

1. Butter a 9-inch cake pan with 1 tablespoon butter. Toss pears with lemon juice.

2. In a large sauté pan over medium-high heat, melt 2 tablespoons butter and sprinkle with 2 tablespoons granulated sugar. Add pears, cut side down, in a single layer. Cook until browned, 2 to 3 minutes. Turn and brown the other cut side. Transfer to a plate.

3. To the same sauté pan, add 6 tablespoons Poire Williams, and sprinkle with the rest of the granulated sugar. Cook until reduced to a syrup, about 1 minute. Pour into cake pan, coating the bottom. Place pears in pan, cut side down, arranging in a pattern in a single layer (there may be a few leftover slices; dice them and scatter over the other pears).

4. In a medium mixing bowl, whisk together the flour, ginger, cinnamon, cloves, nutmeg and salt. Set aside. Preheat oven to 350 degrees.

5. In the bowl of an electric mixer, beat the remaining 8 tablespoons

butter until fluffy. Add brown sugar, and beat on medium-high speed for 3 minutes. Add eggs, and continue beating to combine. Add molasses and fresh ginger. Gradually add flour mixture. In a small bowl, combine the baking soda and 2 tablespoons boiling water, beating with a fork. Add to the batter, and mix well.

6. Pour batter into cake pan over the pears. Bake for 25 minutes. Lower heat to 325 degrees, and bake an additional 15 minutes, until cake springs back when touched in the center. Remove from oven. Cool for 1 hour, then invert onto serving plate. Fold remaining Poire Williams into whipped cream and serve with cake.

Mango-Pineapple Upside-Down Cake

Good
Restaurant,
New York

Eliminate the mango and use all pineapple, and you have the near-classic, made with fresh, not canned, fruit. Good Restaurant is a homey spot in Greenwich Village, where the food sometimes offers surprising touches of sophistication, as this dessert indicates.

TIME: 1 hour 45 minutes, plus cooling   YIELD: 6 servings

8 ounces (2 sticks) unsalted butter, softened
1½ cups plus 3 tablespoons packed dark brown sugar
1 cup diced fresh mango plus ¼ cup finely chopped
1 cup diced fresh pineapple plus ¼ cup finely chopped
1 cup plus 1 tablespoon all-purpose flour

¼ cup yellow cornmeal
1½ teaspoons ground cinnamon
1 teaspoon ground ginger
1 teaspoon baking powder
½ teaspoon salt
½ cup granulated sugar
3 large eggs
⅓ cup sour cream
1 teaspoon vanilla extract

1. Preheat oven to 350 degrees. Use a little of the butter to lightly grease a 9-inch cake pan, and line bottom with parchment or waxed paper.

2. To make the topping, in a small saucepan, melt half the butter with ½ cup plus 3 tablespoons brown sugar. Stir until smooth, and pour into cake pan; allow to cool slightly. Sprinkle diced mango and pineapple over pan, and set aside. Sift together flour, cornmeal, cinnamon, ginger, baking powder and salt and set aside.

3. In the bowl of an electric mixer fitted with a paddle attachment, beat remaining butter until light, about 3 minutes. Add remaining brown sugar and granulated sugar, and beat until light and fluffy, about 5 minutes. Add eggs, one at a time, stopping and scraping down sides of bowl after each addition. Beat in sour cream and vanilla.

4. On low speed, mix flour mixture into batter in three batches. Gently fold in finely chopped mango and pineapple. Pour batter into the cake pan. Bake until top is golden brown and a cake tester inserted into center comes out clean, 50 to 60 minutes. Transfer to a wire rack to cool completely. Run a knife around the edges. Invert onto a platter, peel off paper and serve.

Cranberry Upside-Down Cake

This fresh cranberry upside-down cake could join the usual pies on the Thanksgiving dessert board. For Alice Waters, one of the originators of California cuisine at Chez Panisse in Berkeley, food must be seasonal, as with this autumn confection.

Alice
Waters
∾

TIME: 1 hour   YIELD: 8 servings

12 tablespoons (1½ sticks) unsalted butter	¼ teaspoon salt
¾ cup light brown sugar	1 cup granulated sugar
9 ounces (2⅔ cups) fresh cranberries	1 teaspoon vanilla extract
¼ cup fresh orange juice	2 large eggs, separated
1½ cups all-purpose flour	½ cup whole milk
2 teaspoons baking powder	¼ teaspoon cream of tartar
	Lightly sweetened whipped cream
	Orange liqueur, optional

1. In a 9-inch round cake pan over low heat, melt 4 tablespoons butter and add brown sugar. Stir until sugar dissolves, swirling pan to coat bottom. When sugar starts to caramelize, remove pan from heat and allow to cool.

2. In a small bowl, combine cranberries and orange juice. Toss to coat berries well. Spread berries evenly in pan, and sprinkle with any juice remaining in bowl. Set pan aside. Preheat oven to 350 degrees.

3. In a large mixing bowl, sift together flour, baking powder and salt. Set aside.

4. Using an electric mixer, cream remaining butter with granulated sugar until pale, light and fluffy. Add vanilla, and beat in egg yolks one at a time, scraping bowl once or twice. Add flour mixture alternately with milk, ending with dry ingredients. Set batter aside.

5. Using an electric mixer, whisk egg whites with cream of tartar just until whites are softly peaked. Fold whites into batter one-third at a time. Spoon batter into prepared pan, and spread it evenly over cranberries. Bake until top is browned and cake pulls away slightly from edges of pan, 25 to 35 minutes. Let cake cool for 15 minutes.

6. Invert cake onto a cake plate. Serve with slightly sweetened whipped cream, flavored, if desired, with orange liqueur.

HOLIDAY CAKES

Almost any homemade cake can suit a holiday meal, but like the inevitable pumpkin pie at Thanksgiving, the ones I have gathered for this chapter strongly suggest certain events on the calendar. Fruitcakes and Yule logs for Christmas, flourless Passover cakes and winter-friendly gingerbread are some of the recipes included in this section. But there are other dessert recipes suited for holidays, too, and not just cakes. See page 547 for suggestions for various occasions.

Postmodern Fruitcake ☀

Kay
Rentschler

This updated version of a classic fruitcake depends on good-quality candied fruit. And there is proportionately less fruit in relation to the amount of batter. If you wish, you can substitute Cognac or rum for the water in the infusing syrup. Kay Rentschler was a frequent contributor to the Dining pages of *The New York Times*, until she moved out of New York.

TIME: About 1½ hours, plus 6 hours' macerating   YIELD: 8 to 10 servings

1½ cups chopped pitted dates
¼ cup chopped candied citron,
    plus more for decorating
¼ cup chopped candied orange
    peel, plus more for decorating
¼ cup chopped candied lemon
    peel, plus more for decorating
¼ cup candied cherries, plus more
    for decorating
½ cup hot brewed coffee,
    preferably espresso
¼ cup Cognac
6 ounces (1½ sticks) unsalted
    butter, softened, plus more for
    greasing pan

3 cups all-purpose flour
½ teaspoon ground mace
½ teaspoon ground cinnamon
⅛ teaspoon ground cloves
½ teaspoon salt
1 teaspoon baking soda
1 teaspoon baking powder
½ cup dark brown sugar
2 teaspoons vanilla extract
2 large eggs
2 tablespoons granulated sugar

1. Combine dates and candied fruit in a small bowl. Pour coffee and Cognac over them, and stir to combine. Cover and macerate 6 hours or overnight.

2. Place oven rack in lowest position and a large roasting pan on rack. Fill pan halfway with hot water. Preheat oven to 350 degrees. Grease a 10-inch tube pan. Whisk flour, mace, cinnamon, cloves, salt, baking soda and baking powder together in a medium bowl. Set aside.

3. In a mixer with a paddle attachment, beat butter on medium speed until light and fluffy, 40 seconds. Scrape down bowl, add brown sugar, and beat until light and fluffy, 2 minutes. Mix in vanilla. Add eggs, beating well after each addition.

4. With machine on low speed, add dry ingredients, and mix just to combine. Mix in dates, fruit and macerating liquid. Turn batter into cake pan, smoothing top. Bake in water bath until cake has risen and top is brown, about an hour. Remove cake from oven, cool in pan on wire rack 5 minutes, turn out of pan right-side up onto rack and cool completely.

5. Heat granulated sugar with 1 tablespoon water to a simmer, stirring to dissolve sugar. Simmer until syrup thickens slightly. Remove from heat. Arrange slices of candied fruit on top of cake, and brush with syrup.

Mini Pains d'Épices

Payard
Pâtisserie
and Bistro,
New York

Pain d'épices is French for spice bread, very similar to what Americans know as gingerbread, with the difference that there is a decided flavor of anise in most recipes. Here, the *pains d'épices* are baked into 4 small loaves in disposable foil pans, something that a commercial bakery like Payard Pâtisserie and Bistro is likely to prefer. Fluted paper baker's liners, metal pans and even flexible silicone molds can be used. This is an eggless recipe.

TIME: 1 hour 15 minutes, plus cooling   YIELD: 4 small loaves

Butter for greasing pans
Flour for dusting pans
2 cups nuts, preferably a mix of
    sliced almonds, slivered
    almonds, skinned pistachios,
    skinned hazelnuts, walnut
    halves and pine nuts
1 cup dried fruit cut in ¼-inch
    dice, preferably equal amounts
    of apricots, figs and pitted
    prunes and dates
¼ cup dark raisins
¼ cup golden raisins
Finely grated zest of 1 lemon
Finely grated zest of 1 orange

4 teaspoons baking soda
1 teaspoon pastis or other anise-
    flavored liqueur
¼ teaspoon ground cinnamon
¼ teaspoon freshly grated nutmeg
¼ teaspoon ground cloves
Pinch of salt
1 cup pine honey, or other
    strongly flavored honey
¾ cup sugar
2 tablespoons dark rum
2 pieces star anise, tied in
    cheesecloth
3 cups all-purpose flour, sifted

1. Preheat oven to 350 degrees. Butter four aluminum-foil baby loaf pans, each 5¾ inches by 3¼ inches by 2 inches. Dust the insides with flour, and tap out excess. Place pans on baking sheet; set aside.

2. In a large mixing bowl, combine nuts, diced fruit, dark raisins, golden raisins, lemon zest and orange zest. Mix well. Add baking soda, pastis, cinnamon, nutmeg, cloves and salt. Stir to mix.

3. In a medium saucepan over medium heat, combine 1¾ cups water with honey, sugar, rum and star anise. Bring to a boil, and immediately remove from heat. Remove and discard star anise. Pour liquid into the bowl

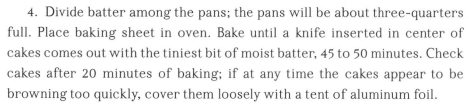

of fruit and nuts, and stir gently. Let mixture rest for 5 minutes, stirring occasionally. Add flour, stir well and let rest for 2 or 3 minutes.

4. Divide batter among the pans; the pans will be about three-quarters full. Place baking sheet in oven. Bake until a knife inserted in center of cakes comes out with the tiniest bit of moist batter, 45 to 50 minutes. Check cakes after 20 minutes of baking; if at any time the cakes appear to be browning too quickly, cover them loosely with a tent of aluminum foil.

5. Transfer cakes to a rack, and cool to room temperature. Unmold, and wrap in plastic film. To serve, cut into thin slices. The cakes are best after ripening for 3 days at room temperature. If sealed in airtight wrap, they may be frozen for a month.

Spicy Gingerbread

Kay
Rentschler

Here is a simple, tender gingerbread given an extra dose of zip with the addition of cayenne. Though it can be served unadorned, a spoonful of crème anglaise (page 533) would be delicious alongside, and it would be an excellent foil for various ice creams. Kay Rentschler wrote for the Dining pages of *The New York Times*, until she moved out of New York.

TIME: About 1 hour, plus cooling   YIELD: 8 to 10 servings

4 ounces (1 stick) unsalted butter, softened, plus more for greasing pan
2 cups all-purpose flour, plus more for pan
1¾ teaspoons ground ginger
1¼ teaspoons ground cinnamon
½ teaspoon unsweetened cocoa
¼ teaspoon ground anise

Pinch of ground cloves
⅛ teaspoon cayenne pepper
½ teaspoon salt
1 teaspoon baking soda
1 cup milk
⅔ cup molasses
½ cup dark brown sugar
2 large eggs

1. Preheat oven to 325 degrees. Grease and flour one 9-inch round cake pan. Sift flour, ginger, cinnamon, cocoa, anise, cloves, cayenne, salt and baking soda into a medium bowl, and set aside.

2. In a small saucepan, combine milk and molasses and warm over low heat, stirring occasionally, until molasses dissolves into the milk. Remove from heat and set aside.

3. In the bowl of a mixer with a paddle attachment, beat butter on medium speed until light and fluffy, about 40 seconds. Scrape down bowl, add brown sugar and beat until smooth and light. Add eggs, one at a time, beating well after each addition.

4. With machine on low speed, add flour mixture in three parts and milk mixture in two. Turn batter into the cake pan, smoothing top. Bake until gingerbread tests clean with toothpick, 40 to 45 minutes. Remove from oven, cool in pan 5 minutes, turn out onto a rack and cool completely.

88   ·   *The New York Times Dessert Cookbook*

Raisin Cake with Port

This rich dessert cake suggests the winter holiday table. You can substitute other dried fruits, like diced dates, for some of the raisins. Candied orange peel would also be suitable to include. And you do not have to splurge on fine aged tawny port. An inexpensive entry-level tawny works just fine. But for a port to accompany the cake, look for a twenty-year-old.

TIME: 1½ hours, plus cooling   YIELD: 8 servings

Florence
Fabricant

4 ounces (1 stick) unsalted butter, softened

1½ cups cake flour

1½ cups dark raisins

1 cup tawny port

½ teaspoon ground cinnamon

1 teaspoon baking powder

¼ teaspoon baking soda

½ teaspoon salt

½ cup honey

2 large eggs

1. Preheat oven to 350 degrees. Use ½ tablespoon butter to grease an 8- or 9-inch springform pan. Dust with a little flour.

2. Place raisins in a small bowl and mix with ½ cup port. Sift together remaining flour with cinnamon, baking powder, baking soda and salt.

3. Beat remaining butter until fluffy. Slowly beat in honey. Beat in eggs one at a time. Beat batter 1 minute. Stir in flour mixture in thirds, alternating with remaining port. Fold in raisins with port. Spread mixture in pan and bake about 55 minutes, until cake tester comes out clean. Cool on a rack, then unmold.

Muscadine Yule Log

Nigella
Lawson

This chocolate Yule log flavored with Grand Marnier and decorated with caramel spikes is not typical but it is dramatic, and worth the effort. Nigella Lawson specializes in grand-looking desserts that are simpler to make than they appear to be.

TIME: 1 hour, plus 2 hours' refrigeration and cooling   YIELD: 8 servings

10 ounces bittersweet chocolate

1 cup heavy cream

2 tablespoons finely chopped candied orange peel

5 tablespoons plus 1 cup granulated sugar

3 tablespoons Grand Marnier

4 large eggs, separated

1 cup confectioners' sugar, plus extra for sprinkling and dredging

1 teaspoon vanilla extract

¼ cup plus 3 tablespoons cake flour

2 tablespoons light corn syrup

1. Finely chop 6 ounces of the chocolate, and place in a mixing bowl. In a small saucepan, bring cream to a boil. Whisk hot cream into chocolate until smooth, then add orange peel and stir to mix well. Set aside to cool and thicken, or chill 40 minutes, stirring occasionally.

2. In a small saucepan, combine 5 tablespoons granulated sugar with ¼ cup water. Bring to a boil, then remove from heat. Stir in the Grand Marnier, then set aside to cool to room temperature.

3. Preheat oven to 350 degrees. Line a 15-by-10-inch jelly roll pan with parchment paper, allowing paper to overlap slightly at ends.

4. Using an electric mixer, whisk egg whites until foamy. Gradually add ½ cup of the confectioners' sugar, and beat until whites form firm, glossy peaks. In a large bowl, whisk egg yolks by hand with ¼ cup confectioners' sugar. Add vanilla, and whisk to blend. Turn mixer to lowest speed, and add yolk mixture to whites, mixing only to combine; do not overmix. Place flour in a sifter, and sift over mixture. Using a rubber spatula, gently fold in the flour. Scrape mixture into jelly roll pan, and smooth the top. Sprinkle cake lightly with 2 tablespoons of confectioners' sugar. Let it sit 5 minutes, then sprinkle with 2 more tablespoons confectioners' sugar.

5. Bake cake until lightly golden and springy to the touch, about 10 min-

utes. Lifting it from the pan with the parchment paper, slide it onto a rack, and cool to room temperature. Place a piece of parchment paper over the cake, then invert cake onto the counter, on the paper. Peel away the baking paper. Brush Grand Marnier syrup over the surface of the cake. Using an offset spatula, spread the chocolate mixture evenly over the syrup. Starting from one of the shorter ends of the cake and using the paper for assistance, roll up the cake. Wrap in plastic wrap, and refrigerate for 1 hour. (The cake can be chilled, and when set, wrapped airtight and frozen for 1 month.)

6. To prepare the cake for serving, in a small saucepan, combine 1 cup granulated sugar, corn syrup and ¼ cup water. Place over medium heat, and bring to a boil. Boil until syrup is a light caramel color, about 5 minutes. Remove from heat and cool for 5 minutes.

7. Line a baking sheet with parchment paper. Drop a small spoonful of the syrup on the paper, to make a dot ½ inch in diameter. Using the tip of a small icing spatula or knife, and starting at the center of the dot, draw caramel out to shape a spike or plume. Continue to shape about 7 spikes. Refrigerate until firm, about 15 minutes.

8. Spread a generous amount of sifted confectioners' sugar on a baking sheet. Chop and melt the remaining 4 ounces of chocolate. Unwrap the cold cake and brush with this melted chocolate, then dust with sifted confectioners' sugar. Return the cake to the refrigerator for 5 minutes to set the chocolate, then transfer to a serving platter. Decorate with caramel spikes before serving.

One-Pan Christmas Cake

Nigella
Lawson

Fruitcake it is, but one that is a keeper. Bake two, one of them without the jam glaze, to be frozen for the following year. It keeps extremely well in the freezer. With this recipe, English cookbook author Nigella Lawson has freshened and updated a classic. Sweetened chestnut puree is sold in cans in fancy food shops.

TIME: About 3 hours, plus cooling   YIELD: One 8-inch cake

2¼ cups golden raisins
1⅓ cups dark raisins
1 cup currants
⅓ cup candied cherries, quartered
6 ounces (1½ sticks) unsalted
   butter
1½ cups muscovado or dark
   brown sugar
¾ cup sweetened chestnut puree
½ cup plus 3 tablespoons dark
   rum

Juice and grated zest of 1 orange
Grated zest of 1 lemon
3 large eggs, beaten
2 cups all-purpose flour
½ teaspoon baking powder
¼ teaspoon ground cinnamon
¼ teaspoon ground cloves
¼ teaspoon ground nutmeg
¼ cup strained apricot preserves
Candied fruits for decorating cake
Nuts for decorating cake

1. Preheat oven to 300 degrees. Line the bottom and sides of an 8-inch-round, 3-inch-high springform pan with a double layer of parchment paper that extends about 2 inches higher than sides of pan.

2. In a large saucepan, combine golden raisins, dark raisins, currants, candied cherries, butter, sugar, chestnut puree, ½ cup rum and the orange juice. Add orange zest and lemon zest, and mix well. Place pan over medium-low heat, and bring to a simmer. Stir until butter has melted, then simmer for 10 minutes. Remove from heat, and allow to stand for 30 minutes.

3. Add eggs, flour, baking powder, cinnamon, cloves and nutmeg to pan. Stir to combine. Pour mixture into prepared cake pan, and smooth surface. To keep cake moist, wrap strip of heavy brown wrapping paper around outside of pan, tying it with string; paper should be twice height of pan.

4. Bake until top of cake is firm and dry, but a toothpick inserted in center comes out slightly sticky, 1¾ to 2 hours. Cool on a rack and remove brown paper. If desired, pierce cake several times with a skewer, and pour

remaining rum into holes. When cake has cooled, remove it from pan and discard parchment paper. Wrap first in waxed paper and then foil, and store in a cool place or refrigerate until ready to decorate.

5. To decorate, combine preserves and 1 tablespoon water in a saucepan. Place over low heat, and stir to make a smooth glaze. Remove from heat, and cool. Paint top of cake with half of the glaze, and decorate it with candied fruits and nuts. Paint a second coat of glaze over decorations.

Orange-Date-Walnut Passover Cake

Rebecca
Esquenazi

Passover cakes must be flourless and must also be made without other starches like cornstarch (which is also an ingredient in confectioners' sugar). To be pareve, suitable for both meat and dairy meals, they must not contain any dairy ingredients. The Intense Chocolate Mousse Cake (page 30) and the Magie Noire (without the icing, page 31) would also be suitable for Passover. This recipe comes from an accomplished home cook.

TIME: 1 hour 15 minutes, plus cooling   YIELD: At least 12 servings

3 cups sugar
1 cup vegetable oil, plus more for
    pan
4 whole oranges
½ to 1 cup orange juice
6 large eggs

¼ teaspoon salt
2 cups matzo meal
2 cups coarsely ground walnuts
1 cup packed chopped dates
2 to 3 tablespoons orange liqueur

1. Make a sugar syrup by stirring 1½ cups of sugar into 1½ cups of water in a heavy saucepan. Bring to a boil, then lower heat and simmer, uncovered, for 40 minutes, or until syrup is reduced to one-third of its original volume. Meanwhile, preheat oven to 350 degrees and grease a 9-by-13-inch cake pan.

2. Coarsely grate zest of oranges. Juice oranges and combine with enough additional orange juice to make 2 cups.

3. In a bowl, beat eggs with remaining 1½ cups sugar. Add orange juice and oil, and continue mixing. Stir in salt, matzo meal, walnuts, dates and orange zest. Turn into greased pan and bake for 45 minutes or until golden. Cut into 2-inch diamonds in pan.

4. Stir liqueur into sugar syrup and pour over hot cake. Let sit a few hours before serving.

CHEESECAKES

A cheesecake is halfway between a cake and a tart. It is often baked in a deep springform pan, and usually has a crust, like a tart, though some are made crustless, baked in a deep pan without a removable bottom that is set into a hot water bath like a pudding. Cheesecakes are easy to prepare and always draw raves. Some recipes result in cracking on top as the cake, which has puffed up during baking, sinks and cools. A dusting of confectioners' sugar, or a thin layer of sour cream or berries or a scattering of nuts is all it takes for the camouflage. Cheesecakes benefit from refrigeration to set the texture, but should not be served ice cold. Dip your knife in cold water for well-defined slices.

Vanilla Cheesecake

But for the crust, made with almonds and brown sugar instead of graham cracker crumbs, this is as typical and simple a cheesecake as you can ask for, and making it with beaten egg whites, no yolks, keeps it light. Warming the cream cheese makes mixing the filling easier to accomplish. The dusting of bee pollen is strictly a trendy finishing touch. Cinnamon or nutmeg, or nothing, are your alternatives. The Tasting Room is a popular wine bar in New York's East Village.

TIME: 1 hour 15 minutes, plus chilling   YIELD: 8 to 12 servings

6½ tablespoons unsalted butter,
   melted
1½ cups ground almonds
3 tablespoons light brown sugar
1½ pounds cream cheese,
   softened

4 large egg whites
1 cup plus 2 tablespoons
   granulated sugar
1½ teaspoons vanilla
1 pint sour cream
Bee pollen, optional

1. Preheat oven to 350 degrees. Butter the bottom and sides of a 9-inch springform pan with 1 tablespoon butter. In a small bowl, combine almonds and brown sugar. Stir in remaining butter. Press nut mixture into bottom of pan.

2. In a saucepan, soften cream cheese over low heat. When very soft, remove from heat, transfer to a large bowl and set aside. Whip egg whites with an electric mixer until they hold soft peaks. Gradually add 1 cup granulated sugar and beat until mixture holds firmer peaks. Fold in cream cheese and 1 teaspoon vanilla. Pour into pan, and bake 40 to 45 minutes, until a toothpick inserted in center comes out only slightly moist. Cake should not be brown at all.

3. Meanwhile, in a small bowl whisk together sour cream, remaining granulated sugar and vanilla. When cake comes out of oven, increase temperature to 450 degrees. Carefully spread sour cream mixture over cake. Return the cake to the oven for 5 minutes to set topping. Do not overcook or it will turn brown. Remove cake from oven and let cool in pan. Chill in refrigerator. To serve, run a knife along edge of pan, and remove sides of pan. Sprinkle with bee pollen (if using), and serve.

Cream Cheese Cheesecake

This is the cream cheese cheesecake with the crumb crust. Chilling the cake is essential to set it, but take it out of the refrigerator an hour before serving, so the flavor can bloom. Dip your knife in cold water for neater slices. Melissa Clark frequently contributes dessert recipes to *The New York Times.*

Melissa Clark

TIME: 1 hour 45 minutes, plus 3 hours' chilling   YIELD: 12 servings

6 tablespoons unsalted butter, melted

1½ cups fine cookie crumbs (chocolate wafers, graham crackers, gingersnaps or shortbread cookies)

1½ pounds cream cheese, at room temperature

1 cup sugar

5 large eggs

1 teaspoon grated lemon zest

1 teaspoon vanilla extract

¼ teaspoon salt

1 cup sour cream, at room temperature

Fresh berries or figs for serving, optional

1. Preheat oven to 325 degrees. Wrap the outside of a 9-inch springform pan in a double layer of foil. Lightly brush inside of pan with 1 tablespoon melted butter.

2. In a bowl, mix together cookie crumbs and remaining butter. Pat mixture evenly into bottom of pan, pressing it down. Bake until crust is firm, about 15 minutes. Cool on a wire rack.

3. In the bowl of a mixer fitted with a whisk attachment, beat cream cheese and sugar for 2 minutes. Add eggs one at a time, scraping down the sides of the bowl frequently. Beat in lemon zest, vanilla and salt. Fold in sour cream by hand.

4. Scrape filling into crust, and smooth top. Bake until cake is barely set, about 50 to 60 minutes. Cool in pan on a wire rack, then cover, and refrigerate for at least 3 hours or overnight. Run a knife around edge of pan. Remove sides of pan and serve the cake with the berries, if desired.

Chocolate Cheesecake

Florence
Fabricant

The lightness of *fromage blanc* balances the richness that chocolate contributes to this cheesecake. This cake can be made a day in advance and refrigerated until ready to serve.

TIME: 1 hour 45 minutes, plus cooling   YIELD: 8 servings

2 cups crushed chocolate wafers
4 tablespoons melted unsalted
   butter
3 cups *fromage blanc*
3 large eggs
1 cup sugar

3 ounces semisweet chocolate,
   melted and cooled
1 teaspoon vanilla extract
1 tablespoon unsweetened Dutch-
   process cocoa

1. Preheat oven to 350 degrees.

2. Mix cookie crumbs with melted butter and press this mixture into the bottom and about 1½ inches up the sides of an 8-inch springform pan. Refrigerate.

3. Puree the cheese in a blender or food processor until perfectly smooth.

4. Beat eggs with sugar until thick and light. Stir in the melted chocolate, the cheese and vanilla. Pour into the prepared crust and bake about 1 hour, until a knife inserted in the center comes out clean. Shut off the oven and leave the cake in another 15 minutes.

5. Remove from the oven and allow to cool 30 minutes. Refrigerate at least 2 hours, then remove the sides of the pan, first running a knife around the edges. Dust with sifted cocoa before serving.

IN CHEESECAKE CITY, A QUEST FOR THE BEST
By Ed Levine

In the cosmology of New York City restaurants, there is no dessert more universal than the cheesecake. In a city of constant ethnic flux, cheesecake is itself a constant, offering something for everyone.

Cheesecake is one of those quintessential New York foodstuffs that in some circles is thought of as unsophisticated. Certainly its name does not roll off the tongue like tiramisu, or tarte Tatin. But cheesecake at its best is a perfect sweet—a smooth, creamy confection with only a hint of tart.

You read that correctly. Any discussion of cheesecake in New York City must begin with a few stipulations. While Italian and postmodern cheesecakes have their place in the pantheon, the proper New York cheesecake has a simple and unchanging list of ingredients: cream cheese, eggs, sugar, vanilla and heavy cream. The result is light as gauze. It also packs the wallop of a professional boxer. Americans understand this and champion it.

Chocolate swirls occasionally visit a cheesecake. So, too, do cherries, blueberries, lemon curds. It is not heretical to enjoy these jazzy renditions, but they are often paint on the lily. Italian bakers and bakeries believe in a different sort of cheesecake, one made with ricotta—which gives their cheesecake a rougher texture.

Restaurant chefs have also weighed in with nontraditional takes on cheesecake. Pumpkin cheesecake with maple syrup and crème fraîche, studded with pieces of pumpkin and macerated raisins; uncooked cheesecake made out of *fromage blanc* bathed in heavy cream, and served on a bed of ice; Oaxacan cheesecake crusted with raw brown sugar and served with guava lime sauce.

Wonderful cheesecakes all. But in the end the best way to satisfy a cheesecake craving is with a creamy piece of ungarnished, undoctored, New York cheesecake.

Sweet Potato Cheesecake

Galatoire's,
New Orleans,
Louisiana

Sweet potatoes are added to cream cheese cheesecakes, especially in the South. This recipe comes from Galatoire's, a legendary New Orleans restaurant. Galatoire's is one of the most historic restaurants in the French Quarter.

TIME: 1½ hours, plus chilling   YIELD: About 12 servings

Graham cracker crust mixture for a pan (page 525)
9 ounces cream cheese, softened
1⅓ cups granulated sugar
¼ cup light brown sugar
1¾ cups cooked mashed sweet potatoes, cooled (about 1 large potato)

2 large eggs, slightly beaten
⅔ cup evaporated milk
2 tablespoons cornstarch
¼ teaspoon ground cinnamon
⅛ teaspoon ground nutmeg
2 cups sour cream, at room temperature
1 teaspoon vanilla extract

1. Preheat oven to 350 degrees. Press crust into the bottom and partway up the sides of a 9-inch springform pan. Bake and cool crust.

2. Beat cream cheese with an electric mixer until smooth. Add 1 cup granulated sugar and brown sugar, beating until smooth. Add sweet potatoes, eggs, evaporated milk, cornstarch, cinnamon and nutmeg, beating until well combined. Pour into crust. Bake until set, 55 to 60 minutes.

3. Whisk sour cream, remaining granulated sugar and vanilla to combine. Spread over warm cheesecake. Return to oven, and bake until just set, 5 minutes. Cool on wire rack. Remove sides of pan, and chill for a few hours or overnight.

Mango Cheesecake

Mango adds a tropical touch to a typical cream cheese cheesecake. The graham cracker crust is richer than usual, thanks to the substitution of brown sugar for white. Nigella Lawson specializes in festive reinventions like this one.

Nigella
Lawson

TIME: 2 hours, plus overnight chilling   YIELD: 8 to 10 servings

8 ounces graham crackers

3 tablespoons dark brown sugar

4 ounces (1 stick) unsalted butter, softened and cut into pieces

2 to 4 mangoes, for approximately 2 cups puree

1½ pounds cream cheese

1 cup superfine sugar

6 large eggs

2 tablespoons lime juice

1. Place graham crackers in the bowl of a food processor and process to fairly fine crumbs. Add dark brown sugar and butter. Process until mixture clumps together like damp sand. Press mixture evenly into bottom of a 9-inch springform pan and refrigerate while preparing filling.

2. Preheat oven to 325 degrees. Peel and cut flesh from mangoes and puree in food processor until smooth. You should have 2 cups puree. Add cream cheese and process until smooth. Add superfine sugar, and, with motor running, add eggs one at a time through the feed tube. Add lime juice, and process until blended.

3. Place springform pan on a double layer of heavy-duty foil. Crimp edges up around pan to make a waterproof casing. Place foil-covered pan in a deep roasting pan. Pour filling into pan and pour boiling water into roasting pan to come about halfway up sides of cake pan, but not higher than foil.

4. Bake until filling is set and wobbles slightly in the center, about 1 hour and 45 minutes. Remove pan from water bath. Discard foil and place pan on a cooling rack. When cool, refrigerate overnight. To serve, remove sides from pan. Place cake on a serving platter.

Goat Cheese Cake with Poached Sour Cherries

Savoy,
New York

Tart sour cherries are seasonal, usually available from local farms from late June to late July. This recipe can also be made with blueberries. Using goat cheese gives the cheesecake a refreshingly bright tanginess. Savoy is a small SoHo restaurant whose chef and owner, Peter Hoffman, is devoted to shopping in the Union Square Greenmarket, where he can buy his goat cheese and, in July, his sour cherries. Canned sour cherries will not work as well as fresh in this recipe. The goat cheese puddings on page 418 are very similar.

TIME: 1 hour, plus 1 hour chilling   YIELD: 24 small cakes or one 9-inch cake

Vegetable oil spray
3 pints (6 cups) fresh sour
    cherries, pitted
2 tablespoons all-purpose flour
9 ounces soft fresh goat cheese
½ cup plus 1 tablespoon superfine
    sugar
¼ cup cornstarch

Pinch of salt
½ vanilla bean, scraped, or ½
    teaspoon vanilla extract
5 large eggs, separated
½ cup granulated sugar
1 cup sweet riesling
1 3-inch cinnamon stick
3 star anise

1. Preheat oven to 350 degrees, with racks positioned halfway and two-thirds down. Place a kettle of water over high heat to bring to a boil. Spray oil in 24 4-ounce metal cups, 2 12-cup muffin pans or a 9-inch springform pan, and set aside. If using a springform, cover the outside of the pan with a double layer of foil.

2. In a mixing bowl, toss 4 cups cherries with flour. Divide cherries among cups or scatter in springform pan. Set aside.

3. Using an electric mixer, beat together goat cheese, ½ cup superfine sugar, cornstarch and salt. Add scrapings of vanilla bean or vanilla extract. Add egg yolks one at a time, mixing well after each addition.

4. In a separate bowl, whisk egg whites to soft peaks. Add remaining tablespoon superfine sugar, and continue to whisk until stiff but not dry. Mix about ½ cup egg whites into cheese mixture to lighten it, then gently

fold in remaining whites. Spoon batter into cups or pan, filling cups about three-quarters full.

5. Place cups, muffin tins or springform pan in one or two baking pans. Carefully pour in boiling water to halfway up sides of cups or springform pan. Cover water-filled baking pans tightly with aluminum foil. Place in oven. If using two pans, place one on middle rack and the other on rack below, switching and reversing pans halfway during cooking to ensure even baking. Bake until cake is puffed and firm to touch, about 20 minutes for individual cakes, about 40 minutes for a large cake. Remove pans from water bath, and allow to cool, then refrigerate until chilled, about 1 hour.

6. While cake cools, in a medium saucepan, combine granulated sugar and ½ cup water. Place over medium heat until sugar is dissolved. Add riesling, cinnamon, star anise and remaining cherries. Bring to a boil, then use a slotted spoon to transfer cherries to a bowl, draining well. Allow to cool. Continue to boil liquid in saucepan until it is reduced by half. Remove from heat, and allow to cool.

7. To serve, drizzle cherry syrup on each plate, and place cake on top. Top cake with poached cherries, and serve.

Ricotta Tart

Pepolino,
New York

Cheesecakes made with ricotta are often called Italian cheesecakes. They tend to be moister and less silky than cream cheese cheesecakes. This one, however, has an unusual pedigree. The recipe came from Italy, from Cibreo, a fine restaurant in Florence where cream cheese is used to make the tart. But because the Philadelphia brand cream cheese that is sold in Italy is not the same as the kind in American stores, the chef, who worked at Cibreo before opening Pepolino, said the results are better with ricotta cheese. *Fromage blanc* can also be used. The recipe yields a cross between a cheesecake and a tart.

TIME: 2½ hours, plus cooling   YIELD: 2 tarts (16 servings)

1¾ cups granulated sugar

11 ounces (2¾ sticks) unsalted butter, slightly softened, in pieces

2 large egg yolks

4 cups cake flour, approximately

2½ pounds ricotta cheese

5 large eggs, lightly beaten

1 teaspoon vanilla extract

2 cups heavy cream

Confectioners' sugar

1. Combine ¾ cup sugar, the butter and egg yolks in a food processor or a large mixing bowl. Process or beat until smooth. Add flour about 1 cup at a time, pulsing until blended if using a food processor, or mixing by hand until a soft, smooth dough can be gathered in a ball. Divide in two, flatten each portion into a disk, wrap in plastic and refrigerate for 40 minutes.

2. Preheat oven to 500 degrees. Roll out one disk on a lightly floured board to a thickness of ⅛ inch. Fit dough into a 9-inch springform pan or a 9-inch round cake pan 1½ inches deep with a removable bottom. In a springform pan, dough should come up 2 inches on sides; with a cake pan, dough should be even with top edge. Repeat with second pan. If you do not have two pans, the second tart can be made after the first has finished baking.

3. In a large bowl or in an electric mixer on low speed, beat together ricotta, remaining granulated sugar, whole eggs, vanilla and cream until well blended and smooth. Ladle filling into prepared pans.

4. Bake 10 minutes. Reduce temperature to 300 degrees and continue baking for 1 hour and 10 minutes, until top is puffed and golden—some cracking is to be expected—and a knife inserted in center comes out clean. Transfer to a rack and cool 10 minutes. Remove outer ring from pan and cool tart to room temperature. Filling will sink as it cools. Tart can be refrigerated. Dust with sifted confectioners' sugar before serving.

Dulce de Leche Cheesecake

Sonora
Restaurant,
Port Chester,
New York

This sumptuous cheesecake is baked like a flan, without a crust. But baking the filling in a graham cracker crust would not be a mistake. And if you double the recipe, you can bake it in a cheesecake pan, 9 inches in diameter and 3 inches deep. *Dulce de leche* is a Mexican milk-based caramel. It is simple, though time-consuming, to prepare at home. When made with goat's milk, it is called *cajeta.* Both *dulce de leche* and *cajeta* can be purchased in fine food shops and Mexican stores. Sonora was a very good Mexican restaurant in Manhattan, and now the chef, Rafael Palomino, has relocated his restaurant to Port Chester, New York.

TIME: 1½ hours, plus 1 hour resting   YIELD: 8 servings

8 ounces cream cheese, at room
  temperature
3 large eggs

½ cup heavy cream
1 cup *dulce de leche* (page 536)

1. Preheat oven to 325 degrees. Place cream cheese in a food processor and process until soft. With machine running, drop in eggs through the feed tube, followed by heavy cream, then *dulce de leche.*

2. Place mixture in a 9-inch pie dish. Put dish in a large pan and add hot water until it comes halfway up the side of pie dish. Place in oven and bake about 1 hour or a little longer, until a cake tester comes out clean and top is fairly firm.

3. Remove pan from water bath. Let cake rest 1 hour, then serve at once. Or refrigerate, but remove from refrigerator one-half hour before serving.

YEAST CAKES
AND PASTRIES

Though bread-baking typically depends on yeast, there are some rich dessert specialties that are leavened with yeast. They are briochelike confections, such as baba au rhum, kugelhopf and some traditional sweet holiday breads like panettone and kulich.

The procedure in making these cakes is similar to baking bread, that is, the yeast is mixed with warm liquid, added to other ingredients and the resulting dough is kneaded to activate the gluten, to make the end result springy but tender. Many electric mixers and food processors come equipped with a dough hook that will do the kneading. But inexperienced bakers should knead by hand, to understand how the ball of dough changes as it is kneaded, and how it should feel when finished. There are few kitchen tasks as relaxing as the rhythm of kneading, turning the ball of dough as you go.

After kneading, the dough must rise and be punched down before it is shaped and put into its pan or pans. It may require a second rising in the pan before baking, so be sure to allow plenty of time.

Most doughs can be set to rise overnight in the refrigerator, so if it is more convenient, the recipe can be started the day before the dough has to be baked. Yeast doughs made with a generous amount of sugar, like the ones that follow, usually take longer to rise. The amount of butter will also retard rising. The dough is bound to be softer and stickier than bread dough.

The recipes must be less precise than those for cakes that are not made with yeast. The amount of flour it will take to form a dough with the proper consistency will vary, depending on how fresh the flour is and how moist or dry your kitchen may be. Similarly, rising time will be affected by the ambient temperature. It is important to allow yeast-risen cakes to cool completely before they are cut, otherwise they may be gummy.

Experience with baking bread will make these recipes easy. But even for those who have never tried yeast-baking, the recipes should not be a challenge.

The golden, buttery results are worth the effort.

Blueberry Kuchen

This yeast cake studded with blueberries is like a sweet summer coffee cake. But it is also a wonderful dessert with vanilla ice cream alongside. Nigella Lawson is an English cookbook author and television personality.

Nigella Lawson

TIME: About 1 hour, plus rising   YIELD: 9 servings

2½ to 3 cups all-purpose flour
½ teaspoon salt
2 tablespoons superfine sugar
1½ teaspoons rapid-rise or other instant active dry yeast
½ cup milk
4 tablespoons unsalted butter, softened, plus more for pan
3 large eggs

½ teaspoon vanilla extract
Finely grated zest of 1 orange
Vegetable oil for bowl
1 tablespoon orange juice
2 cups fresh blueberries
½ cup pecan halves, chopped
2 tablespoons demerara or light brown sugar
¼ teaspoon ground cinnamon

1. Mix 2½ cups flour with the salt, sugar and yeast in a large bowl. In a small saucepan, combine milk and butter, and place over low heat until milk is lukewarm. Pour into a bowl, and add two eggs, vanilla and orange zest; mix until blended. Stir liquid ingredients into dry ingredients to make a soft dough, adding more flour if necessary.

2. Using a mixer with a dough hook, or by hand, knead dough until smooth and springy. Place in an oiled bowl and cover with plastic wrap. Leave to rise in a warm place until double, about 1 hour. (Or let rise in refrigerator overnight, returning to room temperature before proceeding.)

3. Punch dough down. Butter a shallow 12-by-8-inch baking pan and press dough into pan. Cover with a kitchen towel, and leave to rise in a warm place 15 to 20 minutes longer.

4. Preheat oven to 400 degrees. Prepare a glaze by mixing together remaining egg and orange juice until blended. Paint glaze over dough. Spread blueberries on dough in a single layer. Mix pecans with sugar and cinnamon, and sprinkle evenly over blueberries.

5. Place in oven, and bake 15 minutes. Reduce heat to 350 degrees, and bake until dough is risen and brown at edges, about 15 minutes more. Cool about 10 minutes. Cut into 9 rectangles. Serve warm.

Alsatian Kugelhopf

Pâtisserie
Jean, Colmar,
France

Kugelhopf is basically a briochelike coffee cake baked with a yeast dough and studded with raisins. It is typically made in a fluted mold. Bake it in a cylinder with more dried fruits and it becomes Italian panettone. Leftovers are delicious toasted plain or made into French toast. Pâtisserie Jean is in Colmar, France, in the heart of Alsace.

TIME: 3 hours, plus cooling   YIELD: About 8 servings

¾ cup warm milk, approximately
¼ cup granulated sugar
½ teaspoon salt
2 packets (¼ ounce each) active
  dry yeast
4 cups all-purpose flour,
  approximately
¼ cup kirsch or mirabelle,
  optional

⅔ cup raisins, golden, black or a
  combination
2 large eggs, lightly beaten
8 tablespoons (1 stick) unsalted
  butter, softened
8 to 10 blanched almonds
Confectioners' sugar

1. Combine ⅓ cup warm milk, 1 tablespoon granulated sugar, salt, yeast and 2 tablespoons flour in a bowl and mix with a fork to make a paste. Cover and let rise in a warm place until almost doubled in volume, about 20 minutes.

2. Warm kirsch or mirabelle, or ¼ cup water, slightly, and pour over raisins in another bowl. Set aside.

3. In another bowl, combine 3½ cups sifted flour, remaining granulated sugar and milk, and eggs, with yeast paste. Mix to make a soft, elastic, slightly sticky mass, adding more flour or milk as needed. Using wooden spoon or fingertips, work in 6 tablespoons butter.

4. Turn dough out onto a lightly floured countertop and knead vigorously, lifting and slamming dough down seven or eight times until smooth and elastic. Work raisins and their liquid into dough.

5. Spread remaining butter generously around the sides and bottom and into crevices of an 8-inch kugelhopf mold, preferably glazed earthenware. Arrange almonds in indentations in bottom of mold. Gently shape dough into a roll about 10 or 12 inches long and arrange in a circle in mold. Cover

and let rise in a warm spot until dough doubles and is level with rim of mold, about 1 hour.

6. Preheat oven to 450 degrees. Place mold on center rack and bake 10 minutes. Lower heat to 350 degrees and continue baking 40 to 45 minutes, until kugelhopf shrinks slightly away from sides and a slim knife or skewer inserted in cake comes out clean and dry. Cool in mold 5 minutes, then turn out onto a rack and cool at least 4 hours before cutting. For maximum flavor, do not cut for 6 hours.

7. Dust liberally with confectioners' sugar just before slicing.

Kulich

Suzanne
Hamlin

Kulich is the traditional Russian Easter cake, not unlike kugelhopf or panettone with its buttery yeast dough. It is served with a rich, pyramid-shaped cheese pudding called paschka that is made with cream cheese, dried fruits and nuts, with Cyrillic symbols for "He Has Risen" traced on the top. Suzanne Hamlin is a Brooklyn, New York–based food writer.

TIME: About 5 hours, including rising and cooling   YIELD: 8 servings

1 packet (¼ ounce) active dry yeast	3 large eggs, room temperature
½ teaspoon plus ½ cup granulated sugar	1 teaspoon vanilla extract
¼ teaspoon saffron threads	½ cup raisins, slivered blanched almonds or chopped dried apricots
2 tablespoons warm milk	2½ to 3 cups all-purpose bleached flour
4 ounces (1 stick) unsalted butter, softened, plus more for mold	½ cup confectioners' sugar
¼ teaspoon salt	2 teaspoons lemon juice

1. Dissolve yeast and ½ teaspoon granulated sugar in ¼ cup warm water (110 degrees). Let stand until mixture bubbles, about 5 minutes.

2. Soak saffron in milk for 5 minutes. Strain, set aside and discard threads.

3. In the bowl of an electric mixer, beat together butter, ½ cup granulated sugar and salt. Beat in yeast, saffron milk, eggs and vanilla. Slowly add dried fruit or almonds.

4. On low speed, gradually add 2¼ cups flour. Then, by tablespoons, add ¼ cup of flour. Increasing mixing speed, beat until dough is shiny and elastic, about 5 minutes.

5. Add dough hook to mixer and beat on high speed until dough pulls away from sides of bowl, about 2 minutes. Dough should be soft and slightly sticky. Add more flour, a tablespoon at a time, if necessary. If kneading by hand, lightly flour or oil hands and knead until dough starts to pull away from bowl.

6. Cover bowl with plastic wrap, put in a warm place and let dough rise until it has doubled in bulk, 1 to 2 hours.

7. Using an empty 46-ounce can, cut a round of parchment paper to fit bottom. Lightly grease bottom and sides of can. Fit round in bottom, and line sides with parchment, letting paper extend 2 inches above rim.

8. Punch down dough, and knead briefly into a smooth ball. Gently drop ball into can. Cover top lightly with plastic wrap, and put can in a warm place until dough has risen to about 1½ inches below rim, about 1 hour. Preheat oven to 325 degrees. Place oven rack in lowest position.

9. Bake 1¼ to 1½ hours, until a skewer inserted into center comes out clean. Let bread rest in can on a rack for 10 minutes, then gently dislodge it. Peel off parchment, and let bread cool.

10. Before serving, put confectioners' sugar in a glass measuring cup, and gradually stir in lemon juice and 1 teaspoon water. Stir until mixture is like heavy cream. Pour over cake, letting icing drip down sides. Let icing set 5 minutes.

Breton Butter Cake

Prune,
New York

Butter baking is a specialty of Brittany, and this cake is no exception. Although the pastry is leavened with yeast, the dough is folded and layered over butter like puff pastry. The same dough, and handling, can be used to make croissants, by cutting triangles of the folded dough that results from step 3, and rolling and curving them. But do not dust them with sugar. An easy way to soften and shape the chilled butter in step 2 is to place it in a zip-lock sandwich bag, seal the bag and pound it in the bag. Then use scissors to snip off the bag. This cake is also quite unlike another Breton cake, page 59, which is essentially a pound cake. Prune is a small but very dynamic restaurant in New York's East Village whose chef and owner, Gabrielle Hamilton, is among the city's trend-setting women chefs.

TIME: 1 hour 15 minutes, plus rising and chilling   YIELD: 8 servings

1⅛ teaspoons active dry yeast
¾ teaspoon orange flower water, plus more for sprinkling
1⅓ cups all-purpose flour, approximately, plus more for kneading and rolling
2 tablespoons cake flour
⅛ teaspoon coarse salt

2 tablespoons soft unsalted butter
6 ounces (12 tablespoons) chilled unsalted butter
¾ cup sugar, plus more for plate and top of cake
1½ tablespoons unsalted butter, melted

1. In a small bowl, combine yeast with ⅔ cup water and the orange flower water. Let sit until bubbly. In a large bowl, combine the flours, salt and yeast mixture. On a lightly floured surface, knead dough, adding a little more flour if needed, until smooth. Butter a large bowl with half the soft butter and add dough. Cover, and let rise in a warm place until doubled, 30 to 60 minutes. Place in refrigerator to firm up, about 30 minutes.

2. On a lightly floured surface, pound chilled butter into a 5-inch square. Cover with plastic wrap and let come almost to room temperature; it should have an icinglike texture. On a lightly floured surface, roll out dough into a 10-inch disk. Place butter on top and fold dough up and around it to cover.

3. Working quickly, roll out dough so that it is 2 feet long and 1 foot

wide. Using a pastry brush, brush off excess flour. Sprinkle with 3 table-spoons sugar, and fold into thirds as if folding a business letter. Turn 90 degrees, sprinkle with 3 tablespoons sugar, roll out to 2 feet long and 1 foot wide, and fold into thirds. Repeat 2 more times, scraping up sticky areas. Avoid using too much flour.

4. Preheat oven to 425 degrees. Use remaining soft butter to grease a 9-inch glass pie plate. Dust with sugar. Place dough in plate, tucking corners under. Let rise in a warm place until soft and puffy, 1 to 2 hours. Brush surface with melted butter, and sprinkle with a generous amount of sugar and a little orange flower water. Bake until risen and golden brown, 25 to 30 minutes. If top browns before bottom, cover with foil. The bottom should be hazelnut brown. Remove from oven, slice and serve warm.

Brioche Peach Tarts

Bayard's and
Financier,
New York

Brioche dough, made with yeast and rich in butter, is used to make the pastry for these pillowy tarts paved with fresh peaches and garnished with almonds. Eric Bedoucha, the pastry chef at Bayard's, in the historic India House mansion on Hanover Square in Lower Manhattan, also bakes for the Financier pastry shops.

TIME: 3 hours   YIELD: 6 to 8 servings for each tart

1½ cups all-purpose flour, plus
    extra for work surface
¼ cup plus 4 teaspoons granulated
    sugar
1 packet (¼ ounce) rapid-rise
    active dry yeast
⅛ teaspoon salt
2 large eggs, at room temperature

¼ cup milk, slightly warmed
6 ounces (12 tablespoons)
    unsalted butter, softened, diced
8 ripe but firm freestone peaches
2 tablespoons finely ground
    almonds
2 tablespoons bread crumbs

1. Place flour, ¼ cup granulated sugar, yeast, salt, eggs and milk in the bowl of a standing mixer fitted with a dough hook. Beat on medium speed, scraping down sides of bowl once or twice, until dough is smooth, about 10 minutes. Add 8 tablespoons of the butter, and continue beating and scraping down sides of bowl until the butter is completely incorporated and dough is smooth again, about 5 minutes. Dust top of dough lightly with flour, cover the bowl with a damp towel and let dough rise in a warm place until almost doubled, 1½ to 2 hours.

2. Preheat oven to 400 degrees. Butter 2 9-inch fluted tart pans with removable bottoms. Punch down dough, and divide in half. Roll half out on a heavily floured work surface into an 11-inch circle, dusting frequently with flour to prevent sticking. Lay dough over a rolling pin, and transfer it to pan. Press dough into the bottom and sides. Trim any excess with a sharp knife. Let rise until slightly puffed, 15 to 20 minutes. Lightly prick with a fork. Repeat with second half of the dough.

3. Meanwhile, bring a large pot of water to a simmer. Add peaches for 30 seconds, then remove with a slotted spoon to a large bowl of cold wa-

ter. Soak peaches just until cool, about 30 seconds, Drain and peel. If you have a serrated vegetable peeler, you can use it to peel the peaches without putting them in boiling water! Halve, pit and cut each peach into 8 wedges.

4. Mix almonds, bread crumbs and remaining granulated sugar in a small bowl. Sprinkle all but 2 teaspoons of the almond mixture over the dough in each pan. Arrange peach slices on dough so that they overlap. Sprinkle with remaining almond mixture. Dot peaches with remaining butter, and place pans on rimmed baking sheet.

5. Place on bottom rack of oven, and bake 10 minutes. Reduce oven setting to 350 degrees, and bake until tarts are golden brown on top, 25 to 30 minutes. Remove from pans immediately (the crust will steam and soften if left in pan), and transfer to wire rack. Cool briefly, and serve warm.

Brioche Tarts with Blue Cheese, Walnuts and Quince

Charlie
Trotter,
Chicago,
Illinois

These brioche tarts are both sweet and savory. They can double as a cheese course or a dessert. Quince is a popular accompaniment for cheese, especially in Spain. Charlie Trotter of Charlie Trotter's in Chicago is one of the country's preeminent chefs.

TIME: 2 hours, plus chilling   YIELD: 4 servings

1 tablespoon active dry yeast
6 tablespoons warm milk
1 cup plus 1½ tablespoons all-purpose flour
2½ cups plus 2 tablespoons bread flour
6 tablespoons plus 1 teaspoon granulated sugar
1 teaspoon plus 2 tablespoons coarsely chopped rosemary leaves
1 teaspoon finely chopped orange, lemon or lime zest
1½ teaspoons salt

3 large eggs
8 ounces (2 sticks) plus 5 tablespoons unsalted butter, softened
2 cups peeled and cubed quince, pear, apple or persimmon
2 tablespoons light brown sugar
1 cup crumbled blue cheese, preferably Maytag
1 large egg beaten with 2 teaspoons milk
1 cup walnuts or pecans, coarsely chopped
Honey, for reheating tarts

1. Place yeast in a small bowl, and pour in milk. Stir, and allow to sit several minutes. In the bowl of an electric mixer, combine all-purpose flour, bread flour, 3 tablespoons plus 1 teaspoon granulated sugar, 1 teaspoon rosemary and zest. Add yeast mixture, salt and eggs. Mix with dough hook on low speed until mixture is cohesive. Add 8 ounces plus 2 tablespoons butter. Continue mixing, scraping bowl frequently, until dough is smooth and pulls away from sides of bowl, about 20 minutes. Cover; refrigerate at least 5 hours.

2. Divide into 4 equal balls. Pat into flat rounds 4 inches in diameter. Place on a baking sheet, cover with plastic wrap, and set aside in a warm place for 45 minutes.

3. While dough rises, prepare quince: Place a small sauté pan over

medium-low heat, and melt remaining 3 tablespoons butter. Add quince, and sauté until just tender. Sprinkle with brown sugar and cool.

4. Preheat oven to 350 degrees. With fingertips, press dough rounds to create a well in center of each and a rim on the edge. Divide quince among tarts. Layer on blue cheese, letting it fall where it may. Brush tart edges with egg-milk mixture. Sprinkle nuts over tarts, letting some fall onto edges. Sprinkle with remaining 2 tablespoons rosemary. Dust generously with remaining 3 tablespoons granulated sugar, especially over edges.

5. Bake until edges and bottoms are golden brown (lift to check), rotating pan halfway for even baking, 20 to 25 minutes. Serve warm or at room temperature. To reheat, drizzle with honey to give a little sheen.

Baba au Rhum

Alain
Ducasse,
Paris

Babas, drenched in rum syrup and topped with clouds of whipped cream, are show-stoppers. The yeast dough for these babas is mighty adaptable. It can be used to make individual pastries, both large and small, and can also be baked in a Bundt or other tube pan. In that format, especially with macerated fruit piled in the center, it is often called a savarin. There is a recipe on page 128. At Alain Ducasse at the Essex House in New York, as well as at the Alain Ducasse restaurants in Monte Carlo and Paris, baba au rhum is a real production number. The dessert is wheeled to the table in a mahogany and glass cart with a choice of rums. The rum you select for dousing the cake is also poured for sipping. Who can resist such a display in a Michelin three-star restaurant that makes a fine art of elaborate service? I can't.

TIME: 2 hours, plus cooling   YIELD: 8 servings

1 packet (¼ ounce) active dry yeast	4 large eggs
⅓ cup milk	Zest of 1 orange, in strips
1¾ cups sifted all-purpose flour	1 cup dark rum
7 tablespoons unsalted butter, softened	1 cup apricot preserves
1 cup plus 2 tablespoons sugar	1 vanilla bean
	1 cup heavy cream

1. In a large stainless steel bowl, dissolve yeast in milk. Place over medium heat, and stir just until milk is warm. Remove from heat, and stir in ¼ cup flour. Cover, and set aside in a warm place to rise 20 minutes, until spongy.

2. Use 1 tablespoon butter to grease 8 half-cup baba molds, a 6-cup ring mold or a Bundt pan. Place molds on baking sheet.

3. Beat remaining butter in a mixer or food processor. Beat in 2 tablespoons sugar and 2 tablespoons flour. Beat in eggs, one at a time.

4. Whisk mixture into yeast sponge. Beat in remaining flour to make a thick, doughlike batter. Spoon batter into molds. Set aside to rise about 30 minutes, until dough reaches just above tops of individual molds and barely to top of single large mold.

5. Preheat oven to 350 degrees. While babas rise, combine remaining

sugar with 2 cups water in a saucepan; bring to a boil. Remove from heat. Stir in orange zest. Allow to cool to room temperature. Stir in ½ cup rum.

6. Bake individual babas about 20 minutes, larger baba about 40 minutes, until nicely browned on top.

7. When babas are baked, remove from oven and unmold. Dip babas into syrup, turning to saturate; place large ring in a large baking dish, and pour syrup over it. Cool on rack placed over a baking pan to catch drips. Strain preserves into saucepan, and heat until quite warm. Brush on cooled babas.

8. Split vanilla bean, scrape seeds into cream; whip cream, and chill. To serve, split babas lengthwise, spoon a tablespoon of the remaining rum on each portion, and top with whipped cream. For a single baba, fill center of ring with whipped cream and add rum as each portion is cut.

Limoncello Babas with Lemon Cream

Felidia,
New York

Babas are French, but made with that particularly Italian liqueur from Capri, limoncello, they become as Italian as can be. And that's the way Lidia Bastianich interprets them at Felidia, one of her restaurants in New York.

TIME: 2½ hours, plus cooling   YIELD: 12 servings

4 ounces (1 stick) plus 5 tablespoons unsalted butter, softened, plus more for tins

1½ cups milk

1 packet (¼ ounce) active dry yeast

2 cups plus 3 tablespoons bread flour

4 large eggs

6 tablespoons plus ¾ cup sugar

Salt

Grated zest of 11 lemons

3 tablespoons cornstarch

1 large egg yolk

5 tablespoons limoncello liqueur

½ cup heavy cream

1. Butter a 12-muffin tin with 4-ounce cups. Melt 4 ounces of the butter and set aside. In a saucepan over low heat, warm ½ cup milk. Pour it into a large bowl, and sprinkle in yeast. Stir until yeast dissolves. Whisk in ½ cup plus 3 tablespoons flour, and cover bowl with plastic wrap. Let rise in a warm place until mixture has doubled, 30 minutes to 1 hour.

2. Place dough mixture in an electric mixer with paddle attachment or a food processor with dough blade. Add 3 eggs, 1 tablespoon sugar, ½ teaspoon salt and remaining 1½ cups flour and beat yeast mixture until very smooth. Gradually mix in melted butter, and continue to mix until smooth.

3. Spoon dough into muffin tin, filling each mold halfway. Grease a piece of plastic wrap or parchment and cover muffin tin. Set aside until dough rises just above tin, about 1 hour.

4. Preheat oven to 350 degrees. Uncover tin and bake babas until dark golden brown on top, about 20 minutes. Transfer tin to a wire rack to cool.

5. To prepare lemon cream, bring 1 cup milk, 3 tablespoons sugar, zest of 1 lemon and a pinch of salt to a boil over medium heat in a saucepan, stirring until sugar dissolves.

6. Meanwhile, whisk together cornstarch, 2 tablespoons sugar, 1 egg and the egg yolk in a bowl. Pour hot milk mixture gradually into egg mixture, whisking constantly to combine. Return mixture to saucepan.

7. Warm liquid over medium-low heat, whisking constantly, being sure to scrape bottom and sides of pan. As soon as liquid reaches a boil, take pan off heat. Whisk in remaining softened butter a tablespoon at a time. Transfer mixture to a shallow bowl, and lay a piece of plastic wrap on the surface of the lemon cream. Refrigerate until well chilled, about 2 hours.

8. To prepare syrup, combine remaining lemon zest, 2 cups water and ¾ cup sugar in a saucepan, and bring to a boil, stirring to dissolve sugar. Simmer until liquid is yellow, about 2 to 3 minutes. Strain through a fine sieve into a bowl. Stir in limoncello. Let cool.

9. Just before serving, whip heavy cream until it forms soft peaks. Whisk chilled lemon cream well, then gently fold in whipped cream.

10. Slice babas in half vertically. Submerge each baba in limoncello syrup for 10 seconds. Arrange babas on plates, cut sides up, and drizzle with more syrup. Top babas with large dollops of lemon cream, and serve immediately.

Bing Cherry Doughnuts

Oceana,
New York

Doughnuts can be yeast-raised or cakey. When filled, as these fresh cherry jelly doughnuts are, they are usually made with yeast. Oceana is a fine seafood restaurant in Manhattan.

TIME: 4 hours, plus overnight rising   YIELD: 8 to 10 large doughnuts, 12 to 16 medium-size ones

4¼ cups all-purpose flour, approximately

2 packets (¼ ounce each) active dry yeast

1 pound Bing cherries, pitted

1 Granny Smith apple, peeled, cored and finely chopped

1⅔ cups sugar

¼ cup milk

6 large egg yolks, lightly beaten

2 teaspoons salt

½ tablespoon lemon zest

5 tablespoons unsalted butter, softened

Vegetable oil for deep frying

1 pint vanilla ice cream, optional

1. The night before or early in the day, place 2 cups flour, ½ packet yeast and ⅔ cup warm water in a large bowl. Mix with a wooden spoon until blended; cover with plastic wrap. Set aside at room temperature 10 to 12 hours. Mixture should double. Refrigerate if not ready to continue with recipe.

2. Run half the cherries through a juice extractor or food mill or puree in a blender and strain. Place juice in saucepan with apple and ¾ cup sugar. Simmer until thick and jamlike, 10 to 15 minutes. Cool. Chop and add remaining cherries. Refrigerate.

3. Set ⅓ cup flour aside. Place remaining flour on a work surface. Make a well in center, and add risen flour-yeast mixture, remaining yeast, milk, egg yolks, ⅔ cup sugar, salt, lemon zest and butter. Work flour into other ingredients from outside to center, forming a sticky mass. Knead by hand or machine 10 to 15 minutes, adding more flour if needed, until barely sticky and very elastic. Place dough in lightly floured bowl. Cover. Refrigerate at least 1½ hours.

4. No more than 8 hours before serving, roll out dough to about ½ inch thick on floured surface. Allow to sit 20 minutes. Place remaining sugar on a salad-size plate.

5. Meanwhile, in a wok or large saucepan, heat oil 2 to 3 inches deep to 360 degrees (no hotter than 375 degrees). Using a 3½-inch biscuit cutter, cut 8 rounds, or use a 2½-inch cutter to make 12 rounds. Scraps can be kneaded briefly, then rerolled. Place in oil, and fry until brown, 90 seconds or so on each side. Place cooked doughnuts on several thicknesses of paper towel to absorb excess oil, then immediately roll in sugar on plate.

6. Using a pastry tube, fill warm doughnuts with cherry mixture. Or poke a hole in each with the narrow end of a wooden spoon, and force in filling through a funnel. Serve with ice cream, if desired, and with remaining cherry mixture as a sauce.

Savarin

Petrossian,
New York

Savarin, named for the French gastronome and writer Brillat-Savarin, was created by Parisian pâtissiers during the reign of Louis Napoléon. It is essentially the same as a baba au rhum, but baked as a single cake. When the film *Babette's Feast* was shown, Petrossian, the New York restaurant that is owned by the Paris-based caviar company, served the meal from the movie. Recipes for the entire menu, including this dessert, were published in *The New York Times*. I made them and served them to friends as I tested them. The dinner was memorable.

TIME: 2½ hours   YIELD: 8 to 12 servings

1 cake (½ ounce) fresh yeast
⅓ cup warm milk
2½ cups sifted all-purpose flour
4 ounces (8 tablespoons) unsalted
  butter, softened
2⅔ cups sugar

6 large eggs
½ cup dark rum
Candied fruits for decoration
Whipped cream or pastry cream
  (page 532)

1. Dissolve the yeast in the milk in a large bowl. Stir in ½ cup of the flour. Cover and set aside in a warm place to rise for 30 minutes.

2. Beat 7 tablespoons butter in an electric mixer. Beat in 2 tablespoons of the sugar and 2 tablespoons of the flour. Beat in eggs, one at a time.

3. Beat the remaining flour into the risen yeast mixture. Beat in butter and egg mixture to make a thick doughlike batter. Butter a large baba or savarin mold or Bundt pan with remaining butter and spoon batter into the mold. It should fill it halfway. Cover with a cloth and set aside to rise until the dough reaches top of the mold. Preheat oven to 350 degrees.

4. Bake savarin for about 40 minutes, until nicely browned on top.

5. While the savarin is baking, combine the remaining sugar with 5½ cups water in a saucepan and boil until syrupy and reduced by half. Remove from heat and stir in the rum.

6. When the savarin is baked, remove it from the oven and carefully spoon the rum syrup over it, allowing it to saturate the cake completely.

7. Cool completely. Unmold and decorate with candied fruits. If desired, fill the center with whipped cream or pastry cream.

COOKIES, BISCOTTI, BROWNIES AND BARS

I s there any dessert that cannot be enhanced by the addition of a cookie, any dinner that would not benefit from a plate of biscotti or madeleines with the coffee? A repertory of these small bites, most of which are easily made in advance and kept in the pantry or frozen to use later, is an asset for any cook. And depending on the occasion, the cookies and bars can be made larger than the recipe specifies, or miniaturized.

The baker of these treats needs little in the way of specialized equipment. Good, flat, heavy-duty baking sheets that will not warp, both regular and nonstick, are essential. Nonstick Silpat liners can be used on regular baking sheets. Parchment paper is necessary for some recipes. Cooling racks are another must. And that's it.

COOKIES

Most cookies are made by dropping mounds of soft batter on sheets, rolling dough and cutting shapes, or forming logs of dough and slicing them. Teaspoons or a knife can be used to form all but fancy cut shapes. For these, professional cookie cutters are best.

When baking cookies, never crowd them on the sheet; it's better to make a second batch. And depending on the consistency of your oven, it's a good idea to turn the baking pan 180 degrees halfway through so that all the cookies bake evenly. Cookies are delicious warm from the oven, but be sure to allow them to cool if you plan to ice them.

French Butter Cookies ✳

These are as sumptuously buttery and basic as can be. The recipe comes from Poilâne, the chain of bakeries in Paris. Though known for their breads, they have always made a few select pastries, like these cookies, a recipe from Lionel Poilâne, the man who restored credibility to traditional French bread baking and who died in a helicopter accident in 2002. If you wish, you can dust the tops of the cookies with coarse sugar before baking, or brush them with icing after. They can even be sandwiched with a layer of ganache (page 531).

Lionel
Poilâne,
Paris

TIME: 45 minutes, plus chilling   YIELD: About 70 cookies

5 ounces (1 stick plus 2
    tablespoons) unsalted French
    or premium American butter,
    softened

½ cup sugar
1 large egg, at room temperature
2 cups all-purpose flour, plus
    more for rolling

1. Put butter in the bowl of a mixer and, working on low speed, beat until smooth. Add sugar and continue to beat until it is blended into the butter. Add egg and beat, still on low speed, until it is incorporated. Add flour and mix only until it disappears; do not overmix.

2. Transfer dough to a work surface and knead it 6 to 8 times, until it just comes together. Divide dough in half, shape each half into a 4-inch disk, wrap in plastic and chill until firm, about 4 hours.

3. Position racks to divide oven into thirds. Preheat oven to 350 degrees. Line 2 baking sheets with parchment paper.

4. Working with one disk at a time, roll dough out on a lightly floured surface until it is between ⅛ and ¼ inch thick. Using a 1½-inch round cookie cutter, cut out as many cookies as you can. Place cookies on lined sheets. (Gather scraps into a disk, chill them, then roll out and cut.) Bake cookies for 8 to 10 minutes or until set; they should not take on much color. Cool on a rack.

Nathan Family Butter Cookies

Joan
Nathan

Here is another simple butter cookie recipe, one that is thinner and crisper than the preceding one, from Joan Nathan, a cookbook writer and a frequent contributor to *The New York Times*.

TIME: 1 hour, plus chilling   YIELD: 4 dozen

8 ounces (2 sticks) unsalted butter
¾ cup sugar
3 large eggs
1 tablespoon brandy
1 teaspoon vanilla extract
⅛ teaspoon salt
3 to 3½ cups all-purpose flour,
    more if cookie cutters are used

Slivered almonds, slightly
    crushed, for decoration,
    optional
Tinted sugar for decoration,
    optional

1. With an electric mixer equipped with a paddle, cream the butter and sugar together. Add 2 eggs, brandy and vanilla extract.

2. Gradually add salt and 3 cups flour, mixing well. Pour out onto a sheet of plastic wrap, wrap tightly, and chill for at least 1 hour or overnight.

3. Preheat oven to 350 degrees. Divide dough in two, and put half in refrigerator. On lightly floured surface, roll the other half into a circle ⅛ inch thick. (The thinner the dough, the better.) Cut with cookie cutters of your choice, dipping cutters in flour to prevent sticking. Transfer the cutouts to 2 ungreased cookie sheets. Repeat with the remaining cookie dough. Leave as is, or brush with egg yolk, and top with slivered almonds or egg white and tinted sugar.

4. Bake in oven for 10 to 12 minutes, or until cookies are golden, turning trays front to back after 6 minutes. Remove, and cool on wire racks.

A SWEET DREAM FOR SWEET CREAM:
Butter Puts on a French Accent
By Kay Rentschler

Butter is the *ne plus ultra* of fats. It tastes better and can do more than its nearest rivals combined; a single 4-ounce stick is absolutely brimming with talent.

The French have known this all along, of course, and if they did not invent butter, they certainly put it on the map—particularly the northern province of Normandy.

Now, small American dairies are producing butters of exquisite flavor and functionality. These high-fat European-style butters have, until recently, been the guarded cache of pastry chefs. But they are anyone's gamble now, whether slipping silkily across a cracker or under a mixer's blades. Once you have had them out for a spin, it is not easy to go back.

Numbering around a dozen, American artisanal butter-makers produce individualistic butters with attributes controlled by their makers. Though the idea that cows are central to butter-making sounds reductive, it is the treatment of the animals that separates artisanal butter-makers from the rest of the industry. Today's creamery butters come from milk produced by a dairy's own herd, or from those at neighboring farms.

Typically, an artisanal butter-maker credits the quality of the butter largely to the freshness of the milk. First the cream is separated from the milk quickly and then it is aged for 12 hours to let the fat molecules knit back together. It is then churned into butter in small, 500-pound batches. The resulting butter has the flavor of fresh cream and a fat content of 86 percent, earning it a place alongside top European butters. Standard American butter contains 80 percent fat.

Favored by artisanal butter-makers, a batch churn, which resembles a washing machine, aerates the cream to froth it, then spins it until the fat molecules are flung from the liquid and begin sticking to one another. At this point, the cream has broken and tiny particles of butter dance in a great tide of liquid known as buttermilk. When the spinning fat molecules reach a certain size, the buttermilk is drained off. What remains is pure butter with about 85 percent fat.

In big commercial operations, by contrast, reserves of cream from industrial warehouses flow into large continuous churns, where they are forced through a fine filter and are extruded as butter—at a rate of up to 22,000 pounds an hour. The butter, usually reinfused with buttermilk to raise its moisture level and lower its overall fat content to the Agriculture Department's minimum of 80 percent, becomes the product most people buy in supermarkets.

But it is not fat alone that distinguishes regular butter and European-style ones. There is also, for some, the compelling presence of culture.

In traditional French farmhouse butter, the cream that rose to the top of milk was skimmed off and held in a cool place until there was enough of it to churn. In the meantime, natural lactic bacteria, or culture, grew in the cream, consuming the lactose or milk sugars, and converting them to lactic acid. The agreeable effects of the lactic acid upon the cream (the cream thickened and soured slightly) earned this product an honored place in French cooking and a name: crème fraîche.

Butter churned from this cream possesses an equally arresting piquancy. It is the flavor associated with European butter. The flavor was that of hazelnuts, and the compound that produced it, diacetyl.

Adding an active culture to butter-making moves the whole operation a few steps into the mystical zone. Today, of course, milk is no longer left to ripen; the results are difficult to control and not always desirable. Instead, pasteurized cream is inoculated with an active culture (like lactococcus lactis diacetylactis or cremoris) and allowed to ferment until flavor compounds, mainly diacetyl, develop. Then the butter is churned.

Most American salted butters contain 2 percent salt.

All butter is comprised of packed fat molecules, water, natural emulsifiers from the cream and flavor compounds. The presence of water makes butter unique among cooking fats and adds to its charms, providing lift, in the form of steam, for laminated doughs like puff pastry, and offering emulsive properties to glossy sauces.

Pastry chefs esteem plasticity, the ability of a dough to be extensible, cooperative and disinclined to tear. Plasticity is determined by emulsifying agents and water drops that become trapped between particles of fat. The strength of that emulsion is directly related to the percentage of butterfat relative to the percentage of water.

On a very basic level, the plasticity of a high-fat/low-moisture butter becomes manifest when it is used. High-test butter melts slowly in a saucepan and burns at a higher temperature. This, along with its lower moisture levels, takes making brown butter, for instance, into a less combustible realm. In baking, low moisture gives cookies snap and contour, and pie crusts high arches. Crispness rules the day.

Butter's greatest achievement, however, must be the sheer sensory force of the chemical reactions that occur when it reaches the oven. It is then that flavor compounds react together to develop the characteristic caramel-like fragrance and deep buttery flavor that makes us swoon for French and Austrian pastries.

You won't get that with olive oil.

Petit Beurre Cookies

Jean
Georges,
New York

This unusual cookie recipe requires that the butter cookie dough first be baked, then cooled and turned into crumbs, which will then become the "flour" in the final cookie dough. The recipe calls for almond flour, which can be made in a blender or a food processor, or purchased from a baking supply company. Jean Georges in New York is the flagship restaurant of chef Jean-Georges Vongerichten.

TIME: 1½ hours, plus cooling and chilling   YIELD: 10 to 12 fragile cookies

2 cups all-purpose flour
¾ almond flour (ground from ½
   cup blanched slivered almonds)

¾ cup sifted confectioners' sugar
10 ounces (2½ sticks) unsalted
   butter, softened

1. Preheat oven to 325 degrees. In a mixer fitted with a paddle, combine the two flours, confectioners' sugar and 6½ ounces butter. Mix on medium-low until a dough forms. Transfer to a baking sheet and roll out ⅛ inch thick. Shape of dough does not matter; smooth edges for even browning. Bake until barely golden brown at edges, 25 to 35 minutes; be careful not to overbake. Remove from oven and cool completely.

2. Using your fingers, crumble dough into fine crumbs and place in bowl of mixer fitted with a paddle. Add remaining 3½ ounces butter and mix at medium speed. Mixture will gather into small pieces, and then change to a dough, pulling away from sides of bowl. Mix until mixture becomes fluffy and creamy like whipped butter, about 5 minutes longer.

3. Line a baking sheet with plastic wrap. Using a rubber spatula, spread dough on sheet in a thick oval. Cover with plastic wrap, and use a rolling pin to roll mixture to about ⅓ inch thick. Chill until firm, about 1 hour.

4. Preheat oven to 350 degrees. Line a baking sheet with parchment paper. Using a 3-inch cookie cutter, cut circles from chilled dough. Transfer to baking sheet, spacing cookies at least 2 inches apart. (Scraps of dough may be rerolled and chilled for additional cookies.) Bake until edges are golden brown, 7 to 10 minutes. Allow to cool on baking sheet. Transfer baking sheet to refrigerator so cookies become well chilled.

5. Fifteen minutes before serving, use a thin, flexible spatula to remove cookies from sheet.

Chocolate Chip Cookies ✳

Wendy
Israel,
Moomba,
New York

This chocolate chip cookie recipe, from a restaurant that served them with dessert, but which is no longer in business, would please Goldilocks. The cookies are neither too soft or too crisp, but just right. They are made with a generous amount of bittersweet chocolate, chopped by hand, instead of with commercial chips. Use high-quality chocolate, labeled with at least 70 percent cacao. Moomba was a trendy New York restaurant that gave bags of the cookies to guests.

TIME: 1 hour   YIELD: 3 dozen cookies

8 ounces (2 sticks) unsalted
   butter, softened
1 cup granulated sugar
1 cup light brown sugar
3 large eggs
½ teaspoon vanilla extract

3 cups all-purpose flour
2 teaspoons salt
1 teaspoon baking soda
1 pound bittersweet chocolate,
   coarsely chopped

1. Preheat oven to 325 degrees. Grease or line several baking sheets with parchment paper. In the bowl of a mixer fitted with a paddle attachment, cream butter and sugars for 4 minutes, scraping down sides after 2 minutes. Add eggs one at a time, beating well after each addition. Add vanilla extract and beat for one minute. Scrape sides of bowl and beat for another minute.

2. Whisk flour, salt and baking soda together and add to bowl. Beat until combined, about 1 minute, scraping bowl once. Add chocolate and mix until combined.

3. Drop scant ¼-cup amounts of cookie dough onto prepared baking sheets, spacing them 1½ inches apart. Bake cookies for 10 to 12 minutes, or until golden brown. Cool on baking sheets.

The Best Chocolate Chip Cookies

Hazelnut paste (or peanut butter) is the secret ingredient in these cookies. Other nut pastes, including almond, could be used. Bill Yosses worked with legendary french pastry chef Pierre Hermé in Paris, but this recipe is all American!

Bill Yosses

TIME: 50 minutes   YIELD: 4 dozen cookies

4 ounces (1 stick) unsalted butter
1 cup granulated sugar
½ cup light brown sugar
¼ cup unsweetened hazelnut paste or peanut butter
2 large eggs
1 vanilla bean, split lengthwise, pulp scraped out

2⅓ cups all-purpose flour
1 teaspoon baking soda
1 teaspoon salt
12 ounces bittersweet chocolate, chopped into ¼-inch pieces or larger
½ cup chopped nuts, optional

1. Preheat the oven to 375 degrees. Line baking sheets with parchment paper. In the bowl of an electric mixer fitted with a paddle attachment, cream the butter and sugars. Add the hazelnut paste, beating until smooth. Beat in the eggs and the vanilla bean pulp, scraping down the bowl as needed.

2. In another bowl, sift together the flour, the baking soda and the salt. Gradually add the dry ingredients to the butter mixture, and combine at low speed until the dough comes together. Mix in the chocolate pieces and, if desired, the nuts. Drop heaping tablespoons of the dough 2 inches apart onto prepared cookie sheets, flattening them slightly by hand.

3. Bake until lightly browned, 9 to 12 minutes. Cool the cookie sheets on a wire rack before removing the cookies.

My Favorite Cookies

Nigella
Lawson

The salted peanuts add an important flavor element to these cookies. Nigella Lawson's cookbooks are popular in her native England and also in the U.S., where she is known for her simple, delicious recipes that can feed a crowd.

TIME: 50 minutes   YIELD: About 20 cookies

6 ounces (1½ sticks) unsalted
  butter, melted and briefly
  cooled
1 cup packed light brown sugar
½ cup granulated sugar
2 teaspoons vanilla extract
2 large eggs

2¼ cups all-purpose flour
1 teaspoon baking powder
½ teaspoon baking soda
1 cup semisweet chocolate
  morsels
1 cup salted peanuts

1. In a medium bowl, using an electric mixer or by hand, beat together the butter, brown sugar and granulated sugar. Beat in vanilla, eggs, flour, baking powder and baking soda. Fold in chocolate morsels and peanuts.

2. Refrigerate bowl of cookie dough for 20 minutes. Meanwhile, preheat oven to 350 degrees. Line a large baking sheet (or two) with a nonstick liner or parchment paper.

3. Shape chilled dough into fat disks about 2½ inches in diameter and ½ inch thick (slightly less than 3 tablespoons of dough for each cookie). Place cookies on baking sheet 1½ inches apart. Bake until golden brown around the edges and cracked and chewy in the middle, about 15 minutes. If using two sheets, switch position of sheets halfway through baking. Remove cookies from oven while they are still soft in the center or they will lose their chewiness as they cool.

4. Allow cookies to rest on baking sheets for about 3 minutes before transferring them to wire racks to cool. When completely cool, store in an airtight container.

Lemon Wafers

These butter cookies flavored with fresh lemon would be the perfect accompaniment to a fruit dessert. Barbara Kafka is a cookbook author and food writer.

TIME: 40 minutes   YIELD: About 3 dozen cookies

Barbara
Kafka

½ cup sugar
Zest of 2 lemons
4 ounces (1 stick) unsalted butter, cut in 1-inch pieces, plus more for cookie sheets
3 large egg whites

1 cup sifted all-purpose flour, plus more for cookie sheets
Pinch of salt
½ teaspoon vanilla extract
1 tablespoon strained fresh lemon juice

1. In a food processor, combine sugar and lemon zest. Process until zest is finely minced, about 1 minute. Stop the machine, and scrape down sides of bowl with a rubber spatula. Add butter, and process until creamy, about 20 seconds. With processor running, add egg whites. Continue to process, adding flour 1 tablespoon at a time, salt, vanilla and lemon juice. Process until a thick batter is formed. Scrape into a small bowl, and stir to combine thoroughly.

2. Place a rack in center of oven. Preheat oven to 400 degrees. While oven is heating, let batter sit at room temperature, about 15 minutes. Butter and flour 2 cookie sheets.

3. Drop rounded teaspoons of batter on prepared baking sheets, and bake for about 8 minutes, or until edges are golden brown. Remove cookies at once to a rack.

Coconut Tuiles

Claudia
Fleming

Tuiles get their name from the way the cookies are handled after coming out of the oven. The hot, paper-thin disks are usually draped over a rolling pin to cool, giving them a curved shape, like roof tiles. They can also be pushed gently into teacups or muffin tins to make tulip dessert cups for fruit or ice cream. And, of course, they can be used without shaping. In a pinch, they can also be layered with pastry cream or another filling to make mini-napoleons. Claudia Fleming was the pastry chef at Gramercy Tavern in New York.

TIME: 1½ hours, plus chilling   YIELD: 3 dozen

1¼ cups sugar
2½ tablespoons unsalted butter
7 large egg whites, at room
  temperature

2 cups shredded unsweetened
  coconut
¼ cup all-purpose flour

1. In the bowl of an electric mixer set at medium speed, beat sugar and butter until the mixture resembles wet sand, about 2 minutes. Gradually add egg whites, and continue to beat until well mixed.

2. Combine coconut and flour, add to bowl, and mix well. Cover and chill at least 8 hours or overnight.

3. Preheat oven to 325 degrees. Use nonstick baking sheets, or regular baking sheets with nonstick liners. For each tuile, drop a heaping teaspoon of batter onto the baking sheet, leaving 3 inches in between. Dip a small offset spatula or the back of a spoon into cold water to prevent sticking, and gently spread each mound of batter into a very thin, even 4-inch round. Bake until golden, about 15 minutes, turning baking sheet so cookies brown evenly.

4. Using a plastic dough scraper or a spatula, remove tuiles from pans. For traditional curved tuiles, drape the cookies while soft and warm over a narrow rolling pin. If the cookies cool they become less pliable. Warm them briefly in the oven to soften again. They can also be baked in pans lined with parchment but they will not be pliable after they are removed from the paper. Cool finished cookies on wire racks.

Anise Shortbread

Shortbreads are dense, buttery and slightly crumbly. Instead of rolling the dough and using cookie cutters, small shortbread cookies can be made by shaping the dough into a smooth log about 2 inches in diameter, and slicing it in rounds ¼ inch thick, as in the following recipe. Shortbread cookies are typically baked with a decorative fork prick on top. Claudia Fleming was a pastry chef at Montrachet before becoming the founding pastry chef at Gramercy Tavern in New York.

Claudia
Fleming

TIME: 50 minutes, plus chilling   YIELD: 2 dozen

1 tablespoon aniseed
8 ounces (2 sticks) unsalted butter
¾ cup confectioners' sugar, plus
   extra for dusting

1 teaspoon vanilla extract
½ teaspoon anise extract
2 cups all-purpose flour
½ teaspoon salt

1. Preheat oven to 350 degrees. In a small skillet over high heat, toast aniseed, stirring until fragrant, about 2 minutes. Transfer to a plate to cool.

2. With an electric mixer, beat butter and sugar until smooth. Add vanilla and anise extracts, and beat well. Beat in the flour, aniseed and salt until just combined. Form dough into a disk, wrap in plastic wrap, and chill for at least 3 hours.

3. Divide dough in half and roll each piece between two sheets of waxed paper to ⅛ inch thick. Cut out rounds with a 2½-inch cookie cutter, and arrange on an ungreased baking sheet. Prick shortbread with a fork, and bake until light brown around edges, 12 to 15 minutes. Cool on a wire rack. Dust half each cookie with confectioners' sugar.

Toasted Pecan Shortbread Cookies

Florence
Fabricant

Brown rice flour is available at health food stores and from baking supply companies. Nut flours, such as almond or hazelnut, can be substituted, with the pecans replaced with chopped almonds or hazelnuts. Though these delicate treats are rich in butter, they boast brown rice flour, too.

TIME: 1½ hours, plus chilling   YIELD: About 60 cookies

1 cup coarsely chopped pecans
8 ounces (2 sticks) unsalted
    butter, softened
½ cup sugar
¼ teaspoon salt
½ cup brown rice flour
1½ cups all-purpose flour
1 teaspoon vanilla extract

1. Place pecans in heavy skillet over medium heat and cook, stirring, until lightly toasted, about 5 minutes. Remove from pan to cool.

2. Cream butter and sugar by hand or in a mixer. Mix salt with rice flour and fold in by hand or on low speed. Fold in the all-purpose flour, pecans and vanilla.

3. Divide dough in half. Place each portion on a large piece of plastic wrap. Fold long side of wrap over dough and gently roll back and forth to form a log about 12 inches long and 1½ inches in diameter. Repeat with second half. Wrap well in plastic and refrigerate until firm, 1 to 4 hours.

4. Preheat oven to 300 degrees. Remove plastic wrap from dough. With sharp knife, cut dough logs in slices about ¼ inch thick and place 1 inch apart on ungreased baking sheets. Bake until firm and just beginning to color, 35 to 40 minutes. Cool on racks.

Chinese Walnut Cookies

Other nuts, including almonds and pecans, can be used to decorate these buttery cookies. Pichet Ong is a New York–based pastry chef who specializes in Asian-accented desserts.

Pichet Ong

TIME: 50 minutes, plus chilling   YIELD: 5 dozen cookies

5 ounces (about 2 cups) walnut
   halves
1¾ cups all-purpose flour
1 teaspoon baking powder
1 teaspoon baking soda
8 ounces (2 sticks) unsalted
   butter, softened, plus more for
   pans

½ teaspoon salt
¾ cup granulated sugar
⅓ cup light brown sugar
1 large egg
1½ teaspoons vanilla extract

1. Preheat oven to 300 degrees. Toast walnuts on rimmed baking sheet for 10 minutes, shaking nuts halfway through. Cool.

2. In a bowl, whisk together the flour, baking powder and baking soda. Using a mixer fitted with paddle attachment, cream butter on medium speed with ½ cup walnuts and the salt until walnuts break up.

3. Scrape down bowl, add sugars and continue to beat until light and fluffy. Add egg and vanilla, and beat until incorporated. Scrape down bowl and add flour mixture, mixing just until incorporated. Scrape dough onto plastic wrap, wrap tightly and refrigerate for at least 4 hours or up to 3 days.

4. Preheat oven to 325 degrees. Butter 2 baking sheets, or line them with parchment.

5. Scoop ½-inch rounds of dough, and place them 2 inches apart on baking sheets. Press a walnut half on each cookie. Bake cookies, rotating pan halfway through, until lightly golden brown, about 10 minutes. Let cool on a wire rack.

Praline Cookies

David
Cunningham,
Lenox Room,
New York

These delectable cookies are made with praline powder, consisting of toasted nuts coated with caramel, cooled and ground. Almond flour is sold at baking supply companies. The Lenox Room is a popular Upper East Side restaurant, but David Cunningham, whose recipe this is, has moved on.

TIME: 1½ hours, plus chilling   YIELD: 4 dozen

1 cup toasted hazelnuts
1¾ cups sugar
⅔ cup almond flour
12 ounces (3 sticks) unsalted
   butter, softened
2 large eggs

⅛ teaspoon vanilla extract
3¾ cups all-purpose flour
½ teaspoon ground cinnamon
½ teaspoon baking powder
½ teaspoon salt

1. For praline powder, place nuts on a nonstick or lightly oiled baking sheet. In a heavy saucepan combine ¾ cup sugar and ¼ cup water, and bring to a boil over medium heat, stirring until sugar dissolves. Increase heat to medium-high, and boil undisturbed until sugar turns deep amber, about 7 minutes. Immediately pour caramel over nuts. Let cool, then break into 1-inch pieces. Place in a food processor, and grind to a powder. In a bowl, combine praline powder with almond flour, and set aside.

2. In a mixer with paddle attachment, cream butter and remaining sugar until light and fluffy, about 2 minutes. Add eggs one at a time, beating well after each addition. Add vanilla, and beat another minute.

3. Meanwhile, in another bowl, whisk together the flour, cinnamon, baking powder and salt. Add to the butter mixture, and mix until just combined. Stir in the praline mixture until fully combined. Form dough into a disk, wrap in plastic and refrigerate for 3 hours or until firm.

4. Preheat oven to 350 degrees. Grease several baking sheets, or line with parchment paper. Unwrap dough, and put between two pieces of plastic wrap. Roll out to ⅜ inch thick. Cut out cookies using a 2½-inch cutter, and place on baking sheets 1 inch apart. Reroll scraps to cut more cookies. If dough gets too soft, freeze for a few minutes until firm. Bake cookies for 12 to 14 minutes, until pale brown. Cool on racks.

Lemon Cornmeal Cookies

Cornmeal gives these cookies a lush, crumbly texture. Try to find stone-ground cornmeal. Tapika was a popular Southwestern-themed restaurant in Midtown Manhattan, now replaced by a bank.

TIME: 1 hour   YIELD: 2 dozen cookies

Alana
Ford,
Tapika,
New York

Soft unsalted butter for baking
   sheets (optional)
2¼ cups all-purpose flour
¾ cup sugar, more for sprinkling
¾ cup yellow cornmeal
¾ teaspoon baking powder
¼ teaspoon salt

1½ teaspoons grated lemon zest
6 ounces (1½ sticks) unsalted
   butter, cut in cubes
1 large egg yolk
2 large eggs
¼ cup pine nuts

1. Preheat oven to 350 degrees. Grease several baking sheets or line with parchment paper. In the bowl of a mixer fitted with paddle attachment and set on low speed, combine flour, sugar, cornmeal, baking powder and salt, and mix until combined. Add lemon zest and butter, and mix until mixture resembles coarse meal.

2. Whisk the egg yolk together with one whole egg. Add to flour mixture and mix until it is evenly incorporated and dough comes together.

3. Scoop cookie dough 2 tablespoons at a time and form into logs, about 2½ inches long. Place logs 2 inches apart on prepared baking sheet.

4. Whisk remaining egg with 1 tablespoon water. Brush onto tops of cookies. Press about 5 pine nuts into top of each cookie and sprinkle with sugar. Bake for 12 to 15 minutes, until golden brown around edges.

Painted Christmas Cookies

Bill
Yosses

These basic cookies become a holiday arts and crafts project, with painted decorations and even a possible hole for hanging them as tree ornaments. The technique for painting the cookies is unexpected because the designs are applied to the raw dough, and becomes baked on. Bill Yosses, a pastry chef who first became prominent at Bouley, was the chef for Citarella stores and restaurants.

TIME: 1 hour, plus chilling   YIELD: 4 dozen 2½-inch cookies

6 ounces (1½ sticks) unsalted
   butter
¾ cup confectioners' sugar
1 large egg
1 tablespoon vanilla extract
1¾ cups all-purpose flour plus
   additional for rolling

1 cup almond flour
Nonstick cooking spray
Cookie paint (page 546)
Granulated sugar for sprinkling

1. In the bowl of a mixer fitted with a paddle attachment, cream the butter and the sugar on low speed. Add the egg and vanilla, and beat until combined.

2. In another bowl, whisk together the flour and the almond flour. With the mixer on low speed, gradually add half the flour mixture to the butter mixture. Beat until combined. Add the remaining flour, and combine, scraping down the bowl as necessary. Scrape the dough onto a piece of plastic wrap, pat it into a disk, and wrap it tightly. Refrigerate for at least 4 hours or overnight.

3. Preheat the oven to 325 degrees. Line baking sheets with parchment paper. Lightly spray the parchment with cooking spray, and blot with a paper towel. Using paintbrushes, fingers or a small knife, paint designs on the parchment paper. Paint in a single thin layer. Only the paint touching the parchment paper will show up on the baked cookie. For best results, paint designs that are smaller than the cookies.

4. Lightly flour a work surface and a rolling pin, and roll the dough out ⅛ inch thick. Use cookie cutters to cut shapes in the dough. With a spatula, lift the cookies, and dust the tops with a clean pastry brush to remove any

excess flour. Place the cookies, dusted side down, onto the paint. Use a rolling pin or your palm to press the cookies gently and evenly into the paint, taking care not to slide or move them. If you choose to make a cookie ornament, use a skewer to form a hole slightly larger than you want it to be when baked.

5. Sprinkle the cookies with granulated sugar. Bake for 9 to 12 minutes, until the cookies are firm and barely golden at edges. Cool the cookie sheets on a wire rack before removing cookies.

Cocoa Christmas Cookies

Alfred
Portale

Spicy, fruity and rich, these are holiday cookie treats. They keep well and can be frozen before glazing. Alfred Portale is a partner and the executive chef at Gotham Bar and Grill in New York. This is a family recipe.

TIME: 45 minutes, plus chilling   YIELD: About 7 dozen

4 cups all-purpose flour

1 cup unsweetened Dutch-process cocoa

4½ teaspoons baking powder

2 teaspoons ground cinnamon

½ teaspoon freshly grated nutmeg

½ teaspoon ground cloves

½ teaspoon salt

1½ cups plump, moist raisins, coarsely chopped

1 tablespoon orange juice

12 ounces (3 sticks) unsalted butter, softened

1¼ cups granulated sugar

2 large eggs, at room temperature

1 teaspoon vanilla extract

1 cup apricot preserves

¼ cup milk, at room temperature

1½ cups lightly toasted walnuts, coarsely chopped

1 cup confectioners' sugar

3 teaspoons lemon juice

1. In large mixing bowl, combine flour, cocoa, baking powder, cinnamon, nutmeg, cloves and salt. Whisk to combine, and set aside. In small bowl, combine raisins and orange juice; reserve.

2. In a mixer with a paddle attachment, or by hand, beat butter and sugar together until creamy. Add eggs one at a time, beating on medium speed for 1 minute after each addition. Beat in vanilla, preserves and milk. On low speed, gradually add flour mixture, beating only until it is incorporated.

3. Stir nuts and reserved raisins into dough. Cover dough tightly with plastic wrap, and chill for at least 2 hours or for as long as 2 days.

4. Preheat oven to 350 degrees. Roll the dough between your palms to form walnut-size balls. Place on a nonstick or parchment-lined cookie sheet, 1½ inches apart. Bake for 10 to 12 minutes, until tops look dry; the tops may crack, which is fine. Transfer cookies to a rack; repeat with rest of dough.

5. For glaze, combine confectioners' sugar, lemon juice and 3 teaspoons of warm water in a bowl. Whisk until smooth. While cookies are still warm, dip tops into glaze, and place on a rack to cool. The cookies may also be painted with the glaze using a feather pastry brush.

Piped Butter Cookies (Spritzgebäck)

Having a pastry bag and decorating tips on hand is more practical than buying a cookie press because a pastry bag has multiple uses. Kay Rentschler has contributed recipes to *The New York Times.*

Kay
Rentschler

TIME: 20 minutes   YIELD: About 6 dozen tiny cookies

6 ounces (1½ sticks) European-
    style butter, softened
1½ cups sifted confectioners'
    sugar

3 large egg yolks
1 teaspoon vanilla extract
1½ cups all-purpose flour
¼ teaspoon fine sea salt

1. Line 3 baking sheets with parchment paper. Adjust oven racks to middle and lower-middle positions and preheat to 400 degrees. Using mixer with paddle attachment, beat butter on medium speed until light and fluffy, 1 minute. Add sugar and beat until very light and smooth. Add yolks and vanilla and beat to combine. Scrape down bowl.

2. In a medium bowl, whisk flour and salt together. With mixer on low speed, add flour mixture a little at a time to butter mixture, beating until dry ingredients are incorporated and a soft, pliant dough has formed.

3. Using a rubber spatula, transfer one-quarter of the dough into a large pastry bag fitted with a small star tip or into the canister of a cookie press. Use a dot of dough to anchor corners of each parchment sheet onto baking sheets. Pipe or press dough in even rows, allowing ½ inch between cookies. Repeat with remaining dough.

4. Bake until cookie edges are deep brown, 8 to 10 minutes, rotating cookie sheets halfway through. Remove from oven and cool on wire racks.

Spice Drops

Bill
Yosses

The spices add a tantalizing touch of heat to these cookies. Bill Yosses was trained in Paris and began his career in New York working alongside Daniel Boulud and Thomas Keller at the Polo.

TIME: 45 minutes   YIELD: 5 dozen cookies

10 whole allspice berries	1 teaspoon salt
5 whole green cardamom pods	½ teaspoon baking soda
5 black peppercorns	6 ounces (1½ sticks) unsalted
1 clove	butter
1 star anise	1 cup sugar
1 nutmeg	1 large egg
2 cups all-purpose flour	⅓ cup molasses

1. Preheat the oven to 350 degrees. Line 3 baking sheets with parchment paper. In an electric grinder, grind the spices to a powder. Transfer the spices to a large bowl, and whisk in the flour, the salt and the baking soda.

2. In the bowl of an electric mixer fitted with a paddle attachment, cream the butter and sugar. Add the egg and the molasses, and beat until smooth, scraping down the bowl as needed. Gradually add the dry ingredients, and beat until combined.

3. Drop teaspoons of cookie dough 2 inches apart on the prepared cookie sheets. Bake until the cookies are golden brown around the edges, 8 to 11 minutes. Cool the cookie sheets on a wire rack before removing the cookies.

Peanut Meringue Cookies

This recipe proves that it is possible to make a delicious cookie without butter. Marian Burros is a food reporter for *The New York Times.*

Marian
Burros

TIME: 1 hour 15 minutes   YIELD: 2 to 2½ dozen cookies

1 large egg white, at room
   temperature

½ cup sugar
¾ cup whole salted peanuts

1. Preheat oven to 325 degrees. Line a baking sheet with brown, waxed or parchment paper.

2. Beat egg white until stiff. Slowly beat in sugar to make a meringue. Fold in peanuts.

3. Drop meringues by the teaspoonful onto the paper-lined baking sheet. Bake 45 minutes. Turn the oven off, and leave cookies in it for 15 minutes more. Cool before serving. Cookies can be stored between layers of waxed paper in a tightly sealed tin at room temperature for as long as a week.

BISCOTTI

The term "biscotti" is the Italian equivalent of biscuits in French, which has given us the same word, biscuit, in English. But their meanings are very different. The word actually means "twice-cooked." And Italian biscotti are just that: cookies that are baked and then baked a second time to crisp them. French biscuit is the term that is now usually used for a plain cake like a sponge cake, though it can also refer to a savory cracker or a crisp, dry toast. In American usage, a biscuit is a buttery little bun and in England it's a cracker. The German zwieback also means twice-baked, and is often a slice of hard, dry toast.

Almond Biscotti

Florence
Fabricant

Biscotti, biscuits and zwieback are made by baking a cookie, flatbread or toast a second time to crisp it. Soft biscotti are made by serving the sliced cookies warm, without returning them to the oven, as in the beginning of step 6 below. I love to serve them this way. Most of the time, biscotti are served crisp and firm and if you want to store them, you'll have to bake them the second time.

TIME: 1 hour   YIELD: About 60 biscotti

1 cup whole blanched almonds
2¾ cups all-purpose flour, plus
   more for work surface
Pinch of salt
½ teaspoon baking soda

¾ teaspoon baking powder
4 large eggs
1 cup sugar
1 teaspoon almond extract

1. Preheat oven to 350 degrees. Spread the almonds on a baking sheet, place in the oven and toast for about 15 minutes.

2. Meanwhile sift the flour, salt, baking soda and baking powder together and set aside.

3. Beat the eggs lightly, just until they are blended, in a mixing bowl with a whisk or in an electric mixer. Remove 2 tablespoons of the egg

mixture to a small dish and set aside. Beat the sugar into the remaining eggs until blended. Stir in the flour mixture to form a soft dough.

4. When the almonds are toasted, remove them from the oven and transfer them to a bowl. Line the baking sheet with parchment paper.

5. Divide the dough in half and place one portion on a well-floured work surface. With floured hands pat it into a 6-inch square. Scatter half the almonds on the dough and press them into the surface. Roll the dough into a cylinder about 2 inches in diameter and 12 to 15 inches long. Place on the paper-lined baking sheet. Repeat with the remaining dough. Brush the tops of both cylinders with the reserved egg.

6. Place in the oven and bake about 15 minutes, until golden and firm to the touch. Transfer to a cutting board and cut on an angle into slices ½ inch thick. Return the slices to the baking sheet, standing them up, and return them to the oven. Bake another 20 minutes, until they are crisp and dry. Allow to cool completely before storing or serving.

Cornmeal Biscotti

Claudia
Fleming

Though the cornmeal in the dough sets these biscotti apart from the usual, giving them an alluringly crumbly texture, they are made in classic fashion, baked in logs, then sliced and rebaked until crisp. This recipe is from Claudia Fleming, who was the pastry chef at Gramercy Tavern.

TIME: 2 hours 15 minutes   YIELD: About 2½ dozen

½ cup coarsely chopped blanched almonds

¼ cup coarsely chopped skinned hazelnuts

4 ounces (½ stick) unsalted butter

1 tablespoon minced rosemary

1½ tablespoons finely grated orange zest

1 cup all-purpose flour

½ cup coarse yellow cornmeal

½ cup sugar

1 teaspoon baking soda

1 teaspoon aniseed

3 large eggs

1. Preheat oven to 350 degrees. Line 2 baking sheets with parchment. Spread nuts out on a jellyroll pan, and toast them in oven, stirring occasionally, until they are lightly golden around the edges, about 8 to 10 minutes. Let cool on a rack. Keep oven on.

2. In a small saucepan, melt butter over medium-high heat. Turn off heat, and add rosemary and orange zest. Let cool.

3. In the bowl of an electric mixer at low speed, mix together the flour, cornmeal, sugar, baking soda and aniseed. Add 2 eggs, one at a time, mixing well after each addition. Add the cooled, melted butter, and mix to combine. Stir in the nuts. Let dough rest for 5 minutes.

4. Form dough into a log 2 inches wide, and place it on one of the baking sheets. In a small bowl, mix remaining egg with one tablespoon water. Brush this wash over the log, then bake log until it is a deep golden brown, about 30 minutes. Let cool on a rack. Reduce oven temperature to 200 degrees.

5. Using a serrated knife, slice log on a diagonal into pieces ¼ inch thick. Arrange biscotti on 2 parchment-lined baking sheets, and bake until crisp, about 45 minutes to 1 hour. Let cool on a rack.

Pepper-Nut Biscotti

These biscotti are spicy and peppery and are excellent for dipping into strong, sweet wines at the end of a meal. Amy's Bread is a New York company that is known for its artisanal breads and baked goods.

Amy's
Bread,
New York

TIME: 1 hour, plus 30 minutes cooling   YIELD: About 6 dozen

3½ cups all-purpose flour

1 tablespoon freshly ground black pepper

1 teaspoon baking powder

1 teaspoon baking soda

¼ teaspoon salt

6 ounces (1½ sticks) unsalted butter, softened

2 cups sugar

4 large eggs

4 teaspoons grated orange zest

2 teaspoons grated lemon zest

1 tablespoon vanilla

½ teaspoon almond extract

3 cups hazelnuts, whole and pieces, with skins, toasted

1. Position oven racks to divide the oven into thirds, and preheat oven to 350 degrees. Line 2 large baking sheets with parchment paper.

2. In a medium bowl, combine flour, pepper, baking powder, baking soda and salt. Whisk to blend.

3. In a mixer with a paddle attachment, beat butter and sugar until smooth. Add eggs, orange zest, lemon zest, vanilla and almond extract. Beat just until well blended. Add flour mixture, and beat at lowest speed or by hand just until moistened. Mix in nuts until blended into dough.

4. Divide dough into quarters. On a lightly floured surface, shape each into a flattened log 14 inches long, 2 inches wide, and 1 inch thick. Put two logs on each parchment-lined baking sheet.

5. Bake until lightly browned, about 25 minutes, rotating pans between oven racks halfway through baking. Logs should be somewhat firm. Cool logs for 30 minutes, then transfer to a cutting board. Cut each log on a slight angle into ¾-inch slices. Keep slices together, then slide them together to re-form logs. Transfer to baking sheets, and separate slices, leaving about ½ inch of space between each.

6. Bake biscotti again until they are light golden brown and slightly firm in the center of each slice, about 16 minutes. Transfer to a rack to cool to room temperature. Store packed in an airtight container.

Jam-Filled Mandelbrot

Rebecca
Peltz

Mandelbrot are the German-Jewish version of biscotti. *Mandel* means almond and the name translates as almond bread. There are no almonds in this version. This recipe comes from a home cook.

TIME: About 1 hour, plus chilling   YIELD: About 60 cookies

8 ounces (2 sticks) unsalted butter
2 tablespoons vegetable
    shortening or unsalted butter
1½ cups plus 1 tablespoon sugar
1 teaspoon vanilla extract
4 large eggs

4 cups all-purpose flour
1 teaspoon baking powder
Dash of salt
3 cups apricot jam
¼ teaspoon ground cinnamon

1. Cream butter, shortening and 1½ cups sugar in an electric mixer or a food processor. Add vanilla and eggs, one at a time, mixing well. In a bowl, whisk together flour, baking powder and salt. Slowly stir into batter. Transfer to a bowl, cover, and refrigerate overnight.

2. Preheat oven to 350 degrees. Cover 2 baking sheets with parchment paper. Divide dough into 4 oval balls, and roll each out very thin. Spread each with about ¾ cup jam. Roll up into long jelly rolls and place on baking sheets.

3. Mix cinnamon and remaining tablespoon of sugar, sprinkle on rolls and bake for 30 minutes. Remove pans from oven and let cool a few minutes. Using a sharp knife, cut into 1-inch slices. Return to oven and bake about 5 more minutes.

BROWNIES AND BARS, INCLUDING FINANCIERS AND MADELEINES

Brownies, baked in a pan from a batter, then cut into squares, are simpler to make than cookies, and usually serve the same purpose: a sweet treat at the end of the meal or at snacktime. For a dinner party, cut them into 1-inch squares. Always use the best-quality chocolate for the best flavor and texture.

Bars and other soft little cakes, including madeleines and financiers, add a delicious finale to the meal, especially when served warm.

Brownies ✳

These are tiny dessert brownies, meant to be served with ice cream. Their texture is halfway between fudge and cake, as it should be. They can be made without the coffee and/or the nuts. Village, as its name might imply, is a restaurant in New York's Greenwich Village.

Village,
New York

TIME: 1 hour, plus cooling   YIELD: About 6 dozen brownie squares

Nonstick cooking spray
5 large eggs
3¼ cups sugar
1½ teaspoons vanilla extract
½ teaspoon finely ground
   espresso coffee beans
⅛ teaspoon salt

8 ounces (2 sticks) unsalted
   butter, melted and cooled
8 ounces unsweetened chocolate,
   melted and cooled
1⅔ cups all-purpose flour
2 cups walnut pieces, toasted

1. Preheat oven to 375 degrees. Line an 11½-by-17½-inch jelly roll pan with parchment paper, and coat with nonstick cooking spray. In an electric mixer, beat eggs, sugar, vanilla, coffee and salt on high speed until thick, about 5 minutes.

2. Add butter and chocolate, and mix until combined. Add flour, and mix lightly to incorporate. Add walnuts, and mix lightly until combined.

3. Spread batter in pan evenly with a rubber spatula. Bake until brownies have set and a knife inserted in center comes out clean, about 18 minutes. Do not overbake. Let cool in pan, then cut into 1-inch squares.

Brownies with Candied Orange Zest

Philippe
Conticini,
Petrossian,
New York

French brownies, intensified with candied orange zest, cinnamon and walnuts, are baked in an unusual fashion. The batter is close to that of a soufflé. And instead of a typically deep baking pan, a shallow one, like a jelly roll pan, is used. And after the brownies have been baked, they are left to rest for hours before they are cut and ready to serve. The result is a brownie that has a texture at once dense but light, like mousse, or a fallen soufflé. At one time, Philippe Conticini, a Parisian chef, was the pastry chef for the Petrossian restaurant and boutique in New York.

TIME: 1 hour 30 minutes, plus resting   YIELD: 12 brownies

Zest of 1 orange, cut into ⅛-inch
  strips
Juice of half a lemon
Juice of half an orange
2 tablespoons granulated sugar,
  more for pan
9 ounces (2 sticks plus 2
  tablespoons) unsalted butter,
  softened, plus more for pan

11 large eggs, at room
  temperature
2¼ cups confectioners' sugar
11 ounces semisweet chocolate (at
  least 58 percent cacao)
1 tablespoon ground cinnamon
¼ cup chopped walnuts
½ teaspoon fleur de sel

1. In a small saucepan, combine orange zest, lemon juice, orange juice and 2 tablespoons sugar. Bring to a boil, then simmer until zest is tender and liquid is reduced to a syrup, about 10 minutes. Cool. Chop zest and reserve; there should be about 3 tablespoons.

2. Preheat oven to 450 degrees. Line a 10-by-15-inch baking pan with a ¾-inch rim with parchment paper. Butter and sugar the paper. Separate 9 eggs, placing whites in bowl of a mixer and 7 yolks in a medium bowl. (Reserve remaining yolks for another use.) Add 2 whole eggs and ¼ cup confectioners' sugar to yolks; whisk to blend.

3. In a double boiler or microwave oven, melt chocolate. Transfer to a mixing bowl and stir in butter until smooth. Whisk in yolk mixture. Stir in cinnamon.

4. Add remaining confectioners' sugar to egg whites. Beat with mixer until stiff. Add about 1 cup egg whites to chocolate mixture. Fold until

blended. Add chocolate mixture to whites in bowl. Fold until smooth. Fold in reserved orange zest and half the walnuts.

5. Pour into prepared baking pan, and use a spatula to spread evenly to sides. Sprinkle with remaining walnuts and fleur de sel and place in oven. When top is puffed, about 20 to 25 minutes, insert a knife tip into center; if it comes out clean, remove from oven. While cake is still hot, use a paring knife to trim sides, which may have puffed up over rim of baking sheet. Place another baking sheet lined with parchment paper on top of brownie, and invert; remove top pan and sheet of parchment. Allow brownie to rest at room temperature for 8 hours, then cut into 12 rectangles.

Orange Mocha Brownies

Marian
Burros

Orange and chocolate are delicious together. In these brownies, a touch of coffee adds to the complexity. Marian Burros is a food reporter for *The New York Times.*

TIME: 35 to 40 minutes   YIELD: 24 to 30 large brownies; 48 to 60 small brownies

8 ounces (2 sticks) unsalted
  butter, plus more for pan
1½ cups all-purpose flour, plus
  more for pan
4 ounces unsweetened chocolate
4 ounces semisweet or bittersweet
  chocolate
2 cups sugar

5 large eggs
2 tablespoons Grand Marnier
1 tablespoon coffee extract
1 tablespoon grated orange zest
Dash of salt
1½ cups chopped pecans
  (optional)

1. Preheat oven to 350 degrees. Butter and flour a 9-by-13-inch baking pan.

2. Melt butter and chocolate over hot water or in a microwave. Set aside.

3. Beat sugar and eggs thoroughly until creamy, then stir in cooled chocolate mixture. Stir in flour, Grand Marnier, coffee extract, orange zest, salt and optional pecans. Spoon batter in the pan and bake 20 to 25 minutes. A cake tester inserted in the center should not come out perfectly clean. Let cool, and refrigerate for as long as 3 days or freeze for a couple of weeks.

4. To serve, defrost if frozen or return refrigerated brownies to room temperature. Cut into squares or rectangles.

Apricot Dreams

These are apricot bars, layered with tender cake, preserves and crunchy nuts. Marian Burros is a food reporter for *The New York Times*.

Marian
Burros

TIME: 40 minutes   YIELD: 5 dozen

1 cup all-purpose flour
1 teaspoon baking powder
Salt
4 ounces (1 stick) unsalted butter, softened
2 large eggs
1 tablespoon milk

12 ounces apricot preserves
2 tablespoons melted unsalted butter
½ cup chopped nuts (unsalted walnuts, pecans, cashews, pistachios)
¼ cup sugar

1. Preheat oven to 325 degrees.

2. Mix together flour, baking powder and ⅛ teaspoon salt. Beat in softened butter. Mix 1 egg with milk, add and beat until mixture is thoroughly blended.

3. Evenly pat out dough in a jelly roll pan, 10 inches by 15 inches. Spread the preserves over the dough.

4. Lightly beat the remaining egg, and mix with melted butter, nuts and sugar. Spread this mixture over the preserves.

5. Bake 25 minutes in the middle of the oven. Cool slightly, and cut into diamonds or squares. Refrigerate for as long as three days, or freeze for a couple of weeks. If frozen, allow to sit at room temperature about an hour before serving.

Nut Diamonds

Marian
Burros

These tender nut bars are irresistible when still warm, and since they can be cut before they cool, serving them warm is a fine idea. Cooled, they become crisper, more like biscotti. Marian Burros' food reporting has appeared in *The New York Times* for over twenty-five years.

TIME: 40 minutes   YIELD: 5 dozen

Vegetable oil for pan
8 ounces (2 sticks) unsalted
   butter, softened
1 cup light brown sugar
1 teaspoon vanilla extract
1 large egg yolk

1¾ cups all-purpose flour
½ teaspoon salt
½ teaspoon ground cinnamon
½ cup very finely chopped pecans
   or cashews
1 large egg, beaten

1. Preheat oven to 350 degrees. Lightly oil a jelly roll pan, 10 by 15 inches.

2. Cream together butter and sugar. Blend in vanilla and egg yolk. Combine flour, salt, cinnamon and ¼ cup nuts, and stir into sugar mixture. Press dough evenly into pan; it should be very thin. Brush top with beaten egg. Sprinkle remaining nuts evenly, and press in lightly. Bake 25 to 30 minutes, until edges start to brown.

3. Remove from oven, run knife around edges of pan and cut into diamonds or triangles while hot. Cool on racks.

THE PASTRY CHEF'S RICH LITTLE SECRET
By Amanda Hesser

It's a simple almond cake, leavened by egg whites, moistened with browned butter and baked into a small mold. But such simplicity is deceiving: the classic French pastry called the financier is exquisitely refined. It is springy, sweet and nutty with an exterior that's as crisp as an eggshell.

In France, financiers have been a staple of fine pastry shops for more than one hundred years. But in America, they have only recently begun making their way into restaurants. And for the home cook they're something of a mystery: not even bibles of French baking include recipes for financiers.

You may have eaten one without knowing it. Pastry chefs all over New York serve them, often without saying so on the menu. But it is impossible not to notice how different the financier is from any other cake.

The financier (pronounced *fee-nahn-see-AY*) often shows up on plates of petits fours, baked in tiny round, fluted or rectangular molds. The shape may be round in some places, rectangular in others, but the base is rarely anything but almond. It has been that way for more than a century.

Pierre Lacam, in *Mémorial Historique de la Pâtisserie,* published in 1890, wrote that the financier was created by a baker named Lasne, whose bakery on the Rue St.-Denis was near the Bourse, the financial center of Paris. Presumably, the rich little cake was named for the rich financiers who frequented his bakery. The cake was baked in rectangular molds, the shape of gold bars. The recipe has withstood time, even without the support of cookbook authors and culinary preservationists. And it has earned the adoration of those who have tried it.

As obscure as the financier has been, there is little mystery about how to make it. All you need is a whisk, a bowl, a pan and a mere stroke of finesse.

A few steps make or break the cake. The first, browning the butter, is what defines its flavor and adds depth to the almonds. You need to heat the butter over medium-low heat until it begins to brown and smell nutty. It is best to do this slowly and to keep a careful eye on it. Once butter begins to brown, it turns quickly and burns easily. Remove it the moment it attains the color of a chestnut. Undercooking it is equally damaging, for it will lack the necessary aroma.

The second trick is to mix the batter as little as possible. It should be stirred until just blended. If you stir too much, the gluten in the flour will get overworked and the cake will be tough.

The batter then has to rest before baking. A few hours in the refrigerator, and the flavors will harmonize and the batter will firm up, making it easier to pipe into molds.

The one decision you need to make regards texture. If you use almond flour, the cake will be finer but denser. If you grind your almonds, it will be coarser and rustic. I prefer grinding. American butter and flour are not the same as in France. And in the finished cake, the differences translate even more tangibly. Somehow the roughness of home-ground almonds and flecks of almond skin give the cakes a kind of soulful intensity that you find in Parisian pastries.

Financiers do impose just one inconvenience: they must be baked on the day they're eaten. In fact, their texture deteriorates in a few hours. Once they're in the oven and the fragrance begins filling your house, this is hardly a problem.

Classic Financiers

François
Payard,
Payard
Pâtisserie
and Bistro,
New York

Pastry chefs often prepare batters that must rest several hours or even overnight before baking. It's not only a convenience, it lightens the end result. So forget what you have learned about the necessity of popping the cake into the oven to bake as soon as a leavened batter is mixed. The aromatic browned butter, a crucial ingredient, should be nut-brown and fragrant, and removed from the heat just shy of when it looks ready because it will continue to brown off-heat in the pan. François Payard is the owner of Payard Pâtisserie and Bistro in New York.

TIME: 50 minutes, plus resting   YIELD: 12 cakes

9 tablespoons unsalted butter, plus more for molds

1¼ cups confectioners' sugar

¾ cup almond flour or ½ cup whole unpeeled almonds

¼ cup bleached all-purpose flour

1 tablespoon plus 2 teaspoons cake flour

Pinch of salt

1 teaspoon baking powder

4 large egg whites, at room temperature

1 teaspoon vanilla extract

Confectioners' sugar for dusting, optional

1. Generously butter 12 2-by-4-inch rectangular financier molds (measured at the top). Refrigerate.

2. In a small pan over medium low heat, melt butter, occasionally swirling, until it begins to brown, about 5 minutes. Set aside.

3. Sift sugar over almond flour. (If using whole almonds, process with sugar in a food processor until fine.) Add both flours, salt and baking powder, and gently whisk to combine. Add egg whites one at a time, whisking just to combine. Do not overwork or the cakes will be tough.

4. Add vanilla to butter. In a steady stream, whisk butter into flour mixture. Cover with plastic wrap, and refrigerate 3 hours.

5. Preheat oven to 375 degrees. Set molds on a baking sheet. Spoon mixture into a pastry bag that has a ¼-inch round tip. Pipe mixture into molds, filling halfway. Bake 18 to 20 minutes, until browned and springy. Remove from oven, and cool 2 minutes before unmolding. Cool completely on rack. Serve plain or dusted with confectioners' sugar, or warm, with ice cream.

Chocolate Financiers ✳

Jean-Paul
Hévin,
Paris

Chocolate makes these financiers from a Parisian pastry chef irresistible.

TIME: 35 minutes   YIELD: 15 small cakes

4½ tablespoons unsalted butter,
    plus more for molds
4½ tablespoons all-purpose flour,
    plus more for molds
5 ounces bittersweet chocolate,
    finely chopped
⅔ cup heavy cream

½ cup confectioners' sugar, sifted
⅓ cup finely ground blanched
    almonds or almond flour
⅛ teaspoon baking powder
Scant ½ cup egg whites (from
    about 3 large eggs)

1. Preheat oven to 350 degrees. Butter 15 financier molds (each with a capacity of 3 tablespoons), dust with flour and tap out excess. Place on a rimmed baking sheet.

2. Melt butter in a small saucepan over medium heat. Continue to heat, watching carefully, until butter turns a light golden brown. Remove from heat; set aside.

3. Put chocolate in a heatproof bowl large enough to hold all the ingredients. Bring cream just to a boil. Add cream to chocolate in two portions, stirring gently, until a smooth, shiny ganache forms; set aside.

4. Stir together confectioners' sugar, almonds, flour and baking powder. Put egg whites in a bowl, and whisk until slightly foamy. Pour whites over dry ingredients, and blend with a flexible rubber spatula. Add melted butter, and blend. Scrape batter into ganache; gently stir until blended.

5. Spoon batter into molds; they should be three-quarters full. Bake 15 to 18 minutes, or until tops are dry and a knife inserted into center comes out clean. Leave 3 minutes; then unmold, and cool on a rack.

Two-Day Madeleines with Brown Butter ✳

The madeleine was, of course, the little cake made famous by Marcel Proust, whose memories flooded back as he nibbled one dipped in *tilleul* (linden or lime-blossom tea). Madeleines must be baked in special shell-shaped molds. The finest madeleines have a hump on the back, which will only happen if the batter is allowed to rest for several hours or overnight before baking. Eleven Madison Park is another New York restaurant owned by Danny Meyer.

Eleven
Madison Park,
New York

TIME: 1 hour, plus chilling   YIELD: About 60 small madeleines or 24 large ones

7 tablespoons unsalted butter, plus
   more, softened, for molds
5 large eggs
½ cup plus 3 tablespoons sugar
1¼ cups all-purpose flour, plus
   more for molds

Large pinch of sea salt
1 teaspoon baking powder
Grated zest of 1 lemon

1. In a small pan over medium heat, melt butter, and cook until it begins to smell nutty and turns brown. Remove from heat, and strain through a fine sieve into a bowl.

2. In a mixer fitted with a whisk, beat eggs and sugar until fluffy. Remove bowl from mixer, and sift flour, salt and baking powder over eggs. Fold together with a spatula. Pour in butter and lemon zest, and fold together. (At this point you could fold in a number of dry ingredients, like finely chopped nuts, ground cardamom, orange zest or coconut.) Refrigerate batter for at least 2 hours, or overnight.

3. Preheat oven to 375 degrees. Generously butter a madeleine pan (small or large molds). Using a pastry bag, pipe batter into molds so they are three-quarters full.

4. Bake until madeleines form humps and are nut brown around edges, 6 to 8 minutes, longer if using large molds. Remove from oven, and bang pan on a countertop to release madeleines from molds. Carefully lift off any that stick. Place in a napkin to keep warm. Repeat with remaining batter.

Madeleines with Citrus, Molasses and Nutmeg

Jehangir
Mehta

These madeleines are dark and sexy, with the aromatic flavors of anise, citrus and molasses. Jehangir Mehta is a pastry chef in New York.

TIME: 1 hour, plus chilling   YIELD: About 60 small madeleines or 24 large ones

5 large eggs
½ cup plus 2 tablespoons
   granulated sugar
1¾ cups plus 2 tablespoons all-
   purpose flour
1½ teaspoons baking powder
1 teaspoon sea salt
Large pinch ground star anise

1 teaspoon freshly grated nutmeg
8 ounces (2 sticks) unsalted
   butter, at room temperature,
   plus more for molds
¼ cup molasses
2½ tablespoons dark brown sugar
Grated zest of 1 orange
Grated zest of ½ lime

1. In a mixer fitted with a whisk, beat together eggs and sugar until fluffy. Remove bowl; sift flour, baking powder, salt, star anise powder and nutmeg over egg mixture, and fold gently until just mixed.

2. In a small pan, melt butter over low heat. Add molasses and brown sugar, and stir until dissolved. Stir in orange and lime zest. Pour this into batter and fold together. Refrigerate for at least 2 hours, or overnight. Spoon batter into a pastry bag fitted with a small (about ¼ inch) round tip.

3. Preheat oven to 375 degrees. Generously butter a madeleine pan (with small or large molds). Pipe batter into molds so they are three-quarters full. Bake until madeleines form humps and are nut brown around edges, 6 to 8 minutes, longer if using large molds. Remove from oven, and bang pan on a countertop to release madeleines from molds. Carefully lift off any that stick. Place in a folded napkin to keep warm. Repeat with remaining batter.

Madeleines with Orange Confit and Honey

Instead of preparing orange confit, chopped packaged candied orange peel can be used. Artisanal is a brasserie-style place that specializes in cheese.

Artisanal, New York

TIME: 1 hour, plus chilling   YIELD: About 60 small madeleines or 24 large ones

1 cup plus 1 tablespoon granulated sugar

1 orange, unpeeled

5 large eggs, separated

¾ cup light brown sugar

1¼ tablespoons orange blossom honey

½ teaspoon vanilla

Grated zest of 1 orange

1 cup all-purpose flour

¾ cup cake flour

2½ teaspoons baking powder

½ teaspoon salt

9 ounces unsalted butter (2 sticks plus 2 tablespoons), melted; more for molds

1. In a small pan, combine 1 cup granulated sugar with 1 cup water and bring to a boil. Slice orange crosswise as thinly as possible. Remove any pits. Add slices to boiling sugar water, stir, then turn off heat and cover with plastic wrap. Once cool, refrigerate orange confit overnight.

2. Finely chop enough of the orange confit (skin and pulp) to make 2 tablespoons. Reserve rest for another use. In a mixer fitted with a whisk, combine egg yolks, light brown sugar, honey, vanilla, orange zest and chopped orange confit. Whisk until mixture is thick and light.

3. Sift together the flours, baking powder and salt. Sift again over the egg mixture and fold in. Add warm melted butter and fold together.

4. In a mixer fitted with a whisk, whip egg whites until foamy, and slowly add remaining tablespoon granulated sugar. Whip to soft peaks; fold into batter. Refrigerate batter for at least 2 hours, or overnight.

5. Preheat oven to 375 degrees. Generously butter a madeleine pan (small or large molds). Using a pastry bag with a ¼-inch round tip, pipe batter into madeleine molds so they are three-quarters full. Bake until they form humps and are nut brown around edges, 6 to 8 minutes, longer if using large molds. Remove from oven, and bang the pan on a countertop to release madeleines from molds. Carefully lift off any that stick. Place in a folded napkin to keep warm. Repeat with remaining batter.

Quince Beignets with Orange Flower Crème Anglaise

Payard
Pâtisserie
and Bistro,
New York

Quince is an autumn fruit that is rarely used raw. And cooked, its tart, somewhat dry ivory flesh takes on a new personality, turning pinkish and flavorfully rich. In this recipe, slices of quince dipped in batter become quince fritters. The batter is also excellent to use with slices of raw banana or poached apple. François Payard is a third-generation French pastry chef.

TIME: 1 hour, plus chilling   YIELD: 16 beignets

6 large egg yolks

2 cups plus 3 tablespoons
   granulated sugar

1 cup plus 1 teaspoon all-purpose
   flour

2 cups half-and-half

4 broad strips orange zest

2 tablespoons orange flower
   water

1 broad strip lemon zest

1 vanilla bean, split lengthwise

4 medium quinces, peeled

Salt

1 large egg

1 cup beer

4 cups vegetable oil for deep
   frying

Confectioners' sugar, for dusting

1. In a medium mixing bowl, combine egg yolks, 1 cup granulated sugar and 1 teaspoon flour. Whisk together until thick and pale.

2. In a small saucepan, combine the half-and-half and 2 strips orange zest. Place over medium heat and bring to a boil. While whisking the egg mixture, very slowly pour about half the hot cream over the yolks. Pour yolk mixture back into pot.

3. Stirring constantly with a wooden spoon, heat until the crème anglaise is thick enough to coat the back of a spoon, about 5 minutes; if you run your finger down the back of the spoon, the mixture should not run into the track that is made. Remove from heat immediately, and strain the crème anglaise into a bowl. Press a piece of plastic wrap against the surface of the crème anglaise. Refrigerate until cool, about ½ hour, then stir in the orange flower water. Refrigerate until ready to serve.

4. In a medium saucepan combine 4 cups water, 1 cup of the granulated sugar, remaining orange zest, lemon zest and vanilla bean. Place over high

heat to bring to a boil. In the meantime, cut each quince crosswise into 4 slices. Using a thin, sharp knife, cut the core from each slice.

5. Add quince slices to boiling syrup, and reduce heat to low. Poach slices until they can be pierced easily with a knife, about 8 to 10 minutes. Drain on a cooling rack.

6. In a medium mixing bowl, combine the cup of flour, remaining 3 tablespoons granulated sugar, a pinch of salt and the egg. Whisk together to blend thoroughly. Very gradually add the beer, whisking until the batter is smooth and the consistency of heavy cream.

7. In a medium saucepan over medium heat, heat the oil until a bit of batter tossed in sinks, then pops up quickly. Working with 4 at a time, dip slices of quince into batter to coat evenly, then drop into the oil. Fry until golden on both sides, about 3 minutes. Drain on paper towels, and continue with the rest of the quince slices. Dust beignets with confectioners' sugar. Serve hot or at room temperature, accompanied by orange flower crème anglaise for dipping.

Loukoumades (Greek Hanukkah Fritters with Honeyed Syrup) ※

Steven
Raichlen

What fruitcake is to Christmas, fritters are to Hanukkah, a holiday that celebrates the miracle of the lamp in the temple that burned for eight days when there was oil for only one. That's why fried foods, like these Greek loukoumades (or Spanish *buñuelos* or Italian *zeppole*), are de rigueur for the holiday. Steven Raichlen is a cookbook author who specializes in barbecue and grilling.

TIME: 1 hour 20 minutes   YIELD: 32 to 36 puffs (8 servings)

1 cup plus ½ teaspoon sugar
¼ cup honey, preferably Greek
1 cinnamon stick
4 cloves
2 strips lemon zest
2 strips orange zest
2 tablespoons Cognac or brandy
¼ cup extra-virgin olive oil,
   preferably Greek

1 teaspoon grated lemon zest
½ teaspoon salt
1 cup all-purpose flour
2 large eggs
5 large egg whites
Cooking spray for baking sheet
Ground cinnamon for sprinkling

1. In saucepan, combine 1¼ cups water with 1 cup sugar, honey, cinnamon stick, cloves and strips of lemon and orange zest, and boil until thick and syrupy, about 4 minutes. Strain syrup into bowl, and cool to room temperature. Add Cognac, stir and refrigerate. Syrup can be prepared up to a day in advance.

2. Preheat oven to 400 degrees. In heavy saucepan, combine 1 cup water with oil, grated lemon zest, salt and remaining sugar, and bring to boil over high heat. Remove pan from heat, and sift in flour. Stir well with wooden spoon to make thick paste. Return pan to high heat, and cook until dough is thick enough to come away from sides of pan in a smooth ball, for 2 to 4 minutes.

3. Beat 2 eggs and 4 egg whites lightly just to combine. Add to dough one-fourth at a time, beating vigorously with wooden spoon until mixture is smooth before adding next batch. Mixture should finally resemble soft ice cream.

4. Transfer dough to piping bag fitted with a ⅜-inch round tip. Pipe 1-inch balls of dough onto nonstick baking sheet lightly sprayed with oil, leaving 1½ inches between each. (If you don't have a piping bag, use 2 spoons to drop balls of dough onto sheet.) Dip a fork in cold water, and with back of tines, smooth top of each ball. Beat remaining egg white with a pinch of salt until frothy. Lightly brush balls with egg glaze. Sprinkle sheet with a few drops of water.

5. Bake dough balls until puffed, firm and nicely browned, for 40 to 50 minutes. If puffs brown too much before they are cooked through, reduce heat. Remove sheet from oven, and cool for 3 minutes.

6. Using spatula, transfer hot puffs to serving bowl. Pour cold syrup on top, and let soak for 3 minutes. Serve puffs with syrup in bowls. Sprinkle with cinnamon.

SOUFFLÉS AND CRÊPES

The magic of eggs, whites and yolks together in a satiny batter that results in lacy-edged crêpes, or separately to permit the whites to elevate a soufflé, is the basis for all the desserts in this chapter. Though care must be taken in mixing your batter for crêpes, so that the consistency is thin enough to cover the bottom of the pan quickly, and you must be sure not to overbeat the whites for your soufflé, the rest is child's play, for these desserts are more forgiving than most people think. And the payoff is always impressive.

This chapter offers a collection of egg-based batter desserts.

SOUFFLÉS

Calvados Soufflé with Tapioca

La Bourride,
Caen,
France

These individual apple soufflés from Normandy are spiked with Calvados, the brandy of the region. If desired, as they are served, the tops can be split and a scoop of vanilla ice cream added to each. La Bourride is a restaurant in Caen, a city in Normandy, France, which is Calvados country.

TIME: 2 hours   YIELD: 8 servings

1 Golden Delicious apple, halved
1¾ cups milk
1 tablespoon quick-cooking tapioca
1 vanilla bean, split lengthwise
¼ cup all-purpose flour
5 tablespoons granulated sugar, plus additional for coating ramekins

8 large eggs, separated
1 cup Calvados
Soft unsalted butter for ramekins
Confectioners' sugar, for sprinkling

1. Preheat oven to 350 degrees. Place apple on a baking sheet, and bake until just tender but still slightly crisp, for about 15 to 20 minutes. Remove from oven, and allow to cool. Peel and core apple, and then cut into small dice. Set aside.

2. In a small saucepan, combine milk, tapioca and vanilla bean. Place over medium heat, and bring to just under a boil. Remove from heat, and allow mixture to rest for 5 minutes. Remove vanilla bean, and scrape pulp back into the milk. In medium saucepan, combine flour and granulated sugar until blended. Whisk in milk mixture until completely blended. Place over medium-high heat, and boil for 2 minutes, stirring constantly. Remove from heat, and set aside.

3. Place yolks into a medium mixing bowl, and 8 whites into the bowl of an electric mixer. Whisk yolks by hand until light and fluffy. Whisk about ½ cup of the milk mixture into yolks, and then whisk this mixture back into the pan of milk. Place the pan over medium heat, and continue whisking

until mixture is thickened and will coat the back of a spoon, about 2 to 3 minutes. Transfer the hot mixture to a bowl, and place plastic wrap directly on the surface to prevent a skin from forming. Allow to cool.

4. In a small saucepan, bring Calvados to a boil, and reduce by half. Remove from heat, and let cool to room temperature. Fold apple dice and Calvados into pastry cream.

5. Increase oven heat to 400 degrees. Butter 8 1-cup ramekins. Sprinkle granulated sugar into each ramekin, and turn so that inside is completely coated. Place ramekins on a baking sheet. Set aside a fine-mesh strainer filled with a few tablespoons confectioners' sugar.

6. Using an electric mixer with a whisk attachment, whip egg whites until they hold stiff peaks. Fold a third of the egg whites into the pastry cream to lighten it; then, add this back to the remaining whites and fold together. Spoon soufflé mixture into ramekins, filling them almost to top. Smooth by running thumb around edges of rims. Bake until raised and golden, about 15 minutes. Remove from oven, and tap strainer over soufflés to sprinkle with confectioners' sugar. Serve immediately.

Rhubarb Soufflés with Ginger

Amanda
Hesser

This soufflé is made entirely of egg whites and sweetened fruit, without a custard or pastry cream base. It is feather-light. Freshly stewed, sweetened rhubarb can be used instead of jam. And the recipe can be a template for other light fruit soufflés. Pear or apricot puree, prune butter (lekvar) or raspberry coulis (page 536) are some possible ingredients. Amanda Hesser has written on food for *The New York Times* for ten years.

TIME: 35 minutes YIELD: 4 servings

Soft unsalted butter for ramekins
2 to 3 tablespoons granulated
   sugar
¾ cup rhubarb jam or rhubarb-
   strawberry jam
3 teaspoons finely chopped fresh
   ginger

2½ tablespoons lemon juice
5 large egg whites
Pinch of sea salt
1 tablespoon confectioners' sugar,
   plus more for sprinkling

1. Generously butter 4 12-ounce ramekins. Sprinkle a little sugar into each, tilting ramekin so sugar coats bottom and sides. Place in freezer.

2. Preheat oven to 400 degrees. Place baking sheet on bottom rack.

3. Place jam, ginger and lemon juice in a small pan and place over medium-low heat just until the jam becomes runny. Remove from heat and transfer to a bowl.

4. Put egg whites, salt and confectioners' sugar in a large bowl. Whisk or beat with an electric mixer until mixture forms fairly stiff peaks. Remove ramekins from freezer.

5. Using a rubber spatula, add a third of the egg whites to the jam and fold together. Add this jam mixture to egg whites in bowl. Fold until mixed well, and spoon into ramekins, being careful not to smear sides and leaving ½ inch on top. Bake until soufflés have risen 2 inches above ramekins, 8 to 10 minutes. They should be wobbly. Remove from oven. Sprinkle with confectioners' sugar, and serve.

Ruby Red Grapefruit Soufflé

Candied grapefruit is not easy to find (see sources), and making it from scratch is monumentally difficult. Fresh grapefruit segments will do just fine. This recipe comes from Alain Ducasse's Michelin three-star restaurant in New York.

TIME: 40 minutes   YIELD: 4 servings

Alain
Ducasse
at the Essex
House,
New York

2 cups ruby red grapefruit juice
Zest of 1 ruby red grapefruit
⅓ cup crème fraîche
4 large egg yolks
1½ tablespoons cornstarch
1½ tablespoons cake flour
9 tablespoons granulated sugar
1 tablespoon soft unsalted butter
　for molds

9 large egg whites at room
　temperature
½ cup diced, top-quality candied
　grapefruit (page 544) or 4
　grapefruit segments, cut into
　¼-inch pieces
1 tablespoon confectioners' sugar
Grapefruit sorbet, optional

1. In a saucepan, simmer juice until reduced to 1 cup. Remove from heat. Reserve 1 tablespoon grapefruit zest. Stir remainder into crème fraîche. In a small bowl, whisk egg yolks with cornstarch, cake flour and 3 tablespoons granulated sugar. Whisk into juice, return to heat, continue whisking and bring to a boil. Remove from heat, and allow to cool. Fold in crème fraîche.

2. Preheat oven to 350 degrees. Butter 4 1-cup soufflé dishes. Mix remaining grapefruit zest with ¼ cup granulated sugar, and dust dishes with this mixture.

3. Whip egg whites with 2 tablespoons granulated sugar until they hold peaks but are still creamy and not dry. Gently fold into grapefruit juice mixture. Spoon half into ramekins. Sprinkle candied zest or grapefruit pieces into dishes, then add remaining grapefruit juice mixture.

4. Bake 12 minutes, until puffed and golden. Sift confectioners' sugar over tops, and serve at once, with grapefruit sorbet alongside if desired.

Apricot-Honey Soufflé

Amanda
Hesser

Glasses of chilled amaretto liqueur would be delicious alongside. Among the food writing Amanda Hesser has done for *The New York Times* are essays on equipment.

TIME: 50 minutes   YIELD: 4 to 6 servings

Unsalted butter for soufflé dish
¼ cup demerara or light brown
   sugar, for sprinkling
1 cup milk
3 large egg yolks
Sea salt
3 tablespoons honey
1 cup dried Turkish apricots

3 tablespoons Sauternes or other
   white dessert wine
5 large egg whites
1 tablespoon confectioners' sugar
1½ tablespoons finely chopped
   sliced almonds
Vanilla or almond ice cream
   (optional)

1. Generously butter a 1½-quart soufflé dish. Sprinkle demerara sugar into dish, tilting so that sugar coats bottom and sides. Place in freezer.

2. In a small pan, heat milk over medium-high heat until bubbles form around edges. Remove from heat and let cool slightly. Place egg yolks, pinch of salt and honey in a medium bowl and whisk until light and fluffy. Very slowly whisk a third of the milk into eggs, and then add this mixture back to pan. Stirring constantly, cook mixture over medium-low heat, until it thickens to a custard and coats the back of a spoon. Remove from heat, strain into a bowl and let cool.

3. In a small pan, combine apricots and Sauternes. Bring to a boil and stir. Remove from heat and let cool.

4. Preheat oven to 400 degrees. Place a baking sheet on bottom rack.

5. In a blender or food processor, combine custard mixture and apricots and puree. Transfer to a medium bowl.

6. Remove soufflé dish from freezer. Place egg whites, a pinch of salt and confectioners' sugar in bowl of an electric mixer and beat until fairly stiff peaks form, or whisk by hand.

7. Using a rubber spatula, add about a third of the egg whites to the apricot mixture and fold until combined. Add apricot mixture to remaining egg whites in bowl. Fold together until well mixed, being careful not to

overmix. Spoon this mixture into soufflé dish, leaving ½ inch on top. Sprinkle almonds on top. Place on baking sheet and bake 17 to 20 minutes, until risen and still a little wobbly when shaken. Remove from oven and serve, plunging two large spoons into center to lift out pieces. Serve with ice cream if desired.

Ginger Soufflé Cake

City Grill,
Atlanta,
Georgia

These cakes are rich, homey unmolded soufflés served with custard sauce. They are like a lightened version of sticky toffee pudding. The recipe comes from a restaurant in downtown Atlanta, Georgia, located in a former bank.

TIME: 2 hours   YIELD: 6 servings

1¼ cups all-purpose flour
1 teaspoon baking powder
1½ teaspoons ground ginger
1 teaspoon ground cinnamon
½ teaspoon ground cloves
½ teaspoon ground allspice
¼ teaspoon salt
8 ounces (2 sticks) unsalted
    butter, softened

1 cup light brown sugar
5 large eggs
½ cup cultured buttermilk or
    plain nonfat yogurt
½ cup molasses
3 teaspoons vanilla extract
½ cup granulated sugar
1½ cups milk

1. Whisk the flour, baking powder, ginger, cinnamon, cloves, allspice and salt in a bowl until well blended. Set aside. Use some of the butter to grease six 8-ounce soufflé dishes or charlotte molds. Preheat oven to 325 degrees.

2. Beat remaining butter with brown sugar until well-blended. Beat in two eggs, one at a time. Beating at low speed, add the flour mixture alternately with the buttermilk. Stir in molasses and 2 teaspoons vanilla.

3. Separate remaining three eggs. In a clean bowl, beat egg whites until softly peaked. Beat in ¼ cup of the granulated sugar and continue beating until the mixture holds peaks but is not stiff. Fold the egg white mixture into the buttermilk batter. Pour the mixture into the soufflé dishes. Place in the oven and bake 45 to 50 minutes, until firm to the touch on top and a cake tester inserted in the center comes out clean. Remove from the oven and allow to cool almost to room temperature.

4. While the soufflés are baking, beat the remaining granulated sugar with the egg yolks until thick and light. In a heavy saucepan, scald the milk and, whisking constantly, slowly pour about half into the egg yolk mixture. Then stir the egg yolk mixture into the hot milk remaining in the saucepan.

Place over medium-low heat and cook, stirring with a wooden spoon, until the custard has thickened enough to coat the spoon and steam begins to rise from it. Remove from heat, stir in the remaining teaspoon of vanilla, strain into a bowl, cover and refrigerate.

5. Unmold the soufflés by running a knife around the edges and inverting each onto a dessert plate. Spoon some of the custard around each portion and serve.

THE MODERN SOUFFLÉ:
Bastion of Strength
By Amanda Hesser

In the world of dining no drama is more riveting than the one surrounding the soufflé. It starts building early in the meal, when the soufflé must be ordered: the anticipation is sealed, a captive audience guaranteed. Then, when it is finally ready, it is rushed through the dining room like a crying baby to its mother, so that when it arrives at the table—inflated, determined and wobbly—the reaction is inevitably the same: the diner is silenced, in awe of the genius who concocted it.

For the assumption is that to create cooking's most fragile and temperamental dish takes immense skill, the finesse of a dancer, the timing of a comedian.

Which is why chefs have never let it die. Crème brûlée may one day retire, but the soufflé will always persist. And though chefs will never concede the point, it is not because the soufflé takes such talent, but because it is so easy.

Chefs know that soufflés are forgiving. They know it's not necessary to whisper while a soufflé bakes and that opening the oven door will not make a soufflé fall. And they know that soufflés can be made ahead of time, assembled completely, then simply baked to order. Generations of intimidated home cooks could have triumphed with those three small tips.

Meanwhile, chefs have been changing the soufflé, too, keeping it up to date. The classic and often stodgy soufflé—made with pastry cream or béchamel, with a sauce poured in at the table—is being replaced with soufflés made without flour and ingredients so flavorful that no sauce is needed at all.

A soufflé is actually one of cooking's most frivolous pursuits. It should be playful. Think of it as nothing more than an omelet, and few omelets are served without some kind of adornment. This past week, I made many soufflés and discovered that despite my efforts to challenge the classic recipe with loose liquid bases and vigorous folding, it is difficult to fail. And more than that, the possibilities are endless.

Well, to a point. A soufflé may be sweet or savory, flavored with ingredients as varied as cardamom and cheese, but if it is not aerated with egg whites, it is not a soufflé. Some restaurants have begun using the word *soufflé* to describe almost anything. Many pass off oozy chocolate cakes as soufflé cakes. Every cake expands a little in the oven, but that does not make a soufflé.

So, to begin, it is helpful to understand just what a soufflé is. It is, essentially, a flavorful sauce suspended in whipped egg whites and baked in the oven. As the soufflé bakes, the heat causes the air in the egg whites to expand, separating the base into a fluffy custard, sealing in any aromas and bursting vertically out of its baking dish.

When it comes out of the oven and begins to cool, the air contracts and the soufflé deflates, which is why it must be eaten quickly. If you let a soufflé deflate, you will be left with an omelet. (But one that will be much lighter than a typical omelet. Any failed soufflé can simply be turned out of its dish and served without shame, like an unmolded custard.)

A good soufflé is rich with contradiction. It has a firm outer shell, while inside it is impossibly light; it is supported by egg, but its taste is not compromised by it; it defies gravity and yet is fragile. And if it is correctly made, spoonfuls of rich, gauzy foam and all of its contradictions will disappear on the palate. Anyone who can create that experience is worthy of praise.

And anyone who can make an omelet and can whip cream can make a soufflé.

Classic soufflés are made up of two parts: the base and the whipped egg whites. The base is a kind of sauce, often thickened with egg yolks. Many recipes call for about one egg per person. So if you are making a soufflé for four, you would use four to five eggs, reserving the yolks for the base.

Anything else that goes into the base has one of two purposes: flavoring or thickening. Classically sweet soufflés have a base of pastry cream. But pastry cream is time-consuming. A more modern approach would be to use crème anglaise, a simple custard of milk, eggs and sugar, adding pureed or whole fruit, melted chocolate or even something as simple as almond extract for scent. Simpler still: omit the yolks and use a dense fruit puree or jam as a base.

Whatever the base, it needs to be highly flavored so that once the egg whites are folded in, the flavor does not disappear.

Preparing the egg whites is perhaps the most critical part. Recipes often instruct you to add a little salt, lemon juice or cream of tartar before whisking to help the egg whites form smaller, tighter bubbles. I have found that all three work equally well. With sweet soufflés, it is good to add a little confectioners' sugar, which contains cornstarch, a stabilizer, at the beginning (about a tablespoon for every four egg whites). This helps the whites form tight bonds and for the finished soufflés to rise evenly in tall, firm cylinders.

The whites should be whisked until they form peaks somewhere between soft and stiff. If they are too soft, the whites tend not to rise to their potential; too stiff, and they may begin to break down.

Once they are whisked, though, they are extremely durable. Classic French cookbooks will tell you to fold the base and whites together gently. But if the base and whites do not form a homogeneous mixture, the soufflé may rise unevenly and have pockets of egg white. Using a rubber spatula, I fold mine vigorously, turning the bowl as I fold the ingredients over again and again, and I have never had a soufflé flop.

Beyond that, there are just a few details to know. Buttering soufflé molds is not the time to be shy about butter. Many classic recipes say to butter the mold once, put it in the freezer and then butter it again—a great waste of time. Instead, use soft butter and smear it on generously the first time, making sure to cover every inch of the mold. Another method is to add a light dusting of a dry ingredient to coat the butter, which gives the soufflé a kind of lattice to climb while baking. With sweet soufflés, sugar is often used, and with savory ones, bread crumbs or finely grated cheese.

If the coating is too thin or misses a spot, the soufflé mixture could latch on to that spot and leave you with a lopsided soufflé.

The mold should be refrigerated or frozen so that when the soufflé mixture is added, the butter does not slide down the sides. And when filling the molds, the filling should be dropped in the center of the mold and allowed to settle by itself. The filling should be highest in the center and slope down to the sides of the mold; it should not be smoothed over with a spatula as for a cake batter.

When the soufflé is in the oven, you want it to rise as quickly as possible before the sides seal and stop expanding. One way to help this is to place the baking rack on the bottom shelf of the oven and to put a baking sheet on the rack while the oven heats. When the soufflé dish, cool from the freezer, begins to warm, the soufflé will expand without cooking through too quickly.

What puts off many home cooks is the assumption that soufflés are a last-minute affair. But almost any soufflé can be made ahead. Simply complete the recipe up to the point of baking, fill the molds and cover them with plastic wrap, then refrigerate until a few minutes before baking. If the egg whites have been whipped well and the mixture combined thoroughly, it will hold for several hours. The cool temperature helps firm up the ingredients, too.

Though I have made soufflés up to a day ahead, I have found them to be at their peak when baked within four hours. Uniform homogeneous mixtures like chocolate and vanilla hold best. But mixtures like yolkless soufflés may not rise as well.

Even in those cases, the base can be made and the molds prepared, so that all you have to do at the last minute is whisk the egg whites. It's like whipping cream for an apple pie.

Though a soufflé looks most dramatic when it is baked in a standard white ceramic fluted straight-sided porcelain mold, any deep, ovenproof mold can be used. One with straight sides will encourage rising. A collar that extends about two inches above the rim will enhance the look. Simply tie a double-ply strip of parchment paper above four inches wide around the dish just below the rim so that it extends two inches above the dish. Butter and sugar the inside.

Berries with Lemon Soufflé Topping

Soufflés? Puddings? These are classic soufflé cakes that separate into a creamy pudding with a soufflé topping as they bake. If you can't find light cream, use ⅔ cup heavy cream and ⅓ cup whole milk.

TIME: 1 hour   YIELD: 4 servings

Florence
Fabricant

3 tablespoons unsalted butter, softened

¾ cup fresh blueberries

¾ cup fresh raspberries

2 large eggs, separated

⅔ cup granulated sugar

¼ cup fresh lemon juice

1 tablespoon finely grated lemon zest

2 tablespoons all-purpose flour

1 cup light cream

Pinch of salt

Confectioners' sugar

1. Preheat oven to 350 degrees. Use 1 tablespoon of the butter to grease 4 8-ounce ramekins or soufflé dishes. Set the buttered dishes in a baking pan at least 1½ inches deep.

2. Spread berries in the bottoms of the dishes.

3. Beat egg yolks until light. Beat in granulated sugar and remaining butter until mixture is creamy. Beat in lemon juice, zest and flour, and then whisk in the cream. Beat egg whites with salt until they hold peaks but are not dry. Fold egg whites into lemon batter, and spoon mixture over berries in each dish.

4. Pour boiling water into outer pan until it comes halfway up sides of baking dishes. Place in oven, and bake for approximately 40 minutes, until tops are puffed and golden brown.

5. Remove from oven, and allow to cool to room temperature. Dust with sifted confectioners' sugar before serving.

Salzburger Nockerl

Wallsé,
New York

Fresh raspberries ennobled with a glorious soufflé topping is this traditional dessert from Salzburg, Austria. A nockerl is simply an Austrian dumpling, on the heavy side when made for soup, but as a dessert, it is turned into a delicate meringue cloud baked on a bed of fruit. Wallsé is an Austrian restaurant in Greenwich Village, New York.

TIME: 40 minutes   YIELD: 4 servings

½ tablespoon unsalted butter, softened

½ cup granulated sugar

1 cup fresh raspberries

1 tablespoon milk

1 vanilla bean, split lengthwise

4 large egg yolks

1 teaspoon lemon juice

7 large egg whites

¼ cup all-purpose flour

½ tablespoon confectioners' sugar

1. Preheat oven to 400 degrees. Brush butter in the bottom, sides and rim of a 10- to 12-inch shallow oval baking dish or ovenproof platter, or a 9-inch shallow round baking dish. Dust with 1 tablespoon sugar.

2. Spread raspberries in center of dish, leaving about a 1-inch border. Sprinkle milk in border.

3. In large bowl, scrape vanilla seeds and pulp into egg yolks. Beat briefly with whisk until smooth. Whisk in lemon juice.

4. Place egg whites in bowl of electric mixer. Beat on medium speed until frothy. Add 2 tablespoons remaining sugar. Continue beating on medium speed, gradually adding all remaining sugar, until whites are very thick and creamy like softly whipped cream. Continue beating a minute or two longer, until beaters leave marks in surface. Increase speed to high and beat 10 seconds. Whites will be dense, will hold their shape but not be stiff.

5. Fold half the whites into the yolks. Sprinkle with flour. Add remaining whites and fold in.

6. Pile egg mixture in three large mounds close together on top of raspberries, each covering one-third of the dish. If using oval dish, place mounds along length of dish; with round dish place mounds in triangle arrangement. Bake 10 to 12 minutes, until surface is golden brown.

7. Remove from oven, sift confectioners' sugar over and serve.

Viennese Oven Pancakes
(Kaiser Schmarrn) ※

This pancake from Eastern Europe was originally a dish for the poor. But the emperor, or kaiser, was said to have liked it and so it became a popular delicacy. It is a puffy souffléed crêpe that is baked in the oven and then torn apart to serve. Vanilla sugar is sold in small jars, but it can be made by burying a vanilla bean, even a used one, in a canister of granulated sugar. Richard Langer is a food writer.

Richard Langer

TIME: About 30 minutes   YIELD: 4 servings

4 ounces (1 stick) unsalted butter
1¼ cups milk
¾ cup all-purpose flour
Pinch of salt
4 large eggs, separated

1 tablespoon granulated sugar
½ teaspoon vanilla extract
¼ cup golden raisins
Vanilla sugar
½ cup apricot preserves

1. Preheat oven to 400 degrees. Melt half the butter.

2. Whisk milk, flour and salt together. Beat yolks into milk mixture. Stir in melted butter.

3. Beat egg whites with granulated sugar and vanilla until stiff. Fold into batter.

4. Place remaining butter in a 12-inch ovenproof skillet. Place in oven. When butter in skillet melts, swirl it around to cover bottom and sides. Pour batter into skillet, and sprinkle raisins on top.

5. Return skillet to the oven and bake pancake until brown on top, about 20 minutes. Remove from oven and, using two forks, tear it into pieces. Return it to oven for 5 more minutes. You want it to be firm in spots, fluffy in others. Dust pancake with vanilla sugar, and serve with apricot preserves.

Blueberry-Ginger Gratin

Florence
Fabricant

Fresh blueberries tossed with ginger are topped with a souffléed crust and served warm, for an easy way to vary this ubiquitous summer fruit. The combination of sweetly tangy blueberries with the sugary heat of ginger is one of my favorites.

TIME: 1 hour   YIELD: 4 servings

2½ tablespoons unsalted butter
1½ cups blueberries
1 tablespoon slivered crystallized ginger
2 large eggs, separated
½ cup granulated sugar

¼ cup orange juice
2 tablespoons all-purpose flour
½ teaspoon ground ginger
1 cup heavy cream
Pinch of salt
Confectioners' sugar

1. Preheat oven to 350 degrees. Butter an 8-inch gratin dish with ½ tablespoon of the butter. Spread blueberries in dish.

2. Beat egg yolks with the granulated sugar until creamy and thick. Beat in the remaining butter, then beat in orange juice. Whisk flour and ground ginger together and stir in alternately with cream.

3. Beat egg whites with pinch of salt until stiff but not dry. Fold into egg yolk mixture and spread over berrries. Place in oven and bake about 30 minutes, until browned on top.

4. Remove from oven and allow to cool about 15 minutes. Dust with confectioners' sugar, then serve.

Old-Fashioned Peach-Raspberry Duff

It may be called a duff but it is essentially fruit with a soufflé topping. The term *duff* at one time meant "dough" pronounced in a dialect. It has English, Irish and American usage as a term for a pudding. It also shows up as a sailor's dessert and was mentioned in *Treasure Island* by Robert Louis Stevenson. Larry Forgione was one of the first generation of cutting-edge American chefs. His restaurant, An American Place, is now in a department store in New York.

Larry
Forgione,
An American
Place,
New York

TIME: 1 hour   YIELD: 8 to 10 servings

Soft unsalted butter for dish
1 cup fresh apple cider
¾ cup plus ⅔ cup granulated
    sugar
2 tablespoons quick-cooking
    tapioca
6 firm, ripe freestone peaches,
    peeled and cut into medium
    slices

2 tablespoons brandy, optional
1 tablespoon grated fresh ginger
Grated zest of 1 lemon
2 cups fresh raspberries
5 large eggs, separated
2 teaspoons vanilla extract
½ cup all-purpose flour, sifted
Sifted confectioners' sugar, for
    dusting

1. Butter a shallow 9-by-12 baking dish, and set aside. In a large saucepan, combine the apple cider, ¼ cup water, ¾ cup of the sugar and the tapioca. Bring to a boil, and add the peaches, brandy, ginger and lemon zest. Bring back to a boil, reduce heat to low, and simmer for 2 to 3 minutes. Remove from the heat and add the raspberries, stirring to mix. Set aside.

2. Preheat oven to 350 degrees.

3. In the bowl of an electric mixer, combine the egg yolks and remaining ⅔ cup of sugar. Beat until thick and pale in color, about 3 to 4 minutes. Add the vanilla, and beat just to blend; set aside. In another bowl, use a whisk attachment to whisk the egg whites into soft peaks; do not overbeat. Using a rubber spatula, fold the sifted flour into the egg whites. Fold the egg white mixture into the beaten egg yolks.

4. Pour the batter evenly over the fruit in the baking dish, making sure the fruit is completely covered. Bake until golden, about 30 to 40 minutes. Remove from oven and sprinkle with confectioners' sugar. Serve.

Strawberry Pavlova

Nigella
Lawson

The meringue for this Australian dessert confection is baked until it is firm. It becomes the base for berries and whipped cream. Nigella Lawson is an English cookbook author whose *Forever Summer* emphasizes dishes where one simple, fresh main ingredient shines.

TIME: 2 hours, plus macerating   YIELD: 6 servings

4 large egg whites
Pinch of salt
1¼ cups superfine sugar, plus
    more for berries
2 teaspoons cornstarch, sifted
1 teaspoon white-wine vinegar
Vanilla extract

1 pound strawberries, about
    2 pints, hulled and halved or
    quartered
½ teaspoon high-quality balsamic
    vinegar
2 cups heavy cream

1. Preheat oven to 350 degrees. Line a baking sheet with parchment paper, and draw a circle on the paper using an 8- or 9-inch cake pan as a guide. In bowl of an electric mixer, combine egg whites and salt. Begin beating at low speed, slowly increasing to high. Continue until satiny peaks begin to form. Gradually beat in 1¼ cups sugar a tablespoon at a time until meringue is stiff and shiny.

2. Sprinkle in cornstarch, white-wine vinegar and a few drops of vanilla, and fold in gently. Mound onto parchment within circle, and shape into a disk, flattening top and smoothing sides. Place in oven, and immediately reduce heat to 300 degrees. Bake 1 hour 15 minutes. Turn off heat, and allow meringue to cool completely in oven.

3. Meanwhile, in a mixing bowl, combine strawberries, ½ teaspoon vanilla, balsamic vinegar and sugar to taste. Cover with plastic wrap. Let sit at room temperature at least 15 minutes and up to 2 hours.

4. To serve, invert meringue onto a plate, and carefully peel off parchment. (Crisp top of meringue will now be against plate with tender underside facing up.) Whip cream until it is thick enough to hold peaks, and spread it evenly over meringue. Cover cream with strawberries, allowing a small amount of their liquid to dribble onto cream. Serve immediately.

CRÊPES

Crêpe-making is time-consuming, and depends to a large extent on having the proper pan. But given those requirements, serving crêpes for dessert has its advantages. The crêpes can be made well in advance. They take a minimal amount of the most basic ingredients. And they are crowd-pleasers. Fold them over a filling, warm them in a sauce or, for the most effect, flame them, and your guests are guaranteed to be pleased. And never, ever be disappointed if your first crêpe or two does not turn out well. They never do, for reasons that experts have never satisfactorily explained to me, except to say that the seasoning of the pan that occurs when the first crêpes (or breakfast pancakes, for that matter) are cooked makes the difference. Just toss out the first one (or nibble it as you cook) and soldier on. For more on crêpes, see the essay on page 199.

Crêpes Suzette

Allowing the batter to stand for at least thirty minutes, as in this recipe, then thinning it if needed, is a necessary step to assure thin, even crêpes. The standing permits the flour to swell and dissipates any air in the batter from the mixing. In this Nigella Lawson re-creates a forgotten classic, full of flavor.

Nigella Lawson

TIME: 1 hour 20 minutes   YIELD: 4 to 6 servings

1 cup Italian 00 flour or all-purpose flour
Pinch of salt
1 large egg
1¼ cups milk, or more as needed
2 tablespoons melted, cooled unsalted butter
Vegetable oil or nonstick vegetable oil spray, for pan

1 cup freshly squeezed orange juice
Finely grated zest of 1 orange
10 tablespoons unsalted butter
⅓ cup superfine sugar
⅓ cup Grand Marnier, Cointreau or triple sec liqueur

1. In a small mixing bowl, combine flour and salt. Form into a mound, making a small well. Crack egg into well, and mix with a wooden spoon, gradually incorporating flour from sides.

2. Mix in 1¼ cups milk to make a smooth batter. Using a whisk, blend in melted butter. Allow to stand for 30 minutes. Batter should thicken to consistency of heavy cream; if necessary, add more milk to thin.

3. Lightly oil an 8-inch crêpe pan or nonstick skillet. Place over medium-high heat until hot. Pour about 3 tablespoons batter into pan, just enough to coat bottom, tilting pan so batter is even. When pancake has a bubbly surface, after about 30 seconds, carefully flip it with a spatula and brown other side, 20 to 30 seconds. Transfer finished crêpe to a large plate. (First crêpe may tear and need to be discarded.) Repeat until batter is used, re-oiling pan about every fourth crêpe and layering finished crêpes with parchment or waxed paper. Allow to cool, cover with plastic wrap and refrigerate until needed.

4. In a small saucepan, combine orange juice, zest, butter and sugar. Place over high heat and bring to boil; reduce heat to medium low. Simmer until syrupy, 10 to 15 minutes. Remove from heat, and set aside.

5. Fold crêpes into quarters, and arrange in circular pattern, slightly overlapping, in a nonreactive skillet or other shallow flameproof pan. Pour warm syrup on top, and place over low heat until crêpes are warm, about 5 minutes. Place liqueur in pan that held orange syrup.

6. When crêpes are hot, pour liqueur on top; carefully touch a flame to surface to light it. Serve immediately, spooning crêpes and sauce onto each plate.

A MODERN TURN ON THE DESSERT COURSE
By Regina Schrambling

Nothing more than very thin cakes filled with sweetness, crêpes are the antithesis of the over-wrought dessert. They lie low and deliver clear, simple satisfaction. No wonder so many chefs who fancy themselves the Gaudís of sugar have forgotten them.

Other, more elaborate desserts from the Escoffier era are all over New York these days, like bombes and timbales and beignets. But apparently it takes a bold chef to offer simplicity amid all the fussiness on the dessert front. Even classic French restaurants, like Lespinasse and Daniel, have largely abandoned the crêpe. And those who dare serve them make them in substantially altered form, like the open-face apple crêpe at Fleur de Sel.

Over the last few years, crêpes have instead become staples of street fairs and travesties of what they are in France. If you want good crêpes, you may have to make them yourself.

A great one is small and tender and has just enough flavor to make you want to taste the pancake alone, before plowing into the lemon or chocolate inside. At their best, they have a quiet elegance.

The filling can be as elemental as a slathering of good jam, or a sprinkling of fresh berries. Street vendors in France, and in SoHo and Midtown here, fill them with everything from Nutella to a drizzling of Grand Marnier and powdered sugar. The contrast between the filling at the center and the almost austere crêpe makes them so satisfying.

Because crêpes are done in steps, they are the most approachable of showstoppers. The batter, made from milk, eggs, flour and salt, is enormously forgiving. You spread it so thin that it's almost impossible to undercook, and even if you cook it too long, the crêpes will not turn dry and brittle because the batter is so egg-rich and supple. The one tricky part is spreading the batter over the pan: you have to pour it in quickly and rotate the pan even quicker so that the bottom is completely covered. Luckily, as with pancakes, only one side has to look presentable. And crêpes are generally cooked a second time, once they're filled, so you have another shot at getting them right.

Unlike tarts, Bundt cakes and soufflés, crêpes do not need a special pan. You can buy one, made of thin dark steel with a low, slightly sloping rim, but is it worth the investment? A classic seven-inch crêpe pan tested against an all-purpose nonstick skillet proved that the crêpe pan heated evenly, very quickly, and retained the heat through the cooking of many crêpes. All the crêpes got a uniformly speckled brown surface. One serious disadvantage is the handle, which is steel and gets hot fast.

The skillet worked just as well, and it had a rubber shield on the handle. The only downside was that its rounded sides kept the batter from spreading evenly before it set. You have to work to keep the edges of the crepes from thinning out and turning crisp. But that problem was far outweighed by the pan's ability to do so many other jobs besides cooking crêpes.

Apple Crêpes

These crêpes are made with thin apple slices embedded in the batter. Fleur de Sel is an intimate French restaurant in Manhattan's Flatiron District.

Fleur de Sel, New York

TIME: 45 minutes   YIELD: 8 servings

7 tablespoons unsalted butter
1⅔ cups all-purpose flour
4 large eggs
2 cups milk
1½ teaspoons fleur de sel
⅔ cup sugar

2 large Granny Smith apples,
    peeled, cored and cut into
    rounds ¼ inch thick
Whipped cream, ice cream or
    Devonshire cream, for garnish

1. Melt 3 tablespoons of the butter. Let cool. Place flour in a large mixing bowl. Make a well in the center. Add eggs one at a time, stirring in gently to mix eggs gradually with flour. Add milk a little at a time until it is smoothly incorporated. Add salt and 2 tablespoons sugar, and stir to mix. Pass batter through a fine sieve, then mix in melted butter. Refrigerate up to 12 hours.

2. Preheat oven to 250 degrees.

3. Place an 8-inch nonstick omelet or sauté pan over medium heat. Add ½ tablespoon butter and 4 or 5 apple slices. When butter starts to color, turn apple rounds, and pour in ¼ cup crêpe batter, tilting pan to coat it evenly.

4. When batter is set and browning at edges, flip crêpe with a wide spatula. Top with ½ tablespoon butter. Sprinkle evenly with 1 tablespoon sugar. Brown about 1 minute, flip again. Immediately transfer to a baking sheet and place in oven. Repeat with remaining ingredients. Transfer crêpes to individual dessert plates. Top with whipped cream, ice cream or Devonshire cream. Serve.

Apple Caramel Calvados Crêpes ❋

Nigella
Lawson

These crêpes are made with plain crêpe batter and are filled with apples. Nigella Lawson is an English cookbook author and television personality.

TIME: 1 hour   YIELD: 6 servings

8 tablespoons (1 stick) unsalted butter, plus more for pan
1 cup all-purpose flour
1⅓ cups milk
1 large egg
4 teaspoons Calvados or Apple Jack

4 apples, preferably Gala
Juice of half a lemon
2 tablespoons granulated sugar
⅓ cup light brown sugar
⅓ cup light or dark corn syrup
⅓ cup heavy cream

1. Melt 2 tablespoons of the butter. In a blender or food processor, combine flour, milk and egg. Process just until blended. Pour into a pitcher and stir in melted butter and 2 teaspoons Calvados.

2. Place a crêpe pan or small nonstick skillet over medium-high heat. Brush with butter. Allow pan to heat for about a minute. Ladle a scant ¼ cup batter into pan and quickly swirl so batter forms a thin pancake. Return pan to heat and watch for tiny bubbles to form on surface and edges of pancake. Flip pancake; it should be light golden brown. Allow to cook about 30 seconds longer, then transfer to a plate lined with parchment paper. Continue making pancakes, layering each one with parchment. Crêpes may be covered and stored at room temperature for up to a day.

3. Peel, halve and core each apple. Cut the halves into four wedges, and cut each wedge crosswise. Place in a saucepan and add lemon juice, 2 tablespoons butter and granulated sugar. Place over medium heat and cook uncovered, stirring occasionally, for 10 minutes. Cover and continue to cook and stir for another 10 minutes. Allow to cool for 5 minutes.

4. In a small saucepan, combine the remaining 4 tablespoons butter, brown sugar and corn syrup. Bring to a boil; simmer for 2 minutes. Add cream and remaining Calvados. Simmer until thickened, 2 to 3 minutes.

5. To assemble, place a room-temperature crêpe on a plate. Spoon warm apple filling into center, and fold edges over it. Drizzle warm sauce on top. Repeat with remaining crêpes, and serve.

Cornmeal Crêpes and Blackberry Compote

Claudia
Fleming

Cornmeal crêpes are on their way to being tortillas. They have delightful texture and are here served layered with blackberry compote. Claudia Fleming was the pastry chef at Gramercy Tavern, known for refined American cuisine.

TIME: 45 minutes, plus 8 hours' chilling   YIELD: 8 servings

½ vanilla bean, split lengthwise, seeds and pulp scraped out
2 cups milk
⅞ cup all-purpose flour
½ cup heavy cream
9 tablespoons sugar
3 large eggs

Pinch of salt
5 tablespoons yellow cornmeal
Melted butter for pan, if necessary
1 quart blackberries
Sweet-corn ice cream (page 459), or vanilla ice cream

1. Place vanilla seeds in a blender with the milk, flour, cream, 6 tablespoons of the sugar, eggs and salt. Blend until smooth. Pass mixture through a fine sieve, and stir in cornmeal. Cover and chill at least 8 hours.

2. Heat a heavy 8-inch skillet, preferably nonstick, over medium-high heat. (If not nonstick, brush with butter.) Add about 3 tablespoons crêpe batter to pan; swirl so that batter just coats bottom of pan. Pour any excess batter back into bowl. Cook crêpe until bottom is browned and small bubbles appear on top, about 45 seconds. Flip, and cook until browned on the other side, about 30 seconds. Remove to a plate, and repeat with remaining batter, buttering pan occasionally if crêpes begin to stick. Makes about 30 crêpes.

3. To make the compote, combine half the blackberries, 2 tablespoons water and 3 tablespoons of the sugar in a saucepan over medium-high heat. Cook, stirring occasionally, until blackberries give up their juice and sugar dissolves, about 5 minutes. Turn off heat. Stir in remaining berries.

4. To serve, place a crêpe on a plate, then using a slotted spoon, top with some compote. Top with another crêpe and more blackberries, then finish with a third crêpe. Spoon some blackberry liquid around crêpe, and garnish with a scoop of ice cream.

Crêpes Belle Hélène

Nigella
Lawson

Belle Hélène, a combination of pears and chocolate, is used in this crêpe recipe. Nigella Lawson's food writing has appeared as a column in *The New York Times'* Wednesday food section.

TIME: 30 minutes   YIELD: 6 servings

1½ cups sugar

1 vanilla bean, split lengthwise

2 strips lemon zest, each about 2½ inches by ½ inch

3 large Bartlett pears or other pears suitable for poaching, peeled, cut in two lengthwise and cored

1 cup all-purpose flour

1⅓ cups milk

1 large egg

2 tablespoons unsalted butter, melted and slightly cooled, plus more for pan

8 ounces bittersweet or semisweet chocolate, chopped

½ cup strong black coffee or 1 teaspoon instant coffee dissolved in ½ cup water

½ cup heavy cream

1 tablespoon Poire Williams eau de vie, optional

6 scoops high-quality vanilla ice cream

Crystallized violets, optional

1. In a wide saucepan, mix together 1 cup sugar, vanilla bean, lemon zest and 3 cups water. Place over low heat and stir until sugar dissolves. Increase heat to medium and simmer for 5 minutes. Add pear halves and simmer until pears are tender but still keep their shape, about 20 minutes. Transfer pears to a bowl, and set aside. (Vanilla bean may be rinsed, dried and placed in a jar of sugar to make vanilla-scented sugar.)

2. While pears poach, preheat oven to 200 degrees. Mix together the flour, milk and egg until smooth. Transfer to a bowl, and stir in melted butter. Place a nonstick or well-seasoned crêpe pan or 8-inch skillet over medium-low heat. Brush with butter.

3. Pour a scant ¼ cup batter into center of pan; lift pan and swirl it so batter covers bottom thinly and evenly. Return pan to heat, and allow it to sit until bottom of crêpe is lightly browned, about 1 minute. Flip crêpe, and cook other side for 30 to 60 seconds. Transfer to a parchment-paper-lined

baking sheet, and place in oven to keep warm. (Alternatively, crêpes may be allowed to cool for reheating later.) Continue with remaining batter, to make a total of at least 6 crêpes.

4. In a small saucepan, combine chocolate, coffee and ½ cup sugar. Place over low heat, stirring occasionally, until chocolate melts. Add cream, return to a bare simmer, and whisk until smooth. Stir in eau de vie, if using. Pour into a pitcher, and keep warm.

5. To serve, cut pear halves into thin slices. Arrange crêpes on a clean work surface, and cover half of each crêpe with pear slices. Fold crêpes over to make six semicircles. Use a spatula to transfer crêpes to individual serving plates or one large platter. At one side of each semicircle place a scoop of ice cream. Fold other side over to make a fat quarter. Top each quarter with hot chocolate sauce, and garnish with crystallized violets.

Pineapple Upside-Down Crêpes

The Inn
at Little
Washington,
Washington,
Virginia

The process of flipping the crêpes out of the pan seems complicated, but after the first one, it becomes easy. The over-proof rum is used because it is more reliable to flambé, but regular 80-proof dark rum can be used. Warm the rum before flaming it, and stand back. The Inn at Little Washington in Washington, Virginia, is one of the finest country inns in America.

TIME: 1 hour 15 minutes   YIELD: 10 to 12 servings

13 tablespoons unsalted butter
2 cups all-purpose flour
¾ cup sugar
3 large eggs
Pinch of salt
1 cup milk, or as needed
2 large ripe pineapples, peeled, cored and cut lengthwise into quarters

1 cup toasted, coarsely ground macadamia nuts
¾ cup heavy cream, or as needed
½ cup 151-proof rum
10 to 12 miniature scoops vanilla ice cream (page 446) or goat's milk ice cream (page 448)

1. Melt 6 tablespoons butter. Cool. Combine flour, melted butter, ¼ cup sugar, eggs and salt in a food processor or blender. With motor running, add enough milk (about 1 cup) to make a fluid batter. The batter may be covered and refrigerated up to 24 hours.

2. Line large baking sheet with parchment paper, and set aside.

3. Slice pineapple quarters crosswise, ⅛ inch thick.

4. In a 7-inch nonstick pan over medium heat, melt ¼ teaspoon butter, spreading with a spatula. Remove pan from heat, and allow to cool slightly.

5. With pan off heat, ladle in about 3 tablespoons batter and roll around pan until bottom is evenly coated. Sprinkle with 1 tablespoon macadamia nuts.

6. Return pan to medium heat. Just as crêpe sets, but while it is still wet on top, remove pan from heat and arrange pineapple slices in an overlapping circular pattern, completely covering the surface of the crêpe. Use a skewer or a fork to arrange any of the pineapple slices that fall out of place. Shake crêpe slightly to keep it from sticking to pan.

7. Return pan to heat and sprinkle pineapple with 2 teaspoons sugar and about ½ tablespoon cold butter, cut in bits. Use a rubber spatula to loosen edge of crêpe and check underside. When bottom is golden brown, loosen crêpe by running a spatula around the edges and carefully flip crêpe over in pan. Continue cooking until sugar underneath begins to turn a light caramel color. Add 1 tablespoon cream around edges of crêpe, and tilt pan so that cream blends with sugar and runs under edges of crêpe.

8. Spray a flat metal surface like the bottom of a cake pan with nonstick cooking spray. Place sprayed side over crêpe, and invert skillet to remove crêpe. Slide crêpe onto prepared baking sheet. Repeat process, wiping pan clean between crêpes, to make 10 to 12. The sheet of crêpes may be covered and refrigerated up to 4 hours.

9. To serve, reheat crêpes in a 350-degree oven until hot, about 4 minutes. Transfer to serving plates. Pour rum into small pitcher or gravy boat and set aflame. Top crêpes with burning rum. Garnish each plate with a miniature scoop of ice cream.

Souffléed Almond–Dulce de Leche Crêpes

Florence
Fabricant

Souffléed crêpes (or crêpes-soufflés) are simply crêpes that have been made in advance, then filled with a soufflé mixture and baked to set and puff the filling. The drama far exceeds the effort. *Dulce de leche,* a Mexican milk-based caramel, is easy to make, though time-consuming. Fancy food shops sell it in jars.

TIME: 1½ hours   YIELD: 6 servings

1 cup milk
½ teaspoon almond extract
3 large eggs, plus 3 large eggs
    separated
⅓ cup all-purpose flour
⅓ cup plus 2 tablespoons sugar
1½ tablespoons unsalted butter,
    melted and cooled, plus more
    for pan

1 cup *dulce de leche* or *cajeta*
    (page 536)
½ cup sliced almonds, toasted
1 cup heavy cream, whipped

1. Beat milk, almond extract and 3 whole eggs together until well blended. Mix flour and ⅓ cup sugar together and whisk into batter. Whisk in the melted butter. Strain mixture through a fine strainer and set aside for at least 30 minutes.

2. Heat a 6-inch crêpe pan. Very lightly butter it, then pour in a large spoonful of batter. Quickly tilt pan to coat bottom completely, cook until very lightly browned, peel crêpe off the pan, turn it over and briefly cook the other side and remove. Don't worry if any of the crêpes do not turn out well; there should be enough batter to spare. Repeat with remaining batter, buttering pan as needed. Stack finished crêpes on a dinner plate, with the side that was cooked first facing down. You should have about 12 crêpes.

3. Preheat oven to 400 degrees. Butter a jelly roll pan and dust it with 1 tablespoon sugar.

4. Beat remaining egg yolks until thick. Stir in ⅔ cup *dulce de leche.* Beat remaining egg whites until softly peaked. Add remaining tablespoon sugar and beat until stiff but not dry. Stir one-third of the egg whites into

egg yolk mixture, then fold in the rest. Spoon a heaping tablespoon of the soufflé mixture in the center of each crêpe. Roll crêpe around filling and place crêpes, seam down, on baking sheet.

5. Bake until crêpes are puffed, about 15 minutes. Serve at once, with a little *dulce de leche* spooned on top, sprinkled with toasted almonds and whipped cream on the side.

Prune Clafoutis

Alain
Ducasse,
Paris

Clafoutis is a homey French crêpelike cake baked with fruit. It is often made with cherries, but is delicious with prunes. This is a traditional home-style dessert, yet it has not escaped the notice of Alain Ducasse, a Michelin three-star chef.

TIME: 1 hour   YIELD: 6 servings

9 tablespoons unsalted butter, softened

¾ cup very finely ground blanched almonds

1 cup confectioners' sugar

4 tablespoons cornstarch

1 large egg

2 large egg yolks

⅓ cup granulated sugar

1 cup milk

1 pound pitted prunes, halved

1. Use ½ tablespoon butter to grease a 9-inch round shallow ceramic baking dish, like a quiche pan, or a 10-inch ceramic pie plate.

2. Place all but ½ tablespoon remaining butter in food processor or electric mixer. Process or beat briefly until creamed. Sift together almonds and all but 2 tablespoons confectioners' sugar. Add to butter and continue to process or beat until thick and light in color. Add 1 tablespoon cornstarch. Add whole egg and process or beat well. Transfer to large bowl.

3. In a medium-size bowl, vigorously whisk egg yolks and granulated sugar together until creamy. Whisk in remaining cornstarch. Scald milk in saucepan, then add in a thin stream to egg yolk mixture, beating constantly. Transfer mixture back to saucepan and heat, whisking constantly, until thickened. Remove from heat, brush surface with remaining butter and place saucepan in bowl of ice water to cool down the mixture.

4. Preheat oven to 350 degrees. When mixture in saucepan has cooled to room temperature, fold it into almond mixture in bowl. Fold in prunes.

5. Spread batter in baking dish and bake about 30 minutes, until top is lightly browned and knife inserted in center comes out clean.

6. Transfer to rack and allow to cool about 30 minutes. Sift remaining confectioners' sugar over the surface and serve.

CRISPS, CRUMBLES, COBBLERS AND SHORTCAKES

The desserts in this category are the simplest showy crowd-pleasers of all. They require good, fresh fruit, so the expertise depends on marketing skills. But the preparation, normally involving sweetening, piling into a baking dish—no specialized equipment needed either—adding a topping and baking, is less demanding than making a meatloaf. The lack of technical skill needed puts them squarely in the home-style dessert category, yet, recently, chefs have started serving them in restaurants, too, as you will see from several of these recipes. Often best served warm, these desserts can be prepared in advance and reheated just before serving, adding resilience to their many attributes.

Blackberry Nectarine Crisp

Pearl
Oyster Bar,
New York

Summer blackberries and nectarines make for an especially felicitous combination. (See Nectarines and Berries with Flavored Whipped Cream, page 331; and Brandied Berries and Nectarines, page 332.) Pearl Oyster Bar is a popular no-frills New England–style place in Greenwich Village.

TIME: 1 hour   YIELD: 6 servings

7 tablespoons cold unsalted
  butter
¼ cup all-purpose flour
½ cup rolled oats
½ cup firmly packed light brown
  sugar
¼ teaspoon ground cinnamon
¼ teaspoon salt

4 cups freestone nectarines,
  pitted, peeled and cut into
  1-inch chunks (about 3 large
  nectarines)
½ cup granulated sugar
½ teaspoon vanilla extract
1 heaping cup whole blackberries
Vanilla ice cream for serving

1. Preheat oven to 375 degrees. Grease a 2-quart baking dish or 6 8-ounce ramekins with 1 tablespoon butter.

2. In a food processor, pulse flour, oats, brown sugar, cinnamon and salt once or twice to mix. Cut remaining butter into small chunks, add to flour mixture and pulse a few more times, until mixture just comes together into small crumbly clumps. Reserve.

3. In a large bowl, combine nectarines, granulated sugar and vanilla. Pour nectarines into baking dish or ramekins, scatter blackberries on top and sprinkle with the processed mixture. Bake 45 minutes, until bubbling. Serve immediately with vanilla ice cream.

Plum Crumble

This is a recipe to prepare in late summer, when small purple-blue Italian prune plums come on the market. But almost any other fruit can be substituted. Amanda Hesser is the author of *The Cook and the Gardener: A Year of Recipes & Writings from the French Countryside*, which celebrates the simplicity and seasonality of recipes like this one.

Amanda Hesser

TIME: 40 minutes   YIELD: 4 servings

5 tablespoons cold unsalted butter, cut into small cubes, plus more at room temperature for pan

1 to 1½ pounds small ripe Italian prune plums, halved and pitted

2 tablespoons granulated sugar

2 tablespoons plum eau de vie, gin or brandy

½ cup all-purpose flour

Large pinch of sea salt

⅓ cup chopped almonds, toasted

¼ cup almond paste

¼ cup light brown sugar

Vanilla ice cream or whipped cream and crème fraîche, for serving

1. Preheat oven to 375 degrees. Butter a 9- or 10-inch shallow round baking dish. Place plums, cut side up, in the dish; they should fit snugly in a single layer. Sprinkle with granulated sugar and eau de vie.

2. In a food processor, pulse flour, salt, almonds, almond paste and brown sugar until it is like coarse meal. Then add chilled butter cubes and pulse until mixture looks more like peas.

3. Sprinkle almond mixture over plums and bake in oven until bubbling and browned, about 20 to 30 minutes. Let sit for 10 to 20 minutes before serving, to cool and set. Serve with scoops of vanilla ice cream or whipped cream with a little crème fraîche folded in.

Plum and Ginger Crumble

Marian
Burros

The starting point for this crumble is Marian Burros' famous plum torte (page 39). In this version, which is seasoned with ginger, the cake batter has one less egg, making it dry enough to turn into crumbs to top the plums.

TIME: 6. minutes   YIELD: 6 to 8 servings

12 Italian prune plums, halved and pitted
2 tablespoons light brown sugar
1½ tablespoons plus 1 cup all-purpose flour
¾ teaspoon ground cinnamon
¼ teaspoon ground ginger
2 heaping tablespoons finely chopped candied ginger

¾ cup granulated sugar
1 teaspoon baking powder
¼ teaspoon salt
1 large egg, well-beaten
4 ounces (1 stick) unsalted butter, melted
Vanilla ice cream, optional

1. Preheat oven to 375 degrees.

2. Place plums in a bowl. Mix brown sugar, 1½ tablespoons flour, ¼ teaspoon ground cinnamon, ground ginger and candied ginger together and mix with plums. Arrange plums, skin side up, in ungreased deep 9-inch pie plate or shallow baking dish attractive enough to use for serving.

3. In a bowl combine granulated sugar, baking powder, remaining flour, remaining cinnamon and salt and mix well. Stir in egg. Rub together with your fingertips to combine ingredients and make a crumbly mixture. Sprinkle over the plums. Drizzle butter evenly over the top.

4. Bake 30 to 35 minutes. The crumble is done when the top is browned and plums, when pricked with cake tester, yield easily. Remove from oven. Serve warm, plain or with vanilla ice cream.

5. If desired, refrigerate for up to 2 days or freeze well wrapped. To serve, bring to room temperature and warm at 300 degrees.

Intense Chocolate Mousse Cake (page 30)

Berries with Lemon Soufflé Topping (page 191)

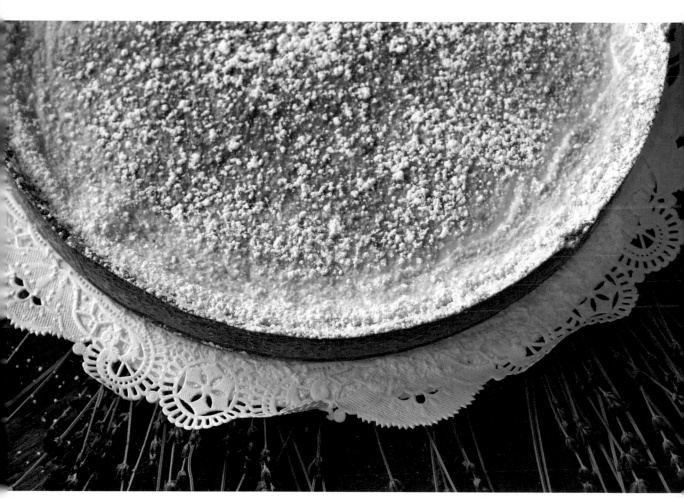

Ricotta Tart (page 104)

Madeleines with Orange Confit and Honey (page 171)

Quick Classic Berry Tart (page 272)

One-Pan Christmas Cake (page 92)

Cardamom Ice Cream (page 452)

Big Apple Pie (page 233)

Strawberries with Pink Peppercorn Sauce over ice cream (page 341)

Strawberry Pavlova (page 196)

Marie Louise's Rice Pudding (page 405)

Double Dip of Chocolate Pudding (page 402)

Mango Cheesecake (page 101)

Chocolate Caramel Mousse (page 431) served with Orange Confit (page 543)

Vanilla Cheesecake (page 96)

Tropical Fruit Trifle (page 382)

Strawberry-Rhubarb Crumble

Strawberries and rhubarb are a classic springtime pairing, one that I find particularly felicitous. Rhubarb has a particular affinity for brown sugar. It is important to serve this dessert as soon as it has cooled a little; otherwise, the strawberries, which do not take well to long cooking, will become faded.

Florence Fabricant

TIME: 45 minutes   YIELD: 6 servings

4 tablespoons unsalted butter
1½ pounds fresh rhubarb
1 pint fresh strawberries, hulled
 and halved
2 teaspoons ground ginger

1½ cups light brown sugar
4 tablespoons whole wheat flour
⅔ cup rolled oats
1 pint vanilla ice cream

1. Preheat oven to 400 degrees. Butter a 6-cup baking dish with ½ tablespoon butter.

2. Remove any leaves from rhubarb stalks. Dice rhubarb. Place in a bowl and mix with strawberries, 1½ teaspoons ginger and 1 cup brown sugar. Spread into the baking dish. Dot with 1 tablespoon butter.

3. With a fork or your fingertips mix remaining brown sugar and ginger with flour and oats. Cut remaining butter in bits and mix in until crumbly. Spread this mixture over rhubarb and strawberries.

4. Place in the oven and bake 25 to 30 minutes, until top is browned and the fruit begins to bubble. Allow to cool 20 minutes, then serve with ice cream.

Roasted Pineapple Crumble with Macadamia Nuts

Florian
Bellanger,
Le Bernardin,
New York

Banana is an unusual ingredient in the caramel that is prepared to sweeten the pineapple and enrich the end result. Care must be taken when making and handling the hot caramel: it will bubble up and may spatter when the hot water is added. Florian Bellanger developed this recipe when he was the pastry chef at Le Bernardin in New York. He is now the executive pastry chef for Fauchon, the French fancy food retailer.

TIME: 1 hour 45 minutes   YIELD: 6 servings

6 tablespoons cold unsalted butter, in pieces, plus more for ramekins

1 cup plus 3 tablespoons granulated sugar

1 vanilla bean, sliced lengthwise, seeds scraped out

6 quarter-size slices peeled fresh ginger (½ ounce)

5 whole cloves, chopped

¼ cup mashed banana (½ large banana)

2 tablespoons dark rum

1 fresh pineapple, peeled

¾ cup (3 ounces) macadamia nuts

1 heaping tablespoon pecans

1 tablespoon unsalted pistachio nuts

1 cup all-purpose flour

3 tablespoons packed dark brown sugar

½ teaspoon salt

⅛ teaspoon ground cinnamon

⅛ teaspoon freshly grated nutmeg

1. Preheat oven to 400 degrees. Butter 6 8-ounce ramekins.

2. In a medium saucepan, combine 1 cup sugar, ¼ cup hot water, the vanilla bean and scrapings, ginger and cloves. Stir the mixture over medium heat until the sugar dissolves. Increase the heat to medium-high, and cook the mixture until it is caramelized and dark golden brown, about 10 minutes.

3. Carefully add 1¼ cups hot water (the caramel will seize and bubble up, so stand back), banana and rum. Stir the mixture over low heat until the caramel is smooth.

4. Pour the caramel into a 9-by-9-by-2-inch pan. Add the pineapple, and roast it, turning it every 10 minutes with tongs or a long-handled fork to coat with caramel, for a total of 50 minutes. Remove the pan to a wire

rack, and let the pineapple cool in the caramel. Reduce the oven temperature to 350 degrees.

5. While the pineapple is roasting, prepare the topping. Place the nuts on a baking sheet with a rim, and toast them in the oven with the pineapple for 8 to 10 minutes, until pale golden brown. Reserve 18 macadamia nuts, then coarsely chop the rest of the nuts.

6. In the bowl of a mixer with a paddle attachment, or in a food processor, combine the flour, remaining butter, brown sugar, remaining granulated sugar, salt, cinnamon and nutmeg. Stir the mixture on low speed or pulse until it resembles pebbles (do not overmix). Add the chopped nuts, and briefly mix them in.

7. When the pineapple is cool enough to handle, cut 2 half-inch-thick slices from it, and cut the slices into thirds. Reserve for garnish. Cut the remaining pineapple lengthwise into quarters, and cut away the core. Dice the pineapple into half-inch cubes. Reserve the caramel.

8. Divide the pineapple among the ramekins. Drizzle 1 tablespoon of the caramel over each. Top with the crumble mixture, filling the ramekins to the top.

9. Bake the ramekins for about 17 minutes, or until the tops are golden brown. Serve warm, garnished with the reserved macadamia nuts and pineapple slices.

Rhubarb-Berry Cobbler

Florence
Fabricant

This springtime dessert amounts to strawberry-rhubarb pie without the bother of making and rolling a full pie crust. Adding raspberries enhances the scarlet color: they keep theirs when strawberries fade during cooking. The pastry topping is extremely easy to make and handles beautifully, so the lattice crust is not a challenge. But any of the crisp and crumble toppings can be used instead.

TIME: 1 hour 20 minutes   YIELD: 6 to 8 servings

9 tablespoons unsalted butter
1½ cups light brown sugar
2 tablespoons cornstarch
1½ pounds rhubarb, in 1-inch pieces, about 5 cups
½ pint strawberries, hulled and quartered
½ pint raspberries

½ teaspoon ground cinnamon
1 cup all-purpose flour, plus more for dusting
½ teaspoon baking powder
¼ teaspoon salt
4 tablespoons milk, approximately
1 tablespoon granulated sugar
1 pint vanilla ice cream (page 446)

1. Preheat oven to 350 degrees. Melt 4 tablespoons butter and brush an 8-inch square or 9-inch round pan, attractive enough for serving, with a little of the melted butter.

2. Whisk brown sugar and cornstarch together in a large bowl. Add rhubarb, berries, cinnamon and remaining melted butter. Toss to combine. Transfer to baking dish.

3. Place flour, baking powder and salt in a food processor and pulse briefly. Dice remaining butter and add. Pulse until coarsely blended. Add milk, pulse briefly, then transfer to a bowl. Gather together by hand to form a soft dough, adding a little more milk if needed. Transfer to a floured board and roll to a rectangle 8 by 10 inches. Cut in 1-inch-wide strips and arrange in lattice fashion over rhubarb mixture. Dust with granulated sugar.

4. Bake about 50 minutes, until pastry is lightly browned. Cool at least 30 minutes before serving with ice cream.

Mixed Berry Cobbler ☀

This cobbler recipe is on its way to becoming a shortcake. Instead of baking the biscuitlike mounds of dough with the berries, they can also be simply split, filled with fresh, sweetened berries, peach slices or other fruit and topped with whipped cream for shortcakes. Scott Campbell, who was the original chef for Vince & Eddie's on the Upper West Side of Manhattan, now has his own place, @SQC, also on the Upper West Side.

Scott Campbell, Vince & Eddie's, New York

TIME: 2 hours, including cooling   YIELD: 8 servings

2 cups all-purpose flour
2 tablespoons baking powder
Pinch of salt
8 ounces (2 sticks) cold unsalted
   butter, plus more for dish
5 tablespoons granulated
   sugar
1 cup half-and-half

1 pint blueberries, rinsed
1 pint strawberries, rinsed and
   hulled
½ pint blackberries, rinsed
½ pint raspberries, rinsed
1½ cups dark brown sugar
Mint sprigs for garnish
1 quart vanilla ice cream

1. Preheat oven to 350 degrees. Line a baking sheet with parchment paper. Butter a 9-by-13-inch baking dish, attractive enough for serving.

2. Place the flour, baking powder and salt in a food processor, and whirl briefly to combine. Dice the butter, add it and pulse until the mixture is uniformly crumbly. Mix 4 tablespoons sugar and half-and-half together, and pour into the food processor. Pulse just until the ingredients are combined to form a soft dough. Do not overmix.

3. Scoop the dough into 8 mounds on the baking sheet, spacing to allow 2 inches between them. Sprinkle with a tablespoon of sugar, and bake 20 to 25 minutes, until lightly browned.

4. While the pastry is baking, combine the berries in a mixing bowl, add the brown sugar, mix gently, then spread in the buttered baking dish.

5. When the pastry is done, place it on the berries, spacing them evenly. Place the baking dish in the oven to continue baking, until the topping is browned and the berries are bubbling, about 30 minutes.

6. Allow to cool for about 30 minutes, then serve, with pastry on each portion. Garnish with mint and vanilla ice cream on the side.

Apricot-Raspberry Cobbler

Florence
Fabricant

The season for fresh apricots is fleeting, usually late June and early July, around the time the first raspberries of the season arrive, hence the argument for joining the two fruits in this cobbler. Later in the summer, I often substitute fresh, peeled peaches or unpeeled nectarines and blackberries.

TIME: 1 hour 10 minutes, plus cooling   YIELD: 6 servings

5½ tablespoons unsalted butter

2 pounds ripe apricots, pitted and halved

1 pint raspberries

1 tablespoon lemon juice

1 cup light brown sugar

2 tablespoons cornstarch

1 teaspoon ground ginger

1 cup self-rising flour

¼ teaspoon salt

3½ tablespoons lowfat milk

Whipped cream or ice cream

1. Preheat oven to 350 degrees. Grease an 8-inch square or 9-inch round baking dish with ½ tablespoon butter.

2. Mix the apricots, raspberries and lemon juice together. Toss with the brown sugar, cornstarch and half the ginger and spread in the baking dish.

3. Mix the flour, remaining ginger and salt. Cut in the butter by hand or by pulsing in a food processor until the mixture resembles coarse meal. Lightly stir in the milk to form a tender dough. Roll out the dough to ⅜-inch thickness on a floured board and cut in strips 1 inch wide. Crisscross the strips over the fruit.

4. Bake about 40 minutes, until the crust has browned and the filling bubbles. Allow to cool to lukewarm, then serve with whipped cream or ice cream.

Pear and Cranberry Cobbler

Cranberries suggest autumn, but dried ones are available all year, so this dessert actually knows no season. The dried cranberries add a delicious note of tartness to this cobbler. I have given the typical biscuit dough topping extra allure with strips forming a lattice top.

Florence Fabricant

TIME: 1½ hours   YIELD: 6 to 8 servings

4 tablespoons unsalted butter, melted
¾ cup light brown sugar
2 tablespoons cornstarch
4 cups coarsely diced peeled pears (about 6 large pears)
1 cup dried cranberries
½ teaspoon ground cinnamon
1 cup all-purpose flour, plus flour for work surface

2 teaspoons baking powder
¼ teaspoon salt
5 tablespoons cold unsalted butter, in small pieces
3 to 4 tablespoons milk
1 tablespoon granulated sugar
Whipped cream

1. Preheat oven to 350 degrees. Grease an 8- or 9-inch square baking dish with 2 teaspoons melted butter.

2. Mix brown sugar with cornstarch in a large bowl. Stir in pears, cranberries, remaining melted butter and cinnamon. Spoon into baking dish.

3. Whisk flour, baking powder and salt together. Cut in cold butter by hand or by pulsing in a food processor until crumbly. Stir in enough milk to form a soft dough. Roll or pat on a lightly floured board to ¼ inch thickness. Cut in 8 to 10 strips 9 inches long and about 1 inch wide. Crisscross strips over fruit in pan. Sprinkle with sugar.

4. Bake about 40 minutes, until crust has browned and filling bubbles. Set aside until just warm and serve with whipped cream.

Plum Cobbler with Hazelnuts

Florence
Fabricant

This cobbler, with its hazelnut pastry, is the equivalent of a deep-dish pie. But it offers a change of pace from the usual summer fruit pie or tart. I love the way the earthy, toasty hazelnuts play off against the vibrant richness of the plums.

TIME: 1 hour   YIELD: 8 servings

3 tablespoons unsalted butter, softened
¼ cup chopped toasted hazelnuts
4 cups mixed pitted plums, cut in chunks (12 to 15 plums, depending on the size)

1 cup light brown sugar
1 teaspoon ground cardamom
3 tablespoons all-purpose flour
Hazelnut pastry (page 525)
¾ cup heavy cream

1. Preheat oven to 400 degrees. Use 1 tablespoon butter to grease a 4-cup, 9-inch square baking dish. Dust bottom with 2 tablespoons hazelnuts.

2. Put plums in a bowl. Mix remaining hazelnuts with brown sugar, cardamom and flour. Toss with plums. Spread plums in baking dish and dot with remaining butter.

3. Roll out pastry ⅛ inch thick to fit top of baking dish with about a 1-inch overhang. Cover fruit with pastry, fold in edges and tuck into pan, forming a thicker border. Brush with a little of the cream and cut a decorative pattern of slits in top.

4. Bake about 40 minutes, until top is nicely browned. Whip cream while cobbler is baking and refrigerate.

5. Allow cobbler to cool at least 1 hour before serving with whipped cream.

Peach and Crème Fraîche Shortcake

The biscuit shortcakes for this recipe can be prepared in advance, and, if you like your shortcakes warm, reheated briefly before they are filled. Amanda Hesser, a food editor and cookbook author, also wrote a long-running "Private Lives" column in *The New York Times Sunday Magazine*, which was collected as *Cooking for Mr. Latte: A Courtship in Recipes*.

Amanda
Hesser

TIME: 50 minutes   YIELD: 10 servings

5 very ripe freestone peaches, peeled, pitted and thinly sliced
½ cup plus 3 tablespoons sugar
2 cups heavy cream
2½ cups crème fraîche

2 cups all-purpose flour
¾ teaspoon salt
1 tablespoon baking powder
4 ounces (1 stick) very cold unsalted butter, in small cubes

1. Place peaches in a medium bowl, sprinkle with ½ cup sugar and stir gently. Set aside at room temperature. Using a mixer or whisk, beat heavy cream until slightly thickened. Add ¼ cup crème fraîche and continue to beat mixture until it will hold soft peaks. Cover and refrigerate.

2. Preheat oven to 375 degrees. In a large bowl, whisk together flour, salt, baking powder and remaining 3 tablespoons sugar. Using a pastry blender or two knives, cut in butter until mixture resembles lumpy corn-meal. Add 1½ cups remaining crème fraîche. Using a wooden spoon, or by hand, fold and press mixture together until a moist dough forms. Do not overwork dough or shortcakes will be heavy.

3. On a lightly floured surface, pat or roll dough into a rectangle about 12 inches by 5 inches and ½ inch thick. Using a knife dipped in flour, cut rectangle lengthwise in half, then each half crosswise into 5 pieces. You should have 10 squares. Place on a baking sheet and spread a thin layer of remaining crème fraîche on top of each shortcake. Bake until risen and golden, 15 to 20 minutes. Transfer to a rack to cool. Shortcakes are best served warm and can be reheated in a low oven for a few minutes.

4. To serve, split shortcakes in half. Place bottoms on plates. Drop 2 heaping tablespoons of reserved cream mixture onto each, allowing some to drip over side. Spoon over some of the peaches with their juices. Place tops of cakes on peaches and spoon on more peaches and juice. Serve.

Strawberry Sour Cream Shortcake

R. W.
Apple, Jr.

This is a strawberry shortcake made as one large cake, not individual portions. R. W. Apple, Jr., is a senior reporter for *The New York Times* who has a particular love for food and frequently writes about it.

TIME: 1 hour   YIELD: 6 servings

4 tablespoons cold unsalted butter
  plus 1 tablespoon softened and
  1 tablespoon melted butter
2 cups sifted all-purpose flour
1 tablespoon baking powder
¼ cup sugar, plus more for
  sweetening
¾ teaspoon salt
3 ounces cream cheese
1 large egg
About ½ cup milk
1 quart fresh strawberries, hulled
  and thinly sliced
1 cup sour cream

1. Preheat oven to 450 degrees. Grease an 8-inch round cake pan with soft butter.

2. Into a large mixing bowl, sift together the flour, baking powder, ¼ cup of the sugar and the salt. Add the cream cheese and chilled butter. Using a pastry blender or two knives, cut the cream cheese and butter into the mixture until it resembles coarse cornmeal.

3. Break the egg into a measuring cup, and beat lightly with a fork. Add enough milk to make ¾ cup. Pour the egg mixture into the flour mixture, and stir. Knead the dough inside the bowl just until it is blended and cohesive, about 20 seconds.

4. Shape half of the dough into an 8-inch disk, and place in cake pan. Pat the dough flat to the edges of the pan. Brush the top of the dough with the melted butter. Shape the remaining dough into another disk and place in the pan on the buttered dough, patting flat to the edges. Bake until golden brown, about 17 to 20 minutes. Remove from heat and allow to cool.

5. Place strawberries in a bowl, add sugar to taste, and mix. Place sour cream in a small bowl, and add sugar to taste, mixing well.

6. To serve, remove the cake from the pan, and use a large knife to pry the layers apart; they should split naturally. Place the bottom layer on a serving plate, and top with strawberries. Place the second layer over the strawberries, and top with sour cream. Serve.

Toasted Brioche Shortcakes with Strawberries

Florence
Fabricant

I often serve this utterly simple version of strawberry shortcakes. Instead of baking cake layers or biscuits, my "shortcake" is actually a dessert French toast. A fancier name for it might be Strawberry Pain Perdu, as *pain perdu*, or "lost bread," is what the French call French toast. Dipping the slices of egg-soaked brioche in sugar before sautéing them contributes to the caramelization of the surface.

TIME: 1½ hours   YIELD: 6 servings

5 large eggs
½ cup whole milk
6 slices, each about ¾ inch thick, brioche or egg bread
3 tablespoons unsalted butter
½ cup sugar

1 pint strawberries, hulled and halved
4 tablespoons red currant jelly, melted
1 cup crème fraîche

1. Beat the eggs with the milk in a large, shallow bowl. Add the brioche slices one at a time, turning in the egg mixture to coat both sides. Set aside to soak at least 1 hour. Most, if not all, the egg mixture should have been absorbed by the bread.

2. Heat the butter in a heavy skillet.

3. Spread the sugar on a plate.

4. Remove the bread from the egg mixture and dip each slice in the sugar, lightly coating both sides. Place in the skillet and sauté over medium heat, turning once, until lightly browned. You may not be able to sauté all the slices at once. Place the finished slices on individual dessert plates.

5. Mix the berries with the jelly and spoon some on top of each brioche slice. Top each with a generous dollop of crème fraîche and serve.

PIES AND TARTS

Pies and tarts are two separate baking entities that often encroach on each other's territory. Shape is the defining characteristic, with pies baked in slope-sided dishes and usually served directly from them. Pies may have one crust or two. Tarts are usually straight-sided, often fluted and, unlike pies, unmolded before serving. But many tart recipes are interchangeable with pie recipes, and vice versa.

When it comes to baking a pie or a tart, the pastry is all-important. Some of the recipes that follow include pastry recipes. But there is also a large selection of pastry recipes in the chapter on Basics (page 519). If you find one you like, and feel you can handle with ease, do not hesitate to call it your own, and to use it for most of the pies and tarts you bake. A good surface for rolling pastry, a heavy rolling pin, a dough scraper to clean your work surface and perhaps lift the pastry, and pie pans are the equipment you will need. Some pastry recipes can be mixed in a food processor or an electric mixer. Most can also be done by hand, by cutting the chilled fat into the flour mixture with your fingertips, two knives or a pastry blender.

The secret to good pastry is in the light hand with which you work it, so the natural, elastic gluten in the flour is not activated. When it comes to adding the liquid, do so gradually. Too much moisture will make your pastry heavy; too little will make it difficult to handle. And if the whole notion of mixing and rolling pastry is too daunting, there are always crusts made of crushed nuts, graham crackers or other cookies, which you will find as part of some of the recipes in the Pies section below as well as in the Cheesecakes section (page 95) and the Basics chapter (page 519).

PIES

Pie-baking derives from the English mother-country. Apples, for example, were not native to the New World, but were planted from seeds carried from England by the earliest colonists. The fruit of the orchards that flourished went mostly into cider, an alcoholic drink that was consumed in prodigious amounts by adults and children. Some estimates put the daily intake of cider—which was safer than water or milk—at some three gallons per person. John Chapman—or Johnny Appleseed, as he was known—took the pips from Philadelphia cider mills to plant in the Ohio Valley.

Now, what does this have to do with pie? Apple pie, of course, is the quintessential American dessert. It is a double-crust confection baked in a slope-sided pan. The shape of a wedge of pie, with one edge sealed, made it easy to carry, and a slice of pie was often a breakfast on the road for a worker or schoolchild. Pioneer women stocked their Conestogas with apples, some of which they dried, so when the fresh fruit was no longer available, they made pie from dried apples. And when these gave out, they soaked crackers in cider vinegar to make mock apple pie. There are pies that are associated with various regions of the country. Key lime pie in Florida is one example. Chiffon pies were often served in New York restaurants. Pecan pie is a Southern specialty that is popular at Thanksgiving, just as New England pumpkin pie is farther north.

As for pie pans, glass will result in a somewhat darker, crisper crust. And since a pie is served from its pan, glass is more presentable at the table than metal. Some cooks, including Amanda Hesser of *The New York Times*, swear by nonstick pie pans, but I do not find them necessary. There is usually enough fat in the pastry so that the crust will not stick to glass or plain metal.

Big Apple Pie

But for its extra-large size, this apple pie is a classic, cinnamon-scented and sealed in a double crust. Its flavor is given a bit of tang with the addition of cider or cider vinegar. Indeed, instead of supermarket cider vinegar, look for an artisanal brand, which will have more body and sweet complexity. You need a deep pie dish for it, otherwise, bake it in a regular pie pan but reduce the filling quantity by half. Suzanne Hamlin is a food writer based in Brooklyn, New York.

Suzanne
Hamlin

TIME: 1 hour 15 minutes   YIELD: 8 or more servings

3 pounds red or golden apples,
    2 or 3 different kinds, peeled,
    cored and sliced
½ cup sugar
½ cup apple cider or apple cider
    vinegar
1½ teaspoons ground cinnamon
⅛ teaspoon salt
Several grindings black pepper

2 tablespoons all-purpose flour
Rich butter pastry, chilled (page
    521)
2 tablespoons unsalted butter
1 egg beaten with 1 tablespoon of
    water
Whipped cream, crème fraîche or
    ice cream, for serving

1. Preheat oven to 425 degrees. Place apples in a large bowl. Add sugar, apple cider or vinegar, cinnamon, salt, pepper and flour. Mix well.

2. Line a deep-dish 9- or 10-inch metal pie pan with half the pastry, leaving a generous top edge. Prick the bottom of the pastry all over with the tines of a fork. Transfer apples to pie tin, mounding slightly in center. Cut butter into bits, and distribute over apples.

3. Cover apples with the other half of the pastry. Trim around edges, and crimp the top and bottom pastry together. Using a pastry brush, paint the top of the pastry with the egg wash. With a sharp knife make a small hole in the center of the pastry. Make five cuts, each about 3 inches long, radiating from the center hole.

4. Put the pie pan on a baking sheet, and bake on the lower level of the oven for 10 minutes. Reduce heat to 325 degrees, and bake for about 50 minutes more, until the crust is deep golden brown. Cool on a rack. Serve warm or at room temperature with whipped cream, crème fraîche or ice cream.

Apple Crumb Pie

Michael
Romano,
Union Square
Café, New
York

This pie is a variation on the following sautéed apple pie. Here, too, the apples are cooked before they are transferred to the pastry, but not long enough to caramelize them (you can eliminate the flour and allow the apples to caramelize). Prebaking the pastry guarantees that the crust will stay crisp. Michael Romano is the executive chef at Union Square Café, the flagship of Danny Meyer's New York restaurants.

TIME: 1 hour 70 minutes, plus chilling   YIELD: One 9-inch pie (6 to 8 servings)

1¼ cups all-purpose flour
½ cup dark brown sugar, packed
4 teaspoons ground cinnamon
4 ounces (1 stick) plus 5
   tablespoons cold unsalted
   butter
Butter pastry (½ recipe, page 520)

1 cup granulated sugar
3 pounds McIntosh or Granny
   Smith apples, peeled and cut
   into 1-inch dice (8 to 9 cups)
1 vanilla bean, cut in half
   lengthwise
Squeeze of fresh lemon juice

1. In a medium bowl, combine 1 cup flour with the brown sugar and half the cinnamon. Cut 4 ounces of the butter into small pieces. Add the butter to the flour mixture and with your hands or a pastry blender work it in until crumbs are formed with lumps about the size of hazelnuts. Refrigerate.

2. Preheat oven to 350 degrees. Adjust the shelf to the lower third of the oven. On a lightly floured surface, roll out the dough ⅛ inch thick. Press into a 9-inch pie pan, and trim excess dough; flute or fold, and press edges to make a border. Prick the bottom of the pie shell with the tines of a fork, and refrigerate or freeze briefly to set crust. Line the dough with foil, fill with pie weights or dried beans and bake for 15 minutes. Remove weights and foil, and continue baking for about 15 minutes, or until crust just begins to brown. Remove from oven, and cool.

3. Combine granulated sugar and remaining cinnamon. In a large skillet or sauté pan, melt the remaining butter over medium heat. Add diced apples and cinnamon-sugar. With a small knife, scrape the seeds from the vanilla bean into the apple mixture, and discard the bean. Cook the apples, stirring, about 5 minutes, or until the edges just begin to soften. Add ¼ cup

flour, and continue to cook, stirring, until the flour is completely absorbed, about 2 to 3 minutes. Remove from heat, and add a squeeze of fresh lemon juice to taste.

4. Pile cooked apple mixture in pie shell, mounding it high in the center. Cover with crumb topping. Bake in preheated 350-degree oven until filling bubbles and crumbs are lightly browned, about 30 to 40 minutes. Serve warm.

Sautéed Apple Pie

Florence
Fabricant

I have always had two problems with the typical two-crust apple pie. First, the apples, as they bake in the crust, give off liquid, so some kind of starch, typically flour or cornstarch, must be added. And, second, the apple filling tends to shrink, so what goes into the oven with a generous dome emerges somewhat flattened. Cutting slits in the top crust to allow steam to escape is necessary, otherwise there will be an empty space between the filling and the crust. A few years ago, I began sautéing the apples before using them to fill the pie. This extra step permits the fruit to cook down, which is why you can start with five pounds of apples. It concentrates the liquid and it also coats the apples with a lovely caramel glaze. This method will also work with a double-crust peach pie.

TIME: 1½ hours   YIELD: 8 to 12 servings

4 tablespoons unsalted butter
5 pounds apples, peeled, cored
  and sliced ½ inch thick
¾ cup plus 1 tablespoon sugar

1 teaspoon ground cinnamon
Rich butter pastry (page 521)
Flour for rolling dough
1 tablespoon heavy cream

1. Melt butter over medium-high heat in a large skillet, preferably not nonstick. (Apples will not caramelize as well in a nonstick pan.) Add apples, sprinkle with ¾ cup sugar, and sauté, turning apples, about 10 minutes, until tender and lightly caramelized. Fold in cinnamon. If you do not have a skillet large enough to hold all the apples, do this step in two stages or in two skillets. Spread cooked apples on a platter to cool.

2. Preheat oven to 400 degrees. Divide pastry in two unequal halves; roll out larger portion on a lightly floured board, and line pie pan. Spoon in cooled apples. Roll out remaining pastry, and cover pan; seal and crimp edges. Cut several decorative slits in top. Alternatively, top pastry can be cut in strips and used to make lattice.

3. Brush pastry with cream, and dust with remaining sugar. Bake about 40 minutes, until pastry is golden. Cool briefly, then serve.

Apple, Pecan and Raisin Pie ✳

Here is another apple pie that calls for sautéing the apples before filling the pie. The yellow Delicious apples, a variety that French chefs favor, are fairly dry-textured, and take well to the sauté pan. Eastville Manor is an inn and restaurant on Maryland's Eastern Shore.

William Scalley, Eastville Manor, Maryland ∾

TIME: 2 hours, plus cooling   YIELD: 8 servings

8 ounces (2 sticks) plus 3 tablespoons cold unsalted butter	6 large Golden Delicious apples
	¾ cup coarsely chopped pecans
	¾ cup raisins
1¾ cups all-purpose flour	1½ teaspoons ground cinnamon
¼ teaspoon salt	1½ cups packed light brown sugar
1 tablespoon granulated sugar	1 cup old-fashioned rolled oats

1. Thinly slice 4 ounces (1 stick) of the butter, and place in freezer until well chilled. In the bowl of a food processor, combine 1¼ cups of the flour, salt, granulated sugar and butter from freezer. Pulse until mixture resembles coarse meal, about 10 seconds. With machine running, add 2 to 4 tablespoons ice water a little at a time until the dough just holds together. Transfer dough to a mixing bowl, and shape into a ball. On a lightly floured surface, roll out dough to ⅛ inch thickness. Fit into a 9-inch pie plate, trim the edge with a sharp knife and crimp the border. Lightly cover with plastic wrap, and refrigerate.

2. Peel, core and slice apples. In a large sauté pan over medium heat, melt 3 tablespoons of the remaining butter. Add apple slices, and saute until soft, 10 to 15 minutes. Remove from heat, and allow to cool.

3. Preheat oven to 325 degrees. In a mixing bowl, combine pecans, raisins, cinnamon and ¾ cup of light brown sugar. Mix well. Add apples, toss lightly and set aside. Slice remaining 4 ounces butter, and place in a food processor. Add remaining ½ cup flour, and pulse until mixture resembles coarse meal. Transfer to a mixing bowl, and add remaining ¾ cup light brown sugar and oats; mix well.

4. Spoon apples into pie shell. Cover with oatmeal topping. Bake until crust is golden brown and filling is slightly bubbly, about 1 hour. Cool before serving.

Bourbon Pecan Pie

Suzanne
Hamlin

Toasting the pecans before baking the pie guarantees that they will have exceptional flavor. Always store your nuts in the freezer for optimum freshness. Suzanne Hamlin is a food writer based in Brooklyn, New York.

TIME: 1 hour 5 minutes   YIELD: 8 servings

1½ cups pecan halves
Butter pastry (½ recipe, page
  520)
3 large eggs
½ cup dark brown sugar
1 cup dark corn syrup
¼ teaspoon salt

6 tablespoons unsalted butter,
  melted
1 teaspoon vanilla
2 tablespoons bourbon
1 tablespoon all-purpose flour
Whipped cream, crème fraîche or
  vanilla ice cream for serving

1. Preheat oven to 350 degrees. Spread pecans on a baking sheet and roast them for about 7 minutes, until toasted. Remove them from the baking sheet, and cool. Increase oven temperature to 450 degrees. Roll out pastry and line a 9-inch pie pan.

2. In a large bowl, beat eggs slightly, and whisk in the dark brown sugar and corn syrup. Whisk in the salt, butter, vanilla and bourbon. Mix flour with pecans, and add.

3. Prick the bottom of the pastry all over with the tines of a fork. Pour the filling into the crust, and put the pan on a flat baking sheet. Place on the lower level of the oven, reduce the temperature to 350 degrees and bake for 35 to 40 minutes, until filling is puffed and firm. Check after 20 minutes; if the crust is browning too quickly, loosely drape a piece of aluminum foil around the edges.

4. Remove to a rack, and serve warm or at room temperature, with whipped cream, crème fraîche or vanilla ice cream.

Black Walnut Pie

Bryan
Simmons

The black walnut is native to the Eastern United States, especially in the Appalachian region. The nuts are rounder, smaller and more assertively flavored than the more common walnuts, often called English walnuts (even though they originated in Persia). They are also more expensive. They can be ordered online from www.black-walnuts.com or Hammons Products at 888-429-6887. Regular walnuts, toasted, can be substituted in this recipe. Bryan Simmons is a home cook who lives in Somerville, Massachusetts.

TIME: 1 hour, plus chilling and cooling   YIELD: One 8-inch pie

1¼ cups all-purpose flour, more
    as needed

Salt

⅓ cup vegetable shortening,
    chilled

3 large eggs

⅓ cup packed light brown sugar

1 cup maple syrup

3 teaspoons apple cider vinegar

½ teaspoon vanilla extract

3 tablespoons unsalted butter,
    melted and cooled

1½ cups coarsely chopped black
    walnuts

Whipped cream or vanilla ice
    cream, optional

1. Stir flour and ½ teaspoon salt together in a large bowl. With a pastry cutter or two knives, cut in shortening until mixture looks mealy. Slowly add 3 tablespoons ice water, tossing mixture until water is absorbed. Shape dough into ball, wrap in plastic wrap and refrigerate 1 hour.

2. On a lightly floured surface, roll dough into a 10-inch round, and place in an 8-inch pie pan, trimming edge and crimping as desired. Refrigerate for 1 hour.

3. Whisk eggs in a bowl until frothy. Add brown sugar, and whisk until smooth. Add maple syrup, vinegar, vanilla and a pinch of salt. Whisk until smooth, and gradually whisk in melted butter.

4. Place rack in lower third of oven, and preheat to 375 degrees. Spread walnuts in pie shell. Pour filling over them. Bake until puffed and partly set, 35 minutes. Pie will set as it cools to room temperature. It may be served with whipped cream or vanilla ice cream.

Blueberry Pie with Lattice Top

Amanda
Hesser

The mixing method for the crust, using a large plastic bag, is fairly unique, but extremely convenient. Amanda Hesser is a food writer and cookbook author, and the food editor of *The New York Times Sunday Magazine*.

TIME: 1½ hours, plus chilling and cooling   YIELD: 8 servings

2 cups all-purpose flour
⅔ cup confectioners' sugar
Kosher salt
⅛ teaspoon baking powder
6 ounces (1½ sticks) unsalted
    butter in small cubes
1½ tablespoons freshly grated
    lemon zest

1 large egg yolk
2 tablespoons heavy cream,
    approximately
5 cups blueberries
3 tablespoons cornstarch
¾ cup granulated sugar
2 tablespoons lemon juice
Whipped cream, for serving

1. In a 1-gallon plastic bag, combine flour, confectioners' sugar, ½ teaspoon salt and baking powder. Wrap butter cubes in plastic wrap. Place both in freezer for at least 30 minutes. Pour contents of flour bag into a food processor and pulse a few times. Add butter and pulse until mixture is reduced to flakes. Lightly beat lemon zest, egg yolk and heavy cream together, add to food processor, and pulse 5 times. Dough is ready if it holds together when you press mixture between your thumb and index finger. If it's too crumbly, add a little more cream.

2. Pile dough onto a countertop. Using the heel of your hand, knead dough bits until they cohere. Form into two balls, one slightly smaller than the other, and flatten each into a disk. Cover with plastic wrap and chill for at least 3 hours.

3. In a large bowl, mix together the blueberries, cornstarch, granulated sugar, lemon juice and pinch of salt.

4. Roll out larger ball of dough between 2 sheets of floured plastic wrap. When it is ⅛ inch thick, remove top layer of plastic and invert dough into a 9-inch pie pan. Gently press into pan without stretching dough. Chill. Roll out other ball of dough, and when it is ⅛ inch thick, slice into ½-inch-wide strips.

5. Remove pie shell from refrigerator and pour berry mixture into it. Arrange strips of pastry in a lattice pattern on top. Cut overhang of dough to ¾ inch, then roll it up and over lattice edge, making a neat rounded border. Crimp border. Chill unbaked pie. Preheat oven to 400 degrees.

6. Bake pie until filling bubbles on edges and crust is golden brown, 40 to 45 minutes. Check after 20 minutes. If crust is browning too quickly, cover it with a round band of aluminum foil. Place finished pie on a rack and let cool to room temperature. Serve with huge dollops of whipped cream.

Blueberry Chiffon Pie

Amanda
Hesser

There are a couple of elements that give this pie real personality. The cornmeal in the pastry provides felicitous crunch. And the chiffon filling is made with a rich custard base. Amanda Hesser is a food writer and cookbook author who has contributed numerous recipes to the Dining section and *The New York Times Sunday Magazine.*

TIME: 1½ hours, plus chilling   YIELD: 8 servings

1¼ cups all-purpose flour
⅓ cup white cornmeal
⅓ cup confectioners' sugar
Kosher salt
9 tablespoons unsalted butter in small cubes
½ vanilla bean, split, insides scraped out
6 large egg yolks

1 cup heavy cream, approximately
2 cups blueberries
¾ cup granulated sugar
Grated zest of 1 lemon
2 tablespoons lemon juice
1 packet plain gelatin, dissolved in ¼ cup warm water
6 large egg whites

1. In a 1-gallon plastic bag, combine flour, cornmeal, confectioners' sugar and ½ teaspoon salt. Wrap butter cubes in plastic wrap. Place both in freezer for at least 30 minutes. Pour contents of flour bag into a food processor and pulse a few times. Add butter and pulse until it resembles tiny pebbles. Lightly beat together vanilla seeds and pulp, 1 egg yolk and 3 tablespoons heavy cream. Add to food processor and pulse 5 times. Dough is ready if it holds together when you press mixture between your thumb and index finger. Add a little more cream if it is too crumbly.

2. Pile dough onto countertop. Using the heel of your hand, knead dough bits until they cohere. Collect dough into a ball and flatten into a disk. Cover with plastic wrap and chill for at least 3 hours.

3. Roll out pastry and press into a shallow 9-inch pie pan. Trim excess pastry to ½ inch from edge, then tuck it under. Crimp edges. Line with foil and pie weights or dried beans. Chill pastry for 30 minutes.

4. Preheat oven to 400 degrees. Bake pie shell for 15 minutes. Remove foil and weights, reduce heat to 350 degrees and bake until pie shell is golden brown, at least 5 minutes longer. Remove from oven and let cool.

5. In a small saucepan, combine blueberries and ⅓ cup granulated sugar. Place over medium heat and cook at a rapid simmer until berries wilt and juices thicken, about 15 minutes. Let cool. Mixture should resemble a loose jam.

6. In a pan, whisk together remaining egg yolks, lemon zest, lemon juice and 2 tablespoons granulated sugar. Cook over low heat until mixture coats back of a spoon, 2 to 4 minutes. Do not overcook or eggs will curdle. Remove from heat and stir in gelatin. While it cools, whip ⅔ cup heavy cream until it holds stiff peaks. Separately, whip egg whites and pinch of salt until foamy, then gradually beat in remaining granulated sugar until whites hold stiff peaks.

7. Fold cooled gelatin mixture into beaten egg whites. Then fold in the whipped cream, followed by blueberries. Mix gently until smooth. Pour into pie shell and chill for at least 3 hours before serving.

Chocolate Banana Cream Pie

Wayne
Harley
Brachman

Very few of the recipes in this book provide leftovers: they are designed to be self-contained desserts. But who wouldn't want leftover chocolate pudding, especially one as delectable as this? The pudding mixture can be halved, though with difficulty because of the quantity of eggs. The bananas can also be omitted, if you prefer. And this dessert can be baked as a straight-sided tart instead of as a pie. Wayne Harley Brachman is a pastry chef known for his old-fashioned diner-style desserts.

TIME: 30 minutes, plus cooling and chilling   YIELD: 8 servings

4 ounces bittersweet chocolate,
   chopped
2 tablespoons unsalted butter
2 tablespoons cornstarch
½ cup unsweetened Dutch-
   process cocoa
½ cup granulated sugar
2½ cups milk
1 large egg

2 large egg yolks
1 prebaked 9-inch pie crust or 9½-
   inch tart shell (rich butter
   pastry, ½ recipe, page 521)
2 ripe bananas, peeled and sliced
   ¼ inch thick
½ cup confectioners' sugar
2 cups heavy cream

1. Using a microwave oven or double boiler, melt together the chocolate and the butter. In a medium bowl, combine the cornstarch, ¼ cup of the cocoa and ¼ cup of the granulated sugar. Add ¼ cup of the milk, and stir to blend. Add the egg and yolks, and whisk until smooth.

2. In a medium saucepan, combine the remaining 2¼ cups milk and the remaining ¼ cup granulated sugar. Place over medium heat until scalded. Slowly drizzle the milk into the cocoa mixture, stirring gently with a whisk to blend the mixture without aerating it.

3. Return the mixture to the saucepan, and cook over medium heat until tiny bubbles boil up for 3 seconds. Do not overcook. Remove from the heat, and strain into a clean bowl. Add the melted chocolate mixture, and stir until thoroughly blended. Place waxed paper directly on the surface of the pudding and let cool at room temperature 1 hour, then refrigerate until completely chilled.

4. To assemble, spoon half the pudding into the baked pie shell (reserve the remainder for another use, or eat it plain). Arrange the banana slices evenly and decoratively over the top. Sift the confectioners' sugar and remaining cocoa together into a bowl, and add the heavy cream; mix well. Whip until the cream is the consistency of shaving cream. Spoon over the bananas in the pie shell, and serve.

Coconut Cream Pie with Macadamia Nut Crust

Herbsaint,
New Orleans,
Louisiana

In classic American baking, coconut custard pie is usually made with the coconut custard baked in the crust. This is a lusher, creamier version, in a macadamia nut crust, with a coconut pastry cream filling from Herbsaint, a New Orleans restaurant.

TIME: 1 hour, plus chilling   YIELD: 16 servings (two 9-inch pies)

2 cups sugar

¼ cup cornstarch

6 large egg yolks

7 cups heavy cream

½ vanilla bean, split, insides
  scraped out

8 ounces macadamia nuts, toasted
  and cooled

1 cup all-purpose flour

9 tablespoons unsalted butter

½ teaspoon salt

2½ cups unsweetened coconut,
  lightly toasted and cooled

1. In a small bowl, whisk together 1 cup sugar and cornstarch. In a medium bowl, whisk 5 egg yolks with ½ cup of the cream. Whisk sugar and cornstarch into yolk mixture.

2. In a medium heavy-bottom saucepan, combine 2½ cups of the cream and the scrapings from the vanilla bean. Place the saucepan over medium heat. As cream just starts to boil, whisk a few hot spoonfuls into the yolk mixture to temper it. Reduce heat under pan to low. Pour yolk mixture into the pan, beating, and stir constantly with a wooden spoon until steam just starts to rise from it and the mixture is thick. Transfer to a shallow container, and place plastic wrap on the surface to keep a skin from forming. Refrigerate until cold and firm, at least 1 hour.

3. Combine nuts and flour in a food processor. Process until nuts are finely ground, pulsing to keep them from becoming pasty. In a mixer with a paddle attachment, cream the butter with ½ cup sugar. Add remaining yolk, and mix thoroughly. Add nut mixture and salt, and mix until smooth. Wrap in plastic wrap, and refrigerate until chilled, about 1 hour.

4. Divide nut dough in half. Roll out half between two sheets of plastic wrap to make a circle 10 inches in diameter. Repeat with remaining dough.

Line two 9-inch tart pans, and chill in freezer until very firm, about 30 minutes.

5. Preheat oven to 350 degrees. Line shells with foil and pie weights, and bake until lightly colored, about 15 minutes. Remove pie weights, and continue to bake until the crust is golden brown, 10 to 15 minutes more. Allow to cool.

6. In bowl of a mixer fitted with a whisk attachment combine remaining 4 cups heavy cream, ½ cup sugar and 2 cups of the chilled pastry cream. (Reserve any remaining pastry cream for another use.) Whisk at high speed until soft peaks form. Add coconut, and continue whisking mixture by hand until very stiff. Spoon into cooled tart shells and smooth tops. Serve immediately, or refrigerate until ready to serve.

Double Crust Peach Pie

Deborah
Tyler

This is a summertime pie that depends on peaches that are ripe but not soft, and full of flavor. Do not compromise on the quality of the fruit. Deborah Tyler is the owner of Pie Kitchen in Nyack, New York, where she is known as "the pie lady."

TIME: 1 hour 30 minutes   YIELD: 8 servings

5 or 6 large ripe freestone
   peaches, peeled, pitted and
   sliced ½ inch thick
¼ cup cornstarch

1 tablespoon unsalted butter,
   softened
¾ cup plus 2 teaspoons sugar
Butter pastry, chilled (page 520)

1. Preheat oven to 450 degrees.

2. Combine peaches with cornstarch, butter and ¾ cup sugar.

3. Divide dough into two equal portions. Roll one on a floured surface into an 11-inch circle. Place rolled dough in a 9-inch pie pan. Use a knife to cut dough flush with top of pan. Spread peach mixture in pan.

4. Roll second ball into an 11-inch circle. Place over top of pie. Lift edges of bottom layer, and tuck top layer below. Crimp. Make 6 cuts on top of pie with a knife. Sprinkle handful of sugar over top. Bake on bottom rack for 10 minutes, and then reduce the oven temperature to 350 degrees and bake 50 minutes longer. Serve warm or cooled.

Key Lime Pie

Originally, the Key lime pie was a boater's recipe. The interaction of the acidic lime juice with the condensed milk caused the filling to thicken without cooking or refrigeration. In this rendition, from Joe's Stone Crab, the famous Miami Beach restaurant, the filling is lightly baked, then frozen briefly for insurance. These days, fresh Key limes, which are smaller and yellower than standard Persian limes, are often sold around the country. Fresh Key lime juice is also available. Try to use Key limes or the juice. They will make the filling yellow, not green, which is as it should be.

TIME: 45 minutes, plus chilling   YIELD: 8 servings

Joe's
Stone Crab,
Miami Beach,
Florida

1 cup plus 2½ tablespoons graham cracker crumbs

5 tablespoons unsalted butter, melted, plus butter for pan

⅓ cup granulated sugar

3 large egg yolks

1½ teaspoons grated lime zest, preferably Key lime

1 14-ounce can sweetened condensed milk

⅔ cup Key lime juice, preferably fresh

1 cup heavy cream

3 tablespoons confectioners' sugar

1. Preheat oven to 350 degrees. In a large mixing bowl, combine graham crackers, butter and granulated sugar. Press mixture into bottom and sides of a buttered 9-inch pie pan, forming a neat border around edge. Bake crust until set and golden, about 5 minutes.

2. Using an electric mixer with a whisk attachment, beat egg yolks and lime zest at high speed until very shiny, about 5 minutes. Gradually add condensed milk, and continue to beat until thick, about 3 to 4 minutes. Reduce speed to low. Add lime juice, and mix just until combined.

3. Pour lime mixture into crust. Bake until filling has just set, about 10 minutes. Cool to room temperature, then refrigerate.

4. Place pie in freezer for 15 to 20 minutes before serving. In an electric-mixer, combine cream and confectioners' sugar. Whip until nearly stiff. Cut pie into wedges; serve very cold, each wedge topped with a large dollop of whipped cream, or top pie with whipped cream before serving.

TEST KITCHEN:
Behind Every Successful Pie Stands the Right Pan
By Amanda Hesser

Like casserole dishes, pie pans are equipment that few cooks put much thought into choosing. Many use what was handed down to them, or they buy something pretty, or they cheap out and go for an aluminum pan from the grocery store.

But these are not prudent decisions, for the pie pan is as crucial to the finished pie as the dough. Different materials hold heat differently, and different designs affect the way the pie cooks. If the fit is wrong, the pie will suffer for it. Because a pie is served in its pan, it ought to be one that you want to look at. And considering the effort it takes to make a pie, you should get it right.

A great variety of materials are available: glass, aluminum, stoneware, nonstick and ceramic. And even more designs. Some are deep, some are shallow. Some have wide rims, some have none.

After testing many pans, I found that a shallow aluminum pan, perforated on the bottom, resulted in pumpkin filling cooked through before the dough, producing a gummy, white, half-cooked dough and a filling on the verge of cracking.

A glass Pyrex pie pan did not get hot enough to cook the pastry before the filling. And with a wet filling like pumpkin, which tends to weep liquid after baking, the pastry should be completely cooked through. One easy solution, of course, is to fully or partially bake the crust (blind-bake) before filling it. It can be done, and often is, with a single-crust pie, but not one with a double crust.

A great bargain, by contrast, is a nonstick pie pan, which held heat well and baked evenly, producing a pumpkin pie with a browned crust, still tender from the butter. But the nonstick coating displayed other problems, not to mention having no aesthetic appeal. While slices were easy to remove from the pan, the surface was so slippery that part of the crust's border simply slid off the pie while it was baking. Form the border closer to the inside of the rim.

Then there was an 8-inch, shallow, wide-lip ceramic pan that is a beautiful dish and also works well. The pastry was as brown as almond skin and not at all doughy, and the wide rim made the pan easy to transport to and from the oven. It was not, however, perfect for pumpkin pie. A dish this shallow seems better suited for double-crusted pies with fruits, like apples, mounded high in the center.

Classic-looking Burgundy-clay pie pans come in bright, happy colors, and some have fluted rims, so even if your pie doesn't look great, what's cradling it does. But it makes the sides of the crust cook quicker than the bottom. It's a problem easily solved by baking the pie closer to the bottom of the oven or on top of a baking stone.

The best pan was the 9½-inch deep-dish stoneware pan. It has an odd design, with ridged sides that have a soft slope and no real lip. Though it is made for thicker pies, like double-crusted peach pies, it worked well with pumpkin pie. and allowed the pumpkin filling to puff up and bake to a soft puddinglike texture without cracking. The gentle slope of the sides also made it easy to lift out slices. More important, though, the pie baked evenly. The entire crust was a deep golden brown, like bread crust, and crisp but tender.

I could not leave out grocery store aluminum foil pans. Typically, they come three to a pack for about $2. They are so cheap for a reason: they are incredibly flimsy. Getting the pie with its loose filling into the oven was a near disaster: the pan almost folded in half. The very bottom layer of the pastry cooked, but not the rest, giving it a cardboard texture. Pie pans just aren't that expensive. You might as well splurge.

Key Lime Chiffon Pie

Marian
Burros

Though the juice of fresh Key limes, or the bottled juice, should be used in the filling, the decorative slices of lime for decoration can be regular Persian limes, which are more attractive. You will need about a dozen Key limes for a cup of juice. Marian Burros is a food writer for *The New York Times.*

TIME: 45 minutes   YIELD: 12 to 16 servings (2 pies)

3 cups crushed gingersnap
   cookies
1⅓ cups crushed pecans
⅔ cup melted unsalted butter
2 tablespoons grated lime zest
2 packages unflavored gelatin
2 cups sugar

½ teaspoon salt
8 eggs, separated
1 cup Key lime juice, preferably
   fresh
3 cups heavy cream
Thinly sliced limes for garnish

1. Preheat oven to 350 degrees. In a food processor, grind gingersnaps and pecans to fine crumbs. Mix in a bowl with butter and 2 teaspoons lime zest. Pat mixture into bottom and sides of two 9-inch pie plates. Bake for 6 minutes. Set aside.

2. Mix gelatin with 1 cup sugar and the salt in a saucepan. In a bowl, thoroughly beat egg yolks with lime juice and ½ cup water. Stir yolk mixture into gelatin mixture. Cook over medium heat, stirring just until mixture comes to a simmer. Remove from heat, and stir in 2 teaspoons lime zest. Chill, stirring occasionally, until mixture mounds lightly when dropped from a spoon, 20 to 30 minutes.

3. In a bowl, beat egg whites until soft peaks form. Gradually beat in remaining sugar. Fold into gelatin mixture. In separate bowl, whip 2 cups cream and fold into filling. Pile into pie shells, and chill until firm. Pies may be made a day ahead.

4. To serve, whip remaining cream and drop mounds on top of pies. Top each pie with slices of lime, and sprinkle with remaining grated zest.

Shaker Lemon Pie ☀

Most lemon pies are open-face. This one is a simple revelation, but, then, the Shaker communities are known for the simplicity of everything they do. Pleasant Hill is in Kentucky.

TIME: 45 minutes, plus resting and cooling   YIELD: 8 to 10 servings

Pleasant Hill
Shaker
Community,
Kentucky

2 large thin-skinned seedless
   lemons, washed, sliced paper-
   thin

2 cups sugar
Butter pastry (page 520)
4 large eggs, well beaten

1. In a bowl, combine lemons and sugar. Allow to stand at room temperature, mixing occasionally, for at least 2 hours or overnight.

2. Preheat oven to 450 degrees. Divide pastry in half and line pie pan. Add beaten eggs to lemon mixture, and stir well. Pour into pie shell, arranging lemon slices evenly. Roll out remaining pastry and cover with top crust. Crimp edges. Cut slits near center of crust.

3. Bake pie for 15 minutes, then reduce heat to 375 degrees. Continue to bake until a knife inserted near rim of pie comes out clean, 20 to 25 minutes. Center of pie will continue to set as it cools. Serve at room temperature or chilled.

Ginger Buttermilk Pie

Richard
Langer

The filling, a kind of custard, is at once tart and creamy. Plain yogurt can be used in place of buttermilk. Richard Langer is a food writer who has contributed to *The New York Times.*

TIME: 1 hour, plus cooling   YIELD: 8 to 10 servings (one 9-inch pie)

1 cup plus 1 tablespoon all-
  purpose flour, plus more for
  rolling dough
½ teaspoon salt
¼ cup canola or grapeseed oil
2 tablespoons milk
1 cup sugar

3 large eggs, beaten
4 ounces (1 stick) unsalted butter,
  melted and cooled
1 cup cultured buttermilk
1 tablespoon lemon juice
1 teaspoon ground ginger

1. Preheat oven to 425 degrees. In a medium bowl, sift together all but 3 tablespoons of the flour, and the salt. In a small bowl, combine the oil and milk, and blend with a fork. Make a well in the center of the flour, and add the oil mixture. Stir with a fork to mix lightly; then add ½ teaspoon cold water. Continue to blend the dough, handling as little as possible, and shape into a ball.

2. On a lightly floured surface, roll out the dough into a 10-inch disk. Fit the dough into a 9-inch pie pan, folding under and fluting the edge. Prick the dough with a fork, and line with foil and pastry weights. Bake 10 minutes, until pastry looks dry. Remove from the oven.

3. While the crust is baking, combine the sugar and remaining 3 tablespoons of flour. Add the eggs, melted butter, buttermilk, lemon juice and ginger. Transfer to the container of a blender or food processor, and mix briefly at the lowest speed or pulse briefly to combine. Do not allow the mixture to become foamy.

4. Pour the filling into the pie shell, and bake 10 minutes. If crust seems to brown too fast, cover the edge with strips of foil. Reduce oven temperature to 350 degrees, and bake until a knife or toothpick inserted into the center comes out clean, about 20 minutes longer. Serve at room temperature.

Chess Pie

Legend has it that the name of the pie comes from the encounter between a Southerner and a waitress in Kentucky. When he asked what kind of pie was served, he was told "jes' pie," hence the name. And it seems that virtually every cook in the South has a supposedly authoritative version of what has become known as Chess Pie. This recipe was sent to Craig Claiborne, the former food editor of *The New York Times*, anonymously, from "A True Southern Belle."

Craig
Claiborne

TIME: 1 hour, plus cooling   YIELD: 8 to 12 servings

Flaky pastry (page 522)
4 ounces (1 stick) unsalted butter,
    softened
2 cups sugar
1 tablespoon flour
2 tablespoons white cornmeal,
    preferably stone-ground
Salt to taste

4 large eggs
¼ cup milk
¼ cup lemon juice
2 teaspoons grated lemon zest
Sweetened whipped cream for
    garnish
Freshly grated nutmeg for dusting

1. Preheat oven to 350 degrees. Place a rack at the lowest position in the oven. Line a 9-inch pie plate with pastry and flute the rim.

2. Place butter and sugar into the bowl of an electric mixer and beat until creamy. Beat in flour, cornmeal and salt. Add the eggs, one at a time, and beat well after each addition. Beat in milk, lemon juice and zest.

3. Pour mixture into the pie shell and place on lowest oven rack. Bake 45 minutes, until filling is golden and firm. Allow to cool to room temperature.

4. Serve in small wedges, topping each with a dollop of whipped cream and a sprinkling of freshly grated nutmeg.

Pumpkin Pie with Ginger

Roland
Mesnier,
The White
House,
Washington,
D.C.

This is a spicy, custardy Thanksgiving classic. But because it comes from a former chef at the White House, it is designed to provide servings for a big table of guests. At the White House for Thanksgiving, they would bake a dozen of them.

TIME: 1 hour 10 minutes, plus cooling and chilling   YIELD: 10 to 12 servings

3 large eggs

2 large egg yolks

1 cup sugar

½ teaspoon salt

1½ teaspoons ground cinnamon

¾ teaspoon ground ginger

¼ teaspoon ground cloves

2¼ cups milk

2⅔ cups unsweetened canned
    pumpkin puree

1 large pie shell (½ recipe,
    page 520)

1 cup heavy cream

Candied ginger, finely cut

1. Preheat oven to 375 degrees. Beat whole eggs and yolks lightly. Beat sugar and eggs by hand or machine until creamy, and beat in salt, cinnamon, ginger, cloves and milk until thoroughly blended. Stir in the pumpkin. Pour into prebaked pie shell.

2. Bake about 1 hour, until a toothpick inserted in center comes out clean. Do not jiggle. Cool pie on wire rack, then chill.

3. To serve, whip cream and pipe around edge of pie; decorate with candied ginger.

Two-Crust Pumpkin Pie

Pumpkin pie is invariably filled with a custard made from the vegetable puree. It's not my favorite. So one year I experimented with this pie, for which I handled the pumpkin like apples in a two-crust pie. It was a great success.

Florence
Fabricant

TIME: 2 hours   YIELD: 8 servings

5 cups peeled, diced pumpkin or butternut squash

⅔ cup raisins

1 cup light brown sugar

3 tablespoons all-purpose flour, plus more for rolling pastry

1½ tablespoons frozen orange juice concentrate, thawed

½ teaspoon ground ginger

¼ teaspoon ground nutmeg

¼ teaspoon ground cloves

Rich butter pastry (page 521)

2 tablespoons unsalted butter

1 tablespoon heavy cream

Vanilla ice cream or orange sorbet for serving

1. Preheat oven to 425 degrees. Combine pumpkin, raisins, brown sugar, flour, orange juice concentrate and the spices in a bowl.

2. Divide pastry in slightly unequal halves. Roll out larger portion on lightly floured board, and line pie pan. Spoon in pumpkin mixture. Dot with butter. Cover with top crust. Seal and crimp edges, brush with cream, and cut a few decorative slits in top for steam to escape.

3. Bake 15 minutes. Reduce the heat to 350 degrees, and continue baking until the crust is golden brown, about 1 hour. Serve warm or at room temperature with ice cream or sorbet.

Kabocha Squash Pie ✳

Pichet
Ong

Kabocha squash are easy to handle, but other kinds of winter squash, including butternut and acorn, can be used instead. Pichet Ong is a New York pastry chef whose desserts combine Western and Asian flavors.

TIME: About 2½ hours   YIELD: 8 servings

1 medium kabocha squash, about 3 pounds

¾ cup (2 ounces) walnuts, toasted and cooled

½ cup light brown sugar

¾ cup graham cracker crumbs (about 7 crackers)

Grated zest of 1 lime

2¼ teaspoons ground cinnamon

1⅛ teaspoons ground ginger

1¼ teaspoons salt

4 tablespoons (2 ounces) unsalted butter, melted

10 ounces (1⅓ cups) cream cheese, at room temperature

1 cup granulated sugar

¾ teaspoon freshly ground nutmeg

1½ tablespoons brandy

2 large eggs, at room temperature

Crème fraîche, for serving, optional

Ginger butterscotch sauce (page 540)

1. Bring an inch of water to a boil in a large covered pot fitted with a steamer basket or rack. Put in squash, cover and steam, replenishing water as needed, until fork tender, about 1 hour. Turn squash over halfway through steaming. Set squash aside until cool enough to handle.

2. Preheat oven to 300 degrees. In a food processor, combine walnuts with a few tablespoons brown sugar and pulse a few times, until nuts are coarsely ground. In a large bowl, whisk nuts with graham cracker crumbs, remaining brown sugar, lime zest, ¾ teaspoon cinnamon, ⅛ teaspoon ginger and ½ teaspoon salt. Pour melted butter over this mixture, and mix with your fingers until butter is distributed. Press evenly into a 10-inch glass pie plate. Bake crust until lightly browned, about 12 minutes, then set aside.

4. When squash is cool, cut it in half and scoop out seeds and pulp. Scoop squash flesh into a measuring cup until you have 2½ cups.

5. In a food processor, process cream cheese with granulated sugar, remaining spices and salt until light and smooth. Scrape down bowl, add squash and process until smooth. Mix in brandy and then eggs, one at a time. Finish mixing by hand with a rubber spatula.

6. Place pie plate on a baking sheet and pour filling into crust. Bake until just set in center, about 1 hour. Let cool, then serve, topped with crème fraîche and drizzled with ginger butterscotch sauce.

Maple Bourbon Sweet Potato Pie

Karen
Barker,
Magnolia
Grill,
Durham,
North
Carolina

Sweet potato pie is a Southern staple. Bourbon and maple syrup set this one apart. Magnolia Grill is an innovative restaurant in Durham, North Carolina, owned by Karen and Ben Barker. Mrs. Barker is the pastry chef.

TIME: 2 hours, plus cooling   YIELD: 8 servings

2 medium or 3 small sweet
  potatoes (about 1½ pounds)
¾ cup heavy cream
6 tablespoons maple syrup
5 tablespoons dark brown sugar
4 tablespoons unsalted butter,
  melted
¼ cup bourbon
3 large eggs
1 large egg yolk

1 teaspoon vanilla extract
¼ teaspoon salt
¼ teaspoon freshly grated nutmeg
¼ teaspoon ground cinnamon
⅛ teaspoon ground cloves
A few grinds of black pepper
1 baked 9-inch pie crust (rich
  butter pastry, ½ recipe, page
  521)

1. Preheat oven to 425 degrees. With a fork, pierce sweet potatoes, and place on foil-lined baking sheet. Roast until soft, about 1 hour, turning once. Cool, peel and put flesh through a food mill, or mash smoothly with a potato masher to make 2 cups of puree.

2. Reduce heat to 350 degrees. In a medium bowl, whisk puree and remaining ingredients to combine. Pour into prepared crust.

3. Place pie plate onto a cookie sheet, and bake until filling is just about set, or when a knife inserted 1 inch from the edge comes out clean, 45 to 50 minutes. Cool pie on wire rack to room temperature.

TARTS

A tart is not a pie. Tart implies a flat, straight-sided shell that is either pre-baked or baked with a filling. A tart pan is often fluted, with a separate bottom, so the sides can be removed after baking for a more glamorous presentation.

As for the pastry, tarts and pies are not particularly different. Find a pastry you like and can handle with ease, and keep it for everything you bake. When fitting your pastry into the tart shell, ease it in, gently pushing down, without stretching it, and allow some overhang. Then you can simply roll your rolling pin over the sharp edge of the tin, which will automatically cut away the excess pastry. Tarts are often made with pre-baked pastry shells. Do not hesitate to fully bake the pastry, fill it, then bake it with the filling. To pre-bake, you will probably have to prick the bottom to keep the pastry from shrinking. But more important is to line the pastry with a sheet of foil and weight it with pastry weights (ceramic or metal) or with dried beans for the first 10 minutes, which also keeps the pastry from shrinking. Then you remove the foil and weights and continue baking until the pastry is golden. This is the method to use to prepare a tart shell for an unbaked filling and, often, for a filling that does require baking.

Among the recipes in this section are French tartes Tatin, the famous caramelized upside-down apple tart (but also made with other fruit). Tartes Tatin are made in pie pans, not loose-bottom tart pans. But with their name, they could only go into the tart section.

Apple Tart

Alex
Witchel

A puff pastry base makes this tart very French. Frozen puff pastry can be used, but try to find a brand that is made with butter (check the ingredient list). Instead of frozen puff pastry, butter pastry or rich butter pastry for a 9-inch pie or tart (pages 520, 521) can be substituted. Alex Witchel is a reporter for *The New York Times*.

TIME: 1 hour   YIELD: 4 to 6 servings

1 lemon
2 to 3 Granny Smith apples
1 frozen puff pastry sheet, 8 to 10
    ounces, thawed, or quick puff
    pastry (page 526)

2 tablespoons superfine sugar
1 tablespoon unsalted butter,
    melted
Crème fraîche for serving,
    optional

1. Preheat oven to 425 degrees. Juice lemon and pour juice into a wide bowl. Peel, halve and core apples. Place in the bowl with the lemon juice and add cold water to cover.

2. Place puff pastry on a large baking sheet. Use a sharp knife to lightly score a half-inch border; do not cut all the way through. (This will allow a frame of pastry to rise above the apple filling.) Refrigerate until needed.

3. Pat apple halves dry, and cut each half into quarters. Thinly slice each quarter. Remove pastry from refrigerator, and sprinkle with 1 table-spoon sugar. Working inside scored lines, place neat rows of closely over-lapping apples, until pastry is covered.

4. Brush apples with melted butter, and sprinkle with remaining sugar. Bake until pastry puffs around apples and fruit is soft and lightly colored, 20 to 25 minutes. Serve warm with crème fraîche, if desired.

Apple Almond Tart with Gingered Streusel Topping ✳

French pastry chefs prefer to bake with Golden Delicious apples because they are sweet, requiring less sugar, and have a fairly dry texture so they hold their shape. Amanda Hesser is working on a new edition of *The New York Times Cookbook*.

Amanda
Hesser

TIME: 1 hour 10 minutes, plus cooling   YIELD: 6 servings

5 tablespoons cold unsalted butter
¾ cup plus 2½ tablespoons sugar
5 Golden Delicious apples, peeled, cored and quartered
12 thin slices peeled ginger
1½ cups plus 2 tablespoons all-purpose flour

¾ teaspoon salt
½ cup vegetable oil
2 tablespoons milk
½ teaspoon almond extract
2 tablespoons minced crystallized ginger

1. Preheat oven to 425 degrees. Place a large nonstick sauté pan over medium-high heat. Add 3 tablespoons butter and 2 tablespoons sugar. When mixture starts to darken, add apples and ginger slices, and toss to coat. Sauté until apples begin to color lightly and juice has cooked down to a sauce, about 10 minutes. Remove from heat, and let cool.

2. In a 9-inch round straight-sided nonstick or glass cake pan, combine 1½ cups flour, ½ teaspoon salt and ½ tablespoon sugar. Gently mix ingredients with fingers and make a well in center. In a small bowl, whisk together oil, milk and almond extract. Pour oil mixture into well, and mix with a fork just enough to dampen. Using your fingertips, pat out dough so it covers bottom of pan and comes up sides about ½ inch (pastry should be about ⅛ inch thick). Place in refrigerator until needed.

3. To make streusel topping, in a small bowl, combine ¾ cup sugar, 2 tablespoons flour, ¼ teaspoon salt and crystallized ginger. Cut in remaining 2 tablespoons cold butter.

4. Lay apples in a fanned circle in pastry-lined pan. Tuck slices of ginger among apple slices. Pour over any excess juices, and sprinkle streusel over top. Bake until slightly browned, about 40 minutes. Serve warm or at room temperature.

Rustic Apple Tart with Cider Sorbet

Charlie
Palmer,
Aureole,
New York

Because the pastry is made into a flat, almost free-form shape without a crimped or fluted edge, it deserves the name rustic. Tarts made like this are also called galettes. Charlie Palmer is one of America's premier chefs, one of the first generation of great American chefs. Aureole is his flagship.

TIME: 1½ hours   YIELD: 8 to 10 servings

3 medium Granny Smith apples,
   peeled and cored
Juice of 1 lemon
3 tablespoons fresh apple cider
½ cup plus 2 tablespoons sugar
3 tablespoons Wondra flour

1 tablespoon plus ¼ teaspoon
   ground cinnamon
3 tablespoons unsalted butter,
   melted
Flaky pastry, chilled (page 522)
Cider sorbet (page 471)

1. Halve apples lengthwise, and cut each half into paper-thin slices. Place slices in a mixing bowl, and sprinkle with lemon juice. Add cider, and toss to combine. Add ½ cup sugar, flour and 1 tablespoon cinnamon, and toss to coat well. Drizzle butter over the top, and again toss to combine.

2. Preheat oven to 375 degrees. Place dough on a lightly floured surface, and roll it, from the center out, into a circle about 9 inches in diameter and ¼ inch thick. Carefully lift dough onto an 8-inch pizza pan or a pizza stone. There will be about an inch of overhang. Fold the overhang under to give the pastry circle a double thickness along the edge. Using fingertips, crimp a neat, fluted rim on the edge.

3. Working from the edge toward the center, make concentric circles of slightly overlapping apple slices, keeping the outside edge of the slices facing the crimped edge of the dough. At the center of the tart, use a few apple slices to make a slightly raised rosette shape. Combine remaining sugar with remaining cinnamon. Sprinkle the top of the apples with cinnamon sugar.

4. Place tart in oven, and bake until crust is golden and apples are barely tender, caramelized and beginning to brown on the edges, about 40 minutes. Remove from oven, and allow to rest for 15 minutes. Cut into wedges, and serve with cider sorbet.

EN ROUTE: SOLOGNE
The Tart That Turned France Upside Down
By William Grimes

LAMOTTE-BEUVRON, FRANCE

In the United States, small towns get to brag if they give birth to a vice-president or a major league pitcher. In France, a dessert can put you on the map, and what after-dinner classic could be more famous than the tarte Tatin, the beguilingly simple combination of thick caramelized apple slices resting on a bed of flaky pastry?

It turns up, in crude outline, on the billboard outside this town in the Loire Valley due south of Orléans, reminding motorists that they are entering "the home of the genuine tarte Tatin." Those who miss the billboard probably make the connection as they pass by the big, square Hôtel Tatin, reputed birthplace of the renowned tart. If not, they will eventually get the point walking along the streets of Lamotte-Beuvron, where every pastry shop—and there are a lot of them for a town of fewer than five thousand people—puts its tartes Tatin front and center in the windows. Jack Lejarre has a silver trophy in his. Last year, the official tarte Tatin booster society, the Confrérie des Lichonneux de Tarte Tatin, declared his tart to be the finest in the land.

Like pizza in New York, or saltwater taffy on the Jersey Shore, the tarts are unavoidable. There are minitarts for a single serving, tarts for six and jumbo tarts for eight. As often as not, the saleswoman who puts the tart in a cardboard box and ties it up with a ribbon will include a flyer that recounts the history of the tart, lists the Ten Commandments of the tarte Tatin lovers (No. 1: "You will love the tarte Tatin with all your heart and soul") and offers a recipe in rhyme, cleverly constructed so that the first letter of each line spells tarte Tatin. There are two ways to interpret the feverish promotion surrounding the tarte Tatin. Either Lamotte-Beuvron, touristically speaking, does not have a lot to work with, or the tarte Tatin is truly a wondrous thing.

The correct answer is B.

Of course, there are bad tartes Tatin. You can find them at the Hôtel Tatin, as a matter of fact. But the good ones can be very good, all the more impressive in their absolute simplicity. The filling has but three ingredients: apples, butter and sugar. There's a crust, usually puff pastry but sometimes pâte brisée, or short crust. And that's it. A thick, buttery layer of firm, caramelized apples sitting on top of crunchy pastry.

The trick lies in the cooking. The tarte Tatin is what the French call a *tarte renversée*, or upside-down tart, which means you can't see the filling as it cooks, because the pastry bottom sits on top. And because you can't see the filling, you cannot know precisely how brown the apples are getting.

Pastry-makers go by feel. They monitor the bubbling cooking liquids, looking for the right color. Sometimes they get distracted, and the tart goes awry. "Sometimes I take my eye off the oven," said Claude Fouquiau, a pastry-maker in Nouan-Le-Fuzelier, near Lamotte-Beuvron. "Those are the tarts I don't sell."

To the amateur eye, they all look pretty much alike. And the investigator who tries to get the inside line on what makes one different from another runs into the French version of the wall of silence. It's a perplexed look that says, "Why on earth would anyone want to know the answer to this?" followed by a shrug and a one-size-fits-all nonexplanation condensed into three little words, "*tour de main.*"

Tour de main means skill or knack. Stunningly nonspecific, the term popped up in every pastry shop I visited, and there were times, as I searched for the perfect tarte Tatin, that I began to suspect that the phrase was being used to disguise a simple, shocking fact. The average French pastry-maker cannot explain what makes his tart different because he has never bothered to look at the competition.

At the shop of Jacques Sailer, Mme. Sailer seemed amazed to hear that Mr. Lejarre, a few hundred feet down the road, liked to caramelize his apples aggressively, producing a tart liberally dotted with large black spots. "Really?" Mme. Sailer said, as if hearing this bit of news for the first time. She seemed genuinely puzzled. "Maybe he just left them in the oven too long," she offered.

It took persistent questioning to move the conversation past *tour de main*. But once over that hurdle, the admirable French enthusiasm for technique took over. Which apples to use, how thin to roll the pastry, how long to caramelize—the list of variables went on and on. The tart is so simple that a millimeter's difference in the thickness of the crust can establish a distinct style, even a separate school. A little too much sugar can make the apples taste candied. Too much butter, and the tart can cloy. Some pâtissiers turn the excess crust upward, creating a rim. Others insist that the crust not overlap the topping. The fine points, in tarte-Tatin-land, can be sliced very fine.

I know. I spent the better part of a morning walking up and down Lamotte-Beuvron, buying one tart after another. Before long, I had a stack of boxes that extended from my outstretched hands to my chin. I looked like a Domino's delivery boy.

After foraging in nearby towns, I had a backseat full of tartes Tatin, which I ferried to my hotel and arranged side by side for a professional tasting. When it was all over, I was wavering in my determination to honor the First Commandment. It's one thing to love a tarte Tatin heart and soul. But a dozen?

All of them start with apples, of course. The Loire Valley abounds in apples, but traditionally the apple par excellence for the tarte Tatin has been the Reine de Reinette, a very handsome orangish-red apple with thin yellow stripes, a firm texture and a nice balance of sweetness and acidity. Its season, however, is short, from October to mid-November, and more popular, well-promoted varieties have pushed it aside. As a result, almost no one uses it for a tarte Tatin.

An exception is Didier Clement, the chef at the Michelin two-star Lion d'Or in Romorantin-Lanthenay. Gala and Golden Delicious, he insists, are too sweet, and sometimes have a slight banana note. When the Reine de Reinette disappears, along with the closely related Reinette Clochard and Reinette Chanteclerc, he moves to a variety called Belle de Boskoop.

But elsewhere in the Sologne, pastry-makers use Gala and Golden Delicious, peeled and cored, then sliced in quarters and arranged in tight-packed concentric circles in a high-sided tart pan liberally smeared with butter and sprinkled with sugar. Mr. Sailer has a trick. He peels his apples the night before so that they dry out a bit. This helps him avoid a serious pitfall, an over-abundance of liquid in the pan, resulting in mushy apples and a soggy crust.

Each pastry-maker has his own opinion about how to caramelize the apples, and how much. Mr. Sailer shoots for a golden brown. Mr. Fouquiau goes a couple of degrees darker, achieving a light chestnut color. The prizewinning Mr. Lejarre pushes his foot all the way to the floor, cooking his apples until they are dark brown with a black spot in the center. Some chefs start their caramelization on the stove top and finish it up in the oven. Others do it all on top of the stove.

"I like an apple that's well perfumed, which is why I use Galas," Mr. Fouquiau said. "Also, they hold their shape well." He seeks out his apples from small producers. He uses butter from the Charente. He rolls out a thin crust—"two to three centimeters." His tart, by a slim margin, scored highest on my personal chart.

He faced worthy competitors. Mr. Lejarre's imposing tart, thick on top but with a very fine crust, seemed analogous to a deep-dish Chicago-style pizza. I did not ask him if he had left his tart in the oven too long.

"Caramelization accounts for the charm of the tart," he said sternly. "It's everything."

The tart came into being, if legend is to be believed, in 1898. Stephanie and Caroline Tatin, the daughters of a baker and pastry-maker in Romorantin-Lanthenay, operated the Hôtel Tatin, a thriving enterprise thanks to its location directly across from the train station, where well-to-do hunters from all over France descended in large numbers in the fall and winter. One evening, overwhelmed by the rush of customers, Stephanie rushed into the kitchen, found that no desserts were ready, and threw a pan filled with peeled apples into the oven, unaware at first that the apples were not sitting on a crust. To retrieve the error, she put a crust on top, and the tarte Tatin was born.

No one really believes the story, not even the tarte Tatin society. Upside-down tarts were made in France long before the late nineteenth century.

But there is no question that the Hôtel Tatin's tart gained a following, although Philip and Mary Hyman, editors of the encyclopedic *Inventory of the Culinary Patrimony of France,* have found that pears were used as often as apples. Even better, it got excellent PR. The great Curnonsky, known as the prince of gastronomes, discovered it in the 1920s and published a recipe in *La France Gastronomique.* Soon afterward, the tart appeared on the menu at Maxim's in Paris, with the prim designation Tarte des Demoiselles Tatin. At that point, its reputation was made.

Fame encouraged innovation. There are flambéed tartes Tatin, mango tartes Tatin and tartes Tatin with flavored icings. Many recipes encourage cooks to add a dollop of crème fraîche with each serving, or to make it with sugar and butter on top as well as on the bottom.

The *confrérie* takes a tough line on such changes. In fact, it came into existence to defend the basic recipe from heresy. But the society does acknowledge that some newfangled tarts do homage to the original, like the dried-apricot-and-almond version served at Durand Dupont in Paris.

And surely the quince glaze that Mr. Clement applies to his tart would not be considered a complete outrage. After all, accident is part of the legend. Who's to say that a newer, better tart might not be just one more mistake away?

Official Tarte Tatin ❋

Tarte Tatin is to France what apple pie is to America. The quartered apples sop up more caramel than slices would, and give the tart its gently domed look after it is inverted. A tarte Tatin mold is a special tin-lined copper pie pan that conducts heat extremely well and enhances browning. A heavy skillet, even cast-iron, can be used. The *confrérie* is an international brotherhood of tarte Tatin aficionados.

TIME: 1 hour   YIELD: 8 servings

4 ounces (8 tablespoons) unsalted butter, softened
1 cup sugar
6 medium Gala or Golden Delicious apples, peeled, cored and quartered

1 thin (⅛-inch) sheet puff pastry, thawed if frozen, cut into a circle 12 inches in diameter, or quick puff pastry (page 526)

1. Spread butter evenly in a 10-inch tarte Tatin mold or heavy 10-inch ovenproof skillet. Spread sugar as evenly as possible on sides and bottom of pan. Beginning at edge of pan, arrange apples, peeled side down, in concentric circles, fitting apples closely together.

2. Preheat oven to 350 degrees. Place pan over high heat, and cook without stirring until sugar caramelizes and turns dark golden brown, 15 to 20 minutes. Remove from the heat, and press gently on the apples with a wooden spoon to help fill any spaces between them. Cover the apples with puff pastry, tucking the edges inside the rim of the pan. Bake until the pastry is golden brown, about 30 minutes.

3. Remove tart from oven, and allow to rest for 5 minutes. Cover pan with a large plate, and quickly invert tart; remove pan. Serve hot or warm.

Ruby Red Grapefruit Apple Tarte Tatin

Dylan
Prime,
New York

Using grapefruit is just one of many variations on the tarte Tatin. Slices of mango can also be used. Dylan Prime is a New York steak house.

TIME: 1 hour 35 minutes, plus chilling   YIELD: 8 servings

1¼ cups all-purpose flour
½ teaspoon salt
7 ounces (1¾ sticks) chilled
    unsalted butter in ½-inch cubes
½ cup sugar
3 medium ruby red grapefruit,
    peeled and in sections, all pith
    and membrane removed

3 Granny Smith apples, peeled,
    cored and sliced ½ inch thick
Whipped cream or vanilla ice
    cream, optional

1. Combine flour and salt in an electric mixer. Using a dough hook, gradually mix in 5 ounces butter (1 stick plus 2 tablespoons) at low speed. Mixture does not have to be smooth; bits of butter can be visible. Add about 2 tablespoons cold water, and mix until dough just holds together. Form into a flattened ball, wrap in plastic and chill 1 hour. Roll dough into a circle 9 inches in diameter and ⅛ inch thick. Place between 2 pieces of plastic wrap, and refrigerate on a small baking sheet.

2. Preheat oven to 375 degrees. Melt remaining butter in a 9-inch cast-iron skillet. Sprinkle sugar over butter, swirl to blend and cook on stove, undisturbed, over moderately high heat until sugar melts and turns deep golden, about 20 minutes. Remove from heat. (Hot caramel can also be made in a nonstick skillet and poured into a deep 9-inch pie pan.)

3. Arrange grapefruit and apple slices in pan: take care, as sugar is hot. Do not worry if caramel hardens before all the fruit is added. Cover fruit with pastry, and neatly tuck edges into pan.

4. Bake 40 minutes, or until pastry is evenly browned. Cool 20 minutes, then carefully invert onto a platter. Serve warm, with whipped cream or ice cream if you like.

Classic Strawberry Tart

There is no point in attempting this strawberry tart without using berries that burst with flavor. Late spring into summer is the ideal season.

TIME: 6 hours, including chilling   YIELD: 6 servings

Florence
Fabricant

Sweet pastry for 9-inch tart shell, baked and cooled (page 522)
1½ to 2 pints ripe strawberries, as uniform in size as possible
⅓ cup heavy cream

1½ cups pastry cream, chilled (page 532)
⅓ cup red currant jelly
1 tablespoon kirsch

1. Sort the strawberries. You will need about 1½ pints, or 20 ounces, to cover the tart. Rinse the berries, remove the hulls, then place them, cut-side down and not touching, on a layer of paper towel on a tray so they can dry completely. If needed, use a hair dryer on a gentle cool setting to make sure the berries are dry.

2. Whip the heavy cream until stiff. Fold the whipped cream into the pastry cream until completely incorporated. Spread this mixture over the bottom of the baked tart shell.

3. Place the berries on the cream in concentric circles as close to each other as possible. The berries should sit on top of the cream, so don't push them down into it. Refrigerate the tart.

4. Place the jelly and the kirsch in a small saucepan, and cook over medium heat until the jelly has melted and starts to bubble. Remove from the heat.

5. Remove the tart from the refrigerator, and using a pastry brush, glaze the berries with the warm jelly mixture, giving them a thin but complete coating. Serve at once, or refrigerate—but not more than a couple of hours, to prevent the pastry from becoming soggy—until ready to serve. Remove the ring from the pan before serving.

Quick Classic Berry Tart

Dorie
Greenspan

This tart can be made even more quickly with a graham cracker crust (page 525), or a nut crust (page 525), which will remove it from the category of classic. Dorie Greenspan is a food writer and cookbook author who specializes in pastry and desserts.

TIME: 15 minutes   YIELD: 8 servings

About 1½ cups pastry cream
   (page 532)
Sweet pastry for 9-inch tart
   shell, baked and cooled
   (page 522)

2 pints fresh raspberries,
   blueberries, strawberries,
   fraises des bois or an
   assortment
⅓ cup red currant jelly

1. Beat pastry cream with a whisk until it is smooth. Fill crust with enough cream to come almost to edge of rim, and smooth top. Arrange berries in concentric circles over top of tart. If you are using strawberries, cut them in half from top to bottom.

2. Bring jelly and 1 tablespoon water to a boil in a microwave oven or over heat. Working with a pastry brush, dab each berry with a spot of jelly. If you would like, you can glaze entire surface of tart, including pastry cream that peeks through berries, although you may need more glaze.

Fresh Apricot Tart

This tart, one of my favorites, takes advantage of the fleeting fresh apricot season. Select apricots that are ripe but not soft. Late in the summer, when fresh apricots are no longer available, try making this tart with Italian prune plums.

Florence
Fabricant

TIME: 1 hour, plus cooling   YIELD: 6 servings

1 cup all-purpose flour
1½ tablespoons granulated sugar
¼ teaspoon salt
7 tablespoons cold unsalted butter, in small pieces
20 fresh apricots, ripe but not soft, pitted and quartered

2 tablespoons apricot or orange liqueur
½ cup good-quality apricot preserves
3 tablespoons light brown sugar

1. Mix flour, granulated sugar and salt in a bowl. Add all but 1 tablespoon butter and, using your fingertips, a pastry blender or 2 knives, blend butter into flour mixture until coarse and mealy. This can be done by pulsing in a food processor. Sprinkle about 3 tablespoons ice water over flour and butter mixture and, using a fork, lightly mix until ingredients begin to cling together and can be formed into a dough. If you mixed the butter and flour together in a food processor, transfer them to a bowl to mix water in by hand.

2. Form dough into a flattened ball and place in freezer 10 minutes.

3. Preheat oven to 400 degrees.

4. Roll dough out between sheets of waxed paper and fit into a 9-inch tart pan. Trim edges. Cover pastry with a sheet of foil, weight with pastry weights or dry beans and bake 10 minutes, until it looks dry. Remove it from the oven and remove the foil and weights.

5. Toss apricots with liqueur.

6. Spread preserves over bottom of pastry. Arrange quartered apricots, skin side down, in a pattern on top. Sprinkle with brown sugar and dot with bits of remaining tablespoon of butter.

7. Place in oven and bake about 30 minutes, until pastry is golden brown and apricots begin to brown around the edges. Allow to cool to room temperature before serving.

Plum Hazelnut Tart

Florence
Fabricant

Though any kind of plums can be used for this tart, the late summer Italian prune plums, which are freestone and fairly uniform in size, work best. Though I prefer hazelnut pastry, almost any other pastry crust, including graham cracker, can be used for this tart.

TIME: 1 hour 15 minutes   YIELD: 8 servings

Hazelnut pastry (page 525)
⅔ cup sugar
1¼ teaspoons ground cinnamon
½ cup ground hazelnuts
¼ cup all-purpose flour
1 teaspoon baking powder
2 large eggs
½ cup heavy cream

1 teaspoon vanilla extract
2 tablespoons unsalted butter, melted
About 2 cups plums: 15 pitted Italian prune plums, quartered, or about 8 pitted sliced mixed plums

1. Preheat oven to 400 degrees. Roll out pastry and fit it into a 10-inch straight-sided tart pan. Prick pastry, line with foil and weight with pastry weights or dry beans, and bake about 6 minutes until it starts to look dry. Remove foil and weights, return to oven and bake about 10 minutes, until pastry begins to color.

2. Mix 2 tablespoons sugar with ¼ teaspoon cinnamon and set aside. Mix remaining sugar and cinnamon with hazelnuts, flour and baking powder in a bowl. Beat eggs, add cream and vanilla and stir into dry ingredients. Stir in butter. Pour into pastry shell.

3. Arrange plums on batter—if using several colors, you may want to create a pattern. Plums will sink partway into batter. Dust with sugar-cinnamon mixture. Bake 30 minutes. Allow to cool before serving.

Pear Tart

This tart, with its phyllo crust, is halfway to being a strudel. The contrast of the tender pears with the fragile crunch of the pastry is magical. Barbara Kafka is a food writer and cookbook author based in New York.

Barbara Kafka

TIME: 1 hour 15 minutes   YIELD: 6 servings

Zest of ½ orange
Zest of ½ lemon
6 tablespoons sugar
¼ teaspoon ground cloves
1 tablespoon orange juice
1½ teaspoons lemon juice
4 firm, ripe Bosc pears (about
   2 pounds), peeled, quartered,
   cored and cut into 1-inch wedges

6 sheets phyllo dough, defrosted
4 tablespoons unsalted butter,
   melted
¾ cup chopped walnuts

1. Place a rack in center of oven, and preheat to 375 degrees. Place orange and lemon zest in bowl of a food processor, and pulse with sugar and cloves until powdery. With the machine running, pour the orange and lemon juice through the feed tube. Process until fairly liquid. Scrape mixture into a medium mixing bowl. Add pears, and gently toss to coat.

2. Place one sheet of phyllo dough lengthwise on a cookie sheet. Brush it with melted butter. Top it with a second sheet, and brush with butter. Place a third sheet of phyllo crosswise to cover half of the previous layers. Leave some of the dough hanging over each side. Brush with butter. Repeat with another sheet of phyllo, this time covering the other half of the layers. Place another sheet lengthwise, and brush it with butter. Place the last sheet on top, but do not brush it with butter.

3. Sprinkle walnuts in the center of the dough, forming a round 8 inches in diameter. Spoon pears over nuts. Loosely fold the phyllo up and over the pears; there will be a space in the center where the pears show through. Parts of the dough should stick up like a pocket handkerchief.

4. Bake for about 25 minutes, or until the phyllo is golden and the pears are tender. Using a spatula, carefully slide tart off pan onto a serving plate.

Madiran Tart with Wine-Soaked Pears

Hélène
Darroze, Paris

The filling of this French tart combines wine-soaked pears with a red wine custard. The recipe comes from a Michelin two-star chef, Hélène Darroze, who is originally from Gascony, in southwest France. Madiran is a wine that comes from that region.

TIME: 1½ hours, plus 2 days' marinating and final chilling   YIELD: 6 to 8 servings

1 bottle plus ¾ cup Madiran or
   other strong red wine
1 cup granulated sugar
Zest of 1 orange
Zest of 1 lemon
1 cinnamon stick
2 vanilla beans, scraped
8 ripe but firm medium-size
   pears, like Forelle or Bartlett,
   peeled, vertically cut in two and
   cored

6 ounces (12 tablespoons)
   unsalted butter, softened
½ cup confectioners' sugar
2 tablespoons finely ground
   almonds
2 large eggs
1½ cups all-purpose flour, plus
   more for rolling
2 large egg yolks

1. Pour wine into a 4-quart saucepan, add ⅔ cup water, ⅓ cup granulated sugar, citrus zests, cinnamon and half the vanilla scrapings (discard bean pods). Bring to a boil, remove from heat, and add pears. Transfer to a bowl, cover and refrigerate 48 hours.

2. Place 2 cups of the wine marinade in a saucepan, and boil until reduced to ¾ cup. Set aside.

3. Cream 7 tablespoons butter, confectioners' sugar and almonds together. Lightly beat 1 egg, add to butter mixture, then fold in flour and remaining vanilla bean scrapings. Dough should be soft but not sticky. Form into a ball and flatten into a disk, dust with a little flour, and chill 45 minutes.

4. Preheat oven to 350 degrees. Roll out pastry on a floured board, lightly dusting surface with a little flour as you roll. Line a 9-inch tart pan with pastry, line with foil and pastry weights and bake 10 minutes. Remove weights and bake 10 minutes longer. Remove from oven and set aside. Reduce heat to 300 degrees.

5. In a heavy saucepan, beat remaining granulated sugar, remaining egg and egg yolks together until thick and light. Whisk in the ¾ cup reduced wine, and cook over medium-low heat, stirring constantly with a wooden spoon, until steam just begins to rise and mixture thickens to the consistency of custard sauce. Do not overcook or eggs will curdle.

6. Remove custard from heat and beat in remaining butter a little at a time. Pour into tart shell and bake 40 minutes, until set. Set aside until cooled to room temperature, then chill at least 2 hours.

7. Drain pears. Slice thinly and rearrange on top of tart and serve, with remaining pears and wine alongside.

Pear Pecan Tart

Michael
Romano,
Union Square
Cafe,
New York

Brown sugar gives the pastry extra richness. Michael Romano is the executive chef at Union Square Café in New York.

TIME: 1 hour 45 minutes   YIELD: 8 servings

2 Anjou or Comice pears

2 cups granulated sugar

2 teaspoons vanilla extract

6 tablespoons unsalted butter, softened

1¾ cups plus 2 tablespoons light brown sugar

1 cup all-purpose flour, approximately

Pinch of salt

3 large eggs

1½ cups coarsely chopped pecans

⅓ cup grated unsweetened coconut

1 tablespoon unsalted butter, melted

1. Peel pears, and halve lengthwise. In a medium saucepan (3 to 4 quarts), combine 2 cups granulated sugar, 2 cups water and 1 teaspoon vanilla. Bring to a boil, reduce heat to low and simmer, stirring, until sugar dissolves. Add pears to pan, and simmer until pears are tender, about 15 minutes. Remove pears with a slotted spoon, and allow to cool.

2. In an electric mixer with a whisk, cream butter and ⅓ cup brown sugar. Add ¾ cup flour, salt and 1 teaspoon vanilla. Knead briefly until smooth. Press into a ball, wrap in plastic and chill 15 minutes.

3. Preheat oven to 350 degrees. On a lightly floured surface, roll dough into 10-inch circle. Transfer to a 9-inch tart pan; trim edges. Line with foil and pastry weights. Bake crust until it begins to color, about 10 minutes. Remove from oven, and set aside.

4. In a medium bowl, combine eggs, pecans, coconut, 2 tablespoons flour and remaining brown sugar. Whisk until blended. Remove cores from pear halves with melon baller or knife. Slice each half into thin wedges while leaving attached at narrow end of pear.

5. Pour pecan mixture into tart shell. Place pears on top, with narrow ends in center of tart. Fan slices so that they lie nearly flat, covering surface of tart. Bake until tart is set and golden brown, about 35 minutes. Remove to cooling rack, and allow to rest 20 minutes before slicing.

Satiny Lemon Cream Tart

The filling for this tart is rich lemon curd. The tart can be decorated with whipped cream, or, if you wish, topped with meringue and lightly browned in the oven. Pierre Hermé is one of France's premier pastry chefs.

TIME: About 30 minutes, plus chilling   YIELD: 8 servings

Pierre
Hermé, Paris

1 cup sugar
Grated zest of 3 lemons
4 large eggs
¾ cup fresh lemon juice
10½ ounces (2 sticks plus 5 tablespoons) unsalted French or premium American butter, at room temperature and cut into tablespoons

One 9-inch baked tart crust (rich butter pastry, ½ recipe, page 521)

1. Place sugar and lemon zest in a large metal bowl. Rub sugar and zest together until sugar is moist and grainy. Whisk in eggs and lemon juice.

2. Place bowl on a pan that is partly filled with simmering water and cook, stirring with whisk as soon as mixture feels tepid. Whisk until mixture thickens and reaches 180 degrees on an instant-read or candy thermometer, about 10 minutes.

3. Strain into blender or food processor and let rest at room temperature, stirring occasionally, until it cools to 140 degrees, 3 to 5 minutes.

4. With motor on high speed, add 5 pats of butter; scrape down sides of container as needed. Repeat until all butter is incorporated. Beat 3 to 4 minutes more.

5. Pour enough curd into tart shell to come up to rim (you will have curd left over, which can be frozen); chill until cool and set.

Meyer Lemon Tart

Alan Tangren,
Chez Panisse,
Berkeley,
California

Alice Waters of Chez Panisse in Berkeley, California, was the first chef to use Meyer lemons in her kitchen. She would obtain them from friends who grew them in their backyards. Now they are grown commercially and are available in summer. They are rounder and juicier than regular lemons, with thinner skins and sweeter flesh. Alan Tangren is one of the many chefs who have worked at Chez Panisse in Berkeley, California.

TIME: 1 hour, plus chilling   YIELD: 8 servings

13½ ounces (3 sticks plus 3 tablespoons) unsalted butter, softened, plus extra for pan

1½ cups sugar, approximately

8 large egg yolks

½ tablespoon milk

12 ounces (about 2⅓ cups) all-purpose flour, plus more for rolling

¼ teaspoon plus ⅛ teaspoon salt

1¼ pounds (5 or 6) Meyer lemons

5 large eggs

1. In the bowl of a mixer, cream together 8 ounces softened butter (2 sticks) and ½ cup sugar. Add 1 egg yolk and the milk, and beat to combine. In a medium bowl, combine the flour with ¼ teaspoon salt. Slowly add the flour to the butter mixture, stirring until completely blended. Gather dough into 2 balls. Freeze one for future use, chill the other for at least 1 hour.

2. Heavily butter a 10-inch tart pan with a removable bottom. On a lightly floured surface, roll out ball of dough to a circle ⅛ inch thick. Transfer to the tart pan, press into the pan and trim the edges. Prick the bottom with a fork, and place the shell in the freezer for 30 minutes.

3. While shell is in freezer, prepare lemon curd: grate zest of lemons. Squeeze lemons to extract 1 cup of juice. In a medium nonreactive saucepan, combine juice and zest. Add remaining 1 cup sugar, remaining 5½ ounces butter and ⅛ teaspoon salt. Place over medium heat, stirring once or twice, until sugar is dissolved and the butter is melted.

4. In the bowl of a mixer, combine eggs and remaining 7 egg yolks until blended. Slowly add hot lemon mixture to eggs until blended. Return mixture to saucepan, and place over low heat. Whisk constantly until mixture thickens to a puddinglike consistency; do not allow it to boil. Remove from

heat, and continue to stir to stop the cooking. Strain lemon curd into a bowl. Adjust sugar to taste; the curd should be tart, but may need additional sugar if the lemons were unripe. Cover with plastic wrap, pressing it right against the surface of the curd. Allow to cool.

5. Preheat oven to 375 degrees. Remove tart shell from freezer, line with foil and pastry weights and bake 10 minutes. Remove foil and weights and bake until lightly golden, 10 to 15 minutes longer. Remove from heat and allow to cool slightly. Spoon lemon curd into tart shell, and smooth the top. Bake until filling has puffed around the edges, about 30 minutes. Cover edges with foil, if necessary, to prevent overbrowning. Cool to room temperature before serving.

Cherry Amaretto Folded Tart

Katie
Fuller,
Macrina
Bakery and
Café, Seattle,
Washington

You will need about half a pound of cherries for this recipe. Washington State is one of the main sources for fresh cherries in season, so it's no surprise that this cherry dessert comes from Macrina Bakery in Seattle.

TIME: 1½ hours   YIELD: 6 servings

2 cups stemmed and pitted sweet
   red cherries
2 tablespoons amaretto liqueur
½ cup plus 1 tablespoon
   granulated sugar
1 cup ricotta cheese
1 teaspoon vanilla extract
½ teaspoon almond extract

1 tablespoon all-purpose flour
2 large eggs, separated
Flaky pastry (page 522)
1 large egg white, lightly beaten
1 tablespoon coarse (decorative
   or sanding) sugar
2 tablespoons confectioners'
   sugar

1. In a medium-size mixing bowl, combine cherries with amaretto and 1 tablespoon sugar. Let stand 20 minutes.

2. In another mixing bowl, combine remaining ½ cup granulated sugar, ricotta cheese, vanilla extract, almond extract and flour. Add egg yolks to ricotta mixture, mixing well until well blended. Using an electric beater, beat 2 egg whites until stiff but not dry, and fold into the ricotta mixture.

3. On a baking sheet lined with parchment paper, place the 12-inch round of dough. It may overlap the edge of the pan. Mound the ricotta mixture in the center of the dough, and top with the cherries; this will occupy about 8 inches of the center. Pull a 4-inch border up around the filling to make a free-form folded tart, folding a tuck every 2 inches, sealing the folds with beaten egg white. Brush the top of the crust with egg white, and sprinkle the center with coarse sugar. Chill by placing the tart, still on the baking sheet, in the freezer for 20 minutes.

4. Preheat oven to 400 degrees. Bake tart until golden brown, 35 to 40 minutes. Sprinkle crust with confectioners' sugar, and serve warm.

Blueberry Tart with Hazelnut Crust ✳

Companies that sell baking supplies, including nuts, often carry ground hazelnuts. You can use blanched hazelnuts, toasted, to eliminate the step of removing the skins. Sophie Parker, who died in 2001, was the chef and owner of Chez Sophie in Saratoga Springs, New York.

TIME: 1 hour and 30 minutes, plus cooling   YIELD: 8 to 10 servings

Sophie Parker, Chez Sophie, Saratoga Springs, New York

∾

1¼ cups whole shelled hazelnuts

8 ounces (2 sticks) unsalted butter, softened

⅓ cup sugar

1 large egg

1 teaspoon vanilla extract

3 cups all-purpose flour

2½ to 3 cups fresh blueberries, washed and thoroughly dried

10 ounces red currant jelly

2 tablespoons brandy

1. Preheat oven to 350 degrees. Spread the hazelnuts on a baking sheet, and bake until toasted and lightly browned, about 10 minutes. Allow to cool, then rub the nuts by hand to remove the crisped skins. Discard the skins, and place the nuts in a food processor. Chop until coarsely ground, and set aside.

2. In the bowl of an electric mixer, combine the butter, sugar, egg and vanilla. Mix at low speed just until blended. Add the ground nuts and all-purpose flour. Mix at medium speed until the dough forms a ball. Divide the dough into three balls, and cover two with airtight plastic wrap to freeze for another use. Press the remaining dough evenly into the sides and bottom of a fluted 9-inch tart pan with a removable bottom. Chill the pan and dough for 30 minutes.

3. Preheat oven to 350 degrees. Prick the crust all over with a fork, and bake until golden, about 20 minutes. Remove from oven, allow to cool, and remove from pan.

4. Arrange fresh berries as close together as possible, in a single layer over the crust. In a small saucepan, combine the currant jelly and brandy. Place over medium heat, and reduce to evaporate the brandy and return the jelly to a thickened consistency, about 5 minutes. Brush the tart with jelly until the berries and gaps between them are well covered; all the jelly may not be needed. Serve at room temperature.

Blueberry Tart with Crème Fraîche and Honey Cream

Amanda
Hesser

Other berries, including raspberries and blackberries, can replace the blueberries, if desired. Amanda Hesser, a food writer and cookbook author, is the food editor of *The New York Times Sunday Magazine*.

TIME: 1½ hours, plus chilling   YIELD: 8 servings

1 cup plus 3½ tablespoons all-purpose flour

¼ cup almonds

⅓ cup confectioners' sugar

½ teaspoon kosher salt

¼ teaspoon baking powder

7 tablespoons unsalted butter, in small cubes

1 ounce cream cheese

1 large egg, beaten

½ teaspoon almond extract

1 teaspoon cider vinegar

⅓ cup granulated sugar

3 tablespoons crème de cassis

2 cups blueberries

¾ cup milk

5 large egg yolks

2 tablespoons orange blossom honey

¼ cup mascarpone or cream cheese

½ cup crème fraîche

1. In a 1-gallon plastic bag, combine all but 1½ tablespoons flour, the almonds, confectioners' sugar, salt and baking powder. Wrap butter cubes in plastic wrap. Place both in freezer for at least 30 minutes, then pour contents of flour bag into a food processor and pulse a few times. Add cream cheese and butter and pulse until mixture resembles tiny pebbles. Add egg and almond extract and pulse 5 times. Sprinkle in vinegar and pulse 5 more times. Dough is ready if it holds together when you press it between your thumb and index finger.

2. Pour dough onto countertop. Using heel of your hand, knead dough bits until they cohere. Collect dough into a ball and flatten into a disk. Cover with plastic wrap and chill for at least 3 hours.

3. In a 1-quart saucepan, stir together the granulated sugar and crème de cassis. Place over medium heat and stir until sugar is dissolved. When it has simmered for 2 minutes, fold in blueberries and remove from heat.

4. In another small saucepan, bring milk just to a boil. In a bowl, whisk

egg yolks until lightened, then whisk in the remaining 1½ tablespoons flour. Slowly whisk milk into eggs, then pour entire mixture back into pan over medium heat. Whisk constantly and bring to a simmer, cooking for 2 minutes, on and off heat so that sauce does not curdle, until it thickens. Pour into a bowl, cover with plastic wrap and cool in refrigerator.

5. Preheat oven to 400 degrees. Roll out pastry and press it into a 9-inch tart pan. Trim edges. Line with foil and pie weights (or dried beans). Chill, then bake for 15 minutes. Remove foil and weights, reduce heat to 350 degrees and bake until base of tart is cooked and dry looking, about 5 minutes. Remove from oven and let cool completely.

6. Remove the pastry cream from the refrigerator and whisk in honey, mascarpone and crème fraîche. Pour filling into tart shell, then spoon blueberries and their juices over top. Chill for at least 1 hour before serving.

Linzer Torte

Richard
Stoltzman

Richard Stoltzman, a concert clarinetist, is also a passionate baker who took courses at Cordon Bleu in London and from a teacher in Vermont. He likens the art of baking, which he is able to do with confidence, to playing music. "I learn a recipe like I learn a score, and then proceed from memory," he said. "You just have to know how much room you have to interpret." His linzer torte, which he first made in 1974 at the request of Rudolf Serkin, is a good example. He said his hands are too warm to handle strips of dough for the top so he made the dough softer and instead of rolling it, he pipes it through a pastry tube. He also added cocoa to it. Otherwise, the recipe, actually a kind of lattice-top pie with ground nuts and spices in the pastry, and a filling of raspberry preserves, hews to the classic. The dessert is said to have originated in Linz, in Austria, though Russwurm, a pastry shop in Budapest, claims to have invented it. For a more traditional Linzer torte, I have simply prepared the hazelnut pastry on page 525, using an 8-inch tart pan, so there will be enough pastry to make the lattice top, filling it with preserves.

TIME: 3 hours   YIELD: 8 servings

1 cup all-purpose flour

2 tablespoons unsweetened cocoa

½ teaspoon ground cinnamon

¼ teaspoon ground cloves

8 ounces (2 sticks) salted butter, softened

½ cup plus 1 tablespoon granulated sugar

2 large egg yolks

2 cups ground almonds

1 cup seedless raspberry preserves

1 large egg white

Confectioners' sugar

1. Whisk the flour, cocoa, cinnamon and cloves together in a bowl.

2. Cream the butter and beat in ½ cup granulated sugar. Beat in the egg yolks. Gradually blend in the almonds and the flour mixture to make a thick batter. Spread about half the batter in an even layer, ⅛ to ¼ inch thick, in the bottom of an 8- or 9-inch round baking pan that has a removable bottom. Spread the preserves in a layer over the batter, taking care not to break the layer of batter, to within ½ inch of the edge.

3. Spoon the remaining batter into a pastry bag fitted with a large plain or star tube ½ inch in diameter. Pipe 3 to 5 parallel lines of batter across the top of the preserves, from one edge to the other. Give the pan a quarter turn and pipe 3 to 5 more parallel lines across the pastry from edge to edge. Pipe the rest of the batter around the edge. Any excess batter can be used to make round cookies on a baking sheet.

4. Refrigerate torte for 1 hour.

5. Preheat oven to 300 degrees.

6. Beat the egg white with the remaining granulated sugar and 1 tablespoon water until frothy. Brush this mixture over the pastry strips and the edging. Place Linzer torte in the oven and bake for 1 hour. Allow to cool completely. To serve, sift confectioners' sugar over the top and remove sides of pan.

Coco-Mamie

Payard
Pâtisserie
and Bistro,
New York

Though the recipe calls for a small pineapple, it's better to consider quality over size. And a larger, golden pineapple is likely to be best-tasting. You will have extra pineapple to use for another dessert. François Payard, the owner of Payard Pâtisserie and Bistro, is a French pastry chef based in New York.

TIME: 1 hour, plus freezing and cooling   YIELD: 6 to 8 servings

3½ tablespoons unsalted butter,
    softened
All-purpose flour for rolling
    pastry
Sweet pastry (page 522)
½ small pineapple, cut into tiny
    dice, about 2 cups

½ cup granulated sugar
1½ cups finely shredded
    unsweetened coconut
1 large egg

1. Use ½ tablespoon butter to grease an 8-inch round fluted metal tart pan, 1¼ inches high, with a removable bottom, and place it on a baking sheet. On a lightly floured work surface, roll the dough into a 10-inch circle about ⅛ inch thick. Fit the dough into the pan, and trim off the excess, level with the top of the pan.

2. Spread the pineapple evenly over the bottom of the crust, and return the crust to the freezer for about an hour. Preheat the oven to 350 degrees.

3. To make the filling, cream the remaining butter and granulated sugar together in a bowl. Stir in the coconut, and when it is well blended, lightly beat the egg and add it. Spread the filling evenly over the frozen pineapple, pressing down lightly on the fruit to get the filling into the crevices. Spread the filling all the way to the edge of the crust.

4. Place the tart in the oven on the baking sheet, and bake for 50 to 55 minutes, or until the crust is baked through and the filling is golden brown and firmly set on top. Transfer the tart to a rack, and cool.

COCOA:
This Time, Chocolate Takes a Powder
By Regina Schrambling

Cocoa has always had an image problem.

For years, it was considered the poor substitute for chocolate, the pallid powder that needed major help from butter and still could not produce a decent brownie. Then it became scorned as the low-fat but sad alternative to chocolate used by so many pastry chefs during the recent reign of nutrition terror. It even lost its cachet as a hot drink once it was replaced by melted semisweet and cream.

But lately cocoa has been turning up on all the best shelves. High-end chocolate producers now make cocoa powders that leave supermarket brands in the dust. In France, every good chocolatier sells bags of cocoa.

Cocoa, even inexpensive cocoa, has a deep, dark intensity of flavor and an amazing versatility that even the best brands of 77 percent chocolate lack. It cannot replace chocolate. But in recipes like the All-in-One Chocolate Cake (page 28), which are designed to make the most of its sharp taste and chemical capabilities, nothing works better than cocoa.

But in their rush to melt high-quality chocolate in increasingly extravagant quantities, chefs and recipe writers lost touch with a remarkable ingredient. It was as if they had abandoned mushrooms after discovering black truffles. One is not better than the other. They just have to be treated differently.

Chefs brave enough to admit they use cocoa tend to sing its praises in florid terms. Cocoa does more than intensify flavor and sharpen edges. It also creates a moist, perfect crumb in a cake, a crisp bite in a cookie. As it blends into dry ingredients, it transforms the results no less than baking powder does.

The big lie of baking is that 3 tablespoons of cocoa powder combined with 1 tablespoon of fat can replace an ounce of chocolate. Every basic cookbook repeats it. But nothing replicates the richness of chocolate.

Cocoa works best in recipes that are designed for it. Buttermilk brings out its tanginess, and the two combine to produce a springy texture in a cake. Even something as simple as the classic Amazon, or black-bottom, cake found in so many cookbooks uses no dairy products or eggs, only vegetable oil and vinegar with cold water. As with buttermilk, cocoa reacts to acid to produce a dark, moist cake.

Some cocoas, particularly the dark, strong imports that are treated with an alkaline substance and are called "Dutch process," are vital in a recipe like a crisp shortbread or plain cookie in which the chocolate flavor is all-important. Alkalization makes a mellow cocoa, but it can also be a way of camouflaging inferior cocoa beans.

The first step of producing any cocoa powder is always the same: after cocoa butter is extracted from cacao, the pods are pressed again to make a cake with no fat, just flavor, which is made into a powder, or cocoa.

Some of the newly available cocoas have a powerful chocolate taste even though no alkali is involved. But the Dutched varieties are almost uniformly exceptional. Cocoa has a huge advantage over chocolate for a home cook because it is simply so easy to work with. No melting is required, only a little sifting at most. It will never seize up or turn bitter as chocolate can. And it does not deteriorate in storage.

Chocolate Caramel Tart

Coarse-textured high-quality sea salt, or fleur de sel, does wonders for caramel. Claudia Fleming created this dessert when she was the pastry chef at Gramercy Tavern in New York.

Claudia Fleming

TIME: 1 hour 15 minutes, plus chilling and setting   YIELD: 12 to 16 servings

8 ounces (2 sticks) salted butter, softened
½ cup plus 1 tablespoon confectioners' sugar
¼ cup unsweetened cocoa
1 large egg yolk
¾ teaspoon vanilla extract
1¼ cups all-purpose flour, plus more for rolling

2 cups granulated sugar
¼ cup light corn syrup
1 cup heavy cream
2 tablespoons crème fraîche
3½ ounces extra-bittersweet chocolate, chopped
Fleur de sel

1. In bowl of an electric mixer, combine 4 ounces butter, confectioners' sugar and cocoa. Beat until smooth. Add egg yolk and vanilla, and beat until blended.

2. Sift flour into dough mixture. Beat on low speed until combined. Scrape dough onto a sheet of plastic wrap, and shape into a disk. Wrap, and chill until firm, at least 1 hour and up to 3 days.

3. Preheat oven to 350 degrees. On a lightly floured surface, roll dough into an 11-inch circle. Fit in a 10-inch tart pan. Line with foil, and fill with dried beans, or pie weights. Bake 15 minutes. Remove foil and weights, and bake until pastry is brown, 10 to 15 minutes. Transfer in pan to a rack.

4. In a large saucepan, bring sugar and corn syrup to a boil. Stir occasionally, until mixture is a deep caramel color. Carefully (mixture will bubble) whisk in remaining butter, ½ cup cream and crème fraîche until smooth. Pour hot caramel into tart, and allow to cool and set, at least ½ hour.

5. Place chocolate in a bowl. In a small saucepan, bring remaining cream to a boil, pour over, and whisk until chocolate has melted and mixture is smooth. Pour over tart, tilting tart for even coverage. Allow to set for at least 1 hour, then sprinkle with a little fleur de sel.

Chocolate-Fantasy Tart

Nicky
Morse

This tart, all chocolate from pastry to topping, is a chocolate-lover's delight. Nicky Morse, a champion drag racer, also likes to bake.

TIME: 1 hour 30 minutes, plus cooling   YIELD: 14 to 16 servings

Nonstick spray for pan
1¾ cups all-purpose flour
¼ cup light brown sugar
¼ cup finely ground pecans
½ ounce unsweetened chocolate, finely grated
½ ounce semisweet chocolate, grated
11 ounces (2¾ sticks) cold unsalted butter, cubed
4 tablespoons whole milk

1 teaspoon vanilla extract
1 teaspoon Kahlúa
6½ ounces unsweetened chocolate, finely chopped
4½ ounces semisweet chocolate, finely chopped
1¾ cups granulated sugar
3 large eggs
3 tablespoons heavy cream
Ice cream or whipped cream for serving

1. Spray an 11½-inch tart pan with removable bottom with nonstick spray. In a large bowl, combine 1 cup flour, brown sugar, pecans, and both grated chocolates. Cut in 9 tablespoons (1 stick plus 1 tablespoon) butter until mixture resembles coarse meal. Add 2 tablespoons milk, vanilla and Kahlúa, and mix just until blended. Pat pastry evenly into pan, and set aside. Allow remaining butter to come to room temperature.

2. Preheat oven to 350 degrees. In a double boiler, melt 3 ounces unsweetened chopped chocolate and 3 ounces semisweet chopped chocolate, and add 8 tablespoons of the butter a little at a time, stirring to mix. Remove from heat. Add 1½ cups sugar and mix well; mixture will look granular. Add eggs one at a time, mixing well after each addition. Add remaining flour and mix well. Pour into pastry shell. Bake until a toothpick in center comes out clean, 40 to 45 minutes. Cool to room temperature.

3. In a medium saucepan, combine remaining butter, milk, sugar and the cream. Bring to a simmer, and immediately remove from heat. Slowly add remaining chopped semisweet and unsweetened chocolates, stirring slowly with a wooden spoon. Pour evenly over cooled pie, and allow to rest until set. Serve with ice cream or whipped cream.

Cider Pecan Tart

This tart has much in common with a pecan pie, but instead of corn or maple syrup, its main sweetener is reduced, concentrated cider. I like to keep cider that I have boiled down in the freezer. It's a great addition to the pan juices for a pork roast. Use freshly pressed apple cider that is unfiltered and cloudy.

TIME: 1 hour   YIELD: 6 to 8 servings

Florence
Fabricant

2½ cups fresh apple cider

4 tablespoons unsalted butter

⅔ cup light brown sugar

2 tablespoons Calvados, bourbon or brandy

1 teaspoon vanilla extract

¼ teaspoon freshly grated nutmeg

3 large eggs, lightly beaten

Rich butter pastry (½ recipe, page 521)

1½ cups pecan halves, lightly toasted

1½ cup heavy cream, whipped (optional)

1. Preheat oven to 350 degrees. Place cider in a saucepan, and cook over high heat until reduced to one cup. Remove from heat, and stir in butter and brown sugar until dissolved. Then stir in Calvados, vanilla, nutmeg and eggs.

2. Roll out pastry and line a straight-sided 9-inch tart pan with it. A pie pan can be used. Spread pecans over pastry.

3. Pour in cider mixture. Bake 30 to 35 minutes, until surface is fairly firm and pastry is golden. Allow to cool to room temperature. Serve with whipped cream, if desired.

Squash Tart

Regina
Schrambling

A tart for an autumn menu, this one has all the right ingredients: squash, cranberries and spices. Pre-baking the crust, then filling and baking the tart, will guarantee a crisp crust. And it will not be over-browned. Regina Schrambling is a food writer and a former reporter for *The New York Times*.

TIME: 1 hour 20 minutes, plus cooling   YIELD: 1 tart (8 servings)

2 cups coarsely grated butternut
　or kabocha squash
⅓ cup maple syrup or honey
⅓ cup heavy cream
½ cup dried cranberries
1 tablespoon minced crystallized
　ginger

½ teaspoon ground allspice
¼ teaspoon ground cloves
¼ teaspoon salt
2 large eggs
1 pre-baked 9-inch tart crust (rich
　butter pastry, ½ recipe,
　page 521)

1. Preheat oven to 350 degrees. Combine squash, maple syrup or honey, cream, cranberries, ginger, allspice, cloves and salt. Mix thoroughly. Taste, and adjust seasoning, adding more spice if you like. Add eggs, and mix well again so ingredients are completely combined. Pour into prepared tart shell. Set pan on baking sheet on shelf in lower third of oven.

2. Bake 50 to 55 minutes, until filling is fully set. Cool completely before cutting.

TARTLETS

Individual tarts, or tartlets, which offer such serving convenience in restaurants, are more complicated for the home cook to prepare. For one thing, having the proper little tartlet molds on hand is essential. And you will need as many, of course, as you expect to serve. The best ones are French, with loose bottoms. Though most of these tartlet recipes include instructions for making the pastry, any pastry recipe that is used for tarts can be adapted for tartlets. You will need nearly double the amount of dough for an 8- or 9-inch tart to make 8 4-inch tartlets. In a pinch, muffin tins can be used. But it pays to butter them lightly, to make the tartlets easy to remove.

Chocolate Tartlets

These rich little confections are meant to be served warm, encased in buttery chocolate pastry. Though they can be prepared in advance and reheated, they will lose the puffy allure they have fresh from the oven. Claudia Fleming was the pastry chef at Gramercy Tavern in New York.

Claudia Fleming

TIME: 1 hour 15 minutes, plus chilling   YIELD: 12 servings

10 tablespoons plus 2 sticks
    unsalted butter, softened
5 ounces extra-bitter chocolate,
    chopped
5 large eggs, at room temperature
⅞ cup granulated sugar
3 tablespoons plus 1½ cups flour

1 cup confectioners' sugar
¼ cup unsweetened cocoa
½ cup ground almonds
Crème fraîche, for garnish
Chocolate sorbet for serving
    (optional)

1. To prepare the filling, put 10 tablespoons butter in a double boiler over simmering water and scatter the chocolate on top of butter. Let butter and chocolate melt. Remove pan from heat, and stir contents until well blended. Transfer mixture to a large bowl, and let cool.

2. In the bowl of an electric mixer, briefly beat 4 eggs to break them up. Add granulated sugar, and beat 5 minutes at high speed, until very pale and thick. Fold a third of the egg mixture into chocolate mixture to lighten it;

then gently fold in the rest, taking care not to deflate the eggs. Sift 3 tablespoons flour over the batter and carefully fold it in. Cover the filling, and chill 2 hours.

3. Meanwhile, to prepare the dough, beat the remaining butter and sugar in an electric mixer until light and creamy. Add cocoa, and beat until well combined. Add remaining egg, and beat until smooth.

4. Sift the remaining all-purpose flour and the almonds into the cocoa mixture. Beat mixture on low speed until combined. Scrape the dough onto a sheet of plastic wrap, and form into a disk. Cover, and chill until firm, about 1 hour.

5. Preheat oven to 350 degrees. On a lightly floured surface, roll the dough to 3/16 inch thick. Using a 3½-inch round cutter, cut out 12 circles of dough, and press them into 12 individual 3-inch tart pans, trimming away any excess dough. Chill tart shells 20 minutes.

6. Line shells with 5-inch squares of foil, and fill with dried beans or pastry weights. Place shells on a baking sheet, and bake 12 to 14 minutes, until pastry is dry. Remove foil and weights, and cool shells on a rack.

7. Divide filling among tart shells, and bake until filling is puffed and slightly cracked on top, 12 to 14 minutes. Remove tarts from pans, and serve immediately, garnished with the crème fraîche. Serve with chocolate sorbet.

Crackling Thin Tarts with Pecans
and Sticky Caramel

The dough for these puff pastry tartlets is baked with a weight to keep them from puffing too much. Anne Rosenzweig has been influential in New York's dining scene.

Anne
Rosenzweig

TIME: 40 minutes   YIELD: 4 servings

⅔ cup light brown sugar
2 tablespoons granulated sugar
⅓ cup light corn syrup
½ cup heavy cream
Pinch of salt
2 tablespoons unsalted butter

4 5-by-5-inch puff pastry squares, thawed if frozen, or quick puff pastry (page 526)
3 cups pecan pieces
Ice cream for serving, optional

1. In a medium heavy saucepan, combine light brown sugar, granulated sugar, corn syrup, heavy cream and salt. Place over high heat, and bring to a boil. Boil for 10 minutes, then remove from heat and add butter. Stir well to mix, and keep warm. (The sauce may be prepared a day ahead of time and stored, refrigerated, in a squeeze bottle. Reheat by placing the bottle in a pot of boiling water until softened and warm.)

2. Preheat oven to 450 degrees. Place puff pastry squares evenly spaced on parchment paper laid on a baking sheet. Chill for 15 minutes. Cover with another sheet of parchment paper, and weight with another baking sheet on top. Bake for 8 minutes, remove top baking sheet and top parchment paper, and continue to bake until golden brown, 2 to 3 minutes. Remove from oven. (The puff pastry may be baked a day in advance and stored, sealed in plastic wrap, at room temperature.)

3. To serve, preheat oven to 450 degrees. Pour warm caramel sauce over pastry squares, and sprinkle an equal number of pecans on each square. Bake tarts until caramel is bubbly and pecans are toasted, about 4 minutes. Serve hot, unadorned or with a scoop of ice cream.

Warm Spiced Pineapple Tartlets

Wylie
Dufresne

Pricking puff pastry will keep the layers from rising too high. Wylie Dufresne is a trend-setting New York chef who owns WD-50 on the Lower East Side.

TIME: 4 hours   YIELD: 6 servings

2 cinnamon sticks

2 vanilla beans

4 ounces (1 stick) unsalted butter, cut into pieces

4 tablespoons finely grated ginger

Generous pinch cracked black peppercorns

1 cup sugar

2 cups freshly squeezed orange juice

1 medium ripe pineapple

Flour for dusting

1 sheet puff pastry (about 14 ounces), thawed if frozen, or quick puff pastry (page 526)

Coconut, vanilla or ginger ice cream

1. Wrap cinnamon in towel and crack with mallet into rough pieces. Place in dry skillet over medium heat, and toast, shaking occasionally, until fragrant, about 2 minutes.

2. Transfer cinnamon to medium saucepan. With paring knife, split vanilla beans lengthwise and scrape out seeds. Place beans and seeds in pan; add butter, ginger, pepper, sugar and juice. Bring to boil over high heat, whisking to dissolve sugar. Remove from heat, cover and steep 30 minutes.

3. Trim top and bottom from pineapple. Cut in half lengthwise; reserve half for another use. Peel remainder, and cut in half again lengthwise. Cut away core, and cut each piece crosswise into ¼-inch-thick pieces.

4. Add pineapple to syrup, and return to a boil. Reduce heat, and simmer gently until tender, 5 minutes. (Don't overcook.) Remove from heat; cool to room temperature.

5. Unfold puff pastry, and roll on floured surface into 13-by-9-inch rectangle. Punch out 6 4-inch disks, then cut out a 1-inch circle from center of each. Prick pastry with tines of fork. Place on parchment-lined baking sheet.

6. Use slotted spoon to lift pineapple onto paper towels to blot dry. (Reserve syrup in saucepan.) Discard any large cinnamon bits. Arrange pineapple pieces over pastry, 6 or 7 pieces on each ring, with narrow end of pieces pointing inward. If necessary, trim pineapple so that pieces fit on pastry rings. Refrigerate baking sheet until tarts are well chilled, 2 to 6 hours.

7. Strain syrup through fine sieve into clean saucepan. Bring to a boil, and cook until sauce turns golden brown and reduces to 1¼ cups, about 12 minutes. Remove from heat.

8. About 30 minutes before serving, preheat oven to 425 degrees. Bake tarts until golden brown and puffed, about 20 minutes.

9. While tarts are baking, warm sauce over low heat; do not let sauce boil.

10. Transfer baked tarts to individual plates. Place small scoop of ice cream in center of each. Drizzle 2 tablespoons warmed sauce over each, and serve immediately.

Plum Tartlets with
Toasted Almond Cream

City
Bakery,
New York

Large, juicy pluots, a cross between a plum and an apricot, are easier to use because they tend to be freestone. Speckled brown-skin Dinosaur pluots have brilliant red flesh, as do Elephant Heart plums. City Bakery is Maury Rubin's pastry shop and café in Manhattan's Flatiron District.

TIME: 1 hour   YIELD: 6 servings

Sweet pastry for 6 4-inch tartlet
  shells (page 522)
7 small to medium plums
  (Shiro, Santa Rosa, sugar), or
  3 large plums or pluots
3 ounces (about 1 cup) slivered
  almonds

¾ cup confectioners' sugar
6 tablespoons unsalted butter,
  softened and cut into 6 pieces
1 large egg yolk

1. Preheat oven to 375 degrees. Line 4-inch tartlet pans with pastry, line pastry with foil and baking weights and bake 10 minutes. Remove foil, and continue baking until golden. Remove from oven and set aside.

2. Halve and pit small plums, and cut each in about 6 slices ½ inch thick. If using large plums, cut 10 to 12 slices from each, ½ inch thick, 1 inch wide and 2 inches long. Set aside. Spread almonds on baking sheet. Toast in oven until golden, about 5 minutes. Let cool, then transfer to food processor or grinder and process until coarsely ground.

3. Place sugar in bowl of electric mixer or in bowl to use with hand mixer. Add butter, and toss lightly to coat. Beat at medium speed until creamy and smooth. Add almonds, and beat 30 seconds. Add egg yolk, and beat to blend.

4. Spread mixture evenly in tartlet shells. Stand 3 plum slices, skin-edge up, in a row down the center of each tartlet. Stand 2 more slices on either side of each row.

5. Bake 25 to 30 minutes, until almond filling is puffed and golden around the edges but soft in center. Plums will brown around the edges. Remove from oven, transfer to wire rack and cool. Filling may sink a bit as tartlets cool.

Santa Rosa Plum Galettes ✳

Demerara sugar is a large-grained light brown variety that originally came from Guyana. True demerara sugar is less refined than granulated sugar. Turbinado sugar or, in a pinch, regular light brown sugar which is made by tinting white sugar with molasses, can be used. Aqua, known for seafood, is one of the restaurants in the Bellagio resort and casino in Las Vegas.

Aqua at Bellagio, Las Vegas, Nevada

TIME: 45 minutes   YIELD: 8 servings

Cream cheese pastry for 8 tartlets (page 523)

1¼ cups (4 ounces) blanched, sliced almonds

½ cup plus 1 tablespoon granulated sugar

4 ounces (1 stick) unsalted butter, softened

3 large eggs

¼ cup all-purpose flour

1 teaspoon vanilla extract

Pinch of salt

10 ripe Santa Rosa plums, pitted and sliced

Demerara sugar for sprinkling

Whipped crème fraîche or vanilla ice cream

1. Preheat oven to 375 degrees. Cut pastry into 8 equal pieces. Roll each piece between sheets of plastic wrap into ⅛-inch-thick rounds (about 6 inches in diameter). Place pastry rounds on 1 or 2 baking sheets that have been lined with parchment paper or nonstick liners. Chill rounds while preparing filling.

2. In a food processor, combine almonds with 1 tablespoon granulated sugar. Pulse until mixture becomes a fine meal (avoid overprocessing). Add butter, 2 eggs, remaining granulated sugar, flour, vanilla and salt and process until combined.

3. In a bowl, beat remaining egg with 1 tablespoon water. Brush this egg wash over prepared pastry rounds. Spoon about 2 tablespoons almond filling in center of each pastry round and spread it to within 2 inches of the edge. Arrange plum slices in a spiral over filling. Sprinkle demerara sugar generously over plums. Fold edges of tart dough up over edges of plums, pleating it as you go.

4. Bake tarts until pastry is golden brown, about 18 to 20 minutes. Serve warm with whipped crème fraîche or vanilla ice cream.

Apple-Honey Tartlets

Florence
Fabricant

The combination of all-purpose and whole wheat flours adds a nuttiness to the cream cheese pastry used for these tartlets. And though a type of honey is not specified in the recipe, pay attention to this ingredient. A strong honey, like buckwheat or acacia, will give the tartlets a more robust flavor, while a wildflower honey will be more delicate. My favorite honey is Tasmanian leatherwood from Australia, which has a hauntingly musky fragrance without being heavy.

TIME: 45 minutes   YIELD: 6 servings

½ cup all-purpose flour
½ cup whole wheat flour
½ teaspoon salt
4 ounces cream cheese, in small
  pieces
4 ounces (1 stick) unsalted butter,
  in small pieces

1 tablespoon sugar
1 teaspoon ground cinnamon
3 apples, peeled, cored and sliced
  thin
¼ cup honey

1. Preheat oven to 500 degrees. Cover a baking sheet with foil or parchment.

2. Mix the flours and salt together in a bowl. Using a pastry blender, 2 knives or your fingertips, blend the cream cheese and butter into the flour to make a tender pastry dough. Roll the pastry on a floured board and cut 6 5-inch rounds.

3. Arrange the pastry rounds on the baking sheet. Mix the sugar and cinnamon together and sprinkle on the pastry rounds. Arrange the apple slices, slightly overlapping, on each.

4. Bake 10 minutes, until the apples begin to brown. Remove from the oven and allow to cool about 10 minutes. Drizzle with honey and serve.

Lemon Meringue Tartlets

If you prefer, you can pipe rosettes of the meringue on the tartlets with a pastry bag and a large star tip. These are simply petit lemon meringue pies. They must be served within hours of being made.

Florence Fabricant

TIME: 1 hour   YIELD: 4 servings

1½ cups graham cracker crumbs
¾ cup sugar
8 tablespoons unsalted butter,
   melted and cooled

4 large eggs, separated
¼ cup lemon juice

1. Preheat oven to 425 degrees.

2. Mix the graham cracker crumbs with 2 tablespoons sugar and 5 tablespoons melted butter. Press the crumbs into the bottom and sides of 4 4-inch tartlet pans. Place in the oven and bake 15 minutes. Remove.

3. Beat the egg yolks and 2 of the whites with 6 tablespoons of the remaining sugar and the lemon juice. Stir in the remaining melted butter. Pour this mixture into the graham cracker tartlet shells, place in the oven and bake about 20 minutes, until set. Adjust the oven rack to the highest position.

4. Beat the remaining whites until softly peaked. Gradually sprinkle in the remaining sugar and beat until stiff. Mound this meringue on the top of each tartlet, using a fork to create many little peaks on the surface. Return to the oven and bake about 15 minutes, until lightly browned. Cool before serving.

Squash and Fennel Tartlets

Payard
Pâtisserie
and Bistro,
New York

The candied pistachios in this recipe make delicious garnishes for other desserts, especially chocolate cakes and puddings. Payard Pâtisserie and Bistro on the Upper East Side is one of New York's best pastry shops.

TIME: 1 hour   YIELD: 8 servings

¼ cup confectioners' sugar

1 large egg white

⅓ cup shelled and skinned
   unsalted pistachio nuts

½ pound packaged puff pastry,
   thawed, or quick puff pastry
   (page 526)

2 cups sugar

Zest of 1 lemon, cut in broad
   strips

Zest of 1 orange, cut in broad
   strips

1 clove

1 star anise

2 small bulbs fennel, trimmed of
   stems and cores and cut into
   thin slices

2 tablespoons unsalted butter

1 butternut squash (about 1½
   pounds), peeled, seeded and cut
   into ¾-inch dice

¼ cup fresh apple cider

Juice of 1 lime

2 cups lemon sorbet for serving

1. Preheat oven to 300 degrees. Line a baking sheet with parchment. Place confectioners' sugar in a small bowl. Spoon half the egg white onto a plate (discard other half). Toss pistachios in egg white to coat them; then toss them in confectioners' sugar until they are lightly coated and do not stick together. Place nuts on baking sheet, and bake until they are brown and start to crack. Remove from oven, and set aside to cool.

2. Increase oven temperature to 400 degrees. On a lightly floured work surface, roll out the puff pastry to ⅛-inch thickness, and cut into 8 4-inch circles. Place on a parchment-lined baking sheet, and put a lightweight wire cooling rack on top of the pastry to keep it from puffing too much. Bake until golden, 5 to 6 minutes. Cool to room temperature on a rack.

3. In a large saucepan, combine sugar, lemon zest, orange zest, clove and star anise with 1 cup of water. Place over high heat, and bring to a boil. Turn off the heat, cover and allow mixture to rest 5 minutes. Using a slotted spoon, remove the zest and spices, and return mixture to a boil. Add

fennel, and reduce heat to medium-low. Poach fennel until it is translucent, about 15 minutes. Cool fennel in the liquid.

4. While fennel is poaching, place a large skillet over medium heat. Melt the butter, and add the squash. Sauté until the squash is very tender, about 15 minutes. Add the cider, and continue stirring until cider evaporates. Transfer squash and pan juices to container of a blender. Add lime juice, and process until mixture is smooth.

5. With a small spoon or a sharp knife, hollow out the center of each pastry round, without cutting through to the bottom, to leave some pastry for a base. Fill each hollow with about 2 tablespoons of squash puree. Top with drained poached fennel, placing some around edge of tartlet, then mounding some in center. Scatter pistachio nuts on top of tartlet and around plate, and top each tartlet with a small scoop of lemon sorbet.

Goat Cheese and Honey Phyllo Tarts with Sautéed Seasonal Fruit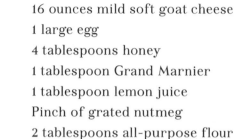

Traci
Des Jardins,
Jardiniere,
San
Francisco,
California

Layering and stacking buttered phyllo is a quick and convenient way to make a substitute for puff pastry. Traci Des Jardins is one of several women chefs who highlight the San Francisco dining scene.

TIME: 90 minutes   YIELD: 9 tarts

16 ounces mild soft goat cheese
1 large egg
4 tablespoons honey
1 tablespoon Grand Marnier
1 tablespoon lemon juice
Pinch of grated nutmeg
2 tablespoons all-purpose flour
1 box phyllo dough, thawed

8 ounces clarified unsalted butter
Sugar
½ cup white wine
1 vanilla bean, split
4 tablespoons unsalted butter
1½ cups fresh fruit, peeled and
  seeded, cut into attractive
  shapes

1. Combine cheese, egg, honey, Grand Marnier, lemon juice and nutmeg in food processor or heavy-duty mixer. Blend well. Gradually sift in flour, and mix until smooth. Place in refrigerator.

2. Place one sheet of phyllo dough on work surface. Brush on a coat of butter. Sprinkle with sugar. Place another sheet of phyllo on top, and repeat, ending with a third sheet of phyllo. Brush with butter, and set stack aside. Repeat, making 6 stacks. Cut each stack into 3 circles 5½ inches in diameter.

3. Combine 5 tablespoons sugar, white wine and vanilla bean in a saucepan, and bring to a boil. Lower heat slightly and cook until mixture has been reduced by two-thirds. Remove vanilla bean. Melt butter in a sauté pan over medium heat, and add fruit. Cook until softened but not mushy, 8 to 12 minutes.

4. Preheat oven to 425 degrees. Spread 2 tablespoons of goat cheese mixture in center of a stacked circle, leaving a margin of about an inch. Place another circle on top. Fold edges up and over to seal all around. Bake on cookie sheet 7 to 10 minutes, or until golden brown.

5. To serve, place fruit and some syrup on a plate, and place warm tart on top.

FANCY PASTRIES

In this section you will find ambitious show-stoppers, the kinds of pastry confections that dazzle shoppers in the best bakeries. They are special-occasion desserts. But most can be prepared partly or completely in advance.

Galette des Rois

Le Passe-
Partout,
Montreal,
Canada

The Galette des Rois is so named because it is traditionally served on Epiphany, the Feast of the Three Kings, January 6. For that occasion, a tiny ceramic charm or figure, or a large dried bean, is often baked inside. The guest who finds it is crowned king or queen. Le Passe-Partout is a tiny restaurant with a big reputation in Montreal.

TIME: 45 minutes, plus chilling and resting   YIELD: 6 servings

½ tablespoon beaten egg yolk
¾ cup plus 2 tablespoons sugar
1 tablespoon plus 2 teaspoons
    flour, plus more for rolling
⅓ cup milk
7 tablespoons unsalted butter
3 large eggs

¾ cup finely ground blanched
    almonds
1 pound frozen puff pastry,
    thawed, or quick puff pastry
    (page 526)
Salt

1. In a medium bowl, whisk egg yolk and 2 tablespoons sugar together until blended. Whisk in flour. Place milk in a small saucepan, and bring to a boil. Gradually whisk boiling milk into egg mixture. Return mixture to saucepan, and bring to a boil while continuing to whisk. It will thicken. Remove from heat, and transfer to a clean bowl. Place plastic wrap directly on surface, cool, and refrigerate until cold.

2. In a food processor, mix butter and ½ cup sugar together until smooth. Add 2 whole eggs and mix until smooth. Add ground almonds and mix again. Add chilled pastry cream and mix until well blended and smooth. Cover and refrigerate 2 or 3 hours.

3. Make a simple syrup by mixing ¼ cup sugar with ¼ cup water in a saucepan. Bring to a boil, remove from heat and allow to cool; reserve at room temperature.

4. Divide puff pastry dough in half. On a lightly floured surface, roll each half into a 10-inch round ⅛ to ¼ inch thick. Transfer dough to a baking sheet and refrigerate for 1 hour.

5. Line a baking sheet with parchment paper or a nonstick liner. Place one round of dough in center of sheet. Spread evenly with almond pastry cream, leaving 2 inches clear around perimeter. (If desired, bury an

almond or other object in the center; this is traditional for Three Kings Day.) Using a pastry brush, moisten rim of galette with cold water, and place second round of dough on top, stretching it to cover pastry cream and rim. Press lightly all around rim of dough to seal. Using a sharp paring knife or pizza wheel, trim ½ inch from edge of galette to make a neat edge. In a small bowl, mix remaining egg with a pinch of salt, and brush across top of galette. Using a paring knife, make a series of shallow incisions in top of galette, starting from center and spiraling toward edge. Allow galette to rest at room temperature for 1 hour.

6. Preheat oven to 425 degrees. Bake galette until light golden brown, about 10 minutes, then reduce heat to 350 degrees and bake until dark golden brown. Glaze top of galette with sugar syrup, and bake 2 minutes longer. Cool on a rack, and serve at room temperature.

THE NAPOLEON COMPLEX:
Delusions of Grandeur Seize Restaurant Kitchens
By Amanda Hesser

What you get from chefs in restaurants today can resemble the conversation at a cocktail party: some of it is smart, and a lot of it is showing off. Consider the ostentatious trend toward greater and greater height on the plate, food sculpture that looks impressive until you try to eat it, and it falls to pieces.

This trend, which drives chefs to build dishes ever higher, can be seen perfectly in the proliferation of dishes named after the napoleon, the classic dessert that has become just about anything you can imagine, as long as it comes stacked high.

It took pastry chefs more than a century of toiling in the kitchen to perfect and popularize the napoleon, a prim rectangle of alternating layers of flaky, buttery puff pastry and vanilla-scented pastry cream.

Then today's aspiring Napoleons of cuisine got hold of it. Some of them saw an opportunity to juxtapose contrasting flavors and textures in imaginative ways; others approached the task like construction workers, brick and mortar layered ever higher. In little more than a decade, they have completely changed the napoleon, often disastrously, sometimes triumphantly.

The clue here is a crisp layer and a soft, creamy layer. If you can imagine the ingredients coming together to form a layered, texturally contrasting dish, in the spirit of the original napoleon, you will probably have found a good variation on the theme.

Without the contrast of textures, and a subtle interplay of flavors, the napoleon becomes something slightly crude—a prosaic stack of raw materials. Why not just add bread and make a sandwich?

Assembling a great napoleon has to be much more than just slapping ingredients on top of one another. But with so many interpretations, the word itself is on the verge of dissolving into meaninglessness.

Where the napoleon is going, as it turns out, is easier to pin down than its origin. The word "napoleon" appears to be a corruption of "napolitain" (Neapolitan), the name of an old French dessert, which is a layering of butter cookies and jam iced with fondant. The napoleon dessert as Americans know it, however, more closely resembles the French pastry called a millefeuille (thousand-leaf)—the familiar layering of puff pastry and pastry cream—which was created sometime in the nineteenth century.

The millefeuille-like pastry was introduced to the United States around the turn of this century. But the word "millefeuille" never stuck. "Napoleon" did. It's much easier to spell and to pronounce.

EDITOR'S NOTE: Do not ask for a "Napoleon" in a pastry shop in France, as I mistakenly did during my student years. They won't know what you are talking about. The term is millefeuille (pronounced meel-FOY, sort of.)

Lemon Curd Napoleon

Substituting phyllo for puff pastry simplifies the preparation, a shortcut that many chefs use. Picholine is an elegant restaurant near Lincoln Center.

TIME: 1 hour   YIELD: 6 servings

Terrance
Brennan,
Picholine,
New York

8 large egg yolks

½ cup lemon juice

Grated zest of 2 lemons

¾ cup granulated sugar

8 ounces (2 sticks) unsalted butter

6 sheets phyllo dough, thawed

½ cup confectioners' sugar

2 cups fresh raspberries, or
    other seasonal berries

1. In the top of the double boiler, combine the egg yolks, lemon juice and zest. Add the granulated sugar, and whisk to blend. Place over simmering water. Whisk until thickened, about 4 minutes. Remove from the heat.

2. Dice half the butter and whisk in, a piece at a time. Place the top of the double boiler in a large bowl of ice water, and stir frequently until chilled. Transfer mixture to a container, cover and refrigerate. It may be stored for up to 3 days.

3. Preheat oven to 400 degrees. Melt and clarify remaining butter. Line 2 baking sheets with parchment paper.

4. Place the phyllo sheets on a work surface, and cover with a slightly dampened cloth. Remove one phyllo sheet, and lightly brush with clarified butter. Top with two more sheets, brushing each with butter. Make a second stack with the remaining three sheets of phyllo, buttering each one. Using a sharp, round 3-inch cookie cutter, cut 12 circles from each stack. Sprinkle generously with confectioners' sugar, and transfer to a baking sheet. Cover phyllo disks with a sheet of parchment paper, and fit another baking sheet on top. Bake until golden, about 5 minutes; do not overcook. Remove top baking sheet and parchment paper, and allow phyllo disks to cool.

5. To assemble, place a dab of lemon curd in the center of each plate, and press a stacked phyllo disk on top of it. Top the phyllo with 1 tablespoon of lemon curd. Arrange 4 raspberries on the curd. Top with another phyllo disk, more lemon curd, and raspberries, continuing until each napoleon has 3 layers of berries. Top with a phyllo disk, and sprinkle with confectioners' sugar. Serve immediately.

Red Raspberry Napoleons

Charlie
Palmer,
Aureole,
New York

Though this napoleon is also made with phyllo instead of the more tradi-tional puff pastry, there is no reason why puff pastry cannot be used in-stead. Aureole is the flagship of chef Charlie Palmer's empire, which extends from New York to Washington, Las Vegas and California.

TIME: 1 hour, plus chilling   YIELD: 4 servings

½ teaspoon unflavored gelatin
3 large egg yolks
1 large egg
Salt
½ cup plus 3 tablespoons
   granulated sugar
¼ cup Wondra flour
2 cups half-and-half, or whole
   milk
1 vanilla bean
2 tablespoons cold unsalted butter

1 package frozen phyllo, thawed
8 ounces unsalted butter, melted
1 cup superfine sugar,
   approximately
5½ cups fresh raspberries
¼ cup orange juice
1 teaspoon grated orange zest
3 tablespoons confectioners'
   sugar
4 sprigs fresh mint, for garnish

1. In a small pan combine gelatin with ¼ cup cold water. Place over low heat, and stir until gelatin has softened, about 1 minute. Remove from heat, and set aside.

2. In a medium mixing bowl, combine egg yolks, whole egg, salt and ¼ cup granulated sugar. Whisk to blend. Add flour, and whisk until smooth.

3. In a large saucepan over medium heat, combine the half-and-half and ¼ cup granulated sugar. Split vanilla bean lengthwise, scrape pulp into pan, then add the bean. Stir to dissolve sugar, bring to a boil, and immedi-ately remove from the heat. Whisk about 1 cup of the hot half-and-half into the egg mixture, then immediately pour the egg mixture back into saucepan. Return pan to medium heat, and whisk constantly until thick-ened, about 2 to 3 minutes. Add reserved gelatin, reduce heat to low, and whisk 2 minutes more. Remove from heat, and whisk in the chilled butter. Pour mixture into a shallow container, and place a piece of plastic film on the surface. Refrigerate until well chilled, about 4 hours.

4. Cut a 2-by-4-inch rectangle of cardboard. Line 2 baking sheets with parchment paper. Preheat the oven to 375 degrees.

5. Spread phyllo on a dry counter and cover with a slightly dampened kitchen towel. Remove one sheet, and brush lightly with melted butter. Sprinkle with a little of the superfine sugar. Repeat with three more sheets, and stack them one atop another. Make another stack with four more sheets. Cut eight 2-by-4-inch rectangles from each stack by placing the cardboard rectangle on the top sheet and cutting all the way through. (Twelve pieces are needed: extra allowed for breakage.) Place stacked rectangles on baking sheets, cover with parchment paper and top each sheet with another baking sheet. If you do not have four baking sheets, use two, baking each batch of pastry separately. Bake until lightly golden, about 5 minutes. Remove from oven, uncover, and allow to cool. Place stacked rectangles on wire racks, and reserve.

6. In a medium saucepan over low heat, combine 2½ cups raspberries, orange juice, zest and 3 tablespoons granulated sugar. Cook, stirring, until raspberries are soft, about 5 minutes. Remove from heat, and transfer to a blender. Process until smooth.

7. Pour sauce through a very fine sieve, pressing to extract all of the puree. Discard the seeds. Pour the sauce into a nonreactive container, and refrigerate.

8. Remove vanilla bean from pastry cream. Set aside 20 raspberries. Place a rectangle of stacked phyllo on each of 4 plates. Spoon a heaping tablespoon of cream onto the pastry, and top with a few raspberries. Add a small spoonful of cream, and top with another rectangle of pastry. Repeat to make another layer, topped by pastry. Lightly sift confectioners' sugar over the top. Serve in a pool of sauce, garnished with 5 raspberries and a sprig of mint.

Bittersweet Chocolate Dacquoise with Halvah Cream

Bill
Yosses

Chocolate and halvah make for a stunningly felicious combination. The best halvah can be found in Middle Eastern stores, not cellophane packages at candy counters. Bill Yosses began his career in Paris, where he worked at La Maison du Chocolat and at Fauchon before returning to New York.

TIME: 3 hours, plus cooling and freezing   YIELD: 8 servings

1½ cups confectioners' sugar, plus more to dust cake

⅓ cup plus 1 tablespoon unsweetened cocoa

6 large egg whites

⅛ teaspoon cream of tartar

¾ cup plus 2 tablespoons granulated sugar

4 ounces bittersweet chocolate, chopped

2½ cups heavy cream

2 cups milk

½ cup tahini (sesame paste)

7 tablespoons honey

⅓ cup cornstarch

2 large egg yolks

1½ cups crumbled halvah

1. Preheat oven to 250 degrees. Line 2 baking sheets with parchment paper; use a marker to trace three 8-inch circles onto paper. Turn paper marked side down.

2. In a large bowl, sift together confectioners' sugar and cocoa powder; set aside. In the bowl of an electric mixer, whip egg whites until foamy. Add the cream of tartar and a tablespoon of the granulated sugar; whip until soft peaks form. With mixer running, gradually pour in rest of the granulated sugar, and whip until very stiff peaks form. Fold a third of the egg whites into the sugar and cocoa mixture. Fold in remaining whites.

3. Transfer mixture to a pastry bag fitted with a large plain tip or to a large resealable plastic bag with a corner cut off. Starting just within the circles marked on parchment paper, pipe rounds of batter, working inward in a spiral. Bake for 2 hours, then turn off oven; allow meringue to dry in oven until oven has cooled completely, at least 4 hours longer or overnight.

4. For ganache, place chocolate in a bowl. In a saucepan, bring 1 cup

cream to a boil. Pour it over chocolate, and let sit for 3 minutes. Starting in center, whisk well to combine. Refrigerate, covered, until thickened but still pourable, 1 to 2 hours.

5. For halvah cream, pour milk into a saucepan, and bring to a simmer. Meanwhile, in a large heatproof bowl, whisk together tahini, honey, cornstarch and egg yolks. Pour a little bit of hot milk into tahini mixture, whisking constantly. Continue to whisk, and add rest of milk to bowl. Pour mixture back into saucepan, and bring to a boil, whisking constantly. Boil, whisking, for 2 to 3 minutes until very thick. Transfer to a bowl, and whisk in half the crumbled halvah. Cover bowl with plastic wrap, and refrigerate until chilled, at least 1 hour.

6. Whip 1½ cups heavy cream just until it is thick enough to hold soft peaks. Gently fold cream and the remaining crumbled halvah into chilled tahini mixture.

7. To assemble, set aside nicest meringue disk for top layer. Place one meringue layer in an 8-inch springform pan. Spread half the halvah cream over meringue. Place another round of meringue over cream. Spread ganache on meringue in an even layer. Chill about 15 minutes to set ganache. Cover ganache with remaining halvah cream. Top with last round of meringue. Cover pan and freeze for 1 to 2 hours.

8. Before serving, run a knife around edge of pan, then remove sides of springform pan. Sift a thin layer of powdered sugar over top. Transfer to a serving platter. To slice, use a serrated knife dipped in hot water. Wipe dry between cuts.

Dacquoise with Poached Pears and Sabayon

Diane Forley,
Verbena,
New York

A classic dacquoise is made with meringue layers like these. In this recipe, the seeds are removed from the vanilla bean so that they will not leave speckles on the pears. Scrape them onto a piece of plastic wrap, enclose tightly, and set aside to use in other recipes. Diane Forley owned Verbena in New York, with her husband, Michael Otsuka. They closed the restaurant and relocated to work in California.

TIME: 2 hours   YIELD: 6 servings

2 cups whole almonds
1¾ cups sugar
8 large egg whites at room
    temperature
4 cups white wine
¼ cup almond paste
1 vanilla bean, sliced in half
    lengthwise, seeds removed and
    reserved for another use
1 orange, peeled and cut into 4
    round slices

Juice of one lemon
1 cinnamon stick
2 pieces star anise
5 cloves
2 tablespoons grenadine
    (optional)
3 Bartlett pears
5 large egg yolks
1 cup heavy cream, whipped until
    stiff

1. To make the dacquoise disks, preheat oven to 250 degrees. Line a baking pan 13 by 17 inches with parchment paper.

2. Using a food processor, chop the almonds with ⅓ cup of the sugar until finely ground. Place egg whites in the bowl of an electric mixer. Whip the whites until soft peaks form; then, gradually add ⅔ cup sugar. Continue to whip until whites are barely stiff. Fold in the almond mixture. Pour into baking pan, and bake until the meringue is dry on the surface but still slightly springy to the touch, about 1 hour and 20 minutes. When the meringue is baked, cover with sheets of foil or waxed paper, invert onto a clean baking sheet and remove parchment paper. Using a cookie cutter or other circular shape, cut into 12 4-inch rounds.

3. While meringue is baking, prepare the poached pears: In a wide nonreactive saucepan 6 quarts or larger, combine the wine and almond paste.

With a wooden spoon, break the paste into pieces. Add ½ cup of the sugar, the vanilla bean, orange slices, lemon juice, cinnamon stick, star anise, cloves and grenadine. Peel the pears, cut in half and remove cores. Place cut side down in the saucepan, and place a clean cotton napkin over them in the pan liquid, to keep them submerged. Place pan over medium heat, and bring to a simmer. Reduce heat to low, and simmer until the pears are cooked through, about 25 minutes. Remove the cloth, and place the pears in a bowl until needed. Strain the poaching liquid, reserving ½ cup for the sabayon.

4. To make the sabayon, reheat the poaching liquid if it has cooled. In a metal bowl briefly beat the 5 egg yolks and remaining ¼ cup of sugar. Fit the bowl over a saucepan with about an inch of boiling water. Continue to beat the egg mixture by hand until it thickens. Transfer to an electric mixer, and beat at medium speed while adding the ½ cup of poaching liquid in a thin stream. Beat until mixture has cooled, about 5 to 7 minutes. Fold in the whipped cream.

5. Place a dacquoise disk on each of six serving plates. Place a small amount of sabayon on each disk, top with a pear half and add more sabayon. Lean a second disk against the pear. Serve immediately.

Banana Turnovers

Kay
Rentschler

Other fruit, like mangoes, peaches, apples or apricots, can be used in place of bananas. A jam filling is another option. Kay Rentschler has contributed many recipes to *The New York Times.*

TIME: 1 hour, plus chilling   YIELD: 6 servings

1 cup half-and-half
3 tablespoons granulated sugar
Pinch of salt
1 tablespoon cornstarch
2 large eggs, separated
1 tablespoon cold unsalted butter
1 teaspoon vanilla extract
Flour for dusting dough

1 pound frozen puff pastry,
    thawed but cold, or quick puff
    pastry (page 526)
2 large ripe bananas
¼ cup confectioners' sugar
Vanilla mousseline (page 534),
    caramel sauce (page 539) or
    vanilla ice cream

1. In a small heavy saucepan, combine half-and-half, 2 tablespoons granulated sugar and the salt; bring to a simmer over medium heat, stirring occasionally.

2. Meanwhile, in a small bowl whisk together cornstarch and remaining granulated sugar. Add 2 egg yolks and stir until mixture is smooth.

3. Ladle about ¼ cup simmering half-and-half into egg yolk mixture and whisk well to combine. Transfer mixture into simmering liquid, whisking vigorously. Allow pastry cream to bubble for 5 seconds, then remove pan from heat. Stir in butter and vanilla. Transfer to a small bowl, place plastic wrap on the surface and refrigerate until chilled.

4. Unfold puff pastry dough on floured surface and dust with flour. Using a pizza cutter, divide dough evenly into six 5-inch squares; arrange squares on work surface with a point facing you.

5. Working quickly, peel bananas and cut into thirds. Slice each third lengthwise in two pieces. Place 1 tablespoon pastry cream in lower center of each dough square, 2 banana slices on top and dab with more cream. Brush dough edges lightly with water. Fold points of each square down to form triangular turnovers. Press edges of each with fork, and refrigerate on parchment-lined sheet pan for 30 minutes. Meanwhile, place oven rack in lower position and preheat oven to 375 degrees.

6. In small bowl, whisk egg whites until frothy; brush on turnovers. Sift confectioners' sugar over surface of each. Bake until well-risen and deeply browned, about 40 minutes, turning sheet pan once halfway through. Serve warm with vanilla mousseline, caramel sauce or vanilla ice cream.

Croustade with Prunes and Armagnac

Ariane
Daguin

This recipe from Gascony, the region in southwestern France that is known for the production of Armagnac and for the cultivation of the plums used for drying to become prunes, illustrates an historic cultural connection. The Moors that occupied Spain also exerted their influence on the southwest of France, which is why phyllo is used. This pastry is also called pastis in the region. Ariane Daguin, who is from Auch in Gascony, and who owns D'Artagnan, a company that sells foie gras, game and other products, including prunes, is a tireless ambassador of the region.

TIME: 1 hour 20 minutes, plus marinating   YIELD: 6 to 8 servings

12 large pitted prunes
¾ cup Armagnac
4 tablespoons unsalted butter

1 tablespoon orange flower water
10 sheets phyllo, thawed
3 tablespoons sugar

1. Place prunes in Armagnac and allow to marinate in the refrigerator for 2 weeks. Drain prunes, reserving Armagnac.

2. Melt butter in a small saucepan; add 1 teaspoon orange flower water and 1 tablespoon reserved Armagnac. (Keep remaining Armagnac for another use, in cooking, baking or to add to drinks.) Remove from heat and set aside.

3. Preheat oven to 300 degrees. Brush some of the butter mixture in bottom and sides of 10-inch pie pan.

4. Spread phyllo on work surface and cover with damp cloth. Cut stack of phyllo sheets in a circle to fit bottom of pie plate. Reserve scraps. Keep phyllo covered when not being used so it does not dry out. Place one circle in pie plate. Brush lightly with butter mixture. Repeat with six more circles, lightly buttering each.

5. Scatter prunes over phyllo. Sprinkle with remaining orange flower water. Butter one circle of phyllo on both sides and place on top. Add another circle and butter top. Crumple last circle of phyllo and place on top. Crumple scraps and place them on top, too, so crumpled phyllo covers the top. Brush with remaining butter and sprinkle with sugar.

6. Bake about 45 minutes, until golden. Serve warm or at room temperature.

Apple Strudel

The convenience of frozen phyllo cannot be underestimated. Making strudel dough from scratch is an extended production. But the Viennese or Hungarian strudel illustrates, better than any other dish, the influence of Turkish or Muslim cooking in Europe. That is why phyllo and strudel are interchangeable. Berghoff, a famous and venerable German restaurant in Chicago, is now closed.

Berghoff, Chicago, Illinois

TIME: 45 minutes   YIELD: 6 to 8 servings

4 large Granny Smith apples, peeled, cored and thinly sliced
¾ cup granulated sugar
½ cup golden seedless raisins
½ cup chopped pecans
1 tablespoon ground cinnamon
¼ teaspoon salt

¼ cup fine dry bread crumbs, more for sprinkling
¾ cup (1½ sticks) unsalted butter, melted
4 16-by-22-inch sheets phyllo, thawed
Confectioners' sugar

1. In a large bowl, combine apples, granulated sugar, raisins, pecans, cinnamon, salt and ¼ cup bread crumbs. Toss until mixed.

2. Preheat oven to 375 degrees. Place 1 sheet phyllo on a work surface, and brush lightly with melted butter. Sprinkle with a scant tablespoon of bread crumbs. Repeat with remaining sheets of phyllo, stacking them.

3. Spoon apple mixture over phyllo to within 1½ inches of edges. Grasping long edges of phyllo, roll up jelly-roll fashion. Place roll on a cookie sheet, seam side down. Brush with remaining melted butter. Bake until golden, about 30 minutes. Allow to cool, then sprinkle lightly with confectioners' sugar.

Strawberry Tiramisu

Florence
Fabricant

The layered Venetian dessert called tiramisu has become a cliché. I made it with strawberries to give it a refreshingly new and summery personality. Its various layers must be prepared separately, so it takes time and effort, but the end result is an unusual strawberry dessert, and a tour-de-force. Even chocolate lovers are not likely to be disappointed.

TIME: 1 hour, plus chilling   YIELD: 8 servings

½ cup kirsch or framboise
½ cup milk
3 large egg yolks
½ tablespoon cornstarch
4 to 6 tablespoons sugar
½ cup heavy cream

1½ pints strawberries
⅓ cup strawberry preserves
8 ounces mascarpone cheese
4 ounces "savoiardi" biscuits or
    ladyfingers
1 tablespoon unsweetened cocoa

1. Mix the kirsch or framboise with ¼ cup water. Set aside.

2. Scald the milk in a heavy-bottomed two-quart saucepan. Remove from heat.

3. Combine the egg yolks and 3 tablespoons sugar in a bowl. Using a whisk or a handheld mixer, beat the egg yolks and sugar until they are thick and light. Beat in the cornstarch, then beat in the hot milk in a thin stream.

4. Return the mixture to the saucepan. Place over medium-low heat and, beating constantly, gradually add ⅓ cup of the diluted liquor. Continue beating until the mixture is thick, light and beginning to simmer. The cornstarch will prevent the eggs from separating but it is important to keep beating the mixture and scraping the bottom of the saucepan.

5. Transfer the mixture to a metal bowl. If you have time, refrigerate it, covered with plastic wrap placed directly on the surface of the custard, for four hours or longer, until thoroughly chilled. Or place it in a bowl of ice and water and continue beating until the mixture is cold, then refrigerate it. Whip the cream until stiff and fold it into the chilled egg yolk mixture. Refrigerate again.

6. Rinse and hull the strawberries and slice them. Sweeten them if necessary. Refrigerate.

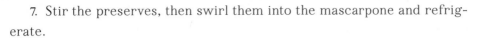

7. Stir the preserves, then swirl them into the mascarpone and refrigerate.

8. Up to an hour before serving, arrange half the biscuits on a square or round platter or in a shallow serving bowl about 9 inches in diameter. Sprinkle them with half the remaining diluted liquor. Top with half the sliced strawberries. Spread with the mascarpone. Top with the remaining biscuits. Sprinkle with the remaining diluted liquor. Top with the remaining strawberries. Spread the whipped cream and egg yolk mixture over the strawberries. Dust lightly with sifted cocoa and refrigerate until ready to serve.

FRUIT DESSERTS

L et's say there are three dessert food groups: chocolate, caramel and fruit. Often, a dessert will involve all three. And even when fruit is not the primary component, some fruit or a fruit sauce might brighten and enliven the plate.

The desserts in this chapter are those that feature primarily fruit. Fruit pies, soufflés, fruit-based cakes, crumbles, cobblers, puddings and frozen confections like sorbets are given in other chapters. These recipes are among the lightest in the book: macerated raw fruit, compotes, fruit soups, terrines and other gelatin-based desserts, poached fruit and baked fruit.

A fruit dessert is only as good as the fruit that you use. Pay attention to the seasons to obtain the ripest, most flavorful fruits. Although making a dessert is not the ideal way to use up fruit that might be bruised or past its prime, because there are many recipes that call for cut-up fruit, some specimens that are not pristine enough for the fruit bowl can be used.

Sometimes, preparing a fruit dessert requires several days of advance planning. Peaches and pears that are beautifully ripe might not be available the very day you need them, but if they are slightly underripe and you have allowed for a couple of days for them to soften just so, you will be ahead of the game. Pears especially are the most flavorful when they ripen off the tree.

The only specialized equipment needed for these desserts, in addition to sharp knives, are a peeler, a pitter for some fruits like cherries, a zester and a melon-baller.

UNCOOKED FRUIT DESSERTS

Shopping, not cooking, is what counts for these desserts. The ripest, most alluringly jewel-like, seasonal fruits are necessary when a dessert carpaccio, a fruit soup or herb-scented berries and cream will end the meal. Indeed, when I am in the market shopping for ingredients and I see some particularly perfect fruit, I might change my dessert plans on the spot, and decide that a simple presentation of fresh fruit is all I have to serve. Similarly, if I am planning goblets of chilled fresh blackberries and nectarines splashed with liqueur, for example, and no ripe nectarines beckon from the fruit stand, I am likely to shift gears, see what fruit does appeal, and make a substitution. That is the way good cooks and chefs approach the market.

Nectarines and Berries with Flavored Whipped Cream

Robin
Reiels,
Flying Fish,
Seattle,
Washington

This simple confection is the very expression of July and August, when nectarines are at their juicy peak, and fresh blackberries are also in the market and at farm stands at prices that do not leave you gasping. It's also the only time you have a shot at finding fresh lavender. The advantage to using nectarines, not peaches, is that nectarines do not require peeling. Try to use a mixture of yellow and white ones. This recipe comes from a popular Seattle restaurant.

TIME: 15 minutes, plus macerating   YIELD: 4 servings

4 cups ripe freestone nectarines, sliced ¼ inch thick (about 4 large)

1 pint raspberries

1 pint blackberries

2 tablespoons good-quality balsamic vinegar

5 tablespoons sugar

Salt

Pinch freshly ground black pepper

2½ cups whipping cream

2 teaspoons fresh lavender flowers

Zest of 1 orange

Mint leaves for garnish

1. In a large nonreactive bowl, mix the fruit, vinegar, 2 tablespoons sugar and pinches of salt and pepper. Let sit uncovered in refrigerator for 30 minutes.

2. Combine cream, remaining sugar, lavender, orange zest and another pinch of salt, and whip until soft peaks form.

3. Put fruit into serving bowls, and spoon a bit of whipped cream on top. Garnish with mint.

Brandied Berries and Nectarines

Florence
Fabricant

The preceding recipe gets a splash of balsamic vinegar while the flavor in this one depends on liqueurs. The dessert couldn't be simpler, so give it some panache with your presentation, piling the fruit into stemmed wineglasses. That's the way I serve many desserts, giving them the grandeur of stemware set on a plate, which leaves room for a cookie or other garnish. And when a dessert is meant to be eaten cold, I chill the glasses in the refrigerator before filling them.

TIME: 20 minutes   YIELD: 6 servings

4 large ripe freestone nectarines
Juice of ½ lemon
½ pint each blackberries and
   raspberries, or all blackberries
2 tablespoons sugar

¼ cup blackberry brandy
½ cup blueberries, optional
6 sprigs fresh mint
Crème fraîche, optional

1. Halve the nectarines, and discard pits. Slice nectarines, and place them in a bowl. Toss with lemon juice.

2. Press half the blackberries and raspberries through a fine sieve into a small saucepan. Add sugar, and heat gently, just until sugar has dissolved, 3 to 4 minutes. Stir in the brandy.

3. Mix remaining blackberries, raspberries and optional blueberries with nectarine slices. Pour sauce over fruit, and mix gently. Cover and refrigerate until ready to serve.

4. Spoon fruit into large stemmed goblets, and garnish with mint and a dollop of crème fraîche, if desired, before serving.

FOR RASPBERRIES, UBIQUITY (AT A PRICE)
By David Karp

There was a time when raspberries were a seasonal delicacy, considered fancy enough to be served by themselves as dessert at fine restaurants.

Now they are always available, but the flavor that once made them such a delight is harder to find.

What about out-of-season raspberries?

Twenty years ago, off-season raspberries fetched more than $20 a pound in New York.

Red raspberry canes are normally planted in late winter and produce two crops. Second-year canes, called floricanes, bloom from late spring to early summer, and first-year canes, called primocanes, from late summer to fall.

The growers dig up dormant plants from northern nurseries, hold them in cold storage, then plant them in Southern California from April to September. The discombobulated plants then bear fruit from late fall to early spring.

That is the rainy season in California, and rain causes raspberries to soften and rot. So growers shield many of the rows in near-transparent plastic tunnels, originally adapted from Spanish strawberry growers. Supported by metal hoops, and open at the sides for ventilation, these structures also protect against wind and mild frost.

Since the equable maritime climate always seems like spring to the canes, workers even strip off leaves by hand to make them go dormant and then bloom again in winter. A year-round crop in California, with help from its fields in Mexico in the winter, resulted in a crucial advantage with supermarket chains. Seventy million pounds of raspberries are a typical California harvest now, most of them around Watsonville, the biggest raspberry district.

How do out-of-season raspberries rate for flavor? Some are mediocre, most are decent or good, but none are great. They are dependably pleasant, but lack the complexity and aroma of the best berries. Part of the problem is that raspberries trucked to distant markets need to be picked firm to arrive in good condition, and most of a berry's aroma develops only with full ripeness.

Black raspberries, also called blackcaps, are a different species, native to the Eastern United States. Alluringly purple-black in color, they are small, round, firm, dry and very seedy, with a distinctive sweet taste of dark cherries. As fresh berries, blackcaps are too seedy for many people, and are rarely sold at supermarkets, but their intense color and flavor drive aficionados wild.

Once used in the edible dye stamped on meat, and as coloring in Dr Pepper soda, blackcaps now are used mostly in processed foods like jam, for which their rich flavor is superb.

Their season is short, usually several weeks in July, and the canes are low-yielding compared with those of red raspberries. Scattered plantings exist in the East and Midwest, but most of the nation's crop, about 1,300 acres of the Munger variety, is mechanically harvested for processing in the Willamette Valley, near Portland, Oregon.

Black raspberries were all but forgotten until two years ago, when a scientific study cited them as being the highest of all berries in anthocyanins, the antioxidant compounds that scavenge harmful free radicals associated with aging and cancer.

This sparked a surge in interest.

Paradoxically, despite the reputed health benefits of their berries, black raspberry plants are extremely susceptible to viruses, and rarely live more than a few years.

Macerated Blackberries ✳

Sitting in a warm place with a dusting of sugar adds to the lushness of the berries. Consider using white rum or gin in place of the kirsch. Richard Langer is a food writer.

Richard
Langer

∽

TIME: 5 minutes, plus resting   YIELD: 2 servings

2 cups fresh blackberries
1 tablespoon sugar

1 tablespoon kirsch, if desired

1. In a small mixing bowl, combine the blackberries, sugar and kirsch. Stir gently to mix.

2. Set aside in a warm spot, like a sunny windowsill, and allow to macerate for 1 to 2 hours.

Grappa-Soused Summer Fruit ✳

A combination of grappa and freshly ground black pepper enhances this mixture of summer berries and fresh figs. Jody and Heather Adams are chefs at Rialto in Cambridge, Massachusetts.

Jody
Adams and
Heather
Adams,
Rialto,
Cambridge,
Massachusetts

∽

TIME: 10 minutes, plus maceration and chilling   YIELD: 4 servings

¼ cup grappa or eau de vie, any
   flavor
¼ cup sugar
Zest of ½ lemon, in strips
1 tablespoon lemon juice
10 mint leaves, torn in half

¼ to ½ teaspoon coarsely ground
   black pepper
2 cups strawberries, hulled and
   cut in half if large
1 cup raspberries
4 large fresh figs, quartered

1. Mix grappa with sugar in a large nonreactive bowl until sugar dissolves. Add lemon zest, lemon juice, mint and pepper.

2. Add fruit; toss, and let sit 2 hours at room temperature. Chill at least 1 hour before serving. For more intense grappa flavor in fruit, macerate overnight in refrigerator.

Pluot Carpaccio with Ginger Sauce

Florence
Fabricant

Pluots, a relative newcomer in the fruit basket, are a cross between apricots and plums. Thanks to the apricot, they are easily pitted, unlike may kinds of regular plums. They tend to be large, sweet and juicy, and often, but not exclusively, ruby-fleshed. They are easy to cut into generous, even slices.

TIME: 45 minutes, plus chilling   YIELD: 6 servings

8 red pluots, ripe but not soft
⅓ cup sugar
1½ teaspoons freshly grated
   ginger

¼ cup ginger liqueur
6 mint sprigs for garnish

1. Cut pluots in half lengthwise, and remove pits. With a mandoline or fine slicing blade on a food processor, use very gentle pressure to slice pluot halves paper-thin, starting with the flat cut side. Reserve uneven slices, scraps and pieces with a hole from pits.

2. Arrange perfectly round slices closely overlapping like petals on each of 6 dessert plates. You should have about 25 slices per plate. Refrigerate.

3. Finely chop remaining pieces; you should have about 1½ cups. Place in small saucepan. Add sugar, ginger and ⅓ cup water. Bring to a simmer, and cook over medium heat about 15 minutes, stirring occasionally, until fruit has nearly dissolved and is like a sauce. Remove from heat, stir in liqueur, transfer to a metal bowl and place bowl in ice water to chill. Refrigerate if not serving right away.

4. To serve, drizzle about 3 tablespoons of sauce over each plate of sliced pluots, and garnish with mint.

Cherries in Barbera

The cherries in this recipe are cooked, but just barely. They then pick up the rich cherrylike flavors of Barbera wine. The recipe comes from Roberto Donna's cooking school in Washington, D.C.

TIME: 1 hour 20 minutes, plus chilling   YIELD: 8 to 10 servings

Il Laboratorio del Galileo, Washington, D.C.

3 pounds cherries, pitted
1 cup sugar
2 whole cloves
½ stick cinnamon

Grated zest of 1 lemon
Grated zest of 1 orange
1 cup Barbera wine
½ pint heavy cream

1. In a large saucepan, combine cherries and remaining ingredients except for cream. Bring to a boil and turn off heat. Cool and refrigerate for 1 or 2 days.

2. When ready to serve, beat cream until soft peaks form. Remove cloves and cinnamon stick from cherry mixture. Spoon cherries and some of the juice into 8 to 10 stem glasses. Top each with a dollop of whipped cream.

Cherries with Chocolate in Ricotta

Regina
Schrambling

The winey richness of ripe cherries can stand toe-to-toe with dark chocolate. Sweetened ricotta cheese dresses the package with flair. Regina Schrambling is a food writer who was a *New York Times* reporter.

TIME: 10 minutes   YIELD: 4 servings

15 ounces part-skim ricotta

¼ cup kirsch, or to taste

¼ cup confectioners' sugar, or to taste

2 ounces bittersweet chocolate, chopped

1 to 1½ pounds cherries, pitted and halved

Cocoa, preferably unsweetened Dutch process, for garnish

2 tablespoons sliced almonds, toasted

1. Whip ricotta with kirsch and confectioners' sugar. Fold in chocolate and cherries. Add more kirsch and sugar if needed. (If time allows, chill at least 15 minutes.)

2. Divide among 4 shallow bowls. Dust lightly with cocoa, and garnish with almonds.

Sour Cherries with Mascarpone Cream

Sour cherries, usually the Montmorency variety, enjoy a brief season, from mid-June to mid-July. They are bright red and usually softer than regular table cherries. Pie-makers love them. In this recipe they are macerated with herbs—use lemon thyme, lemon sage or even lemongrass if verbena is not available—then bedded on mascarpone. In place of mascarpone and cream, 12 ounces of crème fraîche can be used. Sanford is a restaurant in Milwaukee, Wisconsin.

Sandy D'Amato, Sanford, Milwaukee, Wisconsin

TIME: 20 minutes, plus macerating   YIELD: 4 servings

1¼ pounds fresh sour cherries, pitted

½ cup firmly packed fresh lemon verbena leaves

5 tablespoons sugar

½ teaspoon ground mace

¼ cup spätlese riesling

8 ounces mascarpone cheese

½ cup heavy cream

1. In a large nonreactive bowl, mix cherries, lemon verbena, 4 tablespoons sugar, ¼ teaspoon mace and wine. Cover and refrigerate at least 24 hours.

2. Strain and set aside cherries, reserving juice. Remove lemon verbena leaves from strainer, and add to juice.

3. Put juice in a blender, and blend it fine. Strain through a medium sieve, pressing to extract all liquid. Pour juice over cherries, reserving ¼ cup.

4. In a small bowl, soften cheese with a spatula. Slowly stir in reserved juice until mixture is smooth.

5. Combine cream and remaining sugar in another bowl, and beat until soft peaks form. Fold whipped cream into mascarpone.

6. To serve, divide mascarpone into 4 bowls. Pour cherries and juice over cheese. Top each serving with a pinch of remaining mace.

Winter Fruit Salad

Amanda
Hesser

The fruit in this dessert is not cooked, but the heated macerating liquid penetrates and seasons it after an overnight stay in the refrigerator. Bosc pears are not the only variety that is suitable, but their firm flesh, even when ripe, stands up well. Asian pears would be another good option, especially with star anise among the seasonings. Amanda Hesser is a food writer and cookbook author.

TIME: 15 minutes, plus chilling   YIELD: 6 servings

1¼ cups sugar

3 star anise

1 vanilla bean, split in half
   lengthwise

2 2-inch long strips lemon zest
   (peeled with a vegetable
   peeler), preferably Meyer
   lemon

3 ripe but firm Bosc pears

1 firm tart apple

8 dried Turkish apricots, halved

4 dried brown figs, stemmed and
   quartered

1. Place 5 cups water in a medium saucepan. Add the sugar, star anise, vanilla bean and lemon zest. Bring to a boil, and cook until the sugar is dissolved. Remove from heat.

2. Peel and core pears and apple. Slice thinly lengthwise and place in a large heatproof bowl. Add apricots and figs. Pour hot sugar syrup on top, making sure all the fruit is covered. Cover bowl with plastic wrap; poke a few holes in plastic. Chill overnight.

3. Ladle fruit into a serving bowl and serve.

Strawberries with Pink Peppercorn Sauce

Ever since balsamic vinegar imported from Italy began appearing on store shelves in the late 1980s, American chefs have been tempted by the traditional Modenese dessert that simply consists of fresh strawberries drizzled with balsamic vinegar. But the balsamic vinegar they use is the syrupy, artisanal kind, sold in small flasks for $100 or so. In this recipe you need a good-quality brand, aged more than ten years and superior to what is generally on supermarket shelves, but it does not have to be top-of-the-line. For another dessert that combines strawberries and balsamic vinegar, see Zabaglione with Strawberries and Balsamic Meringue (page 400). Susan Spicer is a chef based in New Orleans. Her restaurants are Bayona, Herbsaint and Cobalt.

Susan Spicer

TIME: 30 minutes   YIELD: 4 servings

¼ cup sugar

2 tablespoons Cognac

1 tablespoon good-quality
   balsamic vinegar

1 teaspoon pomegranate molasses

1 teaspoon pink peppercorns,
   lightly crushed

1 pint strawberries, hulled

Vanilla ice cream or mascarpone
   for serving

1. Place the sugar in a saucepan with 1 tablespoon water. Stir to dissolve. Bring to a boil over medium-high heat, and simmer until it is a deep caramel color. Watch carefully because mixture can burn easily. Remove from heat.

2. Carefully pour in the Cognac and vinegar, standing back because mixture can spatter. Return to low heat and swirl mixture to dissolve caramel. Remove from heat and stir in the pomegranate molasses and peppercorns. Dice 1 cup of the strawberries, add to caramel and cook over low heat for one minute. The sauce will be thick and syrupy. Remove from heat and allow to cool to room temperature.

3. Dice remaining strawberries and stir into sauce. Serve over vanilla ice cream or mascarpone.

Cherries with Red Wine Granita

Geoffrey
Zakarian

This early summer refresher highlights the ripe cherry flavor that is typical of the gamay grape, especially in Beaujolais. A simple Beaujolais-Villages will do nicely. Geoffrey Zakarian is the executive chef of two New York restaurants, one named Town and the other Country. This recipe is from Town.

TIME: 20 minutes, plus chilling and freezing   YIELD: 6 servings

1 cup Beaujolais or other gamay
  wine
1¼ cups sugar
1⅓ cups white grape juice
3 hibiscus tea bags

1 stalk lemongrass, trimmed and
  crushed
Grated zest of 1 orange
Grated zest of 1 lemon
2 pounds cherries, pitted

1. Combine wine, 1 cup sugar and grape juice in a saucepan. Simmer just until sugar dissolves. Transfer to a metal bowl, and refrigerate until cool, about 1 hour. Pour into an 8-inch-square metal baking pan, cover and freeze at least 4 hours.

2. Bring 3 cups water to a boil in a medium-size saucepan. Add tea, remove from heat and infuse 5 minutes. Add remaining sugar, lemongrass, orange and lemon zest; simmer until sugar dissolves, and remove from heat. Discard tea bags and lemongrass. Place cherries in a bowl and pour tea mixture over. Cover and refrigerate until cold, at least 4 hours.

3. Spoon cherries with liquid into stemmed glasses. Use a tablespoon to scrape ovals of frozen wine granita and place on top of cherries. Serve.

THE COOLEST SLICE OF SUMMER
By Marian Burros

Melons are the aristocrats of summer fruit, their cool elegance and exotic lushness perfuming dishes with the fragrances of a flower garden. The charming palette of summer colors spans the spectrum, from the creamy white flesh of the honeydew to the brassy firecracker red of the watermelon. In sorbets and chilled soups, in cocktails and salads, or simply eaten out of hand, melons are wonderful restoratives for the long, hot summer.

Melons have been admired for just these qualities through the centuries, the admiration reaching something of a frenzy in sixteenth-century France, when they appeared at every meal and moved the poet Marc-Antoine de Gérard, Sieur de Saint-Amant to verse: "O precious food! Delight of the mouth! Oh, much better than gold, masterpiece of Apollo! O flower of all the fruits! O ravishing melon!"

The extraordinary abundance and variety of melons available today would send the poet into a new frenzy.

How do you choose a good melon? There are some rules, starting with the fact that all melons should feel heavy. A good sign of ripeness for most melons is a clean break between the melon and stem rather than a cut in the stem itself, because when most melons are perfectly ripe, they separate naturally from the plant.

Avoid melons that are too firm or too soft or that have sunken spots on the skin.

A ripe melon can be stored in the refrigerator for a couple of days, but it is better to eat it before it has been refrigerated.

Just keep in mind that room-temperature melons have the best flavor but that in the heat of summer, the well-chilled melon is most appealing.

FRUIT SOUPS

How do you dress up a bowl of ripe fruit to make it suitable for an elegant dinner party? The answer is fruit soup. A well-seasoned, fairly thin fruit puree is spooned over perfectly sweetened fruit, sometimes with a scoop of sorbet, and served in a flat soup plate. Jewel-like color and refreshing flavors are the goals. A small serving of fruit soup can also be offered as a palate-cleanser after a heavy main course and before the regular dessert.

Watermelon Soup with Red Summer Berries and Lime ✳

Patrice
Caillot,
Osteria
del Circo,
New York

Make life easy by using seedless watermelon. And make it colorful by preparing two soups, one red and one golden, and pouring them slowly into the bowls, side by side. Osteria del Circo is the casual restaurant owned by the Maccioni family of Le Cirque fame.

TIME: 20 minutes, plus maceration   YIELD: 6 servings

4 pounds watermelon
½ cup sugar
½ cup lime juice
1 cup blackberries, halved

1 cup raspberries, halved
1 cup cherries, pitted and halved
1 cup strawberries, hulled and
　sliced

1. Remove rind and seeds from watermelon. Cut flesh into chunks, and puree in blender. Strain into bowl (there should be about 4 cups).

2. Mix puree with sugar and lime juice. Chill 2 hours.

3. To serve, divide fruits into six chilled soup bowls. Pour watermelon mixture over them, and serve immediately.

Bing Cherry Soup

The restaurant uses white zinfandel (a pink wine), diluted regular zinfandel or rosé for this Bing cherry soup. But consider Beaujolais as well. The gamay grape has a decidedly cherrylike flavor, to complement the fruit, especially when it is a Beaujolais of the most ordinary variety. See also the recipe for Cherries with Red Wine Granita, page 342. Monkey Bar is a steakhouse in Midtown Manhattan.

Monkey
Bar, New York

TIME: 1 hour, plus chilling   YIELD: 6 servings

4½ pounds Bing cherries, pitted
½ vanilla bean
6 ounces candied orange peel or orange slices
8 cups white zinfandel, or 6 cups zinfandel and 2 cups water, or 8 cups rosé wine

Lemon or raspberry sorbet or vanilla ice cream, for serving
Candied orange peel or biscotti, for optional garnish

1. Put 4 pounds of the cherries into a deep, wide, heavy pan. Add vanilla bean, candied orange, and wine. Bring to a boil, lower heat and simmer 30 to 40 minutes, until thickened and reduced by half.

2. Let cool for a few minutes, then transfer to a food processor in batches and pulse briefly, just until fruit is finely chopped. Transfer fruit and liquid to a fine-meshed sieve placed over a large bowl. Press hard with a wooden spoon to extract all the liquid. Cover, and chill liquid 4 hours or overnight. Halve remaining cherries and refrigerate.

3. To serve, ladle liquid into shallow bowls. Divide halved cherries among the bowls. Put a scoop of sorbet or ice cream in the center. Garnish with candied orange peel or a biscotti, if desired.

Red Wine and Berry Soup

Bayard's,
New York

The depth of flavor obtained from this combination of berries is beyond compare. Use a young pinot noir. Bayard's is in the historic India House mansion in lower Manhattan.

TIME: 3 hours   YIELD: 8 servings

1 bottle medium-body red wine
1 cinnamon stick
1 clove
1 vanilla bean, split lengthwise in
    half
¾ cup sugar
½ lemon, sliced

1½ pints strawberries, hulled
1½ pints raspberries
1 pint blueberries
½ pint blackberries
Vanilla frozen yogurt, ice cream
    or raspberry sorbet, optional
Fresh mint sprigs

1. Combine wine, cinnamon, clove, vanilla, sugar and lemon in a saucepan. Bring to boil.

2. In a bowl, combine 1 pint strawberries, 1 pint raspberries, ½ pint blueberries and all the blackberries. Puree in two batches in a food processor. Add to saucepan, return to simmer, strain, cool to room temperature, and then refrigerate for 2 hours.

3. Slice remaining strawberries, and divide among eight soup plates. Scatter in remaining berries. Pour cooled soup over; add a scoop of ice cream or sorbet, if desired, and garnish with mint.

Melon and Organic Strawberry Soup with Fruit Sorbet

The litchis give this fruit soup an exotic perfume. Fresh rambutans, available in late spring from Guatemala, are a fine substitute. Bouley Bakery is one of chef David Bouley's Tribeca restaurants.

Bouley Bakery, New York

TIME: 15 minutes, plus chilling   YIELD: 6 small servings

1 small melon (Cavaillon, cantaloupe or ½ a honeydew), skin and seeds removed, cut into 1-inch cubes
1 tablespoon acacia or other honey
⅛ teaspoon salt
2 tablespoons flat mineral water
1 pint strawberries, preferably organic, hulled

1 pint strawberry-moscato sorbet (page 473)
½ pint raspberries
½ cup skinned and seeded fresh litchis, or ½ cup drained canned litchis (available in Asian markets and specialty food stores)

1. In a blender, combine melon, honey, salt and mineral water. Blend until smooth and creamy, and then transfer mixture to a bowl. Rinse container of blender.

2. Puree strawberries in blender until smooth. Strain through a fine sieve to remove seeds, and then transfer mixture to a bowl. Cover both bowls of pureed fruit, and refrigerate until chilled, at least 1 hour. Chill 6 soup plates.

3. To serve, pour 3 tablespoons of melon puree into each chilled soup plate. Pour 3 tablespoons of strawberry puree into center of each bowl, to make concentric circles of fruit puree. Place a scoop of sorbet into center of each bowl, and garnish with raspberries and litchis. Serve.

Lavender-Cavaillon Melon Soup

Picholine,
New York

Only summertime can welcome this melon soup seasoned with fresh laven-der. If you cannot obtain the herb fresh, dried lavender can be used. Pi-choline is a French-style New York restaurant owned by Terrance Brennan.

TIME: 45 minutes, plus chilling   YIELD: 6 servings

½ cup sugar

12 branches fresh lavender, with
flowers

2 cups grüner veltliner or dry
muscat wine

4 Cavaillon melons (or 1 very
large or 2 medium cantaloupes)

2 tablespoons orange juice

1 tablespoon lemon juice

1 tablespoon lime juice

Pinch of salt

6 fresh figs, quartered

6 scoops cantaloupe (page 474) or
orange sorbet, optional

1. Place sugar in a saucepan and stir in ¾ cup water. Add 6 branches lavender. Simmer until sugar dissolves. Place saucepan in a bowl of ice water to chill. Strain when cool.

2. Place wine in saucepan and cook until reduced to 1 cup. Chill.

3. Remove skin and seeds from melons. Cut enough of the flesh in ½-inch dice to make 1½ cups. Refrigerate. Chop remaining melon and puree in a food processor to yield 4 cups.

4. Add wine, orange juice, lemon juice and lime juice to melon puree. Stir in ½ cup lavender syrup. Add salt. Refrigerate.

5. To serve, fold remaining lavender syrup into diced melon and place a mound of melon in the center of each of 6 chilled shallow soup plates. Add figs. Spoon melon soup around. Top each portion, if desired, with sorbet. Garnish with a branch of lavender and serve.

Champagne Melon Soup with Raspberry Ice Balls

To cut mint in thin strips, stack the leaves, roll them tightly, and slice with a sharp knife. Michel Richard, who rose to fame in Los Angeles, is now based in Washington, D.C.

Michel
Richard

TIME: 1 hour 15 minutes, plus freezing   YIELD: 4 servings

2 cups raspberries
Sugar
1 ripe honeydew melon
2 ripe cantaloupes

2 tablespoons lemon juice, or to
     taste
12 large mint leaves
1½ cups Champagne

1. In a blender, combine raspberries with 4 tablespoons water. Puree until smooth. Line a strainer with cheesecloth, and set over a bowl. Pour in puree, and twist cloth to squeeze out puree. Stir in 4 teaspoons of sugar, or to taste. Spoon mixture into an ice cube tray that makes round balls or another decorative shape. Freeze until firm.

2. Cut honeydew melon in half, and remove seeds. Using a melon baller, remove flesh from melon to within ¾ inch of peel. Set aside melon balls. Using a large spoon, scrape out and reserve remaining flesh. Discard peels.

3. Cut cantaloupes in half, using a straight cut or saw-toothed design. Remove seeds. Using a melon baller, remove flesh to within ¼ inch of peel; reserve any extra flesh. Cut a slice off bottoms of cantaloupes so they stand securely. In a large bowl, mix honeydew and cantaloupe melon balls with lemon juice. Place an equal amount of melon balls in each cantaloupe melon half, and refrigerate.

4. In a blender, puree any honeydew or cantaloupe flesh that has not been shaped into balls. Press through a fine strainer, and add 2 teaspoons of sugar. Refrigerate.

5. To serve, spoon 2 tablespoons of melon puree over melon balls in each cantaloupe half. Allow to sit at room temperature for 30 minutes. Meanwhile, cut mint leaves into very thin strips, and dust lightly with sugar. Arrange 4 frozen raspberry balls in each melon half, and sprinkle with mint. Set each melon half in a soup bowl. At the table pour Champagne directly into cantaloupe halves, and allow to fizz out and over cantaloupes.

JELLIED FRUIT DESSERTS

No, we do not offer your garden-variety Jell-O mold. But recently, gelatin-based fruit desserts have become popular. In place of preflavored gelatin, they call for plain gelatin mixed with fruit juices and purees. Though many recipes suggest a tablespoon of plain gelatin as the equivalent of a single packet, there is actually only 2½ teaspoons in a packet. Most of the time, the difference is not significant. Leaf gelatin can also be used. A guide for substitution is given in the Introduction, on page 10. When using either kind of gelatin it is important to heat it only until it can be dissolved, and never subject it to high heat.

Raspberry Green Tea Terrine ⁕

Florence
Fabricant

∽

The tart-sweetness of the raspberries plays deliciously against the gently tannic tea. Be sure to use whole leaf tea, which these days is even available in the convenient tea bag form.

TIME: 15 minutes, plus chilling   YIELD: 6 servings

6½ cups fresh raspberries, about
   3 pints
Juice and grated zest of 1 lime
8 tablespoons sugar

1¼ cups freshly brewed green tea
2 envelopes unflavored gelatin
Whipped cream, crème fraîche or
   sweetened plain yogurt

1. Place 6 cups of the raspberries in a bowl. Toss with lime juice, zest and 2 tablespoons sugar.

2. Place ¼ cup of the tea in small bowl, add gelatin and stir to soften. Transfer to a small saucepan, stir in remaining tea and heat gently just until gelatin dissolves. Stir in 6 tablespoons sugar. Pour hot gelatin mixture over raspberries. It should just cover the berries.

3. Transfer mixture to a 6-cup loaf pan or porcelain terrine. Alternatively, mixture can be spooned into 6 large wine goblets. Refrigerate at least 1 hour, until the mixture is firm, then serve in slices or individual servings with cream on the side or as a topping and with remaining fresh raspberries for garnish.

Berry Terrine in Muscat de Beaumes-de-Venise Jelly

The Tonic,
New York

Unlike the preceding recipe, which provides for individual molds, this one results in a loaflike terrine, with layers of jellied fruit made by allowing successive additions to set before adding the next. The Tonic had a brief run in New York's Chelsea district. It has closed.

TIME: 5 hours   YIELD: 6 servings

1½ envelopes plain gelatin	1 vanilla bean, split lengthwise
1 cup orange juice	1 tablespoon pink peppercorns
1 half bottle (350 milliliters) muscat de Beaumes-de-Venise	1½ pints raspberries
	½ pint blueberries
⅔ cup sugar, plus more for berries	½ pint strawberries, hulled and sliced

1. Soften the gelatin in ½ cup orange juice. Combine the remaining juice with the muscat, sugar, vanilla and peppercorns in a saucepan, and bring to boil. Remove the saucepan from heat, stir in the gelatin to dissolve, and then strain.

2. Puree 1 pint of the raspberries, strain, and sweeten to taste. Refrigerate puree until ready to serve.

3. Line a 6-cup oblong terrine with plastic wrap. Pour in a thin layer of the muscat mixture and the remaining raspberries. Refrigerate until set, about 1 hour (or freeze for about 30 minutes). Add the blueberries and half of the remaining muscat mixture, and refrigerate 1 hour. Then add the strawberries and the remaining muscat mixture, and refrigerate at least 3 hours, until firm.

4. To serve, unmold the terrine and peel off the wrap. Serve in thick slices with raspberry puree drizzled around.

Jiggling Fruit Mold with Berry Compote

Fifty-Seven
Fifty-Seven
Restaurant,
New York

This is a pretty presentation, with the shimmering, unmolded jelled fruit syrup bedded on top of a berry compote and garnished with whipped cream. Fifty-Seven Fifty-Seven was the restaurant in the Four Seasons Hotel in New York. It has closed.

TIME: 1 hour 15 minutes, plus chilling   YIELD: 4 servings

4 cups raspberries
1 cup sugar
Salt
1 envelope plain gelatin
3 cups (1½ pints) mixed berries
   like blueberries, blackberries,
   raspberries and strawberries

1 tablespoon finely grated orange
   zest
½ cup unsweetened heavy cream,
   whipped

1. Place the 4 cups raspberries with 2 cups water and ½ cup sugar in a saucepan. Add a pinch of salt. Bring to a boil, stirring, and simmer for 3 or 4 minutes. Remove from the heat, and set aside for an hour.

2. Line a fine-meshed sieve with a double layer of cheesecloth, and strain the cooked berries, pressing down gently so no pulp or seeds get into the liquid. Discard the pulp; there should be 2 cups of berry juice.

3. Soften the gelatin in ¼ cup cold water for 5 minutes.

4. Put the reserved berry juice in a saucepan. Add the softened gelatin. Warm over low heat, stirring, until the gelatin dissolves.

5. Spray or brush four ½-cup molds with flavorless oil. (You can use metal molds, ramekins or coffee cups.) Fill with the berry juice. Refrigerate, covered, for 4 hours or overnight.

6. Place remaining mixed berries in a saucepan with ½ cup water, remaining sugar, orange rind and a pinch of salt. Bring to a simmer, and cook, stirring, for 3 to 4 minutes until the fruit has almost dissolved and is syrupy. Remove from the heat, transfer to a bowl, cool and refrigerate, covered, for 4 hours or overnight.

7. To serve, spoon berry compote onto 4 dessert plates. Dip the bottom of each mold into warm water, and unmold onto the compote. Put a dollop of whipped cream on the side of each, and serve.

Hibiscus Gelée

Hibiscus tea can be substituted for dried flowers. Some produce markets even sell pomegranate seeds. Bill Yosses was the executive chef for Joseph's restaurant in New York.

Bill
Yosses

TIME: 3½ hours   YIELD: 6 to 8 servings

2 cups flat bottled water

1¼ cups sugar

1¾ ounces (about 1¼ cups) dried
    hibiscus flowers

2½ packets unflavored gelatin

2 cups pomegranate juice

2 star fruits

2 bananas, peeled and sliced

2 tablespoons pomegranate seeds

¾ cup diced pineapple or sliced
    strawberries for serving

¾ cup diced mango for serving

Plain yogurt for serving

1. In a saucepan, bring water to a boil. Add sugar, stirring until dissolved. Remove from heat, wait 20 seconds, add hibiscus. Steep 10 minutes. Set a sieve over a bowl, strain and press to extract liquid.

2. Meanwhile, put gelatin in a small bowl and add ½ cup cold water. Set aside 5 minutes.

3. Put hibiscus mixture in a saucepan over medium heat. Bring to a simmer. Turn off heat, and add softened gelatin. Whisk until dissolved. Strain liquid into another bowl, and stir in pomegranate juice.

4. Cut 1 star fruit into ¼-inch slices. In a decorative 6-cup mold, arrange half the slices in a single layer. Pour enough hibiscus liquid into the mold to not quite cover star fruit. Place mold in freezer or refrigerator 5 to 20 minutes to set gelatin. Arrange half the banana over the gelatin, and gently pour half of the remaining hibiscus liquid into the mold. Scatter pomegranate seeds over the liquid and place mold in freezer or refrigerator for 20 to 45 minutes to set. Gently pour remaining hibiscus liquid into the mold, and scatter remaining banana and star fruit slices over the top. Refrigerate until set, about 2 hours.

5. To serve, cut remaining star fruit into ¼-inch slices. Place in a bowl with pineapple or strawberries and mango, and combine. Invert mold onto a serving dish. Lift off the mold, and serve gelée in slices with some of the mixed fruit and dollops of the yogurt.

Melon Ball "Martini"

Artisanal,
New York

Whisking the set gelatin breaks it up into a softly frothy mixture for a delightful contrast with the melon. Except for watermelon, any type of ripe melon can be used. Artisanal is a brasserie-style restaurant in Manhattan that specializes in cheese.

TIME: 30 minutes, plus chilling   YIELD: 6 servings

1 teaspoon plain gelatin
2 cups Sauternes wine
¼ cup lime juice
2 tablespoons crystallized ginger,
   slivered

1 teaspoon lime zest, slivered
8 cups small melon balls (from
   about 7 pounds whole melons)

1. Soften gelatin in 1 tablespoon cold water. Place Sauternes in a saucepan, add lime juice, bring to a simmer and remove from heat. Whisk in gelatin. Refrigerate until jelled.

2. Whisk thoroughly and chill for 2 hours. Mix ginger with lime zest and set aside.

3. Place a tablespoon of the gelatin mixture in each of 6 martini glasses. Add melon and spoon on remaining gelée. Top with slivers of lime-marinated ginger and serve.

Sweet Aspic

This aspic begs for the addition of fresh fruit. Consider citrus segments. Verbena was a charming restaurant in Manhattan owned by Diane Forley and Michael Otsuka.

Verbena,
New York

TIME: 10 minutes, plus chilling   YIELD: 4 servings

½ cup sugar
3 sheets of gelatin or 2 teaspoons
   unflavored gelatin

2 cups blood-orange juice,
   tangerine juice or grapefruit
   juice

1. Make a simple syrup by mixing the sugar and ½ cup water in a small saucepan. Bring to a boil, stirring until the sugar is dissolved. Remove from the heat, and let cool.

2. Soften the gelatin sheets in enough cold water to cover for about 5 minutes. Squeeze out excess water. If using powdered gelatin, sprinkle it over ¼ cup cold water, and allow to soften for 5 minutes. In a saucepan, mix the softened gelatin with the juice and sugar syrup. Warm gently, stirring, until the gelatin is dissolved.

3. Transfer to a decorative serving dish or four ½-cup molds sprayed with flavorless oil. Or divide mixture among four stemmed glasses.

4. Cover and chill for 4 hours or overnight. If using molds, loosen the aspic by running a blunt knife around the edges. Invert onto a plate and serve.

COOKED FRUIT DESSERTS

Some fruits must be cooked. Quince is a prime example. Apples, too, are often better poached or baked with a caramel burnish. And while a fresh, ripe pear drizzled with honey can be the perfect partner for a wedge of cheese, that same pear, peeled and poached whole, can also provide the perfect finale to dinner. If you keep dried fruits on hand to plump in warm syrup, then spike, perhaps, with red wine or port, and serve with a cloud of cream, you will never be at a loss for dessert. This section has recipes for these and many more.

Plums with Vanilla ☀

Amanda
Hesser

∽

Welcome late summer with the small dark plums that are sometimes called Italian prune plums because they are dried to make prunes. Amanda Hesser is the food editor of *The New York Times Sunday Magazine*.

TIME: 15 minutes   YIELD: 4 servings

2 pounds small oval purple plums,
   pitted and thinly sliced
2 tablespoons sugar
Grated zest of 1 lemon

½ vanilla bean, split lengthwise,
   seeds and pulp scraped out
Vanilla ice cream, crème fraîche
   or yogurt sorbet, for serving

1. In a medium saucepan, combine plums, sugar, lemon zest, vanilla seeds and 2 tablespoons water. Place over medium heat, stirring occasionally, until plums give up their juice and soften, 5 to 10 minutes. Taste, and adjust seasoning, adding more sugar, lemon zest or vanilla if desired.

2. Let cool 20 minutes. Serve with ice cream, crème fraîche or yogurt sorbet.

Plum Compote

With this recipe, the timing is everything. Watch your plums like a hawk because they can go from tender to collapsed in seconds. Smallish plums like Santa Rosas work well. Marian Burros is a food reporter for *The New York Times.*

Marian
Burros

TIME: 20 to 30 minutes, plus chilling   YIELD: 6 servings

¾ cup sugar
1 cup dry white wine
4 whole cloves
1 3-inch stick cinnamon
Zest of ½ lemon

16 large, firm, ripe red or black
    plums, stemmed
Vanilla ice cream, frozen yogurt,
    crème fraîche or whipped
    cream, for serving

1. Combine the sugar, wine, one cup of water, cloves, cinnamon and lemon zest in a saucepan large enough to hold the plums. Bring the ingredients to a boil, and cook, uncovered, for 5 minutes.

2. Add plums, and bring mixture back to a boil; lower heat, and simmer plums for 10 to 20 minutes, depending on their ripeness, until they are tender but still hold their shape. Some plums will be ready before others; remove them as they are. Then when they are all cooked, return the plums to the syrup, remove from heat and let cool.

3. Chill plums in the syrup. Serve over vanilla ice cream or frozen yogurt with some of the syrup, or serve with the syrup topped with whipped cream or crème fraîche.

Spiced Plum Compote with
Sour Cream Sauce

Marian
Burros

Spices and plums are terrific companions. If you slightly undercook the plums, a good idea since they will be drenched with hot syrup, you can guarantee they will not fall apart. Always use pure maple syrup; no other kind is suitable. But you can replace it by sweetening the cream with maple sugar. Marian Burros is a food reporter for *The New York Times* who writes strong, simple recipes.

TIME: 30 minutes   YIELD: 6 servings

3 pounds firm plums or pluots,
   preferably freestone
8 whole cloves
½ teaspoon ground cinnamon

½ cup sugar, or more, to taste
1 cup sour cream, preferably
   reduced-fat
2 tablespoons maple syrup

1. Wash, dry and stem plums. Cut into 1-inch-thick wedges.

2. Heat a heavy skillet large enough to hold plums until it is quite hot. Add plums, cloves and cinnamon, and sprinkle with sugar, stirring to dissolve sugar; less-ripe plums will require more sugar. Cook plums 5 to 10 minutes, depending on ripeness; riper plums need less cooking. Cook until plums are tender but not falling apart. Remove plums with a slotted spoon and place in a bowl.

3. Strain liquid, return to pan and boil liquid until it reduces and becomes syrupy, about 15 minutes. Pour over plums and cool.

4. In a small bowl, combine sour cream and maple syrup. Serve plums warm or at room temperature with 2 tablespoons sauce on top of each serving.

Prunes in Red Wine

This is a typical European dessert, often made with Beaujolais and served in bistros in France, or, using Chianti, served in Italian trattorias. But any robust red wine will suit this preparation. It's important not to skimp on the quality of the prunes. Big ones, and especially the excellent *pruneaux* (prunes in French) from Agen in southwest France, are best to use.

Florence
Fabricant

TIME: 30 minutes, plus cooling   YIELD: 6 servings

3 cups pitted prunes
½ teaspoon mace
2 cinnamon sticks
1 lemon, cut in half

1½ cups dry red wine
Crème fraîche, mascarpone or
   heavy cream

1. Place prunes in a heavy saucepan with mace, cinnamon, lemon halves and wine.

2. Bring to a simmer and cook very slowly for 20 minutes. Allow to cool to room temperature in pan.

3. Remove lemon and cinnamon.

4. Serve prunes in their sauce topped with a dollop of crème fraîche, mascarpone stirred to smooth it, or heavy cream.

Poached Quince

Bill
Yosses

These poached quince with their rich spices can be served plain, over ice cream (including the cardamom ice cream, page 452) or with crème anglaise (page 533). Bill Yosses was pastry chef at the original Bouley in New York.

TIME: 30 minutes, plus cooling   YIELD: 1 quart

2 cups sugar

4 pieces star anise

4 black peppercorns

3 green cardamom pods

2 cinnamon sticks

2 dried bay leaves or 1 fresh

1 whole nutmeg, quartered

4 quince, peeled, cored and cut
  into eighths

1. In a saucepan, combine sugar and spices with 1 quart water. Bring to a boil, stirring occasionally, until sugar has dissolved. Turn off heat and let spices steep for 5 minutes.

2. Pour the liquid through a sieve set over another saucepan. Discard the spices. Cut a round of parchment paper just small enough to fit inside the saucepan. Add the quince to the liquid and place the parchment paper over the fruit to keep it submerged. Bring the liquid to a simmer. Simmer gently, over medium heat, until the quince are tender, about 15 minutes.

3. Let cool in poaching syrup. Quince can be stored in syrup, in refrigerator, for up to a week.

Muscat-Macerated Fruit

This recipe offers one of many possible ways to soften and enrich dried fruit. Morrell Wine Bar & Café in New York is owned by the Morrell family, which is better known for their wine shop.

Morrell
Wine Bar
& Café,
New York

TIME: 10 minutes, plus cooling   YIELD: 3 cups

1¼ cups mixed dried fruit, like
    apricots, figs, cherries,
    cranberries and currants
¾ cup muscat wine, like Beaumes-
    de-Venise
2 tablespoons honey

3 allspice berries
1 cinnamon stick
1 vanilla bean
Vanilla bean pound cake, for
    serving (page 63)

1. In a small saucepan, combine all ingredients with ¾ cup water. Bring mixture to a simmer, and cook for 2 minutes, stirring to dissolve sugar.

2. Turn off heat, and let mixture cool. Remove vanilla bean and spices before serving with vanilla bean pound cake.

Blackberry Pears with Pear-Verbena Sorbet

François
Payard

Vitamin C powder is ascorbic acid, used to prevent the peeled fruit from browning. Lemon juice is a decent substitute. François Payard's first job in New York was as pastry chef at Le Bernadin.

TIME: 30 minutes, plus chilling and freezing   YIELD: 4 servings

5 fresh lemon verbena leaves or
   1 tablespoon dried
1 15-ounce can pear halves in light
   syrup, frozen overnight
3 tablespoons plus 1¼ cups sugar
½ teaspoon lime juice

Poire Williams eau de vie, optional
Pinch vitamin C powder (available
   at pharmacies) or 1 tablespoon
   lemon juice
4 perfectly ripe Bartlett pears
3 pints fresh blackberries

1. Pour ¼ cup boiling water over the verbena in a small bowl. Cover with plastic wrap, and infuse 10 minutes. Strain, and reserve. Remove frozen pears and juice from can. Puree in a food processor. Add 3 tablespoons sugar, lime juice, verbena infusion and Poire Williams, if desired. Pour the mixture into an ice cream maker, and freeze according to the manufacturer's instructions. Transfer to a container and freeze.

2. To make the pears, dissolve the vitamin C powder in a large bowl of cold water or add lemon juice to the water. Keep close at hand. One by one, peel the pears, leaving their stems, and drop them into the water.

3. Puree the blackberries in a blender or food processor, and strain into a pot deep enough to hold the pears in one layer. Add 1 quart water and the remaining sugar, and bring to a boil. Lower the heat to a simmer, and add the pears. If the pears aren't submerged in the syrup, weight them with a saucer. Poach pears 10 to 15 minutes, or until a sharp knife pierces them easily. Remove from the heat, cover the pot with a kitchen towel, and cool to room temperature. Chill, still covered, overnight.

4. To serve, drain pears, reserving syrup, and cut each crosswise at the point where the neck of the pear meets its round belly. Use a melon baller to scoop out the core in both top and bottom. For each serving, stand the bottom of a pear in a martini glass or dessert bowl. Pour some blackberry syrup around the pear, place a scoop of the sorbet on the pear, and set the top of the pear on the sorbet. Serve.

Pears Poached in Sherry

The Spanish marriage of almonds and sherry infuses the pears with deep, rich flavor and color.

TIME: 30 minutes, plus cooling   YIELD: 6 servings

Florence
Fabricant

6 large ripe pears
4 tablespoons fresh lemon juice
1 750-milliliter bottle amontillado
   or oloroso sherry

½ cup sugar
1 cinnamon stick
¼ cup sliced almonds
Pinch of salt

1. Peel pears. Halve and remove cores. Immerse in water to cover mixed with half the lemon juice.

2. Bring sherry to a simmer in a saucepan large enough to hold pears. Add sugar and cinnamon and simmer until sugar dissolves. Drain pears and add. Cook over low heat until tender, about 15 minutes.

3. While pears are cooking, toast almonds by heating in a dry skillet for several minutes, stirring. Remove from heat when golden. Toss with salt.

4. When pears are done, remove them from saucepan with slotted spoon and place in serving dish. Boil down cooking liquid until reduced to 1 cup and syrupy. Stir in remaining lemon juice. Pour syrup over pears, scatter almonds on top and set aside until barely warm before serving.

Buttered Rum Winter Fruit

Florence
Fabricant

Here you have a winter dried fruit compote with a difference, the buttered rum flavor, making it echo a hot toddy. Serve the compote with slices of pound cake.

TIME: 30 minutes, plus chilling   YIELD: 8 servings

3 tablespoons unsalted butter

4 tablespoons light brown sugar

3 pounds mixed dried fruit

½ cup dark rum

6 cups freshly brewed Earl Grey
   tea

2 cinnamon sticks

1 star anise

½ teaspoon whole cloves

1 cup crème fraîche

1 teaspoon ground cinnamon

1. Heat butter in a heavy 3-quart saucepan. Add sugar and cook over medium-high heat until sugar melts. Fold in fruit and cook, stirring, until fruit starts to soften, about 5 minutes.

2. Warm rum in a small saucepan. Pour over fruit, light match and, standing back a bit, ignite rum in pan. Stir gently with a long spoon until flames subside. Add tea, cinnamon, anise and cloves. Bring to a simmer.

3. Simmer gently until fruit is tender, about 20 minutes. Remove from heat, then chill in syrup.

4. Serve in glass dishes or goblets, each topped with crème fraîche and a pinch of cinnamon.

Berry Tartare

Chateaubriand,
New York
∽

Cooked berries become the sauce and the syrup to hold the chopped berries together. This recipe comes from a New York restaurant that had a brief flash of light, then faded like yesterday's shooting star. But its marvelous and simply made berry tartare deserves to be remembered.

TIME: 1½ hours, including chilling   YIELD: 4 servings

1½ pints raspberries
1½ pints blueberries
1 pint strawberries, hulled
¼ cup sugar
1½ teaspoons raspberry vinegar

1 tablespoon Chambord liqueur or
   crème de cassis
4 tablespoons mascarpone
4 small mint sprigs

1. Rinse berries, and drain on paper towels (berries must be dry).

2. Place 1 cup each of raspberries and blueberries plus a few sliced strawberries in a saucepan with sugar, vinegar and liqueur. Cook over low heat about 20 minutes, until soft. Puree in a food processor, and then force through a sieve. Refrigerate until cold, for at least 1 hour.

3. Meanwhile, finely chop remaining berries by hand, and put them into a sieve suspended over a bowl to drain for 30 minutes. Transfer to a bowl.

4. When sauce is cool, mix a few tablespoons of it with the chopped berries. Form ¾-cup portions of berry mixture into cylinders on each of four dessert plates, using a round mold or a 6- or 7-ounce can with top and bottom removed. Lift off molds. Drizzle remaining sauce around tartare, and then place a couple dollops of mascarpone on each plate. Garnish with mint, and serve.

Sugar-Dipped, Pan-Seared Apples with Warm Apple Butter ✳

Kay
Rentschler

∾

Apples turned into puree, and also caramelized, are combined for this two-step dessert. Fuji apples can be used in place of Cortlands, but since they are larger, purchase them by weight, not number. Kay Rentschler has contributed many recipes to *The New York Times*.

TIME: 1 hour 15 minutes   YIELD: 4 servings

3 pounds fresh Cortland apples,
    about 12 medium
1 cup fresh apple cider
Pinch salt
9 tablespoons sugar

2 tablespoons unsalted butter,
    melted
2 cups lightly sweetened whipped
    cream

1. Quarter and core all but 3 apples, then cut each quarter in half lengthwise.

2. In a large, heavy saucepan, combine apple eighths, cider and salt. Cover and cook over medium heat until apples are soft and pulpy, about 25 minutes. Pass apples through a food mill or a fine stainless-steel sieve set over a medium bowl, then return pulp to saucepan. Add 6 tablespoons sugar and cook uncovered over medium-low heat, stirring frequently, until liquid has evaporated and puree is quite thick, 20 to 30 minutes.

3. Peel and core the 3 reserved apples and cut each into 12 wedges. Place apples in a bowl, add melted butter and toss well to coat. Sprinkle remaining sugar over apples and toss well to coat. Heat a large, heavy skillet over medium-high heat. Lay apple slices individually in hot skillet and sear without turning, until slices caramelize slightly, 7 to 10 minutes. Turn wedges and brown other side, 5 minutes.

4. Divide apple puree among 3 to 4 plates. Top with slices and serve with whipped cream.

Spiced Baked Apples with Maple Caramel Sauce

Though Rome apples are often considered to be "baking" apples, they are really too large for gracious service. Winesaps and Empires would be excellent, as would Cortlands. Melissa Clark is a frequent contributor to *The New York Times*.

Melissa
Clark
∽

TIME: 1 hour 10 minutes YIELD: 4 servings

4 teaspoons unsalted butter, more
  for pan
4 tart baking apples, like Winesap
  or Empire
⅓ cup plus 4 teaspoons maple
  syrup
4 teaspoons brown sugar
4 teaspoons chopped pecans
4 teaspoons chopped golden
  raisins

¼ cup dry white wine or water
3 cardamom pods
2 whole cloves
1¼-inch-thick slice fresh ginger
  root
1 2-inch piece cinnamon stick
Brandied custard sauce (page 534)

1. Preheat oven to 375 degrees. Butter a small cake or baking pan. Use a vegetable peeler to peel a strip of skin from around stem of each apple. Use a melon baller or grapefruit spoon to scoop out core of each apple, leaving at least ¼ inch at base. Stand apples in pan and use a paring knife to make 6 vertical cuts in the core area, surrounding cavity, being sure not to pierce through bottom of apple.

2. Place 1 teaspoon butter and 1 teaspoon maple syrup into cavity of each apple. Mix together brown sugar, pecans and raisins, and stuff one-quarter of this mixture into each apple. Pour remaining maple syrup and the wine into bottom of pan, and add cardamom, cloves, ginger and cinnamon.

3. Bake apples, basting with liquid in pan every 5 to 7 minutes, until tender yet not collapsed, 45 minutes to an hour. Serve warm or at room temperature, with custard if desired.

Applesauce with Wine and Vanilla

Steven
Raichlen

This recipe can be simplified by using apples that have been quartered but not peeled or cored. Force them through a sieve before pureeing. Steven Raichlen is a cookbook author who specializes in grilling and barbecue.

TIME: 30 minutes   YIELD: About 4 cups (8 servings)

3 pounds fragrant apples, like
    Galas or McIntoshes
    (6 to 8 apples), peeled, halved
    and cored
1 cinnamon stick or 1 teaspoon
    ground cinnamon
1 2-inch piece vanilla bean, cut in
    half lengthwise

2 strips lemon zest
1½ tablespoons lemon juice, or to
    taste
¼ cup sugar, or to taste
2 tablespoons dry white wine

1. Place apples in a large, heavy saucepan with other ingredients and 2¼ cups water. Bring to boil.

2. Reduce heat, and simmer apples, covered, until soft, for 20 to 30 minutes. Remove pan from heat, and let cool slightly. Discard cinnamon stick and vanilla bean.

3. Puree apples and pan juices in a blender or food processor: the blender will yield a silky puree; the processor, a chunkier applesauce. Strain and refrigerate until ready to serve.

Orange Poached Figs

Midsummer into fall is the season for fresh figs. There would be nothing wrong with spooning these over ice cream. Barbara Kafka is a food writer and cookbook author.

Barbara
Kafka

TIME: 30 minutes   YIELD: 4 servings

12 medium or 16 small fresh black
   figs, stems removed
¼ cup sugar
⅛ teaspoon freshly ground black
   pepper
One 2-inch piece of vanilla bean,
   split lengthwise

7 tablespoons orange juice
Juice of 1 lemon
2 tablespoons sweet Marsala,
   optional

1. Place figs upright in saucepan just large enough to hold them comfortably in one layer. Sprinkle with sugar and pepper. Add vanilla bean, and pour citrus juices over figs.

2. Cover pan, and slowly bring to boil over medium heat. Lower temperature, and simmer very gently for 10 to 15 minutes for medium figs, 5 to 10 minutes for small, or until cooked through but not falling apart. Add Marsala, if desired, and stir. Serve warm.

Poached Pineapple, Cranberries and Pecans

Kay
Rentschler

The combination of cranberries, ginger and pecans over pineapple suggests an autumn or winter dessert, and one that provides a light change of pace from rich pies and puddings. Kay Rentschler has contributed many recipes to *The New York Times.*

TIME: 20 minutes   YIELD: 4 servings

1 ripe pineapple, peeled, quartered
    vertically and cored
½ cup sugar
Pinch of salt
¼ cup crystallized ginger,
    chopped fine

⅓ cup dried cranberries
⅓ cup coarsely chopped pecans
2 cups lightly sweetened whipped
    cream

1. Cut each pineapple quarter into ½-inch pieces.

2. In a 10-inch skillet over medium heat, bring sugar, salt and 1 cup water to a simmer. Stir once or twice to dissolve. Add pineapple, ginger, cranberries and pecans. Poach, stirring frequently to coat fruit with syrup, until pineapple is just tender, about 5 minutes.

3. Remove skillet from heat and pour fruit and nuts into a colander set over a large shallow bowl. Allow to drain well. Pour pineapple syrup back into skillet and simmer over medium heat, until syrup is thick and has reduced to ⅓ cup, about 5 minutes. When fruit mixture is completely cooled, transfer it to a serving bowl, pour reduced syrup over it, cover with plastic wrap and refrigerate until ready to serve.

4. To serve, spoon whipped cream over fruit.

Baked Rhubarb Compote with Fresh Strawberries

For this dessert, I cooked the rhubarb but left the strawberries raw, with the end result that each of these fruits has the maximum flavor.

Florence
Fabricant

TIME: 30 minutes   YIELD: 6 servings

Unsalted butter for baking dish
1½ pounds fresh rhubarb, cut in
    1-inch pieces
¾ cup light brown sugar

½ teaspoon ground cinnamon
1 pint ripe strawberries, hulled
    and sliced
Whipped cream or ice cream

1. Preheat oven to 350 degrees. Lightly butter an 8-inch-square baking dish.

2. Mix the rhubarb with the sugar and cinnamon. Spread in the baking dish, cover and bake 20 minutes. Allow to cool about 30 minutes, then fold in the strawberries. Serve warm or cold with whipped cream or ice cream.

Baked Apricots

Florence
Fabricant

Ripe apricots in season, especially if they are a trifle softer than you might like to eat out of hand, is what you want for this recipe.

TIME: 45 minutes   YIELD: 4 servings

3 tablespoons unsalted butter, plus more for baking dish
12 ripe fresh apricots, halved and pitted

¼ cup sugar
2 tablespoons Cognac
½ pint vanilla ice cream (page 446)

1. Preheat oven to 500 degrees. Lightly butter a baking dish large enough to hold apricot halves in a single layer.

2. Sprinkle baking dish with 1 tablespoon sugar. Arrange apricots, cut side up, in dish. Sprinkle with remaining sugar. Dot with 3 tablespoons butter.

3. Bake 20 minutes, remove from oven and sprinkle with Cognac. Set aside to cool 15 minutes.

4. Place a scoop of vanilla ice cream on each of 4 chilled plates. Arrange 6 apricot halves on each plate and spoon any of the syrup in the baking dish over the ice cream. Serve at once.

Chilled Braised Apricots with Yogurt, Honey and Pistachios

There is a strong suggestion of the Eastern Mediterranean, especially Turkey, in this dessert. The season for good apricots is a short one, June into July. Buy one piece of the fruit from your market and taste it to be sure the fruit is ripe but firm-textured and sweet with a hint of acid tartness. In fact, this is not a dessert to plan on, but one to consider when the apricots are appealing. Kay Rentschler has contributed recipes to *The New York Times*.

Kay Rentschler

TIME: 30 minutes, plus chilling   YIELD: 4 to 6 servings

2 lemons
2 cups granulated sugar
1½ pounds apricots (about 7 medium), halved
7 ounces whole milk yogurt, preferably sheep's milk

2 tablespoons confectioners' sugar
Pinch of salt
¼ cup wildflower honey
2 tablespoons shelled unsalted pistachios, chopped

1. Preheat oven to 300 degrees. Peel skin from lemons, avoiding white pith, and toss strips into a large saucepan. Squeeze juice through a strainer into the saucepan. Add granulated sugar and 2 cups water. Cover and bring to a boil, stirring once. Remove lid and simmer until mixture reduces slightly, about 10 minutes.

2. Pit apricots and place cut-side down in a single layer in a small roasting pan. Apricots should be snug. Strain reduced hot syrup over them. Cover fruit with foil directly on them and braise in oven for 5 minutes. Turn apricots over, replace foil, and braise 5 minutes more. Remove apricots from oven, turn again and cool. Transfer apricots, covered by their liquid, to a shallow container with cover, and refrigerate 4 hours or overnight.

3. Remove apricot halves from their liquid and drain on paper towels. Pour syrup in a saucepan and reduce over high heat until slightly thickened, about 10 minutes. In a small bowl, stir yogurt, confectioners' sugar and salt together until smooth. Spoon warm sauce on each plate, topped by 2 or 3 apricot halves. Spoon yogurt into their centers. Drizzle with honey and sprinkle with nuts.

Roasted Summer Fruit

Karen
De Masco,
Craft,
New York

This summer dessert is simplicity itself. And with a streusel topping (see list of recipes in Basics, page 527), it becomes a lovely fruit crumble. Karen De Masco is the pastry chef of Craft in Manhattan.

TIME: 30 minutes   YIELD: 4 servings

½ cup sugar
1 tablespoon light corn syrup
4 ripe but firm large yellow
   peaches, halved and pitted
   (8 firm apricots, 8 firm Italian
   prune plums, 4 firm nectarines
   or 4 large, firm pluot plums
   may be substituted)

4 sprigs fresh lavender, basil,
   lemon verbena or mint
1 tablespoon unsalted butter
⅓ tablespoon heavy cream
Vanilla ice cream for serving
   (optional)

1. Preheat oven to 375 degrees. Place sugar in a 10-inch nonstick oven-proof skillet. Drizzle with syrup. Cook over medium heat, stirring, until mixture liquefies. Continue cooking until mixture is light caramel in color.

2. Place fruit in pan, cut side down. Top with herbs. Place in oven and bake 5 minutes, until caramel has darkened and fruit is tender but still holds its shape. Use spatula to turn fruit cut side up, return to oven and roast another 3 to 5 minutes, until edges of fruit have browned. Do not cook long enough for fruit to collapse.

3. Remove from oven. Discard herbs. Transfer fruit to a serving dish or to individual plates. Lift off skins, if desired, especially from peaches, if thick.

4. Place pan on top of stove, and swirl in butter. Cook a few seconds over low heat. Whisk in cream to make caramel sauce. Pour sauce over and around fruit, and serve warm, with ice cream on the side if desired.

Rum-Glazed Mango and Papaya

Regina
Schrambling

Here is another example of lightly cooked mango, doused with rum caramel and garnished with coconut. Though it's not specified in the recipe, a few pinches of sea salt before sprinkling on the coconut brings up another dimension of flavor. Regina Schrambling was a food reporter and editor for *The New York Times.*

TIME: 15 minutes   YIELD: 4 servings

1 large ripe mango, preferably
  Mexican
1 medium-size ripe papaya, about
  1 pound
3 tablespoons unsalted butter

3 tablespoons sugar
3 tablespoons dark rum
½ cup shredded toasted
  unsweetened coconut for
  garnish

1. Peel and seed fruit, and cut into fairly even slices.
2. Melt butter in a large skillet over medium-high heat. Add sugar, and carefully swirl until browned. Very carefully add rum, a tablespoon at a time (it will spatter) and cook until evaporated. Gently add fruit, and continue swirling until well coated.
3. Divide among serving plates, and sprinkle heavily with coconut.

Glazed Mango with Sour Cream Sherbet and Black Pepper

Alain
Ducasse at
the Essex
House,
New York

The Alain Ducasse restaurant serves this dessert as a palate cleanser, after the main course and before the guests are served their soufflés or chocolate extravaganzas. Buttery caramelization does wonders for mangoes, a fruit that is usually served raw.

TIME: 30 minutes   YIELD: 4 servings

⅔ cup sugar
1 stalk fresh lemongrass, in
    pieces
⅔ cup passion fruit nectar (sold
    in fancy food shops)
2 tablespoons plus ⅓ cup lemon
    juice

2 large mangoes, ripe but not soft
4 tablespoons unsalted butter, plus
    butter for baking sheet
⅓ cup lemon juice
Freshly ground black pepper
Sour cream sherbet (page 467)
1 teaspoon coarse black pepper

1. Mix half the sugar with ¼ cup water in a small saucepan, simmer until sugar dissolves, add lemongrass and set aside to cool 20 minutes.

2. Stir in passion fruit nectar and 2 tablespoons lemon juice. Refrigerate.

3. Peel mangoes. Cut in thirds horizontally, leaving the pit in middle section. Place each portion without pit cut-side down on a work surface, and with a large knife cut into 8 slices perpendicular to the cutting board. Gently push down on slices so they spread out and overlap slightly.

4. Sliver enough mango flesh left around the pits to make ½ cup. Set slivers aside.

5. Butter a baking sheet large enough to hold mangoes in a single layer. Heat the broiler.

6. Melt remaining butter in a large nonstick skillet. Use a spatula to place each sliced mango third in the pan so they keep their shape. Cook over medium heat about 5 minutes, sprinkling with two tablespoons sugar and basting with pan juices.

7. With spatula, transfer mangoes to baking sheet, place under broiler, and broil until edges just start to color. Do not overcook. Set mangoes aside.

8. Add remaining sugar to juices in skillet, and cook over medium heat

until juices start to caramelize. Add remaining lemon juice, and continue to cook, stirring, until amber colored. Season lightly with pepper. Spoon on mangoes.

9. Place a sliced caramelized mango third in each of 4 shallow soup plates. Spoon passion fruit sauce around each, and scatter raw mango slivers around. Top each with a large oval scoop of sour cream sorbet, sprinkle ¼ teaspoon coarse pepper on top and serve at once.

Marbleized Apricot Fool

Florence
Fabricant

A fool is an old-fashioned name that is thought to have come from the French *fouler,* meaning to crush or press or puree. When fresh apricots are no longer in season, this dessert can be made with dried ones. Simmer dried halves in half the nectar or juice and a tablespoon of granulated sugar about 15 minutes, cool, then puree them with the cream without straining them first, as in step 2.

TIME: 20 minutes, plus chilling   YIELD: 6 servings

12 large pitted prunes	20 ripe apricots, pitted and
5 tablespoons apricot nectar or	chopped
orange juice	1½ cups heavy cream
1 tablespoon light brown sugar	Ground cinnamon, for dusting

1. Quarter prunes, place in a small saucepan with half the nectar or juice and the brown sugar and simmer 10 minutes, until soft. Set aside to cool.

2. Place apricots in a food processor and puree. Strain puree through a sieve to remove bits of skin. Return apricots to food processor with ¾ cup cream and remaining nectar or juice and process about 30 seconds, until smooth. Remove from processor, then process prune mixture.

3. Drop alternating spoonfuls of prune and apricot purees into 4 goblets. Lightly marbleize them by tracing through them with a knife. Do not overmix. Chill at least 2 hours before serving.

4. Whip remaining cream. Top each serving with a dollop of whipped cream and a light dusting of cinnamon.

CHARLOTTES, SUMMER PUDDINGS AND TRIFLES

Some dessert recipes have become classics over time. The short list comprises charlottes, summer puddings and trifles, all of them English dessert traditions. All are elaborate but none are difficult to prepare, though some advance planning is often necessary so that once the various components are assembled, they have time to meld together to achieve the proper flavors and textures.

Pear and Rum Raisin Charlotte ※

King George III of England experienced the humiliation of losing the American colonies. His wife, Queen Charlotte, had a better time of it, giving her name to a dessert, the charlotte, as in apple charlotte or charlotte Russe. A charlotte consists of a mold lined with buttered bread, filled with a fruit mixture and baked. A lining of sponge cake or ladyfingers can take a chilled mousse filling. Baked charlottes can be made in advance and reheated.

Florence
Fabricant

TIME: 3 hours   YIELD: 6 to 8 servings

2 tablespoons soft unsalted butter
1 cup golden raisins
6 tablespoons dark rum
8 ripe but firm pears, preferably
    Bosc, peeled, cored and
    coarsely chopped
⅓ cup sugar (approximately)

1 teaspoon vanilla extract
12 thin slices firm-textured white
    bread
10 tablespoons unsalted butter,
    clarified
Whipped cream, crème fraîche or
    crème anglaise (page 533)

1. Use some of the softened butter to lightly coat a 5- to 6-cup charlotte mold, soufflé dish or deep round baking dish. Place the raisins in a small dish and add the rum.

2. Melt the remaining softened butter in a large, heavy skillet. Add the pears and sugar and cook over medium-high heat for about 10 minutes, until the pears have softened almost to a puree and most of the liquid has evaporated.

3. Stir in vanilla, the raisins and rum. Continue cooking over low heat another 10 minutes or so, until the mixture forms a thick puree. Adjust sweetening to taste. Remove from heat.

4. Preheat oven to 425 degrees. Cut 8 of the bread slices in half to form rectangles and the rest in half diagonally. Heat some of the clarified butter in a skillet and sauté the pieces of bread until they are golden brown on one side only, adding more butter as needed.

5. Fit the triangles, sautéed side down, in the bottom of the baking dish so they fit exactly. Trim away any excess and reserve. Arrange the rectangles, sautéed side out, around the sides of the dish, overlapping slightly. Fill the center with the pear mixture and, if necessary, trim the bread rectangles to be level with the fruit. Scatter all trimmings on top.

6. Cover the top with foil and bake about 30 minutes. Remove from the oven and allow to cool for 1 hour. Unmold the charlotte. Serve with whipped cream, crème fraîche or crème anglaise.

Raspberry Charlotte

Benoit,
Paris

A charlotte, or perhaps Charlotte, usually consists of a firm, pureed filling served in a case of pastry or ladyfingers. There are special deep, slightly sloping charlotte molds with heart-shaped handles. This recipe, from a restaurant in Paris that is more than one hundred years old, uses *fromage blanc,* raspberry puree and gelatin to make a classic charlotte encased in ladyfingers. A similar cheese-based dessert, made without gelatin and ladyfingers, is the Coeur à la Crème (page 442).

TIME: 1¼ hours, plus draining and chilling   YIELD: 6 to 8 servings

1¾ cups *fromage blanc*

8 cups raspberries

½ cup plus 1 tablespoon superfine
  sugar

1¾ teaspoons unflavored gelatin

One 3-ounce package soft
  ladyfingers (about 24)

1. Place a fine sieve lined with cheesecloth over a bowl, and drain *fromage blanc* at room temperature for 3 hours, or in the refrigerator for 8.

2. In a blender, food processor or food mill, combine 4 cups raspberries with 1 tablespoon sugar and 1 tablespoon water. Let sit about 10 minutes. Puree until smooth.

3. Transfer puree to a sieve placed over a bowl. Push puree through sieve. It should yield 1 cup. Discard solids.

4. In a dish, combine gelatin with 2 tablespoons water, and let sit for 10 minutes. In a saucepan, heat ¼ cup raspberry puree until nearly boiling. Add gelatin mixture; stir to dissolve. Remove from heat, and cool.

5. In a mixing bowl, whisk together drained *fromage blanc* with remaining raspberry puree and remaining sugar. Whisk in cooled gelatin-raspberry mixture.

6. Gently fold 2 cups whole raspberries into *fromage blanc* mixture. Transfer mixture to a 1-quart mold, cover with plastic, and refrigerate overnight or up to 2 days.

7. To assemble charlotte, invert chilled mold over a plate. Dip mold in hot water to help it release. Place ladyfingers standing up all around the sides of the charlotte. Decorate top with remaining 2 cups whole berries.

Tropical Fruit Trifle ✳

Bill
Yosses

Tropical fruit gives a sunny disposition to this trifle, an English dessert that consists of layers of cake, cream or custard, and sometimes jam. A large glass bowl is a must, so the rainbow stratification of the fruit is visible. The usual English trifle bowl has straight sides and is footed. For the sponge cake you can use the recipe for the sponge roulade (page 48), or a double recipe for yellow layer cake (page 529). Bill Yosses, a pastry chef who first became prominent at Bouley, was the chef for Citarella stores and restaurants.

TIME: 2½ hours, plus chilling   YIELD: 12 to 15 servings

2 cups sugar

Grated zest of 3 limes, plus strained juice of 2 of them

½ vanilla bean, split lengthwise

1 pineapple or 2 large Asian pears, peeled, cored and cut into ½-inch dice

1 large red papaya, 2 medium-size yellow papayas or 2 mangoes, peeled, seeded and cut into ½-inch dice

½ teaspoon unflavored gelatin

4 large egg yolks

1 cup heavy cream

1 cup plain yogurt

1 cup crème fraîche or sour cream

2 8- or 9-inch sponge cake layers, homemade or store-bought

9 kiwis, peeled and cut into ½-inch dice

Slices of tropical fruit for garnish

1. To make fruit compote, place ¾ cup sugar in a skillet. Add one-fourth of the lime zest, 1 piece vanilla bean and ½ cup water to the pan. Heat the syrup, stirring until the sugar dissolves. Simmer for 5 to 7 minutes until very reduced.

2. Add 4 cups pineapple or Asian pear to syrup, reserving rest for garnish. Cook gently until fruit is glazed and softened but holds its shape, 2 to 6 minutes. Remove vanilla bean. Place fruit in a bowl and let cool.

3. In clean skillet, add ¾ cup sugar, another fourth of the lime zest, other piece of vanilla bean and ½ cup water. Make a syrup as in Step 1. Add 4 cups papaya or mango to syrup, reserving rest for garnish. Cook gently until fruit is glazed and softened, but holds its shape, 2 to 4 minutes. Remove vanilla bean. Place fruit in a bowl and let cool.

4. To make yogurt cream, simmer an inch of water in the bottom of a double boiler. In a small bowl combine gelatin with 2 teaspoons cold water and set aside. Place egg yolks, remaining sugar, remaining lime zest and juice in the top of double boiler. Whisking constantly, heat yolks over simmering water until thickened, 5 to 7 minutes. Take egg mixture off heat and whisk in gelatin until it dissolves, about 20 seconds.

5. Whip cream until thickened and soft peaks just begin to form. Whisk yogurt and crème fraîche into yolk mixture, then whisk in whipped cream.

6. Trim cake layers so they fit into a large glass bowl. Split each in half horizontally. Place one layer in bowl. Starting at edge of bowl so that fruit shows through glass, place kiwis in one layer on cake. Spread a quarter of the yogurt cream over kiwis and top with another cake layer. Using a slotted spoon, scoop a layer of papaya on the cake, then another quarter of the cream and a third layer of cake. Top with remaining fruit, another quarter of the cream and final cake layer. Spread remaining cream on top. Cover trifle with plastic wrap and refrigerate for at least 3 hours and up to 3 days. Before serving, press pieces of sliced tropical fruit on top.

Summer Pudding

Jane
Grigson

The name of this English summer delight refers to the way the dessert is prepared, in a standard pudding bowl, the kind used for Christmas plum pudding and other steamed puddings. But in summer, when long steaming would not be welcome, the pudding filling, made entirely of berries, is only cooked briefly, then refrigerated, weighted and finally unmolded. Its bread case becomes thoroughly saturated with berry juices, for a gorgeous presentation. Jane Grigson, the author of this recipe, was as English as the pudding itself.

TIME: 30 minutes, plus overnight marinating and chilling   YIELD: 8 to 10 servings

2 pounds (about 7 cups) mixed raspberries, blackberries, currants and blueberries

⅔ cup superfine sugar

About 1½ pounds good-quality white bread, preferably unsliced

Whipped cream or crème fraîche for serving

1. In a bowl, combine berries and sugar. Cover and rest at room temperature overnight.

2. Transfer berry mixture to a large saucepan, place over medium heat and bring to a simmer. Cook gently to allow fruit to release juices, about 2 minutes. Remove from heat and set aside.

3. Slice bread ¼-inch thick and remove crusts. Cut a circle of bread to fit bottom of a round 5-cup bowl. Cut wedges of bread to fit around sides of bowl, leaving no gaps. Place ¼ cup of berries and juice in a small bowl, cover and refrigerate. Pour half the remaining berries and juice into bread-lined bowl. Place a slice of bread in center of bowl. Top with remaining half of the berries and juice.

4. Cut slices of bread to completely cover top of bowl. Fit a plate snugly in bowl. Weight with a heavy can and refrigerate 24 to 72 hours. To serve, remove plate and run a thin knife around inside of bowl. Place a large serving plate with a rim over top of bowl, then invert. Remove bowl. Outside of pudding should be completely soaked with juice. Use reserved juice to brush on any blank spots. Garnish pudding with reserved berries and juice. Serve with whipped cream or crème fraîche.

Holiday Trifle

This trifle offers a touch of the exotic, with its cardamom, pistachios and yogurt. Instead of the pandoro or panettone, slices of brioche can be used. Nigella Lawson's recipes in her "At My Table" column in the food section of *The New York Times* are focused on celebrating and entertaining.

Nigella
Lawson

TIME: 1 hour 15 minutes, plus optional day or overnight refrigeration
YIELD: 8 servings

4½ cups dried apricots
6 cardamom pods, lightly crushed
¾ cup superfine sugar
Juice of 1 lemon
Juice of ½ an orange or tangerine
½ pandoro cake (a 1-pound piece), or panettone

1 cup heavy cream
1 cup Greek yogurt
3 tablespoons honey
¼ cup raw shelled pistachio nuts, chopped into splinters
¼ cup sliced almonds

1. In a saucepan, combine apricots, cardamom pods, sugar, lemon juice and orange juice. Add 6 cups water and stir. Place over high heat to bring to a boil, then reduce heat to low and simmer for 30 minutes. Drain apricots. Strain liquid to remove cardamom pods and seeds. Reserve liquid.

2. Return apricot liquid to saucepan and boil until reduced to about 1½ cups, 15 to 20 minutes. Set aside to cool.

3. Slice pandoro vertically into ½-inch-wide wedges. Arrange half of the slices across bottom of a trifle bowl. Top with half the apricots and half the syrupy apricot liquid. Arrange remaining pandoro slices evenly in bowl, and top with remaining apricots and liquid. If desired, cover with plastic wrap and refrigerate for a day or overnight to allow liquid to be absorbed into cake.

4. To serve, whip heavy cream until peaks form. Add yogurt, beating again just until combined. Layer whipped cream mixture on top of trifle and drizzle with honey. Mix pistachios with almonds, and sprinkle on top. Serve immediately.

CUSTARDS, PUDDINGS AND MOUSSES

The soft, mellow, wiggly, creamy and often cloudlike desserts in this category range from the simplest delicate custards to the nostalgia of childhood puddings to elaborately conceived, often fragile mousses. Heavy saucepans, good whisks and spatulas, a sturdy electric mixer and attractive, often ovenproof baking dishes, bowls and especially ramekins are what the cook must have on hand. A double boiler or one improvised by setting a stainless steel mixing bowl to nest partway into a saucepan of simmering water, or a saucepan with sloping sides and a somewhat rounded edge, often called a Windsor, is particularly useful when whisking eggs over heat for a custard.

CUSTARDS

Many custards and puddings are baked in a water bath to ensure even cooking. The baking dish sits in a larger pan filled halfway with hot water. Putting a small kitchen towel under the baking dish in the larger pan will keep the dish from sliding.

Custard-making is a skill that comes in handy for a wide range of desserts. Soft stovetop custards, custard sauces, pastry cream and ice creams depend on a mixture of eggs or egg yolks, sugar and hot liquid, all cooked together until the eggs thicken the sweetened liquid, usually milk or cream. Making custard in a double boiler is slow but less likely to result in overcooked eggs that have curdled and ruined the end result. But experienced cooks, often impatient, make custard over direct heat, whisking the mixture or stirring it with a wooden spoon until steam just begins to rise. A sure way to stop the cooking is to plunge the bottom of the saucepan into cold water. Another way to be sure the egg yolks will not curdle is to beat them with a teaspoon of cornstarch before heating them, a chef's trick that works not only for custard but also for sauces like crème anglaise. After the custard is properly cooked, it is often strained to smooth it. And while it cools, it's a good idea to place a piece of plastic wrap or parchment directly on the surface to prevent a skin from forming.

Baked Custard

This custard can also be baked in six old-fashioned heavy ceramic custard cups. This typical English recipe is by Nigella Lawson.

Nigella
Lawson

TIME: 1 hour 15 minutes, plus cooling   YIELD: 6 servings

2½ cups whole milk
1 vanilla bean, split lengthwise, or
   2 teaspoons vanilla extract
2 large eggs

3 large egg yolks
¼ cup sugar
Freshly grated nutmeg

1. Preheat oven to 350 degrees. Combine milk and vanilla bean, if using, in a small saucepan. Heat just until warm, then remove vanilla bean, and reserve for another use. If not using bean, add vanilla extract after milk is warmed.

2. In a medium bowl, whisk together the eggs, yolks and sugar. Pour in vanilla-infused milk, whisking until smooth. Strain mixture into a 4- to 5-cup glass or ceramic pie or quiche dish about 9 inches in diameter. Sprinkle with nutmeg.

3. Place dish on a folded kitchen towel in a larger baking pan, and add boiling water to come halfway up the sides of the dish. Place in oven and bake until custard is set, about 1 hour. Remove from oven, and transfer dish to a rack to cool for at least 10 minutes before serving. Serve while slightly warm, preferably about 30 minutes after removing from oven.

Maple Caramel Custard

Florence
Fabricant

Be sure to use pure maple syrup, not a blend. The syrup, however, does not have to be grade A, the finest, which is somewhat lighter and definitely more expensive than grade B, the cooking variety, which is less delicate. Unlike maple syrup, maple sugar is less widely sold. Specialty food shops and mail-order from syrup companies are the best sources. You can use light brown sugar instead, but the flavor of the custard will be less pronounced.

TIME: 1 hour, plus chilling   YIELD: 4 servings

⅓ cup granulated sugar
¼ cup pure maple syrup, warmed
3 large eggs
2 large egg yolks

½ cup maple sugar
2 cups milk
1 cup half-and-half
1 teaspoon vanilla extract

1. Preheat oven to 350 degrees.

2. Swirl the granulated sugar and 3 tablespoons water together in a skillet, preferably nonstick, until the sugar dissolves. Cook over medium-high heat without stirring until the mixture turns amber. Remove from the heat and pour into a 4-cup baking dish, tilting the dish to coat the bottom with the caramel. Drizzle the warm maple syrup over the caramel.

3. In a medium bowl, beat the eggs and egg yolks together. Beat in the maple sugar and stir in the milk, half-and-half and vanilla. Pour into the baking dish.

4. Set the dish in a larger pan and add boiling water until it comes halfway up the sides of the dish. Place in the oven and bake 45 minutes, until a knife inserted in the center comes out clean.

5. Allow the custard to cool to room temperature, then refrigerate for 6 hours or overnight. Run a knife around the edges and invert it into a serving dish with enough rim to catch the maple-caramel sauce.

Thai Coffee Crème Caramel

In Southeast Asia, not just Thailand, coffee is often made with sweetened condensed milk, giving it uncommon richness and a distinctive flavor. This caramel custard flavored with coffee uses sweetened condensed milk. Patricia Yeo, who rose to prominence on the New York scene at AZ, is now at Sapa.

Patricia Yeo, Sapa, New York

TIME: 1 hour, plus chilling   YIELD: 4 servings

7 large egg yolks
Finely chopped zest of half a
    lemon
2 teaspoons vanilla extract

1 tablespoon coffee extract
1 14-ounce can sweetened
    condensed milk
1 cup sugar

1. In a large bowl, combine egg yolks, lemon zest, vanilla extract and coffee extract. Add condensed milk, then fill can to top with water, and add to mixture. Stir well, and allow to sit for 20 minutes.

2. Meanwhile, preheat oven to 300 degrees. Set aside four shallow 1-cup ramekins. Put sugar in a small heavy saucepan over medium-low heat. Stir once or twice as it slowly melts, then begins to boil. Stop stirring, and watch carefully. When sugar has darkened to the color of a hazelnut, remove from heat, and carefully pour a tablespoon or two into each ramekin, swirling so it spreads up the sides about ½ inch.

3. Bring about 4 cups of water to a boil. Strain egg mixture through a fine sieve into a bowl. Pour mixture into ramekins, and place them in a baking pan. Pour boiling water into pan so that it comes about halfway up the sides of the ramekins. Bake until custard is just set, about 30 minutes. Refrigerate custards for several hours or overnight.

4. To serve, run a thin knife around the inside of each ramekin and invert ramekins over a plate with a lip (to contain caramel sauce). Tap bottoms to release custard.

Crème Brûlée

Amanda
Hesser

Though crème brûlée is French, other cuisines have also staked their claims. In England it's burnt cream, and in Spain, crema catalana. Anyone who plans to serve crème brûlée with any frequency should have a kitchen blowtorch fueled with butane on hand. This gadget is extremely easy to use and far more reliable than trying to caramelize the sugar on top of the custard under the broiler. The blowtorch can be used for other recipes, when a quick surface browning is required. The key to crème brûlée is to have an extremely rich custard base, one made with cream, not milk, more like a pot de crème than a standard custard. The thick cream, in a shallow ceramic or pottery ramekin, must be thoroughly chilled for the burnt caramel glaze to set and become crisp and glassy. Though a deeper container can be used, with a shallow dish you will have a larger surface of the delicious burnt sugar. Amanda Hesser lived in France and based her book *The Cook and the Gardener* on her time there.

TIME: 1 hour, plus chilling   YIELD: 6 servings

2 cups heavy cream
1 cup milk
1 vanilla bean, split lengthwise
¼ cup plus 1 tablespoon
   granulated sugar

6 large egg yolks
⅓ to ½ cup turbinado sugar or
   light brown sugar

1. In a medium saucepan, scald the cream and milk with the vanilla bean. Remove from heat and let steep for 15 minutes. Remove vanilla bean and discard.

2. Preheat oven to 300 degrees. In a medium bowl, whisk together the granulated sugar and egg yolks until light and fluffy. Strain cream and milk and add a little at a time to egg mixture, whisking until well blended.

3. Pour mixture into four shallow 1-cup ramekins. Place dishes in a roasting pan and pour enough hot water in pan to come halfway up the sides of the baking dishes.

4. Bake until mixture is just set in center (it should still wiggle when shaken), about 30 to 35 minutes. Remove dishes from roasting pan and let cool completely. Refrigerate 2 to 24 hours.

5. Set out baking dishes 20 minutes before serving. Sprinkle turbinado sugar in a thin even layer over the dishes, covering the cream completely. Light the blowtorch and, holding it so the flame just touches the surface, begin caramelizing the sugar, working in circles from center to edges of baking dish. If sugar begins to burn, remove torch flame and blow on the sugar. Serve immediately. Custards can also be caramelized under a broiler, but must be done one at a time and watched carefully.

Vanilla Pots de Crème

Mark
Bittman

Pots de crème are essentially custards, but extremely rich, tender ones because they are made with cream, not milk. Because they are baked in the oven, they are easier to make than stovetop custards. Mark Bittman writes the "Minimalist" column for *The New York Times.*

TIME: 1 hour, plus chilling   YIELD: 4 servings

2 cups heavy cream, light cream
   or half-and-half
2 vanilla beans or 1 teaspoon
   vanilla extract

6 large egg yolks
½ cup sugar

1. Preheat oven to 300 degrees. Pour cream into a small saucepan. Split vanilla beans in half lengthwise and scrape seeds into cream along with pods. Heat cream until steam rises. Cover pan, turn off heat and let steep for 10 to 15 minutes. If using vanilla extract, just heat cream and let cool while you proceed. Extract will be added later.

2. Beat yolks and sugar together until light. Remove vanilla bean, if used, from the cream and pour about a quarter of the cream into the egg mixture, then pour sugar-egg mixture into cream and stir. If you are using vanilla extract, add it now and stir. Pour mixture into 4 6-ounce ramekins and place ramekins in a baking dish; fill dish with water halfway up the sides of the dishes. Cover with foil.

3. Bake 30 to 45 minutes, or until center is barely set. Heavy cream will set faster than half-and-half. Cover and refrigerate until chilled before serving.

Baked Butterscotch Pudding (A Custard)

Though it's called a pudding, the recipe is essentially for a baked custard. Its amber color, as well as its flavor, suggest butterscotch. Never reveal that it was made without butter. Craftbar is one of chef Tom Colicchio's New York restaurants.

Karen
De Masco,
Craftbar,
New York

TIME: 1 hour, plus chilling   YIELD: 4 servings

1 cup milk
2 cups heavy cream
¼ cup packed dark brown sugar
¾ cup granulated sugar
6 large egg yolks, at room
    temperature

1 teaspoon kosher salt
1 teaspoon vanilla extract
Crème fraîche, for serving

1. Preheat oven to 300 degrees. In a medium saucepan, warm milk, cream and brown sugar to dissolve sugar. In a deep, heavy saucepan of at least 3-quart capacity, mix together granulated sugar and ¼ cup water. Place over medium heat and bring to a boil. Monitor closely, swirling pan so sugar cooks evenly.

2. When sugar is a very light golden caramel, remove it from heat. Put on oven mitts and slowly whisk about a cup of the milk mixture into the caramel to stop it from cooking. It will bubble up violently. Stir until smooth. Add remaining milk mixture.

3. Put egg yolks in a large bowl and beat lightly. Whisk in about ½ cup of the milk mixture into eggs to temper them. Add eggs to milk and caramel mixture and whisk to combine. Stir in salt and vanilla and strain.

4. Bring a kettle of water to a boil. Pour custard into 4 crème brûlée dishes or ramekins. Place dishes in a baking dish and pour in enough boiling water to come halfway up the sides of the dishes. Cover pan tightly with aluminum foil. Bake for 15 minutes, then lift up aluminum foil to let out some steam. Reseal pan, turn it 180 degrees and continue baking, checking every 10 minutes. Pudding is done when sides are set but center is still wobbly when you shake dish, about 25 to 30 minutes.

5. Remove from water bath and let cool to room temperature, then chill. Serve with a dollop of crème fraîche.

Buttered Orange Cream

Clarissa
Dickson
Wright

This custard is flavored with orange and exotic rosewater, made with orange juice instead of milk and enriched with butter and, just before serving, whipped cream. Clarissa Dickson Wright was popular on British television as one of the "Two Fat Ladies" on a cooking show.

TIME: 25 minutes   YIELD: 6 servings

Grated zest and juice from 2
  large, juicy oranges
¼ cup superfine sugar
5 large egg yolks
1 teaspoon rosewater

4 ounces (1 stick) soft unsalted
  butter, cut into large cubes
½ cup heavy cream
6 teaspoons finely chopped soft
  candied orange peel (page 546)

1. Place 2 inches of water in the bottom of a double boiler, and bring to a simmer. In the top of the double boiler, mix together the orange zest and juice, sugar and egg yolks.

2. Place orange mixture over simmering water. Stir gently with a whisk, scraping sides of pan, until the mixture is thick and custardy. Remove the orange mixture from the heat, and place the pan into a shallow bowl of ice water. Stir in rosewater. Quickly whisk butter in, one cube at a time, allowing each cube to emulsify before adding the next. Allow the mixture to cool to room temperature, then remove the bowl from the ice water.

3. Whip cream until it holds soft peaks, and gently fold into the orange mixture until blended. To serve, place an equal portion of the orange cream in each of six large stemmed glasses. Sprinkle a teaspoon of candied orange peel into each glass, and carefully fold in so the peel is suspended throughout the cream. Serve immediately.

Îles Flottantes with Berries

Île flottante, or floating island, is a French confection, made by oven-poaching meringues, unmolding them and setting them on pools of custard. Amanda Hesser is the food editor of *The New York Times Sunday Magazine.*

Amanda
Hesser

TIME: 1 hour   YIELD: 6 servings

3 cups milk

6 large egg yolks

1¼ cups plus 1 tablespoon sugar

½ teaspoon vanilla extract

½ teaspoon almond extract

Pinch of sea salt

Unsalted butter for ramekins

¼ teaspoon cream of tartar

5 large egg whites

1 cup raspberries or blackberries, or a mixture

1. In a medium saucepan, heat milk until bubbles form around edges but do not let it boil. Remove from heat. In another medium saucepan, whisk egg yolks with ¾ cup sugar until light and fluffy. Whisk in hot milk and place pan over medium heat. While stirring constantly with a wooden spoon, heat mixture until it thickens enough to coat the back of the spoon. Move pan off heat occasionally so mixture does not curdle. Strain into a bowl. Stir in vanilla and almond extracts and salt. Cover with plastic wrap punctured with a fork, and let cool to room temperature.

2. Meanwhile, preheat oven to 325 degrees. Bring a kettle of water to a boil. Butter 6 8-ounce ramekins and line with parchment paper. Butter again.

3. In a medium bowl set over a pan of simmering water, dissolve cream of tartar in 2 tablespoons warm water. Add egg whites and ½ cup sugar and whisk vigorously for a minute over medium heat. Remove from heat and continue whisking until soft peaks form.

4. In a small bowl, stir together berries and remaining tablespoon sugar. Fold into egg whites. Divide mixture among ramekins, tapping ramekins on counter to remove any air bubbles. Place ramekins in a roasting pan, and pour in enough hot water from the kettle to come halfway up their sides. Place in oven and bake until risen and firm, about 15 minutes. Remove ramekins from water bath and let cool to room temperature.

5. Unmold meringues into 6 wide, shallow bowls. Peel off parchment. Spoon vanilla sauce around each. Serve.

Zabaglione with Strawberries and Balsamic Meringue

Esca,
New York

Zabaglione, the custard made with egg yolks, wine and sugar, is the sauce for this strawberry dessert. Crisp meringue and high-quality balsamic vinegar complete the flavor profile. Esca is an Italian seafood restaurant.

TIME: 4 to 5 hours, including cooling and chilling   YIELD: 4 servings

5 large eggs, separated, at room temperature

Pinch of salt

½ cup confectioners' sugar, sifted

1 teaspoon plus 1 tablespoon aged balsamic vinegar

½ teaspoon vanilla extract

¾ cup granulated sugar, approximately

⅓ cup prosecco or Champagne

¾ cup heavy cream

1 pint ripe strawberries, rinsed, hulled and diced

1. Preheat oven to 250 degrees. Line a baking sheet with parchment.

2. Using an electric mixer, beat the egg whites with salt until very foamy. Continue beating, adding the confectioners' sugar gradually, until stiff and shiny. Beat in 1 teaspoon vinegar and the vanilla. Spread meringue about ½ inch thick on parchment. Place in oven, and bake 2 hours. Turn off oven, and allow to cool in oven at least 1 hour, until crisp. Break up.

3. Have a large metal mixing bowl that will fit over a large pot of simmering water and a large bowl of ice water ready. Off heat, place the egg yolks in a mixing bowl. With a large whisk, beat yolks and ½ cup sugar until yolks have lightened and start to thicken. Place bowl on pan of simmering water, and continue beating, gradually adding prosecco, until mixture is custardy, 10 to 15 minutes. When zabaglione is very thick and whisk leaves a trace in bottom of bowl, place in bowl of ice water to cool. Stir once or twice.

4. Beat the cream until it just holds peaks. Refrigerate. When the zabaglione is cold, fold in whipped cream. Refrigerate.

5. Sweeten the strawberries with ¼ cup sugar, or to taste. Fold in remaining balsamic vinegar. Divide strawberries among 4 old-fashioned glasses or goblets. Top with crumbled meringue, then with zabaglione. Garnish with a few pieces of meringue, and serve.

PUDDINGS, INCLUDING STEAMED PUDDINGS

Stovetop puddings, including rice and tapioca puddings, are given in this section. But most of the puddings are baked in the oven. Soufflé dishes and ramekins are the containers that are best for baked puddings. English-style steamed puddings are usually done in pottery bowls. And shallower baking dishes that can go from oven to table are excellent for bread puddings. Another option, for individual puddings, is muffin tins.

Mellow Chocolate Pudding

Brown sugar gives mellow warmth to this pudding. It is a subtle variation of the classic, simple combination of sugar, cornstarch and cocoa cooked in milk and was one of the first recipes I learned as a child. Once you can prepare chocolate pudding like this, regardless of the kind of sugar you use, you'll never buy the packaged mix again.

Florence
Fabricant

∾

TIME: 20 minutes, plus cooling   YIELD: 6 to 8 servings

½ cup unsweetened cocoa
⅔ cup light brown sugar
½ cup cornstarch
1 teaspoon cinnamon

½ teaspoon vanilla extract
3 cups whole milk (low-fat or
    skim can be used)
Softly whipped heavy cream

1. Mix cocoa, brown sugar, cornstarch and cinnamon in a heavy saucepan. Gradually whisk in milk.

2. Place over medium heat and cook slowly, stirring with a wooden spoon, until mixture comes to a boil and thickens.

3. Transfer to a serving dish or individual goblets or bowls and cover by placing plastic wrap directly on the surface. Using wooden spoon, scrape all remaining pudding from saucepan and lick it off spoon.

4. Allow pudding to cool until just warm, or refrigerate until ready to serve. Serve with whipped cream.

Double Dip of Chocolate Pudding

Sheila
Lukins
∽

The usual way to make chocolate pudding is to mix cocoa, sugar and cornstarch and add hot milk. The cornstarch is the thickener. Here, however, the double dip comes with the addition of semisweet chocolate and, just in case all this is not rich enough, some butter, too. Sheila Lukins, one of the founders of the Silver Palate, is a food writer and the author of many cookbooks.

TIME: 30 minutes, plus chilling   YIELD: 4 servings

½ cup sugar

3 tablespoons unsweetened cocoa

2½ tablespoons cornstarch

Pinch of salt

1 large egg plus 2 large yolks

2 cups milk

4 ounces semisweet chocolate,
  chopped

2 tablespoons unsalted butter

1 teaspoon instant espresso
  powder

1 teaspoon vanilla extract

Heavy cream or whipped cream,
  for serving

1. Combine sugar, cocoa powder, cornstarch and salt.

2. Whisk egg and yolks together in a small bowl. Add sugar mixture, and whisk to a smooth paste. Set aside.

3. Scald milk in a medium heavy saucepan over medium heat. Remove from heat immediately. Add ½ cup hot milk to egg mixture; whisk until smooth. Slowly pour this mixture back into saucepan with the hot milk. Whisk constantly until smooth.

4. Place saucepan over medium heat, and cook, whisking constantly, until thickened, 5 to 7 minutes. Remove from heat, add chopped chocolate, butter, instant coffee and vanilla. Continue whisking until smooth.

5. Transfer pudding into four individual serving dishes or one bowl. Place plastic wrap directly on surface. Cool to room temperature. Refrigerate until chilled, 1 hour or more. Serve with cream, whipped or plain.

Baked Chocolate Pudding for Two

Half pudding, half soufflé, this is the perfect dessert for an intimate dinner, say, on February 14. The recipe can be doubled to provide more servings.

Florence
Fabricant

TIME: 1 hour, plus resting   YIELD: 2 servings

2½ tablespoons unsalted butter,
   softened
½ cup sugar
1½ ounces unsweetened chocolate
¼ cup lowfat milk
2 large egg yolks

½ teaspoon vanilla extract
3 tablespoons all-purpose flour
1 large egg white
¼ cup fudge sauce (page 537),
   optional
½ cup heavy cream, whipped

1. Preheat oven to 325 degrees. Butter a 2-cup soufflé dish with ½ tablespoon of the butter and line the bottom with waxed or parchment paper.

2. Cream the remaining butter with the sugar. Melt the chocolate in the top of a double boiler. Stir in the milk, then blend into the butter mixture. Beat in the egg yolks and stir in the vanilla and the flour.

3. Beat the egg white until it holds peaks and fold into the chocolate mixture. Spoon the batter into the prepared dish, place the dish in a pan of boiling water that comes halfway up the sides of the dish, place in the oven and bake about 40 minutes, until the top is firm to the touch.

4. Remove from the oven and allow to sit in the warm water for at least 30 minutes. It will sink a bit.

5. Thin fudge sauce by adding 1 tablespoon warm water. To serve, run a knife around the inside of the baking dish, unmold pudding onto a plate, peel off the waxed paper and spoon the fudge sauce around the pudding. Serve with whipped cream on the side.

Chocolate Orange Pudding

Barbara
Kafka

This orange-scented chocolate pudding is meant to be prepared in a microwave oven. But it can also be baked in a conventional oven preheated to 325 degrees. Cover the filled baking dish with foil and place it in a larger pan of hot water. Bake it about 30 minutes, until set. Unmold it if you wish. Barbara Kafka is a food writer and cookbook author who has made cooking in a microwave oven one of her specialties.

TIME: 30 minutes   YIELD: 8 servings

Nonstick vegetable spray
½ cup slivered almonds
Zest of ½ medium orange
½ cup light brown sugar
½ pound semisweet chocolate,
    chopped

½ teaspoon baking soda
¼ pound unsalted butter
3 large eggs
⅓ cup heavy cream
1 teaspoon triple sec

1. Coat a 1½-quart soufflé dish with nonstick vegetable spray and reserve.

2. Place almonds in the work bowl of a food processor, and process until finely chopped. Add orange zest and sugar, and finely chop again. Add chocolate, baking soda and butter, and process until smooth.

3. Add eggs, cream and triple sec, and process until combined. Pour into prepared dish, and cover tightly with microwave plastic wrap. Cook at 100 percent power for 6 minutes. Prick plastic to release steam.

4. Remove from oven, and uncover. Allow to stand, covered with a heavy plate, for 10 minutes.

5. Unmold pudding onto serving plate, and serve warm.

Marie Louise's Rice Pudding

Rice, cooked slowly in milk with sugar, will swell and become delectably tender. In this recipe, from French-born chef Christian Delouvrier's aunt, there is an extra touch, a drizzle of caramel. He is now involved in restaurants in Florida.

Christian
Delouvrier

TIME: About 2½ hours   YIELD: 6 to 8 servings

½ cup long-grain rice
1 very small bay leaf or ½ large
   bay leaf, preferably fresh
1 quart milk

1 cup sugar
½ vanilla bean, split lengthwise
½ cup crème fraîche

1. Preheat oven to 350 degrees. Put rice and bay leaf in a small saucepan, and add 2 cups water. Bring to a boil, then immediately drain rice. Transfer rice and bay leaf to an 8-inch square baking pan, and stir in the milk, ½ cup sugar and vanilla bean.

2. Cut a piece of parchment paper to fit inside pan, and place it directly on top of rice mixture. Place pan inside a larger baking pan and fill larger pan with enough very hot water to reach halfway up sides of small pan. Bake rice until it is very tender and most of the liquid is absorbed, about 2 hours.

3. Meanwhile, prepare caramel syrup. In a small saucepan over medium-high heat, combine remaining sugar with 2 tablespoons water. Cook, stirring, until sugar dissolves. Raise heat to high, and let mixture cook without stirring until it caramelizes and turns a very deep amber, about 7 minutes. Carefully add ⅓ cup hot water (it will sputter). Simmer caramel, stirring, until mixture is smooth. Set aside to cool.

4. As soon as rice comes out of oven, peel off parchment paper. Transfer pan to a rack to cool. Pluck out vanilla bean and bay leaf.

5. Using a whisk or an electric mixer, beat crème fraîche until it holds soft peaks. Fold it into cooled rice mixture. Serve rice pudding in bowls with a drizzle of caramel syrup on top.

Brûlée Coconut Rice Pudding with Lime Syrup ✳

**Tadashi
Ono**

This rice pudding is up to all kinds of tricks. It is made with coconut milk in addition to whole milk, which changes the flavor of the usual comfort food dessert. A crème brûlée topping is applied at the end (it's optional, said the chef, but who could resist?). Italian arborio or Spanish bomba rice are good short-grain varieties for this dish. Tadashi Ono is a French-trained Japanese chef who is now at Matsuri in New York.

TIME: 1 hour, plus cooling   YIELD: 6 servings

1½ cups sugar
4 limes, zest grated, juiced
3 cups whole milk
3 cups canned unsweetened
    coconut milk

1 vanilla bean
¾ cup short-grain rice
1 teaspoon salt
6 teaspoons palm sugar or light
    brown sugar, optional

1. Set a small pot of water to boil. In a separate saucepan or a 10-inch skillet, combine ½ cup sugar and ½ cup water and bring to a boil. Cook for a few seconds, until sugar dissolves. Place lime zest in boiling water for 10 seconds, drain through a sieve and plunge into ice water. Set aside. Add lime juice to sugar syrup. Cook over medium heat until it darkens to caramel, about 20 minutes. Cool briefly, then stir in lime zest and set aside.

2. Put the rice in a deep bowl and run cold water over it, stirring with your hand. Drain and repeat until water runs clear. Combine milk and co-conut milk in a wide, deep, heavy-bottom saucepan, and turn heat to medium high. Split vanilla bean lengthwise and scrape out seeds. Add the seeds to saucepan, along with the rice, 1 cup sugar and salt. When liquid begins to boil, lower heat to a simmer. If the mixture starts to brown, turn heat down. Stir occasionally at first, then more and more frequently, until mixture becomes thick and like oatmeal, about 25 minutes.

3. Spoon pudding into 6 ramekins, and cool to room temperature. You can refrigerate for up to a day, but the puddings are best at room tempera-ture. If desired, sprinkle top of each pudding with palm or brown sugar and use a blowtorch or run puddings under broiler one at a time until sugar bubbles and browns. Serve drizzled with lime syrup.

Green Tea Rice Pudding
with Candied Ginger ✳

Though sweet rice desserts are served in Asia, it has taken fusion cooking for rice pudding to appear on menus of Asian restaurants in America. Here, it is based on the homestyle classic, but tweaked with the addition of Asian ingredients like coconut (as in the previous recipe) or green tea (in this one). The result is usually a lovely reinvention. Powdered green tea, or matcha, is sold in Asian stores, tea shops and, increasingly, more general food markets as well as online. Kay Rentschler has contributed recipes to *The New York Times.*

Kay
Rentschler

∽

TIME: 45 minutes, plus chilling   YIELD: 6 servings

¾ cup medium- or short-grain
   rice
½ teaspoon salt
2 cups whole milk
2¼ cups half-and-half
¼ cup sugar

¼ cup honey
¼ cup minced candied ginger,
   more for garnish
2 tablespoons matcha (Japanese
   powdered green tea)

1. Bring 2 cups water to boil in a heavy 3-quart saucepan. Add rice and salt, cover and simmer over low heat, stirring occasionally, until grains have expanded and water is absorbed, 10 to 15 minutes.

2. Add milk, half-and-half, sugar and honey. Bring to a simmer over medium-high heat. Reduce heat to medium-low and cook, uncovered, stirring occasionally, until mixture begins to thicken, about 20 minutes. Reduce heat to low, add ¼ cup candied ginger and cook, stirring frequently, until pudding is creamy, about 15 minutes more. Remove from heat.

3. Bring ½ cup water to a simmer in a small saucepan. Remove from heat and cool slightly. Sprinkle matcha over surface and whisk until no lumps remain and liquid is frothy. Whisk matcha into pudding. Transfer pudding to a bowl, cover and chill at least 4 hours or overnight. To serve, spoon into bowls and garnish with more minced candied ginger.

Tapioca Pudding with Dried Fruit Compote ✳

Marian
Burros

∾

Like rice pudding, tapioca is enjoying a renaissance. In this recipe the pudding, made from scratch from tapioca pearls, not an instant mix, is enriched with egg yolks like a custard, lightened with egg whites, and embellished with the addition of whipped cream, spices, sweet wine and fruit compote. Marian Burros is a food reporter for *The New York Times.*

TIME: 45 minutes, plus overnight soaking   YIELD: 8 servings

½ cup pearl tapioca
1 cup mixed dried fruit, like
    apples, cherries, pears or
    peaches, but not prunes or
    raisins
1½ cups fresh apple cider
8 tablespoons sugar
2 large eggs, separated

2½ cups skim milk
½ teaspoon ground cinnamon
¼ teaspoon ground nutmeg
Salt
1 tablespoon sweet Marsala
⅓ cup heavy cream, optional
⅔ cup nonfat plain yogurt,
    optional

1. Soak the tapioca in 2 cups of water in the refrigerator overnight.

2. Cut the large pieces of dried fruit so that they are no larger than ½ inch square. Place all the fruit in a medium saucepan with the cider and 1½ tablespoons sugar. Bring the mixture to a simmer and cook for 30 minutes; drain.

3. Beat the egg whites until foamy. Gradually beat in 3 tablespoons of sugar until soft peaks form. Set aside.

4. Drain the tapioca. Place it in a medium saucepan and mix with the remaining sugar and the milk, cinnamon, nutmeg, egg yolks and a few pinches of salt. Let the mixture stand for 5 minutes.

5. Cook the tapioca mixture over medium heat, stirring often, for 20 to 40 minutes, until the tapioca becomes translucent and the mixture thickens. Gradually add the egg-white mixture, stirring just until blended; stir in the Marsala and the stewed fruit.

6. Cool for 20 minutes.

7. While the pudding is cooling, whip the cream, and fold the cream into the yogurt. Serve the pudding warm or chilled, with a few dabs of the whipped cream-yogurt mixture, if desired.

Lemon Coconut Cake (page 55) served with Raspberry Coulis (page 536)

Chocolate Black Pepper Cake (page 34)

Limoncello Babas with Lemon Cream (page 124)

Plum Crumble (page 215)

Baked Chocolate Pudding for Two (page 403)

Baked Butterscotch Pudding (page 397)

Goat's Milk Ice Cream (page 448)

Vietnamese Coffee Tapioca Affogato with Condensed Milk Ice Cream
(page 492)

Hot Fudge Sauce used in a sundae (page 538)

Cherry Sauce used in a sundae (page 542)

Ginger Buttermilk Pie (page 254)

Magie Noire Cake (page 31)

Warm Vanilla Cakes (page 76)

Spicy Gingerbread (page 88)

Crêpes Belle Hélène (page 204)

Blueberry Kuchen (page 111)

Red-Berry Tapioca Pudding ✳

The brilliant ruby color of currant juice gives this tapioca pudding its personality. It starts as a thick sauce which becomes bound with a mixture of fresh berries. Kay Rentschler is a food writer who has contributed recipes to *The New York Times*.

Kay
Rentschler

TIME: 1 hour, plus chilling   YIELD: 6 to 8 servings

¾ cup filtered or bottled water
¼ cup small pearl tapioca
18 ounces red currants on the
    stem
1 pound small strawberries or
    fraises des bois

6 ounces raspberries
8 ounces blueberries
Pinch of salt
10 tablespoons sugar
Crème anglaise (page 533) or
    vanilla ice cream, for serving

1. In a small bowl, pour ¼ cup filtered water over tapioca, stir once, cover and let sit at room temperature for 30 minutes.

2. Meanwhile, wash currants on their stems in a large bowl of water; pick through, and discard damaged or unripe berries. Place two-thirds of the berries with stems in a 3-quart saucepan with remaining ½ cup filtered water. Cover and simmer, stirring once, for 5 minutes. Remove from heat and let rest, covered, for 5 minutes more. Pour berries and juices through a fine-mesh sieve into a 2-cup glass measuring cup, pushing lightly on berries to extract liquid. There should be 1 cup juice.

3. Pluck remaining currants from stems. Rinse and hull strawberries. Sort through raspberries, and discard soft or damaged berries; do not wash. Wash, drain and pick over blueberries.

4. In saucepan from currants, combine currant juice, salt, sugar and tapioca over low heat, and bring to a simmer. Cook, covered, stirring frequently, until sauce has thickened and most of the pearls are transparent, about 5 minutes. Add strawberries and blueberries, and warm fruits to release juices, stirring frequently, for 2 to 3 minutes.

5. Add raspberries and remaining currants. Simmer mixture 2 to 3 minutes. Remove from heat, transfer to a bowl that can be used for serving, cover surface directly with plastic wrap and chill well. Serve with vanilla sauce or ice cream.

Coconut Tapioca

Tadashi
Ono

Two kinds of tapioca add textural interest to this Asian-themed pudding made with coconut milk and seasoned with cilantro made into a syrup by whirling it in a blender with corn syrup. When the chef specifies cilantro leaves, he is not kidding. You must first pluck the leaves from the stems before making the sauce, and you will need nearly half of a bunch of cilantro. Would you be making a mistake by folding some finely slivered crystallized ginger into the pudding before serving it? Not at all. Tadashi Ono is a French-trained Japanese chef who is now at Matsuri in New York.

TIME: 1 hour 15 minutes, plus chilling   YIELD: 6 servings

5½ cups milk
1 cup sugar
¼ cup large-pearl tapioca
¼ cup small-pearl tapioca
1 13½-ounce can unsweetened
    coconut milk

¼ cup cilantro leaves, tightly
    packed
⅓ cup light corn syrup
Passion fruit or other tropical
    fruit sorbet (page 472)

1. Place milk and sugar in a large heavy saucepan. Bring to a simmer over high heat, stirring occasionally to dissolve sugar. Add the large-pearl tapioca, reduce heat to low, and simmer, stirring frequently, for 15 minutes. Add small-pearl tapioca and continue simmering until tapioca pearls are soft, another 35 to 45 minutes.

2. Transfer tapioca to a large bowl while still warm. Stir in the coconut milk. Let the mixture cool, then cover and chill 10 to 24 hours.

3. While tapioca is cooking, bring a small saucepan of water to a boil. Fill a bowl with ice cubes and water. Plunge the cilantro leaves first into the boiling water for 15 seconds, then drain, and immediately plunge them into the ice water. Drain and pat dry.

4. Combine the corn syrup and cilantro in a blender or food processor, and puree. Let the mixture rest for 30 minutes, then strain, discarding the solids. Refrigerate until ready to use.

5. To serve, divide tapioca mixture among six soup plates. Dot each serving with ½ teaspoon of cilantro syrup. Place a scoop of passion fruit or other tropical fruit sorbet in the center. Serve immediately.

Ginger Pudding

The sweet heat of ginger enlivens these individual steamed puddings, which make a lovely dessert in cold weather. Despite the richness of the puddings, the ginger, which has digestive qualities, is excellent to serve at the end of a meal. Pass a tray of plain bittersweet chocolates alongside. Nicola Butt is the pastry chef at the Dartmoor Inn in Lyford, England.

Nicola
Butt

TIME: 1 hour 10 minutes   YIELD: 12 servings

2 12-ounce jars ginger preserves
  or ginger marmalade
1 teaspoon baking soda
½ pound (2 sticks) unsalted
  butter, more for greasing
  ramekins, at room temperature
¾ cup plus 2 tablespoons light
  brown sugar
3 teaspoons ground ginger
Pinch of salt

4 large eggs, lightly beaten
2 cups self-rising flour
4 to 6 pieces stem ginger in syrup,
  finely chopped
7 tablespoons syrup from stem
  ginger in syrup
¾ cup dry sherry
¾ cup heavy cream
1 teaspoon lemon juice

1. Preheat oven to 350 degrees. In a saucepan, combine preserves and baking soda. Place over low heat, and stir just until fluid. Set aside. In a mixer, blend 11 tablespoons butter, ¾ cup brown sugar, 2 teaspoons ground ginger and salt. At low speed, add eggs, then preserves. Add flour and mix.

2. Bring a kettle of water to a boil. Lightly butter 12 1-cup ramekins. Place chopped ginger and a little syrup in each. Reserve 5 tablespoons syrup. Divide batter among ramekins. Cover each ramekin with foil, and put in a large baking dish. Add boiling water to about halfway up the sides of the ramekins. Bake until puddings have set, about 40 minutes.

3. In a medium saucepan, bring sherry to a boil, then simmer until syrupy, about 15 minutes. Add 5 tablespoons ginger syrup, remaining butter, brown sugar, ground ginger and heavy cream. Bring to a boil, then reduce heat to low. Simmer, whisking until mixture is slightly thickened and smooth. Remove from heat, and whisk in lemon juice. Set aside. Keep warm.

4. Place each ramekin on a plate. Remove foil, and top each with about 1½ tablespoons of sauce. Serve warm.

Apricot Steamed Pudding

Barbara
Kafka

This is another microwave oven pudding that can also be made conventionally. First simmer the apricots in a saucepan to soften them. Then bake the pudding in the soufflé dish, covered with foil, in a baking pan filled with hot water to come halfway up the sides of the soufflé dish, about 40 minutes at 325 degrees. Barbara Kafka is a food writer and cookbook author who has made cooking in a microwave oven one of her specialties.

TIME: 1 hour   YIELD: 6 to 8 servings

1 cup dried apricots
1 cup granulated sugar
2 tablespoons lemon juice
8½ ounces (1 stick plus 1
   tablespoon) unsalted butter, cut
   in small pieces

2 large eggs
2 cups very fine, fresh white
   bread crumbs (from 5 slices of
   bread)

1. In a 1½-quart glass or ceramic soufflé dish, stir together the apricots, 1 cup water and ½ cup sugar. Cover tightly with microwave plastic wrap. Cook at 100 percent power for 7 minutes. Prick plastic wrap to release steam.

2. Remove from oven, and uncover. Scrape mixture into a blender, and puree. Scrape down sides of blender. Add lemon juice, and blend until smooth. Put puree into a medium bowl, and let stand 15 minutes or until cool.

3. Place a 2-quart soufflé dish on parchment paper. Lightly trace around the base with a pencil. Cut out the paper disk just inside the pencil marking. Grease the dish and both sides of the paper using 1 tablespoon of the butter. Place paper in the dish.

4. Place the remaining sugar and butter in the work bowl of a food processor, and process until smooth. With processor running, add the eggs one at a time to combine. Add the apricot puree, and process until completely incorporated.

5. Return apricot mixture to the bowl, and gently fold in the bread crumbs until well combined. Pour the mixture into the prepared soufflé dish. To remove the air bubbles, firmly rap dish on counter. Cover tightly

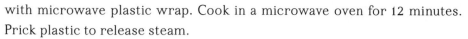

with microwave plastic wrap. Cook in a microwave oven for 12 minutes. Prick plastic to release steam.

6. Remove from the oven, and uncover. Cover with a heavy plate, and let stand for 15 minutes. Unmold, peel off parchment paper, let cool about 5 minutes and serve.

Steamed Banana Pudding

Kay
Rentschler

There are no apologies for the richness of this pudding with its bananas, dates, nuts and sherry. The fresh, soft bread crumbs can be made from white, whole wheat or oatmeal bread. It's a fine substitute for Christmas plum pudding. Kay Rentschler has contributed recipes to *The New York Times.*

TIME: About 2 hours   YIELD: 8 servings

3 ounces unsalted butter, softened, plus more for greasing pan

¾ cup all-purpose flour

1 cup soft bread crumbs (from 2 ounces bread)

1 teaspoon ground cinnamon

¼ teaspoon ground nutmeg

½ teaspoon salt

½ teaspoon baking soda

¼ cup dried currants or chopped pecans (optional)

3 tablespoons dark brown sugar

8 ounces Medjool dates, pitted (about 12 dates)

¼ cup dry sherry

2 large eggs

1½ teaspoons vanilla extract

4 very ripe bananas (12 ounces unpeeled weight)

Whipped cream, caramel sauce (page 539) or vanilla mousseline (page 534), for serving

1. Preheat oven to 325 degrees. Bring a large pot of water to boil over high heat. Generously butter an 8-cup pudding or soufflé mold.

2. Stir flour, bread crumbs, spices, salt and baking soda together in a medium bowl. Add currants or pecans, if desired, and toss to combine.

3. In food processor, cream butter and brown sugar until light and fluffy, stopping machine frequently to scrape down sides. Add dates and pulse until fine. With machine running, drizzle in sherry; scrape bowl.

4. In another small bowl, whisk eggs and vanilla together; pour slowly into processor with machine running.

5. Peel and quarter bananas, and add to processor; pulse until finely chopped. Transfer mixture to medium bowl.

6. Fold dry ingredients lightly into banana mixture. Turn into prepared mold, and cover snugly with a greased lid or aluminum foil. Place pudding

in large roasting pan; pour hot water halfway up the side of the mold. Bake until pudding has risen and tests clean with toothpick or skewer, 1½ to 2 hours. Cool 5 minutes in pan, then invert onto rack. Slice and serve warm with whipped cream, caramel sauce or vanilla mousseline.

7. To rewarm, place pudding on sheet pan, cover with clean, damp cloth and heat in 300-degree oven for 20 to 30 minutes.

Sticky Toffee Pudding

Nicole's,
New York

An outrageously rich English specialty worthy of its name, it's a dessert to serve in small portions in cold weather. Nicole's is the New York restaurant for the designer Nicole Farhi's store in Midtown Manhattan.

TIME: 45 minutes   YIELD: 4 to 6 servings

½ pound (2 sticks) unsalted butter, softened, plus more for ramekins

6 ounces dates, pitted and roughly chopped

1 teaspoon baking soda

¾ cup plus 1½ cups sugar

2 large eggs, lightly beaten

1¼ cups all-purpose flour

1 teaspoon baking powder

1 teaspoon ground ginger

½ teaspoon ground cinnamon

¼ teaspoon ground cloves

Pinch of salt

1 teaspoon pure vanilla extract

2 cups heavy cream

Crème anglaise (page 533)

1. Butter 6 6-ounce ramekins. Preheat oven to 350 degrees. Combine dates and 1¼ cups water in a saucepan, and simmer until dates are soft, about 10 minutes. Add baking soda, and mix well. Mixture will foam up.

2. Cream 4 tablespoons of the butter and ¾ cup sugar in an electric mixer until pale and fluffy. Beat in eggs. In a bowl, combine flour, baking powder, ginger, cinnamon, cloves and salt.

3. Add date mixture and dry ingredients to butter mixture, a third of each at a time, and mix well. Add vanilla. Divide batter among ramekins, filling each no more than ¾ full.

4. Place on a baking sheet, and bake 30 to 35 minutes, until just firm.

5. Meanwhile, place ¼ cup sugar in a deep heavy saucepan, and cook over medium heat, stirring with a wooden spoon, until sugar liquefies and turns light brown. Add remaining sugar ¼ cup at a time, allowing each batch to brown before adding next. When all sugar is in pan, keep cooking until it turns dark brown. Add remaining butter, and stir until melted. Remove from heat and stir in cream, standing back because mixture may spatter. Return to heat; keep warm.

6. Turn out hot puddings into wide, shallow serving bowls. Pour crème anglaise around each one. Pour toffee sauce into a jug, and pass alongside.

Steamed Lemon Pudding

This steamed pudding is on its way to being a soufflé, but it is less dramatic, and can be unmolded. Unsweetened whole milk yogurt can replace the buttermilk. Craft is chef Tom Colicchio's flagship restaurant in New York.

Karen
De Masco,
Craft,
New York

TIME: 45 minutes, plus cooling   YIELD: 6 servings

1 tablespoon unsalted butter
¾ cup plus 2 tablespoons sugar
5 tablespoons all-purpose flour
Finely grated zest of 2 lemons
3 large eggs, separated

1 cup cultured buttermilk
¼ cup lemon juice
1 pint blueberries, optional
⅔ cup heavy cream, whipped,
  optional

1. Preheat oven to 375 degrees. Lightly butter six 4-ounce ramekins or foil muffin cups. Dust each with 1 teaspoon sugar, shaking out any excess.

2. In a small bowl, mix remaining sugar with flour and lemon zest. In a large bowl, lightly beat egg yolks, and stir in buttermilk and lemon juice.

3. Whip egg whites until softly peaked. Whisk sugar mixture into the buttermilk mixture. Fold in beaten egg whites in thirds. Spoon batter into prepared containers. Place in baking pan, and add hot water to pan to come halfway up sides of ramekins or tins. Cover pan completely with foil.

4. Bake about 15 minutes, until batter begins to puff. Remove foil, and bake another 15 minutes or so, until tops begin to brown and are springy to touch. A little cracking is fine.

5. Remove from oven, and serve warm. If you make the pudding in advance, allow it to cool to room temperature, and unmold to serve, or reheat in warm water bath, and serve warm. Fresh blueberries and whipped cream can be served alongside.

Goat Cheese Pudding
with Poached Cranberries

Sam
Hayward

These little cheese puddings are bright, tangy and fresh-tasting. Their cranberry topping suggests fall or winter. But with fresh raspberries and raspberry coulis (page 536), they are appropriate for spring and summer. Sam Hayward is the chef at Fore Street Grill in Portland, Maine.

TIME: 1½ hours   YIELD: 6 servings

1 pound fresh soft goat cheese, at
    room temperature
1 large egg
2 large egg yolks
1¾ cups sugar

½ vanilla bean, or ½ teaspoon
    vanilla extract
½ teaspoon lemon juice
1 pound fresh cranberries, rinsed
    and drained

1. Preheat oven to 325 degrees. Place cheese in a food processor, and process until completely smooth, about 1 minute. Set aside.

2. In the bowl of an electric mixer with a paddle attachment, combine egg and yolks. Beat until light and frothy. Slowly add ¾ cup sugar, and continue to beat until thick and pale. Split the vanilla bean, if using, and scrape the pulp out. Add to mixture (or add extract). Add lemon juice and goat cheese. Beat on medium speed until very smooth.

3. Divide mixture among six 4-ounce soufflé dishes or ramekins. Place in a baking dish, and pour boiling water into the pan to reach halfway up the sides of the dishes. Bake until puddings are firm but do not puff, 20 to 25 minutes. Place cups on a rack to cool to room temperature.

4. While puddings cool, in a saucepan combine remaining cup of sugar with 1¼ cups water. Place over high heat, and bring to a boil. Add half the cranberries, remove from heat, and allow to steep until berries collapse and color the liquid, about 15 minutes. Pour into a fine-meshed sieve set over a bowl, and drain for 30 minutes. Do not force berries through sieve.

5. Place cranberry syrup in a clean saucepan, and place over high heat to bring to a boil. Add remaining cranberries, reduce heat to a bare simmer, and poach berries until tender but still intact, about 4 minutes. Allow to cool at room temperature. To serve, top each custard cup with a portion of cranberries and syrup.

BREAD PUDDINGS

What would we ever do without stale or leftover bread? Bread puddings are one of the many marvels that can be accomplished with it. A basic bread pudding is essentially bits of the bread, often soaked first in milk to soften them, then baked with a custard mixture to bind them. Fruit can be added to the mixture. And a sauce of some kind might be spooned over each serving. Almost any kind of bread is suitable, with or without crusts.

Apple Bread Pudding with Calvados Sauce

Florence
Fabricant

Apples and the French apple brandy, Calvados, are used in this lightly caramelized bread pudding, made with bits of baguette, crust and all. Slightly stale bread is best. I find that placing the baking pan on a kitchen towel makes it more stable and less likely to slide around in the hot water bath.

TIME: 1½ hours   YIELD: 6 to 8 servings

6 tablespoons unsalted butter

3 cups apples, peeled, cored and sliced ½ inch thick

1 cup sugar

½ cup Calvados

3½ cups torn baguette in ½-inch pieces

2 cups half-and-half

½ vanilla bean, split lengthwise

3 large eggs, beaten

¼ teaspoon grated nutmeg

1½ cups fresh cider

1½ teaspoons cornstarch

1. Butter a 6-to-8-cup soufflé dish or other baking dish. Preheat oven to 325 degrees.

2. Melt 2 tablespoons butter in a large skillet over medium-high heat. Add apples, and sauté about 5 minutes, until apples start to brown. Add 3 tablespoons sugar. Sauté a minute or two, until sugar caramelizes. Transfer to a bowl. Add half the Calvados.

3. Melt remaining butter in the skillet over low heat. Add bread, and toss a few minutes to coat with butter. Spoon half the apples into the baking dish, and top with half the bread. Repeat.

4. Place half-and-half and vanilla bean in a saucepan. Scald. Stir in ½ cup sugar. Remove from heat. Whisk a little of this mixture into eggs, then slowly whisk eggs into half-and-half. Strain into baking dish, and dust with nutmeg. Place dish on a kitchen towel in a roasting pan. Add simmering water to come halfway up the sides of the baking dish. Bake 40 minutes, until just set.

5. Meanwhile, boil cider until reduced by half. Sift remaining sugar with cornstarch and whisk into cider. Simmer until thick. Add remaining Calvados. Serve warm on pudding.

Morning Bread Pudding

Overnight chilling and morning baking give this pudding its name. Consider it as a dessert for a weekend brunch. It will benefit from a garnish of berries or other fresh fruit. And, of course, can be served for dinner, too. Amanda Hesser is the food editor for *The New York Times Sunday Magazine.*

Amanda Hesser

TIME: 1 hour, plus overnight resting   YIELD: 6 servings

¾ cup plus 2 tablespoons sugar

6 tablespoons unsalted butter

12 to 15 slices brioche or challah bread about ½ inch thick and about 3 inches round

8 large eggs

¼ cup mascarpone cheese

1 cup milk

¼ teaspoon almond extract

¼ cup coarsely chopped toasted almonds

About ¾ cup *fromage frais* or *fromage blanc,* for serving

1 In a small, heavy saucepan, combine ¾ cup sugar and the butter. Place over medium-low heat. Bring to a boil for a few minutes. It will begin to brown. Adjust heat and stir occasionally with a wooden spoon so that it browns evenly. When it reaches a dark brown, remove from heat and pour into a 9-inch ceramic or Pyrex pie dish. Swirl the caramel around the base and 1 inch up the sides of the dish. Place in refrigerator until caramel is cold.

2. Place heel of bread in center of dish (or two slices stacked on top of each other). Arrange slices, overlapping, around center. They should fill the pie dish snugly. In a large bowl whisk together eggs, remaining 2 tablespoons sugar and mascarpone cheese, until very smooth. Add milk and almond extract. Pour over the bread, to saturate all of it. Cover with plastic wrap and refrigerate overnight.

3. In the morning, take pie dish out of refrigerator and discard plastic wrap. Preheat oven to 375 degrees. Bake pudding 15 minutes, then sprinkle almonds over pudding. Continue baking until moist but not wet in the center, about 15 to 20 minutes more. Remove from oven and run a knife around edge of dish, loosening bread from sides. Place a serving plate over top of dish and, using potholders, hold pudding and invert plate. Lift off pie dish. Scrape any extra caramel from pie dish over pudding. Serve, cutting it into wedges and spooning *fromage frais* onto each plate.

White Chocolate Sourdough Bread Pudding with Almonds

Charlie
Trotter

The Chicago chef Charlie Trotter takes no prisoners. If you have the ambi-
tion to peel and to julienne kumquat rinds, you are well on your way to
preparing this recipe. But were you to substitute candied orange or lemon
peel, or a mixture, you would be doing just fine. Similarly, if your local deli
or supermarket does not happen to sell fresh goat's milk, which the chef is
using to make *cajeta,* you can buy *cajeta* or substitute *dulce de leche,* either
homemade (page 536) or purchased in a jar. Again, the recipe will be just
fine, because its main elements will still be in place: the acidity of the
bread, the sweet tartness of the citrus and the intense richness of white
chocolate and milky caramel. As for what to do with the leftover kumquat
pulp, try forcing it through a sieve or food mill, then freezing the juice you
get to use later to season a sauce for duck or fish.

TIME: 1 hour 15 minutes   YIELD: 4 servings

12 large kumquats
1½ cups plus ⅓ cup sugar
9 ounces white chocolate,
  chopped
6 large egg yolks
1⅓ cups heavy cream
4 cups crustless sourdough bread
  in ½-inch cubes

½ cup sliced almonds, toasted
1 cup fresh goat's milk
¼ cup plus 2 tablespoons whole
  milk
¼ teaspoon cornstarch
¼ teaspoon baking soda
4 small scoops top-quality vanilla
  or chocolate ice cream.

1. Peel kumquats; reserve pulp for another purpose. Julienne the rinds.
Fill a small pan with 2 inches of water, and boil. Drop in rinds to blanch; return to a boil, and drain. Blanch two times more.

2. In a medium saucepan, combine 1½ cups sugar with 1½ cups water.
Place over medium-low heat, and bring to a simmer. Add rinds, and simmer 15 minutes. Drain, and spread out on a plate to dry.

3. Preheat oven to 350 degrees. Place chocolate in a large heatproof
mixing bowl. Place egg yolks in a small bowl, and whisk until blended. In
medium saucepan, bring cream to a boil. Whisk about ¼ cup hot cream
into yolks, then pour yolk mixture into cream. Cook over low heat, stir-

ring, until mixture coats back of a wooden spoon and steam begins to rise. Pour cream mixture over chocolate, and let stand 5 minutes. Stir until smooth. Add bread cubes, stir until completely coated, and let stand until liquid is absorbed, about 10 minutes.

4. Stir in half the kumquat rinds and half the almonds. Place four buttered ring molds, such as 4-inch English muffin rings, on a baking sheet. Fill molds with bread mixture, patting lightly to compress. Bake until just set, 8 to 10 minutes. While puddings are baking, prepare caramel sauce.

5. In a medium saucepan, combine goat's milk and whole milk. Place over medium heat, and bring to a boil. In a small bowl, combine cornstarch and baking soda. Add a little hot milk, and stir until smooth. Add mixture to pan of milk, stir well, and remove from heat. In a deep saucepan, combine remaining ⅓ cup sugar with ¼ cup water. Cook over medium heat until dark amber, about 10 minutes. Add milk mixture, reduce heat to low, and stir constantly until mixture reaches saucelike consistency, about 5 minutes.

6. To serve, spread a circle of caramel sauce on each of 4 dessert plates. Place a pudding in center, and carefully remove mold, loosening with a spatula. Top with a scoop of ice cream. Garnish with remaining kumquat rinds and almonds.

Caramelized Chocolate Bread Pudding

Suzanne
Goin

Is there a dessert that does not benefit from the addition of chocolate? Bread pudding is certainly high on the list, especially when it has been made with buttery, eggy brioche. Hallah can also be used, as can stale Italian panettone. Suzanne Goin is the executive chef and co-owner of Lucques and A.O.C. restaurants in West Hollywood, California.

TIME: About 1½ hours   YIELD: 6 servings

About 3 tablespoons soft unsalted
   butter
5 to 6 half-inch-thick slices
   brioche from a loaf
4 large eggs
3 large egg yolks
2 cups heavy cream
1¾ cups milk
⅔ cup light brown sugar

2 teaspoons vanilla extract
¾ teaspoon ground cinnamon
½ teaspoon freshly grated nutmeg
½ teaspoon kosher salt
4 ounces bittersweet chocolate,
   chopped
1 tablespoon turbinado or light
   brown sugar (optional)

1. Preheat oven to 325 degrees. Place a large roasting pan in the oven, and bring a kettle of water to a boil. Generously butter brioche slices on one side and cut in half diagonally. In a large bowl, whisk together the eggs, egg yolks, heavy cream, milk, brown sugar, vanilla, cinnamon, nutmeg and salt.

2. Sprinkle chocolate in an 8-cup casserole or baking dish at least 3 inches deep. Lay slices of bread, butter side up, over chocolate, overlapping slices like fish scales. Use just enough bread to cover all the chocolate. Pour egg mixture on top, making sure to soak all the bread. When kettle comes to a boil, place the casserole inside the roasting pan in the oven and pour enough boiling water into the roasting pan to come halfway up the sides of the casserole. Bake until custard is just set, 40 to 60 minutes, depending on dimensions of casserole. Pudding is done when the bread in the center rises up and is bouncy to touch. Remove from oven.

3. If you have a kitchen blowtorch, sprinkle sugar over top of pudding, and use torch to lightly caramelize sugar. If you do not have a blowtorch, skip this step (a broiler will curdle custard). Pudding should be served warm, not hot.

Roasted-Fruit and Brioche Bread Pudding

Roasted summer fruit combined with brioche and custard make for a delicious dessert. And the fruit-scented caramel sauce is just the embellishment it needs. Karen De Masco is the pastry chef of Craft in New York.

TIME: 1 hour   YIELD: 8 servings

Karen
De Masco,
Craft,
New York

1 tablespoon unsalted butter	2 large eggs
1 cup sugar	1 large egg yolk
1 tablespoon light corn syrup	1½ cups heavy cream
8 roasted peach, nectarine or pluot halves, or 16 roasted apricot or plum halves (page 374), caramel sauce reserved	1½ cups whole milk
	1 vanilla bean, split
	5 cups crustless brioche in small cubes

1. Preheat oven to 400 degrees. Lightly butter 8 1-cup ovenproof ramekins, and dust with a little sugar.

2. Place 5 tablespoons sugar in a small nonstick skillet. Drizzle with syrup. Cook over medium heat, stirring, until mixture liquefies. Continue cooking until mixture turns into caramel. Pour caramel into ramekins to coat bottoms.

3. Cut roasted fruit in thick slices, and arrange in bottoms of ramekins.

4. Whisk eggs, egg yolk and remaining sugar in a large bowl. Place cream and milk in a saucepan with vanilla bean, and heat until beginning to bubble around edges. Do not allow to boil. Slowly whisk hot liquid into egg mixture. Add brioche cubes, lightly pressing with back of spoon so they become saturated. Remove vanilla bean. Spoon the soaked brioche into ramekins.

5. Place ramekins in a large baking pan. Add hot water halfway up the sides of the ramekins. Place in oven, and bake until tops of puddings are lightly browned and crusty, about 40 minutes.

6. Run a sharp knife around edges, and unmold puddings onto individual plates. Gently reheat caramel sauce reserved from roasted fruit, whisking, until just warm. Pour around puddings and serve.

Maple-Banana Bread Pudding

Florence
Fabricant

Brioche adds richness to a classic custard-based bread pudding. But I like to make this pudding with other breads, like whole grain or raisin varieties, especially from good artisanal bakeries. Why not make it with my own leftover bread? Because when I bake bread there are rarely enough leftovers!

TIME: 1½ hours, plus cooling   YIELD: 6 servings

1½ tablespoons unsalted butter

3½ cups 1-inch cubes stale or lightly toasted brioche or hallah

1⅔ cups whole milk

⅓ cup maple syrup

Pinch of nutmeg

2 large eggs, lightly beaten

1½ cups diced banana (about 2 bananas, not too ripe)

1 tablespoon light brown sugar

¾ cup heavy cream, whipped

1. Preheat oven to 350 degrees. Butter a 6-cup round baking dish with ½ tablespoon butter.

2. Place bread pieces in mixing bowl. Heat milk and syrup in saucepan until syrup dissolves into milk. Add nutmeg. Pour over bread and allow to sit about 30 minutes to saturate. Stir in eggs. Fold in diced banana.

3. Transfer mixture to baking dish. Sprinkle with brown sugar and dot with remaining butter. Bake 35 to 40 minutes, until it is starting to look crusty on top. Serve warm, with whipped cream.

Eggnog Bread Pudding

A little rum, a little nutmeg and you can give a simple custard mixture a whiff of holiday eggnog. A finale for a small New Year's Eve dinner can't be better than this one. And by doubling or tripling the recipe you have a dessert for a New Year's Day buffet.

Florence
Fabricant

TIME: 1 hour, plus cooling   YIELD: 6 servings

1 cup raisins
½ cup dark rum
Unsalted butter for baking dish
4 cups stale French bread pieces
    without crust, torn in 1-inch
    chunks

⅔ cup sugar
3 large eggs
2 cups half-and-half
½ teaspoon freshly grated nutmeg
1 teaspoon ground cinnamon

1. Place the raisins in a bowl and pour the rum over them. Set aside.

2. Preheat oven to 350 degrees. Butter a fairly shallow 2-quart baking dish.

3. Place the bread pieces in a large mixing bowl. In a separate bowl beat ½ cup of the sugar with the eggs until blended. Stir in the half-and-half and the nutmeg. Fold in the raisins and rum. Pour over the bread and allow to sit about 10 minutes until the bread becomes saturated.

4. Mix the remaining sugar with the cinnamon. Transfer the bread mixture to the baking dish and sprinkle the cinnamon sugar over the top.

5. Bake about 35 minutes, until lightly browned. Allow to cool until still slightly warm, then serve.

Individual Ginger-Pear Bread Puddings

Florence
Fabricant

Ginger and pears are lovely together. To give this dessert even more panache, you can add an ounce of chopped bittersweet chocolate to each dish, scattering it on top of the pears. And for really daring, extreme chocolate lovers, I have even used high-quality (not supermarket) unsweetened chocolate.

TIME: 1 hour, plus cooling YIELD: 4 servings

3 tablespoons unsalted butter

3 ripe pears, peeled, cored and
 diced

5 tablespoons sugar

¼ cup crystallized ginger, diced

2 cups French bread pieces
 without crust, torn in 1-inch
 chunks

2 eggs

1¼ cups milk

2 tablespoons sliced almonds

⅔ cup heavy cream, softly
 whipped

1. Heat 2 tablespoons of the butter in a heavy skillet. When the butter is just beginning to brown, add the pears and sauté briefly over high heat until they just start to soften. Sprinkle them with sugar, stir, then remove from the heat. Fold in the ginger.

2. Preheat oven to 350 degrees. Butter 4 1-cup soufflé dishes,

3. Place the bread in a bowl. Beat the eggs and milk together just to blend them and pour this mixture over the bread. Press the bread to saturate it and allow it to soak about 10 minutes.

4. Divide half the bread mixture among the baking dishes. Spoon the pear mixture on the bread in each dish, using it all, then top with the remaining bread. Sprinkle with the almonds.

5. Bake about 25 minutes, until the topping is lightly browned. Serve with whipped cream.

MOUSSES, PANNA COTTAS AND CREAMS

These are puddinglike chilled desserts made with egg whites (mousses) or gelatin (panna cottas). Italian panna cottas, which have suddenly become extremely popular, are what their name implies, cooked cream. Gelatin is added to the cream mixture so the dessert can be unmolded. Almost any panna cotta can be lightened by using unflavored yogurt in place of half the cream. But the yogurt cannot be cooked because it will curdle. It must be added to the mixture after the gelatin has dissolved, as in step 4 of the recipe for Buttermilk Panna Cotta (page 436). Mousses can be served in parfait glasses, stem glasses or cups, or, if they are suitable for unmolding, like panna cottas, they can be placed on a plate and garnished with fruit or a sauce.

Chocolate Mousse

Craig
Claiborne
and
Pierre
Franey

This chocolate mousse is as classic as it gets. For decades, Craig Claiborne and Pierre Franey were the star cooking team for *The New York Times*.

TIME: 20 minutes, plus chilling   YIELD: 12 servings

8 ounces semisweet chocolate, chopped

6 large eggs, separated and at room temperature

¼ cup liqueur (Grand Marnier, amaretto or Chartreuse) or port

6 tablespoons sugar

2 cups heavy cream, plus additional for whipped cream garnish, if desired

1. Place a double boiler or small saucepan over low heat, and melt chocolate. When chocolate is almost melted, remove pan from stove and beat with a wooden spoon until smooth.

2. Place egg yolks in a heavy saucepan and add 3 tablespoons water. Place pan over very low heat and beat constantly with a wire whisk until yolks start to thicken. Add liqueur and continue beating until mixture reaches the consistency of hollandaise sauce. The mixture has become a sabayon. Remove from heat.

3. Fold in melted chocolate. Transfer mixture to a large bowl.

4. Beat egg whites until softly peaked. Add 4 tablespoons sugar and continue beating until stiff. Stir about one-fourth of the egg whites into the chocolate mixture, then fold in the rest. Refrigerate until cold.

5. Beat cream until softly peaked. Add remaining sugar and beat until stiff. Fold into the mousse. Divide mousse among 12 individual goblets, cover and chill until ready to serve, or transfer mousse to a serving bowl, cover and refrigerate. Serve with additional unsweetened whipped cream, if desired.

Chocolate Caramel Mousse

The combination of orange and chocolate, with the intensity of caramel, are the signatures of this mousse. Scott Carsberg is the chef at Lampreia in Seattle, Washington.

Scott Carsberg, Lampreia, Seattle, Washington

TIME: 1 hour, plus chilling   YIELD: 16 servings

1 cup sugar
5 tablespoons unsalted butter, cut into bits
3 cups heavy cream

8 ounces unsweetened or bittersweet chocolate chips or chunks, about 1½ cups
Orange confit (page 543)

1. Place sugar in a heavy skillet over medium heat. When sugar warms and begins to liquefy, stir in ½ cup water with a wooden spoon. Cook, stirring occasionally until mixture caramelizes to a medium amber. Remove from heat. Stir in butter a bit at a time. Briefly warm 1 cup of the cream in a small saucepan, then, standing back in case of spatters, stir in warm cream until blended. Transfer to a metal mixing bowl and set aside until cool enough to touch.

2. Meanwhile beat remaining cream until it holds soft peaks. Refrigerate. Melt chocolate over very low heat or in a double boiler or microwave.

3. Mix melted chocolate into caramel. Allow to cool to room temperature, then gently stir in ⅓ of the whipped cream. Place bowl in a larger bowl half-filled with ice and water to speed cooling. Add remaining whipped cream to mousse mixture and gently fold, just until combined. Cover and refrigerate until set, about 4 hours.

4. Scoop mousse with a spoon dipped in hot water. Serve alongside a piece of orange confit.

Pumpkin Mousse

Marian
Burros

This mellow pumpkin mousse can also be spooned into a baked 8-inch pie or tart crust, either flaky pastry (page 522), or a hazelnut crust (page 525), chilled and served as a pie or tart. Marian Burros is a food reporter for *The New York Times.*

TIME: 25 minutes, plus chilling   YIELD: 6 servings

1 envelope unflavored gelatin

2 cups unflavored canned
   pumpkin or fresh pumpkin
   puree

⅓ cup light brown sugar

2 tablespoons pure maple syrup

1 teaspoon ground cinnamon

½ teaspoon ground ginger

⅛ teaspoon ground cloves

⅛ teaspoon ground mace

Pinch of salt

8 ounces *fromage blanc*

2 tablespoons Grand Marnier

2 tablespoons finely chopped
   crystallized ginger

3 large egg whites

3 tablespoons granulated sugar

½ cup heavy cream

Strips of crystallized ginger for
   garnish

1. Soften gelatin in ¼ cup cold water. Place ½ cup water, pumpkin, brown sugar, maple syrup, cinnamon, ground ginger, cloves, mace and salt in a 2-quart saucepan. Add gelatin and cook over very low heat to melt the gelatin.

2. Remove from heat, and whisk in *fromage blanc* and Grand Marnier. Stir in crystallized ginger. Transfer to a bowl and set aside.

3. Whip egg whites until foamy. Slowly beat in granulated sugar, and beat until whites hold peaks. Fold into pumpkin mixture. Chill 1 hour.

4. Whip cream until soft peaks form. Fold into pumpkin mixture.

5. Spoon the mousse into individual parfait glasses, coupes or wine-glasses. Cover each glass with plastic wrap, waxed paper or foil, and refrigerate for a few hours or overnight. Decorate with strips of crystallized ginger.

Blanc-Manger

Blanc-manger (sometimes rendered as one word), is a French dessert that was famously difficult to get right. The name means "white food" and the pure whiteness of it was essential, so the almonds had to be blanched, pounded, then squeezed through a linen napkin and finally diluted. The almond milk that resulted was then sweetened, strained twice through a silk sieve (no less), and jelled with isinglass. Pâtisserie Rollet-Pradier has been on Paris's Left Bank since 1859.

TIME: 20 minutes, plus chilling YIELD: 6 servings

1½ cups cold heavy cream
¾ cup whole milk
¾ cup ground blanched almonds
½ cup sugar
1 envelope plain gelatin

1 to 2 tablespoons kirsch or 2
  teaspoons vanilla extract
1 cup raspberries or assorted soft
  ripe fruit cut in small cubes
Raspberry coulis (page 536)

1. Fill a large bowl with ice cubes and cold water. Have ready a smaller bowl that fits into the ice-water bath.

2. Whip cream until it holds soft peaks. Refrigerate.

3. Bring milk, almonds and sugar to a boil over medium heat, stirring occasionally until sugar dissolves. While milk heats, put gelatin and 3 tablespoons cold water in a microwave-safe bowl or a saucepan. When the gelatin is soft, about 2 minutes, heat it in a microwave oven for 15 seconds or cook it over low heat to dissolve. Stir the gelatin into the hot milk mixture. Remove the saucepan from heat.

4. Pour the hot almond milk into the small reserved bowl, and set the bowl into the ice-water bath. Stir in kirsch or vanilla, and continue to stir until the mixture is cool but still liquid.

5. Fold the cold whipped cream into the almond milk, then fold in the berries. Spoon the blanc-manger into an 8-inch cake pan 2 inches high or a mold, and refrigerate until set, about 2 hours. The blanc-manger can be covered and kept in the refrigerator for up to 24 hours.

6. To unmold, dip the pan up to its rim in hot water for 5 seconds, then wipe the pan and invert the blanc-manger onto a serving plate. Serve immediately or chill until needed. Serve raspberry coulis on the side.

Panna Cotta with Pomegranate

Jamie
Oliver

Bejeweling a pale panna cotta with deep garnet pomegranate seeds that have been macerated in sugar and grappa is a brilliant touch. Vodka can be used in place of grappa. Jamie Oliver is an English chef and restaurateur who has a program for training disadvantaged young people in restaurant jobs.

TIME: 45 minutes, plus chilling   YIELD: 4 servings

¾ cup milk

Finely grated zest of 1 lemon

1½ cups heavy cream

2 vanilla beans, scored lengthwise

1½ teaspoons unflavored gelatin

½ cup confectioners' sugar

⅓ cup pomegranate seeds

3 tablespoons grappa

1 teaspoon granulated sugar

1. In a small saucepan, combine milk, lemon zest and ¾ cup cream. Scrape pulp from vanilla beans into mixture, and add beans as well. Place over low heat and simmer gently for 10 minutes.

2. Remove from heat, and sprinkle gelatin over hot liquid. When gelatin looks spongy, after about 2 minutes, stir until gelatin dissolves. Allow mixture to cool a bit, then transfer to a bowl. Place in refrigerator, stirring occasionally until mixture is thick enough to coat the back of a spoon, about 15 minutes.

3. In a small bowl, mix remaining ¾ cup cream and confectioners' sugar until smooth. Add to gelatin mixture, stir, then strain into 4 half-cup molds or cups. Cover and chill until set, at least 1 hour.

4. To serve, in a small bowl mix pomegranate seeds, grappa and sugar. Stir until sugar is dissolved. Dip each mold into hot water to loosen panna cotta, then invert onto a dessert plate. Spoon pomegranate mixture on top of and around each panna cotta, and serve.

Saffron Panna Cotta

This panna cotta is given a whiff of the exotic and a gorgeous color with a generous pinch of saffron. This may be the signature dessert of Babbo. The recipe is from *The Babbo Cookbook* by Mario Batali (Clarkson Potter, 2002) and used with permission of the publisher, a division of Random House.

Babbo,
New York

TIME: 30 minutes, plus chilling   YIELD: 6 servings

3½ cups heavy cream
¾ cup sugar
Grated zest of 1 lemon
Large pinch saffron (60 to 65 threads), pounded with mortar and pestle

1 envelope unflavored gelatin plus 1 teaspoon, softened in ¼ cup water
1 cup milk

1. In a medium saucepan, combine heavy cream, sugar, lemon zest and saffron threads. Bring to a boil, stirring gently, and then remove from heat. Stir gelatin into cream mixture to dissolve it. Let mixture rest for 15 minutes to develop flavor and color.

2. Strain mixture through a fine-mesh sieve or chinois, and then stir in milk. Pour mixture into six chilled 1-cup ramekins or dessert cups. Chill before serving.

Buttermilk Panna Cotta
with Sauternes Gelée ✳

Claudia
Fleming

∽

Unflavored whole milk yogurt can replace the buttermilk, if desired. And an everyday generic Sauternes, not the finest Château d'Yquem or Château Rieussec, is the wine you will need. Claudia Fleming was the pastry chef at Gramercy Tavern in New York.

TIME: 50 minutes, plus chilling   YIELD: 7 servings

1⅔ cups Sauternes
13 tablespoons sugar
One 2-inch piece of vanilla bean,
    split lengthwise and seeds and
    pulp scraped out

2½ leaves gelatin, or 2 teaspoons
    powdered unflavored gelatin
1¼ cups heavy cream
1¾ cups cultured buttermilk

1. In a small saucepan, whisk together the Sauternes, 6 tablespoons of the sugar and the vanilla seeds. Place the saucepan over medium-low heat, and reduce the liquid at a bare simmer (turn the heat to low if necessary) until it measures 1 cup, about 45 minutes.

2. If using leaf gelatin, fill a bowl with cold water, and add 1 leaf of the gelatin. Soak until softened, 3 to 5 minutes. Powdered gelatin will be used in step 4.

3. Meanwhile, in a saucepan over medium-high heat, warm the cream with the remaining 7 tablespoons sugar, stirring until it dissolves. Take the pan off the heat.

4. Remove the gelatin leaf from the water and squeeze it dry in a clean dish towel. Add it to the warm cream, and stir until the gelatin dissolves. Or, if using powdered gelatin, stir in 1 teaspoon at this point. Add buttermilk to the pan, and stir well. Strain the mixture through a fine sieve into a glass measuring cup; pour the mixture into 7 8-ounce ramekins, bowls or parfait glasses. Chill until firm, about 3 hours.

5. While the panna cottas are chilling, soften the remaining 1½ leaves of gelatin in a bowl of cold water for 3 to 5 minutes. Drain the gelatin, and squeeze dry. Add it to the warm Sauternes, and stir until the gelatin dissolves, or add remaining powdered gelatin as you stir. Strain mixture

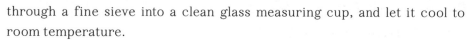

through a fine sieve into a clean glass measuring cup, and let it cool to room temperature.

6. When the panna cottas are set, stir the Sauternes mixture to redistribute the vanilla seeds. Very gently pour a thin stream of the Sauternes down the insides of the ramekins to coat the tops of the custards (do this slowly to avoid puncturing the creams). Chill until the Sauternes gelée is set, about an hour.

Lemon Panna Cotta

Esca,
New York

At Esca, a New York restaurant that serves only seafood, Italian-style, a panna cotta sharpened with lemon makes for a perfect finale.

TIME: 40 minutes, plus chilling   YIELD: 6 to 8 servings

3 cups heavy cream
1¼ cups milk
1 vanilla bean, split, and seeds
   scraped

Zest of 8 lemons
½ cup sugar
3½ sheets gelatin (scant ½ ounce)
   or 1 envelope unflavored gelatin

1. Put cream, 1 cup milk, vanilla bean halves and seeds and lemon zest in a medium saucepan. Simmer for 5 minutes, stirring often. Remove from heat, and allow to steep for 20 to 30 minutes.

2. Strain mixture through a fine-mesh sieve, and return to saucepan. Add sugar. Bring just to a boil over medium heat. Lower heat, and cook 2 minutes, stirring constantly, until sugar dissolves. Set saucepan aside.

3. If using sheet gelatin, snap sheets in half, and place in a bowl of ice water for 5 minutes. Gently heat remaining ¼ cup milk in a small pan. Squeeze moisture out of gelatin, and stir into warm milk one sheet at a time, until gelatin is thoroughly dissolved. If using packaged gelatin, sprinkle on top of the ¼ cup milk in a small pan, and let stand for 2 minutes. Gently heat, stirring constantly for 2 minutes, until gelatin dissolves.

4. Whisk dissolved gelatin into hot lemon cream. Place saucepan in a bowl of ice water, and stir constantly for 5 minutes, to make sure gelatin is evenly distributed.

5. Pour mixture into 6 to 8 shallow bowls, ramekins or custard cups. Refrigerate, uncovered, until just firm, about 2 to 3 hours. Best served within 24 hours.

Blackberry and Vanilla Bean Custard Parfait ✳

This dessert comes from Roxanne's, a restaurant in Larkspur, California, which has since closed, and which served no food that was heated to more than 118 degrees. Forget baking or even making custard, since eggs then cannot be cooked enough to thicken. But one of the more effective ingredients for desserts that the restaurant used was homemade nut milks, especially from cashews. This is an excellent, surprising dessert parfait created by Roxanne Klein.

Roxanne's, Larkspur, California

TIME: 45 minutes, plus overnight soaking   YIELD: 4 servings

1 cup raw cashews, soaked overnight in water and drained

1 cup meat from fresh young (green) coconut; if not available increase soaked cashews to 2 cups

¼ teaspoon seeds from vanilla bean, preferably Tahitian

⅓ cup pure maple syrup

1 sprig fresh lavender or thyme

1 pint fresh blackberries

3 tablespoons honey, preferably thistle

2 tablespoons chopped unsalted nuts

1. For the custard, place half the cashews and coconut in a blender with ¼ to ½ cup water, as needed, to blend until smooth. Add remaining cashews and coconut, vanilla and maple syrup. Blend. Refrigerate until cold.

2. Crush lavender or thyme in a mortar. Place in a large bowl, and add blackberries and honey. Gently crush together with back of a spoon, leaving some berries whole.

3. Layer cashew custard and berries in 4 martini glasses or goblets, top with nuts and serve.

Butterscotch Pudding

David Burke,
davidburke
&
donatella,
New York

David Burke, a chef who loves clever tricks, has come up with a shortcut to butterscotch pudding for his New York restaurant, davidburke&donatella, made simply by melting butterscotch candies in cream. The hardest part about making the dessert is crushing the candies. Place them, unwrapped, in a double zip-lock plastic bag, take a mallet, a meat pounder or an ice crusher to them and whack away.

TIME: 20 minutes, plus chilling   YIELD: 6 servings

8 ounces butterscotch candies,
   crushed
Scrapings of 1 vanilla bean

3¾ cups heavy cream
½ packet unflavored gelatin

1. Mix candies with vanilla bean scrapings and stir into a heavy saucepan with 1¾ cups of heavy cream. Simmer until the candy melts.

2. Whisk gelatin into remaining cream and add to the saucepan. Heat gently until mixture is smooth. Remove from heat and stir.

3. Strain the pudding, pour it into stemmed glasses or ramekins and chill 6 hours, until set.

Bitter Chocolate Cream

The intensity of this chocolate cream, created by the Michelin three-star chef Michel Bras of Laguiole, France, and served like a petit four at the end of dinner, is such that it takes only a tiny bite to satisfy.

Michel Bras, Laguiole, France

TIME: 20 minutes, plus chilling   YIELD: 8 servings

1 cup heavy cream, preferably
  ultra-pasteurized
4 ounces unsalted butter
¼ cup praline powder (page 535)

⅓ cup unsweetened Dutch-
  process cocoa
2 ounces bittersweet chocolate

1. Combine cream, butter, ¼ cup water and praline powder in a heavy saucepan and cook over low heat until the butter and praline have melted.

2. Transfer cream mixture to a food processor and process just until the ingredients are well mixed. Add the cocoa and chocolate and process until smooth.

3. Transfer to individual 2-ounce ramekins or other tiny cups and chill for 2 hours. Serve with coffee.

Coeur à la Crème

Craig
Claiborne
and
Pierre
Franey

Coeur à la crème is a French classic, made by draining cheese overnight in a special white porcelain heart-shaped mold that has little holes on the bottom. The molds come in assorted sizes, and this dessert can be made using 6 individual ½-cup molds instead of one large one. The berry sauce is essential, making the dessert perfect for Valentine's Day. Craig Claiborne and Pierre Franey were for many years the star food writing team for *The New York Times* and wrote several cookbooks together.

TIME: 20 minutes, plus overnight chilling   YIELD: 6 servings

1 cup small-curd cottage cheese
 or *fromage blanc*
1 cup cream cheese
½ cup crème fraîche or sour
 cream

½ cup heavy cream
Strawberry sauce (page 541) or
 raspberry coulis (page 536)
Granulated sugar for serving

1. Line a 3-cup heart-shaped coeur à la crème mold with cheesecloth, allowing some to overhang.

2. By hand, with an electric mixer or in a food processor, combine the cheeses and crème fraîche or sour cream. Beat until well blended. Whip the heavy cream and fold in.

3. Pack the cheese mixture into the mold, cover the top with the overhanging cheesecloth, then with plastic, and place in a dish with a rim. Refrigerate overnight.

4. To serve, uncover the top of the mold, unmold the heart onto a serving plate and peel off the cheesecloth. Serve, with sauce on the side and sugar for guests to use to taste.

FROZEN DESSERTS

The most famous frozen dessert is, of course, ice cream, with dairy—milk, cream or a combination—as its main ingredient. But there are other frozen desserts as well: without dairy, frozen mixtures become sorbet, ices or granitas, which are primarily made with fruit. Granitas are frozen without churning, and so they have an icy, grainy quality and are served by scraping the frozen mixture into serving dishes. Frozen desserts also include an array of festive but not formal confections, such as kulfis, melbas and semifreddos, while on the showstopper side there's baked Alaska. No matter how classic the frozen dessert, making it in a modern electric ice cream maker is immeasurably easier than the old-fashioned method of hand-churning over a slurry of ice and salt.

ICE CREAMS

There are essentially two categories of ice cream, made with or without a custard base. The custard ice cream is often called French ice cream. Dairy-based ice creams made without cream, like those made with buttermilk, whole milk or yogurt, for example, are usually called sherbets. For best results the base must be very cold before churning, so allow time for it to chill. You can speed it up by placing a metal bowl containing the base in a larger bowl of ice and water. With any dessert churned in an ice cream maker, allow time to transfer the frozen mixture, which will be fairly soft straight from the machine, to containers, and to freeze them for at least four hours or overnight. Ice creams that have frozen hard should be placed in the refrigerator for an hour before serving to temper them.

Vanilla Bean Ice Cream ✳

Florian
Bellanger

〜

This is a classic French-style vanilla ice cream. There is really no substitute for using whole vanilla beans. They will give the ice cream those telltale little specks. Florian Bellanger is the executive chef for the American branch of Fauchon, the Paris-based fancy food and catering company.

TIME: 20 minutes, plus chilling and freezing   YIELD: 1 pint

1½ cups whole milk
1 cup heavy cream
2 vanilla beans, split, pulp scraped

1 tablespoon light corn syrup
8 large egg yolks
⅔ cup sugar

1. In a medium saucepan, combine milk, cream, vanilla beans and pulp and corn syrup. Place over medium heat until steaming. Meanwhile, in a medium bowl whisk egg yolks and sugar until light in color and fluffy. Whisk about ⅓ of the hot milk mixture into eggs, then whisk egg mixture back into pan. Continue to heat mixture until it is thick enough to coat the back of a spoon. Strain into a bowl set over ice water, and allow to cool, or chill in refrigerator.

2. Transfer mixture to an ice cream maker, and freeze according to manufacturer's instructions. Transfer to a plastic container, and freeze.

Chocolate Ice Cream

When it comes to making chocolate ice cream, a custard base will always yield a richer, smoother confection. Kay Rentschler has written recipes for *The New York Times.*

Kay
Rentschler

TIME: 1 hour, plus chilling and freezing   YIELD: About 1 quart

6 ounces bittersweet chocolate
4 large egg yolks
½ cup sugar

2 cups milk
¼ cup heavy cream
2 tablespoons instant coffee

1. Using a microwave oven or double boiler, melt chocolate, then place in a large bowl. In a small bowl, mix together the egg yolks and sugar.

2. In a medium saucepan, combine milk, cream and instant coffee and bring to a simmer. When steam starts to rise, remove from heat quickly. Whisk about ¼ cup into egg mixture. Slowly pour egg mixture into remaining milk mixture, and reduce heat to low. Simmer, stirring with a wooden spoon, until thick enough to coat back of spoon. Immediately pour into chocolate. Stir well, cool and refrigerate for about 6 hours.

3. Place in an ice cream maker to freeze, and store in freezer until needed.

Goat's Milk Ice Cream

The Fat
Duck,
Bray,
England

Goat's milk does not dramatically change the taste of this ice cream, which is essentially a pure cream confection, made without additional flavorings. But the fat in goat's milk, which forms in tiny globules that are smaller than those in cow's milk, means the ice cream will be ultra-smooth. The Fat Duck is a Michelin three-star restaurant in Bray, England, near London, where Heston Blumenthal, the chef and owner, is not afraid of wild but delicious experiments. This recipe is not as outré as his bacon-and-egg ice cream.

TIME: 20 minutes, plus cooling, chilling and freezing   YIELD: About 1½ quarts

3¼ cups fresh goat's milk   ⅞ cup sugar
1⅔ cups heavy cream   6 large egg yolks

1. In a heavy-bottomed saucepan combine the goat's milk, cream and half the sugar; bring the mixture to a simmer. Meanwhile, whisk together the egg yolks and the remaining sugar in another bowl.

2. Remove cream mixture from the heat, and add a little to the egg yolk mixture to warm it, stirring constantly to keep the yolks from cooking. Pour the egg yolk mixture into the saucepan, and cook it over low heat, stirring constantly with a wooden spoon, until it thickens very slightly, 3 to 4 minutes. Strain the mixture into a bowl, and let cool completely. Cover and chill until thoroughly cold, at least 4 hours.

3. Freeze in an ice cream maker according to the manufacturer's instructions. Transfer to containers and freeze to harden.

Mint Chocolate Chip Ice Cream

Here's a popular flavor made with fresh mint and chocolate chips. Oceana is a fine seafood restaurant in New York.

David
Carmichael,
Oceana,
New York

TIME: 1 hour, plus chilling and freezing   YIELD: About 1½ quarts

1 quart heavy cream
6 cups packed fresh mint leaves
   (about 4 ounces), 5 cups of the
   mint coarsely chopped

1 cup sugar
10 large egg yolks
10 ounces bittersweet chocolate,
   chopped

1. In a medium saucepan, bring cream and 5 cups chopped mint to a simmer. Turn off heat, and let steep 5 minutes. Strain out mint, and return cream to saucepan.

2. Add ¾ cup sugar to cream, and bring to a simmer. Whisk together egg yolks and remaining sugar. Remove the cream from heat, and add a little to egg mixture to warm it, stirring constantly. Pour the egg mixture into the cream, stirring constantly. Return the custard to heat, and cook over low heat, stirring constantly with a wooden spoon, until mixture thickens enough to coat back of spoon. Remove from heat, strain and pour into bowl. Cover with plastic wrap placed directly on the surface.

3. Cool completely, then refrigerate until cold, at least 4 hours.

4. Meanwhile, prepare mint chips. Melt the chocolate in the top of a double boiler over simmering water. Cool slightly. Lay a 12-by-24-inch sheet of parchment paper on a work surface. Pour the melted chocolate onto the parchment, spreading evenly to cover entire surface. Lay the remaining cup of whole mint leaves onto the chocolate until half the surface is covered, being careful not to overlap. Lift the parchment under the plain chocolate and fold over the mint-covered chocolate to cover it. Place in the refrigerator for 20 minutes to set.

5. Remove chocolate from the refrigerator, and peel off parchment. Break chocolate into large pieces, and then roughly chop. Refrigerate until needed.

6. Freeze ice cream mixture in an ice cream maker, following manufacturer's instructions. Using a spatula, fold in chocolate mint chips by hand. Place in freezer for at least 2 hours before serving.

Cherry Ice Cream

Shelley
Lance

No commercial cherry ice cream ever tasted like this one. Shelley Lance is the pastry chef at the Palace Kitchen in Seattle, Washington, a city in cherry country.

TIME: 1 hour, plus macerating and chilling   YIELD: 2 quarts

3½ cups sugar

1 pound cherries, about 2½ cups stemmed, pitted and quartered

⅓ cup brandy or Cognac

3 cups heavy cream

3 cups milk

2 vanilla beans, split lengthwise

12 large egg yolks

1. Prepare the cherries and ice cream custard base the day before making the ice cream. To macerate the cherries, in a medium saucepan, combine 2 cups of the sugar with 2 cups water. Bring to a simmer, stirring to dissolve sugar. Add the cherries, and simmer 5 minutes. Remove from heat, and transfer cherries and syrup to a bowl. Stir in brandy. Cover, and refrigerate overnight.

2. To prepare the ice cream custard, in a medium saucepan, combine the heavy cream, milk, vanilla beans and remaining 1½ cups sugar. Heat until just beginning to steam, stirring to dissolve the sugar. Remove from the heat. In a separate bowl, whisk the egg yolks until well combined. Add a ladleful of the hot milk mixture to the eggs while whisking vigorously, to warm the yolks. Add the warmed yolks to the hot milk mixture in the saucepan, and return the pan to medium heat. Cook, stirring, until the mixture is thick enough to coat the back of a spoon, about 5 minutes. Immediately pour it through a fine strainer into a clean bowl. Remove the vanilla beans from the strainer, and scrape the pulp from the vanilla beans into the custard. Cover the bowl with plastic wrap placed on the surface of the custard. Cool in a bowl of ice and water. Refrigerate overnight.

3. To finish the ice cream, place a strainer over a bowl and drain the syrup from the cherries. Set the cherries aside, and discard the syrup or reserve for another use. Freeze the chilled custard in an ice cream maker according to the manufacturer's instructions. Using a rubber spatula, fold in the cherries. Transfer ice cream to 2 one-quart containers, cover, and place in a freezer for a few hours or until completely firm.

Lavender-Blueberry Ice Cream

The blueberries and the fragrance of the lavender combine to give this ice cream a beautiful pastel tone and a haunting flavor. Capsouto Frères is a venerable French bistro in New York. Good purveyors of herbs and even some shops that sell fragrances and bath products sell dried lavender. For fresh, it takes a specialty farm stand or your garden in summer.

Capsouto
Frères,
New York

TIME: 45 minutes, plus chilling and freezing   YIELD: 1 pint

4 fresh or dried lavender flowers
1 cup milk
½ cup sugar
6 large egg yolks, lightly beaten
½ cup heavy cream

½ cup cold crème fraîche
1 cup fresh blueberries, pureed in
    a blender and pressed through a
    sieve
2 teaspoons vanilla extract

1. Place lavender and milk in a small saucepan. Bring to a simmer, remove from heat and allow to rest for 30 minutes.

2. Whisk sugar and egg yolks together in a heavy saucepan or the top of a double boiler. Whisk in the lavender-infused milk and the cream. Cook, stirring constantly, over medium heat, or over water in a double boiler, about 5 minutes, until thickened enough to coat the back of a spoon. Take care not to let simmer or eggs will curdle. Remove from heat and cool to room temperature.

3. Transfer to a metal bowl, cover with a piece of plastic wrap placed on the surface, and refrigerate until cold. Strain to remove lavender. Fold in the crème fraîche, blueberry puree and vanilla. Place in an ice cream maker and churn according to manufacturer's directions. Serve at once or place in container and freeze until firm. Use within 2 days.

Cardamom Ice Cream

Laura
Saynay,
Clementine,
New York

Cardamom, which has a spicy sweetness, lends an exotic touch to this French custard-based ice cream. Clementine was a New York restaurant on lower Fifth Avenue.

TIME: 45 minutes, plus chilling and freezing   YIELD: 2 quarts

3½ cups heavy cream
1½ cups milk
1 cup sugar

4 tablespoons cardamom pods,
    lightly crushed
12 large egg yolks

1. In a large heavy-bottomed saucepan, combine the heavy cream, milk and ½ cup of the sugar. Bring to a boil, and immediately remove from heat. Add crushed cardamom pods, cover and allow to steep for 20 minutes. Pour through a fine strainer into a clean saucepan, and discard the contents of the strainer.

2. In a large mixing bowl, combine yolks with remaining ½ cup of sugar. Whisk until blended. Place milk mixture over medium heat, and bring just to a boil. Remove from heat. Gradually whisk 2 cups of the hot liquid into eggs, then pour egg mixture into saucepan of milk. Whisk constantly over medium-low heat until thick and creamy, about 3 to 4 minutes.

3. Remove saucepan from heat, and strain contents into a mixing bowl. Place bowl in a container of ice water to cool or refrigerate until cold. When ice cream base has chilled, freeze in an ice cream maker, according to manufacturer's instructions.

A CITY AT THE MELTING POINT
By Ed Levine

The two little girls, sisters, weren't so much eating their peach ice cream cones as wearing them. There were bits of fruit on their T-shirts and rivulets of cream on their chins. Up in Brooklyn Heights the air was still and humid, but down on the banks of the East River there was a breeze running, and it ruffled the girls' hair. Still, stickiness radiated off them like heat.

Their mother smiled, and took a bite of her own cone, strawberry, purchased like the others at the Brooklyn Ice Cream Factory, a converted fireboat house that sits at the head of a small pier jutting into the river.

"I've been living in Brooklyn my whole life," she said, "and yet every time I come here I feel like I'm on vacation."

That's just what an ice cream cone is in the heat of summer: a five-minute mini-vacation, a sloppy, messy, delicious respite from the sweltering heat. And there is no better place to take that vacation than in the five boroughs of New York.

New York occupies an important place in the nation's ice cream culture for many reasons, and yet as a city we don't get much respect as an ice cream town. Boston often proclaims itself to be the ice cream capital of America, a distinction that is attributable to both regional hucksterism and, perhaps, the popularity of mix-ins, which Steve Herrell introduced at Steve's In Somerville in 1973. And the ice cream at his new chain, Herrell's, is really good. But long before anyone in Boston had ever mixed Reese's Peanut Butter Cups or bits of Heath Bar into a scoop of vanilla ice cream on a cold granite slab, New York's ice cream makers were changing the ice cream we ate and how we ate it.

Indeed, the very first ice cream shop in America may have been in New York; on May 12, 1777, Phillip Lenzi placed an advertisement for his Manhattan ice cream shop in the *New York Gazette and Weekly Mercury*. And less than a hundred years later, Charles Ranhofer, the chef at Delmonico's, New York's fanciest restaurant, would prefigure modern pastry chefs by making ice creams in flavors like asparagus, pumpernickel-rye and rice.

Certainly a case can be made that the ice cream cone was invented here, by a Wall Street restaurateur, Italo Marchiony. In 1903, he applied for and received a patent for his cone-making machine. Sedutto's, the nation's first so-called superpremium ice cream—high in butterfat, with plenty of egg yolks, less air whipped into it and a better class of solid ingredients flavoring the whole—was founded in New York in 1922. As was Schrafft's, which lives on now in only one location—the New York–New York hotel and casino in Las Vegas.

And Häagen-Dazs, like Ed Koch, Billy Joel and Jennifer Lopez, was born in the Bronx.

Reuben Mattus, a Polish immigrant and small-time ice cream maker in the Bronx, was the father. In 1959, he found his business squeezed for shelf space and wildly undersold by larger national brands like Sealtest and Borden.

About to go out of business, he decided to risk all on a high-butterfat, no-additive ice cream with extremely little air whipped into it, to be sold only in pints.

The ice cream was an immediate sensation in New York, and spawned a number of short-lived New York–based imitators, including Frusen Glädje (Frozen Happiness in Swedish), and Alpen Zauber (Alpine Magic), made in Brooklyn but, according to the packaging, "inspired by the Swiss commitment to excellence."

In 1983, Mr. Mattus sold Häagen-Dazs to Pillsbury, which in turn sold it to Nestlé in 2001. Remarkably, the recipe and the ensuing quality hasn't changed significantly. It is the only mass-produced superpremium ice cream that to this day is made without gum or stabilizers. These are used even in New York's highest quality artisanal ice creams to prevent the crystallization—or freezer burn—that occurs in ice cream when it sits in a freezer too long. Häagen-Dazs remains one of the city's best ice creams.

And while I have always thought of myself as the quintessential high butterfat, dense ice cream fellow, I had a revelation the other day when I spent a couple of hours with Mark Thompson at the Brooklyn Ice Cream Factory. Mr. Thompson's ice cream is extremely old-fashioned, with less butterfat than Häagen-Dazs, quite a bit of air, and no eggs. The resulting ice creams are creamy, ethereally light and perfectly balanced. They practically float into your mouth and leave no heavy film on your palate.

"You don't need all that butterfat and all those eggs to make great ice cream," he told me proudly. "You just need wonderful ingredients, a great ice cream maker, a little bit of know-how, and a lot of passion."

Licorice Ice Cream

Not everyone loves licorice, so be sure of your audience before attempting this ice cream from the kitchen of one of San Francisco's top chefs.

TIME: 1 hour, plus chilling and freezing   YIELD: About 1½ quarts

Gary
Danko,
San
Francisco,
California

3 cups heavy cream
1½ cups milk
½ vanilla bean
½ cup unbrewed licorice root tea
   or chipped licorice root

10 large egg yolks
1 cup sugar
⅓ teaspoon kosher salt

1. In a large saucepan, combine 1½ cups cream, the milk and vanilla bean. Place over medium heat and bring almost to a boil. Remove from heat, stir in licorice root, cover and steep for 20 to 25 minutes.

2. In a heavy saucepan, combine egg yolks, sugar and salt. Mix with a whisk until well combined. Strain milk mixture into a pitcher and whisk into egg yolk mixture. Place over medium heat, stirring constantly, cooking until mixture is lightly thickened and coats the back of a spoon. Remove from heat and whisk in the remaining heavy cream. Strain, cool and refrigerate overnight.

3. Pour into an ice cream maker and freeze according to manufacturer's directions. Store in a covered container in freezer.

Poire Williams Ice Cream ✳

Charlene
Reis,
Chez Panisse,
Berkeley,
California

This is the ice cream to serve with a pear tart. Charlene Reis is one of the pastry chefs at Chez Panisse in Berkeley, California.

TIME: 15 minutes, plus chilling and freezing   YIELD: 1½ quarts

6 large egg yolks
2 cups heavy cream
1 cup half-and-half

⅔ cup sugar
3 tablespoons Poire Williams eau
    de vie

1. In a small bowl, whisk the egg yolks just enough to break them up. Set aside. Place the cream in a medium mixing bowl, and set aside.

2. In a small saucepan, combine the half-and-half and sugar. Place over medium heat, stirring occasionally, just until steam rises. Do not boil. Slowly add about ½ cup of the hot mixture to the egg yolks, whisking vigorously to combine well. Pour the mixture into the saucepan, and simmer, stirring constantly, over low heat until it forms a custard thick enough to coat the back of a spoon, about 5 minutes.

3. Strain the custard into the bowl of cream. Add the Poire Williams, and stir to mix well. Cover and refrigerate until well chilled, at least 30 minutes. Freeze in an ice cream maker according to manufacturer's instructions. Transfer to containers and return to freezer to harden.

Apricot Pit Ice Cream

In place of the apricot pits, you can use twenty-four small Italian amaretto cookies to steep in the warm mixture of milk and cream, because their main flavoring agent is apricot pits, which impart a flavor that is similar to almonds, only somewhat more bitter. Vong is the Thai fusion restaurant in New York that is owned by chef Jean-Georges Vongerichten, who worked in Bangkok for several years.

Vong,
New York

TIME: 45 minutes, plus chilling and freezing   YIELD: 1 quart

45 to 50 apricot pits
2 cups milk
1½ cups heavy cream

¼ cup plus 3 tablespoons sugar
7 large egg yolks

1. Wrap apricot pits in a heavy dish towel. On the floor or on a sturdy cutting board, crack pits open using a hammer or a meat mallet, exposing kernels. Watch your fingers.

2. In a medium saucepan, combine apricot kernels and shells with milk and heavy cream. Bring to a boil. Remove from heat, place in a bowl and let cool. Cover and refrigerate overnight.

3. The next day, bring the milk mixture to a boil. Strain through a fine sieve. Meanwhile, in a large bowl, whisk together the sugar and the yolks until light and fluffy. Whisk about ½ cup hot milk into the egg mixture, and then whisk the egg mixture into the milk. Pour into a large saucepan, place over medium-low heat and, stirring constantly with a wooden spoon, cook until thick enough to coat the back of the spoon. Remove from heat immediately. Let cool, and then strain. Transfer to a bowl, cover and chill at least 4 hours.

4. Pour into an ice cream maker, and freeze according to manufacturer's instructions. Transfer to a container and freeze until firm.

Mulled-Wine Ice Cream

Vox,
New York

A spicy wine mixture is the basis for this custard ice cream. Vox was a New York restaurant that enjoyed its 15 minutes of fame and is now closed.

TIME: 1 hour, plus chilling and freezing   YIELD: 1½ pints

1 750-milliliter bottle merlot
1 cup plus 2 tablespoons sugar
3 cinnamon sticks
1 tablespoon whole allspice
Zest of 1 orange

1 vanilla bean, split lengthwise
½ teaspoon orange oil or 1
   tablespoon grated orange zest
1 cup heavy cream
4 large egg yolks

1. In a medium saucepan over high heat, combine the wine, ⅔ cup sugar, cinnamon, allspice, orange zest, vanilla and orange oil or grated zest, and bring to simmer. Reduce heat to low, cover pan, and simmer for 30 minutes.

2. Uncover pan, and increase heat to medium. Simmer mixture until it is reduced by half, about 20 minutes. Let cool, and then strain, discarding solids.

3. To make the base, in a small saucepan, bring cream and ⅓ cup sugar to simmer. In a bowl, whisk together yolks and remaining 2 tablespoons sugar.

4. Remove cream from heat, and add a little to yolk mixture to warm it, stirring constantly to keep yolks from curdling. Pour yolk mixture into hot cream, stirring cream constantly as you pour.

5. Return custard to the stove. Cook over low heat, stirring constantly with a wooden spoon until it thickens enough to coat back of spoon. Remove from heat. Strain custard through a fine-mesh sieve. Let cool, and then combine with mulled wine. Chill until cold, for at least 4 hours. Freeze in an ice cream maker according to manufacturer's instructions.

Sweet-Corn Ice Cream

You will need a summer day to appreciate the sweet-corn ice cream. Try it with blueberry pie. With her husband, the chef Gerry Hayden, Claudia Fleming has opened the North Fork Table and Inn in Southhold, New York.

TIME: 45 minutes, plus resting, chilling and freezing   YIELD: About 3½ cups

Claudia
Fleming

4 ears fresh sweet corn, shucked   ¾ cup sugar

2 cups milk   9 large egg yolks

2 cups heavy cream

1. Using a large knife, slice corn kernels off cobs, and place in a large saucepan. Break cobs into thirds, and add them to pot with milk, cream and ½ cup of the sugar. Bring to a boil, stirring, then turn off heat. Using an immersion mixer, puree corn kernels. (If you don't have an immersion mixer, remove kernels with slotted spoon, puree in a blender, and return to pan.) Let rest 1 hour.

2. Bring mixture back to a simmer, then turn off heat. In a small bowl, whisk egg yolks and remaining sugar. Add a cup of the hot mixture to yolks, stirring constantly so they do not curdle. Add yolk mixture to the saucepan, stirring. Cook over medium-low heat, stirring constantly, until custard coats spoon, about 10 minutes.

3. Pass custard through a fine sieve, pressing down hard on the solids. Discard solids, let custard cool, then cover and chill at least 4 hours. Freeze in an ice cream maker according to manufacturer's directions.

TEST KITCHEN:
For the Finale, Here's the Ice Cream Maker
By Suzanne Hamlin

Kitchenware shops call September to December the buying season for ice cream machines. Sales of machines, at $40 to more than $1,000, are booming. Retailers say that sales surge now, not in the summer months, because the machines are terrific gifts and a boon to home entertaining.

Ice cream isn't all that the machines make. Most are also adept at sorbet, gelato, frozen yogurt and frozen margaritas.

For many buyers, nostalgia still counts. White Mountain, which makes almost the same wooden tub and metal canister ice cream makers it introduced 145 years ago, has two models, one electric, the other hand-cranked. Both use rock salt and crushed ice and make equally good ice cream in about 30 minutes. But the hand-cranked outsells the electric model 3 to 1. A newfangled gadget is a round of plastic shaped like a soccer ball. You put the ice cream mixture in the middle, with rock salt and crushed ice around it, and toss the ball back and forth to chill and thicken the ice cream. Interactive ice cream, anyone?

With the high quality of many commercial ice creams, though, why make ice cream at all?

Nothing beats the impact of freshly made ice cream, with that moment of instant gratification, the rush of rich, supersmooth coldness and the slow, mouth-filling meltdown.

It is a taste that commercial ice cream, no matter how good, can never quite match.

And the custom-made flavors! Where else can you find really fresh peach, burnt caramel, peppermint stick, blackberry, ginger or lemon ice cream? Or mango-lime, three mint or blueberry-zinfandel sorbet?

From its ingredients, ice cream should be simple to make. What is it, after all, but a combination of milk or cream, sugar, maybe eggs, flavoring and ingredients like fruit and nuts?

But getting that smooth rich texture like frozen velvet demands intense fine-tuning by both human and machine.

Fundamentally, ice cream becomes ice cream when the mix is frozen slowly but surely by churning (not whipping), until it reaches a semisolid state. Churned too slowly, it never quite comes together; too quickly, it can produce globules of butterfat.

All ice cream machines work on the same principle. The mix, churned by a dasher, is slowly frozen in a canister. The freezing element can be ice and salt, which is packed around the sealed canister, or a coolant, which is sealed in the canister and activated by prefreezing in a home freezer.

Or in the most expensive machines, starting at about $250, the freezing element is built into the machine, which is an electrically powered refrigeration unit with a compressor. Just plug them in—the machines do all the work.

But regardless of the kind of machine you use, be sure your ice cream or sorbet mixture is very cold before freezing.

Lemon-Buttermilk Ice Cream

Wayne
Harley
Brachman,
Mesa Grill
and
Bolo,
New York

Stirred, unflavored yogurt can replace the buttermilk. Pastry chef Wayne Harley Brachman created this ice cream when he was working at Mesa Grill and Bolo restaurants in New York.

TIME: 1 hour, plus freezing   YIELD: 1 quart

¼ cup fresh lemon juice   1 cup heavy cream
¾ cup sugar   6 large egg yolks
1 cup milk   1 cup cultured buttermilk

1. In a small saucepan, combine lemon juice and ¼ cup of sugar. Place over medium-low heat, and stir until dissolved. Remove from heat, and allow to cool, then refrigerate.

2. In a medium heavy-bottomed saucepan, combine the milk, heavy cream and ¼ cup of sugar. Place over medium-low heat until steam rises from the surface. Remove from heat.

3. In a medium mixing bowl, combine egg yolks with remaining ¼ cup sugar. Whisk to blend. While continuing to whisk yolks, slowly drizzle about a cup of the hot milk mixture into them, to gradually warm them. Add yolk mixture to saucepan. Return saucepan to medium-low heat, and stir with a wooden spoon until mixture has thickened enough to coat the back of the spoon.

4. Strain mixture into a bowl, and place in a bowl of ice water until cold or refrigerate until cold. Stir in buttermilk. Add lemon syrup and stir well. Freeze in an ice cream maker, according to the manufacturer's instructions, then transfer to a container and freeze to harden.

GELATOS, FROZEN YOGURTS AND SHERBETS

Take a step down from ice cream, in terms of butterfat, and you have gelato at about 10 percent fat, as compared with 14 to 16 percent for traditional ice creams. You accomplish a lower fat content without tricking up this dessert with phony substitutes. Frozen yogurt brings the fat count even lower and indeed, by using fat-free yogurt in place of whole milk, lower still, though at some loss of satisfying richness. Sherbet is even more restricted. And then there is sorbet, all fruit. I'll never forget a trip to Paris in the early 1970s, having discovered Berthillon, the now-legendary sorbet-maker on the Île St.-Louis. The vibrancy of those fruit flavors were like no sherbet—the American term—that I had ever tasted. Sherbet, which has a milk base, does not have the vibrancy of sorbet, an inexact translation if there ever was one. But in defense of sherbet, the dairy component adds a lush delicacy, especially for citrus flavors, that can be very alluring.

Lemon Gelato

Nigella
Lawson

It's the milk, without any cream, that makes this recipe a gelato, and not an ice cream. Whereas most ice creams have a fat content of 12 to 18 percent, gelato is really an ice milk, at around 10 percent. Nigella Lawson is an English cookbook author and television personality.

TIME: 40 minutes, plus chilling and freezing   YIELD: About 1½ pints

2 cups whole milk
Pared or grated zest of ½ lemon

5 large egg yolks
½ cup sugar

1. In a small saucepan combine milk and lemon zest. Place over medium-low heat just until steaming; do not boil. Remove from heat, cover and allow mixture to infuse for about 20 minutes.

2. In a medium bowl, whisk together egg yolks and sugar. Strain infused milk, then whisk it into yolk mixture.

3. Pour mixture into a clean saucepan, and place over medium-low heat. Stir constantly with a wooden spoon until it forms a custard thick enough to coat back of spoon, about 10 minutes. Do not overheat or it will curdle.

4. Cool mixture by placing bottom of pan in several inches of ice water; give it a stir. Transfer to a bowl and refrigerate until well chilled, at least 1 hour. Freeze in an ice cream maker according to manufacturer's instructions.

Balsamic Apple Frozen Yogurt

This frozen yogurt is made without a custard base. Since a whole cup of balsamic vinegar is required, the very finest artisanal kind is not necessary. But look for a good quality one all the same, with twelve or more years of age on it. As an alternative consider using a good, aged Spanish sherry vinegar in place of the balsamic. Aquavit is a Scandinavian restaurant in New York.

TIME: 15 minutes, plus draining and freezing   YIELD: About 1 quart

1 quart plain low-fat or fat-free
  yogurt
1 cup unfiltered apple juice or
  fresh apple cider
1 cup balsamic vinegar

2 tablespoons sugar
Juice of 1 lime
Pinch of sea salt
½ cup cultured buttermilk

1. Line a fine strainer with cheesecloth. Pour yogurt into strainer, set over a bowl and drain at least 8 hours or overnight.

2. In a medium-size saucepan, bring apple juice to a boil. Add balsamic vinegar, and boil until mixture is reduced by half. Reduce heat, and add sugar, lime juice and a pinch salt. Simmer for 2 minutes, remove from heat and let cool.

3. In a large bowl, combine drained yogurt and buttermilk. Whisk until blended.

4. Pour cooled balsamic liquid into yogurt mixture, and whisk until thoroughly blended.

5. Transfer to an ice cream maker, and freeze according to manufacturer's instructions.

Rosemary-Lime Sherbet

Local,
New York

This is a sherbet that is on its way to being an ice cream that is made without a custard base. Half-and-half is fairly rich. Be sure to use only the leaves of the rosemary, not the stems. The flavors of this confection are very refreshing, so this sherbet would be delicious to complete a rich dinner. Local restaurant, which was in the theater district in New York, has closed and the chef, Franklin Becker, has moved on.

TIME: 20 minutes, plus chilling and freezing   YIELD: About 1 quart

¾ cup sugar

3 cups half-and-half

2 tablespoons chopped fresh
    rosemary

¼ cup light corn syrup

Juice of 3 limes

1. In a large saucepan, combine sugar, half-and-half, rosemary and corn syrup. Whisk lightly and bring to a boil, making sure mixture does not boil over, then strain into a bowl. Let cool, then chill in refrigerator. Remove from refrigerator and slowly whisk in lime juice. If mixture shows signs of curdling, whisk harder or transfer to a blender and process briefly.

2. Pour mixture into an ice cream maker and freeze according to manufacturer's instructions.

Sour Cream Sherbet

This sherbet is tart and refreshing. The restaurant Alain Ducasse in New York calls it a sorbet and serves it as a palate-cleanser before the regular dessert, but because of the dairy content, sherbet is more on target. There is no French word for sherbet.

TIME: 15 minutes, plus freezing   YIELD: 1 quart

Alain
Ducasse at
the Essex
House,
New York

1 cup sugar

1 pint sour cream

3 tablespoons lime juice

½ tablespoon finely grated lime zest

1. Combine sugar and ¾ cup water in a saucepan. Simmer until sugar dissolves.

2. Whisk sour cream in a large bowl until smooth. Gradually whisk in sugar syrup. Whisk in lime juice and zest. Refrigerate until cold. Transfer to an ice cream maker and freeze according to the manufacturer's instructions.

Fromage Blanc–Lemongrass Sherbet

Vong,
New York

Cheese sherbet? Why not! This sherbet, with its fragrant lemongrass component, has a lovely texture, thanks to the *fromage blanc*. Vong is chef Jean-Georges Vongerichten's Thai restaurant in New York, with branches in other cities.

TIME: 20 minutes, plus chilling and freezing   YIELD: About 1 quart

¾ cup plus 2 tablespoons sugar   1 stalk lemongrass, smashed
⅓ cup light corn syrup   2⅔ cups *fromage blanc*

1. In a large saucepan, combine sugar, corn syrup, lemongrass and 2 cups water. Bring to a boil, then remove from heat and let cool. Cover and refrigerate until thoroughly chilled.

2. Strain liquid through a fine sieve. Stir *fromage blanc* into liquid. Taste and adjust sweetness if necessary. Pour into an ice cream maker and freeze according to manufacturer's instructions.

Lemon-Buttermilk Sherbet

This can be a buttermilk sherbet or a frozen yogurt, either way scented and flavored with vanilla and lemon. It's up to you. The New York restaurant Local has closed.

Local,
New York

TIME: 15 minutes, plus chilling and freezing   YIELD: About 3½ cups

½ cup sugar
2 cups cultured buttermilk
   or unflavored whole milk
   yogurt

1 inch-long piece vanilla bean,
   split lengthwise and pulp and
   seeds scraped out
Juice and zest of 1 lemon

1. In a small saucepan, combine sugar with ½ cup water. Bring to a boil, then remove from heat and let syrup cool. Chill in refrigerator.

2. In a large bowl, whisk together the buttermilk, sugar syrup, scrapings from vanilla bean, lemon juice and zest. Taste and adjust flavor, adding more sugar or lemon juice if needed. Pour into an ice cream maker and freeze according to manufacturer's instructions.

SORBETS, GRANITAS AND ICES

This is the dairyless frozen confection category. These desserts involve fruit puree or juice, or some other liquid, like espresso or chocolate, that has been frozen, either churned in an ice cream maker for a smooth sorbet, or scraped from a metal pan in crystals for granitas and ices. They are among the simplest frozen desserts to make. And assuming you start with a chilled base, like juice or coffee, the advance preparation can be minimal. But there are a few things you have to know. First, the sweeter the mixture, the less hard it will freeze and the smoother it will be. Similarly, the addition of alcohol, like grappa or wine, will inhibit freezing, also making for a somewhat creamier texture. Many of these recipes start by making simple syrup: sugar and water boiled together.

Chocolate Sorbet ☀

Claudia
Fleming

∾

Cold, intense chocolate sorbet is made with a combination of cocoa and bittersweet chocolate. Claudia Fleming was the celebrated founding pastry chef at Gramercy Tavern in New York.

TIME: 45 minutes, plus chilling and freezing   YIELD: 1 pint

⅞ cup sugar
¾ cup unsweetened Dutch-
   process cocoa

8½ ounces bittersweet chocolate,
   chopped

1. In a medium saucepan, combine 2 cups water and the sugar, and bring to a boil over high heat, stirring occasionally. Gradually add cocoa powder, whisking until smooth. Reduce heat to low, and cook mixture at a gentle simmer for 30 minutes, until syrupy.

2. Put chocolate in a large bowl, and add half the cocoa syrup, whisking until chocolate is melted and mixture is smooth. Add remaining syrup, and whisk. Strain through a fine sieve, and let cool. Stir in 1 cup water.

3. Chill mixture, covered, until very cold, at least 4 hours. Pour into an ice cream maker and freeze according to manufacturer's directions.

Cider Sorbet

Apples cooked in cider and pureed form the base of this sorbet. Charlie Palmer is the owner of Aureole in New York and several other restaurants.

Charlie
Palmer

TIME: 45 minutes, plus chilling and freezing   YIELD: About 5 cups

2 pounds Granny Smith apples (about 4) peeled, cored and finely chopped

1 cup fresh or hard apple cider

1 cup sugar

1 3-inch cinnamon stick

1 teaspoon freshly grated orange zest

⅓ cup lemon juice

1. In a medium saucepan, combine apples and ⅓ cup apple cider. Bring to a boil, then reduce heat to low. Simmer, stirring frequently, until apples have softened, about 15 minutes. Remove from heat and allow to cool. Stir to blend into a smooth puree, or puree in a blender or food processor.

2. In a medium saucepan, combine sugar, 1 cup cold water, cinnamon stick and orange zest. Bring to a boil over high heat and boil for 1 minute. Remove from heat and add lemon juice. Allow to cool at room temperature or in a bowl in ice water. Strain through a very fine sieve, discarding solids.

3. Measure out 2½ cups of the apple puree, and combine in a bowl with the strained sugar syrup and the remaining ⅔ cup of cider. Stir to blend well. Refrigerate until cold. Pour mixture into an ice cream maker and freeze according to manufacturer's instructions.

Passion Fruit Sorbet

Claudia
Fleming

Pineapple contributes texture to this sorbet, without overriding the distinctive tart sweetness of the passion fruit. Claudia Fleming is the author of *The Last Course: The Desserts of Gramercy Tavern* and is a James Beard Award winner for best pastry chef.

TIME: 1 hour 15 minutes, plus chilling and freezing   YIELD: 1 quart

1 cup peeled, cored, cubed
   pineapple
1 cup sugar

1⅓ cups unsweetened passion
   fruit juice or puree

1. Place pineapple and 2 tablespoons of the sugar in a food processor or blender, and puree until very smooth. Let mixture rest for 1 hour.

2. Meanwhile, in a small saucepan, combine remaining sugar with 1 cup of water, and bring to a simmer over medium heat. Simmer mixture, stirring, until sugar dissolves, about 3 minutes. Remove from heat, and allow to cool.

3. Strain pineapple mixture through a medium-mesh sieve. Measure out ⅔ cup of pineapple puree, and reserve the rest for another use.

4. In a large bowl, whisk together the pineapple puree, passion fruit juice, and sugar syrup. Cover and chill at least 3 hours or overnight. Pour mixture into an ice cream maker and freeze according to manufacturer's instructions.

Strawberry-Moscato Sorbet

The moscato wine is not a super-syrupy Muscat dessert wine, but an Italian table wine that is very slightly sweet. Eleven Madison Park is one of restaurateur Danny Meyer's most elegant places in New York.

TIME: 15 minutes, plus chilling and freezing   YIELD: About 1 quart

Eleven
Madison
Park,
New York

1 cup very ripe strawberries,
    rinsed, hulled and quartered
1 cup Italian moscato wine

½ cup orange juice
1 cup plus 2 tablespoons sugar
2 tablespoons light corn syrup

1. In a food processor, puree strawberries. Add moscato, orange juice, sugar, corn syrup and 1½ cups water. Puree. Strain through a fine sieve. Taste, adding sugar if necessary. Refrigerate until completely chilled.

2. Stir mixture, then pour into an ice cream maker and freeze according to manufacturer's instructions.

Cantaloupe–Star Anise Sorbet

Sono,
New York

Muskmelons, crenshaws or ripe honeydews can also be used. Sono restaurant in New York, where Tadashi Ono was the chef, has closed. Mr. Ono is now at Matsuri restaurant.

TIME: 30 minutes, plus resting, chilling and freezing   YIELD: About 1½ quarts

2 very ripe cantaloupes, peeled, seeded and cut into large chunks

12 star anise
¾ cup sugar
¼ cup light corn syrup

1. In a food processor, puree cantaloupe until smooth. This should yield at least 4 cups. In a large saucepan, combine 4 cups cantaloupe puree, star anise, sugar, corn syrup and 1 cup water. Place over medium-low heat and stir just until sugar is dissolved. Remove from heat and let rest for at least 2 hours at room temperature.

2. Strain through a fine sieve, pressing out as much juice as possible. Refrigerate until cold. Pour into an ice cream maker and freeze according to manufacturer's instructions.

Apple Granita with Calvados

For this granita, the alcohol is added afterward, at the table. Brasserie Flo is one of Paris's classic restaurants.

Brasserie Flo, Paris

TIME: 30 minutes, plus cooling and freezing   YIELD: About 4 cups (4 to 6 servings)

4 large Granny Smith apples, cored, quartered and thinly sliced

4 cups filtered clear apple juice

5 tablespoons sugar

1 tablespoon lemon juice

Pinch of salt

¼ cup chilled Calvados, or to taste

1. Place a shallow metal pan in freezer. In a nonreactive saucepan, combine apples, apple juice, sugar, lemon juice and salt. Bring to a boil, then simmer uncovered until apples are very tender, about 20 minutes.

2. Pour mixture into a bowl through a sieve, pressing as much apple pulp through as possible. Cool to room temperature.

3. Pour apple mixture into chilled pan. Place in freezer. Stir every 20 minutes until it thickens into coarse crystals, about 1 hour.

4. Stir granita and mound into small cups. Splash with Calvados. Serve immediately.

Mint Ice

Bill
Yosses

If you freeze this ice in shallow trays, you can scrape it to use it like a granita. Bill Yosses began cooking with David Bouley at Montrachet in New York City's TriBeCa.

TIME: 20 minutes, plus cooling and freezing   YIELD: About 1½ pints

2 cups sugar   3 bunches fresh mint

1. In a saucepan, combine sugar with 2 cups water, and bring to a boil, stirring until sugar is dissolved. Let cool.

2. Bring a saucepan of water to a boil. Fill a large bowl with water and ice. Plunge mint, stems and all, into boiling water for 10 seconds. Remove mint to ice water. Let cool.

3. Squeeze excess water from mint. Place mint in a blender with cooled syrup and puree. Strain through a fine sieve. Transfer to a covered container and freeze, stirring from time to time, until firm, at least 4 hours. Or transfer to an ice cream maker, freeze according to manufacturer's directions, then freeze until very firm.

ICE CREAM DESSERTS, PARFAITS AND SEMIFREDDOS

Start with ice cream and you can construct all sorts of impressive desserts. Satisfyingly old-fashioned sundaes are inevitably better when made with top-quality homemade ice cream and sauce. Fanciful layered parfaits and dazzling baked Alaskas crowned with toasted swirls of meringue are a few that are represented in these recipes, and which can end a dinner with great panache. Then there are the semifreddos. The term means half-cold. These are delicious, flavored cream and meringue-based confections that are easy to prepare and do not need an ice cream maker, but which are more fragile than regular ice cream.

Clementine "Creamsicle" Sundaes ✳

Poached clementines in wine and liqueur combined with vanilla ice cream result in creamsicles for grownups.

Florence
Fabricant

TIME: 45 minutes, plus chilling   YIELD: 4 servings

⅔ cup dry white wine
⅓ cup Grand Marnier
½ cup sugar
Juice and finely slivered zest of
   2 oranges

12 clementines
½ pint vanilla ice cream
   (page 416)
4 mint sprigs

1. Combine wine, Grand Marnier, sugar, orange juice and zest in a 3-quart saucepan. Bring to simmer and cook until sugar dissolves. Remove from heat.

2. Peel the clementines and divide in segments. Add segments to the saucepan, return to simmer and, using slotted spoon, immediately remove segments to a bowl.

3. Boil down the cooking liquid until syrupy. Pour over clementine segments and refrigerate at least four hours.

4. Place a scoop of ice cream in each of 4 goblets, spoon clementines and syrup over and serve garnished with mint.

Vanilla Bean Kulfi with Rosewater Oranges

Tabla,
New York

Kulfi is a dense Indian-style ice cream that is not churned. Tabla is an Indian-fusion restaurant in New York.

TIME: 2½ hours, plus freezing   YIELD: 8 servings

5½ cups heavy cream
2 cups milk
1½ cups sugar
1 vanilla bean, split lengthwise
Pinch of salt

3 sprigs fresh rosemary
½ teaspoon rosewater, or to taste
6 small oranges, preferably blood
   oranges

1. In a large, wide pot, bring cream, milk, ¾ cup sugar and vanilla bean to a simmer over low heat. Cook, stirring often, until mixture is reduced by one half, about 2½ hours. Stir in salt.

2. Strain mixture, then pour it into a 1-quart loaf pan or soufflé dish. Cover with plastic and freeze until solid, about 4 hours.

3. Meanwhile, in a small saucepan, combine remaining ¾ cup sugar with ½ cup water and rosemary. Bring mixture to a simmer and stir until sugar dissolves. Turn off heat and let infuse until syrup cools. Remove rosemary, then stir in rosewater.

4. Peel oranges down to the flesh and cut them into segments, removing white membranes. Toss with rosewater syrup.

5. To serve, unmold kulfi and slice it into 8 portions. Top with oranges and syrup.

Vanilla Roasted Figs with Wildflower Honey Ice Cream

The combination of roasted figs and honey ice cream is incomparable. This recipe comes from the French Laundry, chef Thomas Keller's restaurant in Yountville, California.

Thomas
Keller

TIME: 30 minutes, plus chilling and freezing   YIELD: 6 servings

2 cups milk
2 cups heavy cream
½ cup wildflower honey
12 large egg yolks

¼ cup plus ½ tablespoon sugar
18 ripe figs
4 vanilla beans, split lengthwise
3 tablespoons unsalted butter

1. In a large saucepan, combine the milk, cream and honey. Place over medium heat, and stir until honey is dissolved. Remove from heat.

2. By machine or by hand in a metal bowl, whisk egg yolks and ¼ cup sugar until thickened and lightened. Gradually whisk in the milk mixture. Return mixture to saucepan and stir over medium-low heat until mixture coats the back of a wooden spoon and reaches 175 degrees. Do not overheat. Remove from heat and transfer to a mixing bowl. Chill by placing it in a larger bowl filled with ice and water, and allow to cool to room temperature.

3. Strain mixture into a container. Cover, and refrigerate for at least 5 hours, or overnight. Freeze in an ice cream maker according to manufacturer's directions. Transfer to a covered container. Freeze for several hours, or until hardened.

4. Slice off and discard tops of figs. Cut split vanilla beans into 2-inch pieces. Make a small slit in top of each fig, and insert a piece of vanilla.

5. Preheat oven to 400 degrees. In an ovenproof pan just large enough to hold all the figs standing upright, melt butter over medium heat. Add remaining sugar, and stir to dissolve. Stand figs in the butter, and add any remaining vanilla bean pieces to pan. Place pan in oven and bake until figs are thoroughly heated, about 10 minutes.

6. To serve, place a scoop of ice cream into each of six bowls. Arrange three of the figs, warm or at room temperature, around each scoop. Serve.

Mastic Ice Cream with Commandaria and Fig Sauce

Molyvos,
New York

Mastic, a resin from a type of evergreen that grows in Greece, especially on the island of Chios, adds a slightly piney flavor note and fragrance, which was especially prized by the Arabs and Turks. Mastic crystals are sold in good spice shops, in stores that specialize in Middle Eastern ingredients and online. The figs are simmered with Commandaria, a venerable sweet wine made in Cyprus, originally by the knights of the order of St. John. Sweet sherry or tawny port can be substituted. Molyvos is a New York restaurant that serves country-style Greek food.

TIME: 30 minutes, plus chilling and freezing   YIELD: 1 quart

¾ tablespoon mastic crystals	1 bottle (750 milliliters)
2¾ tablespoons plus ½ cup sugar	Commandaria liqueur
2 cups whole milk	2 cinnamon sticks
2 cups heavy cream	1½ cups dried brown figs,
15 large egg yolks	stemmed and quartered

1. Put the mastic and ¾ tablespoon sugar in a coffee or spice grinder and pulverize into a powder.

2. In a large heavy saucepan over medium heat, bring the milk, heavy cream and ¼ cup of the sugar to a boil. While the mixture is heating, combine ¼ cup sugar with the egg yolks in a mixing bowl. With a wire whisk, beat until mixture is pale yellow.

3. Temper the yolks by gently pouring 1 cup of the hot cream mixture into the yolk mixture, whisking constantly until well mixed. Return the remaining cream mixture to the stove over low heat. Stir in the yolk mixture. With a wooden spoon, stir slowly over very low heat until the mixture thickens and coats the spoon, about 6 minutes. Do not let it boil.

4. Strain the hot mixture through a fine-mesh sieve into a stainless steel bowl. Stir in the ground mastic and sugar mixture, stirring until it has dissolved. Let cool for about 10 minutes, stir again and refrigerate until thoroughly chilled. Freeze in an ice cream maker according to manufacturer's directions. Transfer to a container and freeze to harden.

5. In a deep saucepan, combine the Commandaria, remaining 2 table-

spoons sugar and cinnamon sticks. Bring to a boil over medium heat and boil for 3 minutes. Reduce to a simmer and cook over low heat until the alcohol cooks out, about 2 minutes.

6. Add the quartered figs and, over medium-high heat, cook until the figs are soft and the liquid has reduced by half and has a syrupy consistency, about 8 minutes. Refrigerate until ready to serve, for up to 1 week. Serve cool or warmed, over mastic ice cream.

Peanut Sherbet with Peanut Sauce and Peanut Brittle ☀

Zarela
Martinez
∾

All peanuts all the time describes this dessert. Using salted peanut butter to bring the flavor around is essential. Zarela Martinez owns Zarela's, a New York City Mexican restaurant.

TIME: 3 hours, plus freezing   YIELD: 6 to 8 servings

⅓ cup sugar

3 cups skim milk

1¼ cups creamy peanut butter, not unsalted

2 12-ounce cans evaporated milk

1 14-ounce can condensed milk

1 cup cachaça, white rum or other sugarcane spirit

½ teaspoon vanilla extract

½ cup chopped Mexican peanut-sesame brittle (page 501)

1. In a small saucepan over medium heat, combine sugar with ⅓ cup water and bring to a boil, stirring occasionally. Simmer until sugar dissolves.

2. In a blender or food processor, combine syrup, skim milk and ¾ cup peanut butter, and process until smooth. Transfer to a bowl. Cover and chill until thoroughly cold. Transfer mixture to an ice cream maker, and freeze according to manufacturer's instructions.

3. To make peanut sauce, in a blender or food processor, combine evaporated and condensed milks, cachaça, remaining peanut butter and vanilla and process until smooth. Transfer to a tightly covered container, and store in refrigerator for up to one month.

4. To assemble sundaes, pour a little bit of peanut sauce into a tall glass. Place two scoops of peanut sherbet on top. Sprinkle with crushed candy and serve.

Gingersnap Ice Cream with Caramel Oranges ※

Claudia
Fleming

∽

Molasses, spices and oranges are the flavor notes achieved in this dessert that plays the flavors found in gingersnaps with the tart sweetness of oranges. Claudia Fleming was the pastry chef at Gramercy Tavern.

TIME: 45 minutes, plus chilling and freezing   YIELD: About 5 cups

½ cup fresh ginger, peeled and
   sliced
3 cups whole milk
1 cup heavy cream
⅓ cup sugar
4 cinnamon sticks
1 tablespoon cracked black
   peppercorns

½ whole nutmeg, crushed
2 cracked cardamom pods
12 large egg yolks
½ cup dark brown sugar
2 tablespoons molasses
Caramel oranges (page 545)

1. Bring a small saucepan of water to boil. Add ginger, and blanch for 1 minute. Drain ginger and transfer to a large saucepan.

2. Add milk, cream, granulated sugar, cinnamon, pepper, nutmeg and cardamom to saucepan and bring to simmer. Turn off heat and let spices infuse for 20 minutes. Meanwhile, in a bowl, whisk yolks, brown sugar and molasses.

3. To make the base, bring milk mixture back to the boil and remove from heat. Add a little hot milk mixture to yolk mixture to warm it, stirring constantly to keep yolks from curdling. Pour yolk mixture into the rest of the hot milk mixture, stirring constantly.

4. Return custard to the stove, and cook it over low heat, stirring constantly with wooden spoon, until it thickens enough to coat back of spoon. Remove from heat, and strain custard through fine sieve. Chill until thoroughly cold, for at least 4 hours.

5. Pour into an ice cream maker and freeze according to manufacturer's instructions. Serve ice cream topped with caramel oranges.

Pumpkin Parfait

Mark
Bittman

This frozen pumpkin parfait would be a perfectly refreshing alternative to pumpkin pie at the end of Thanksgiving dinner. Mark Bittman writes the "Minimalist" column for *The New York Times* and is the author of *How to Cook Everything*.

TIME: 20 minutes, plus freezing   YIELD: 12 servings

1 pound canned pureed
   unseasoned pumpkin, or 2 cups
   fresh puree
2¼ cups heavy cream
¾ cup milk

¾ cup plus 2 tablespoons sugar
½ teaspoon ground ginger
¼ teaspoon ground nutmeg
1 teaspoon ground cinnamon
2 tablespoons dark rum

1. Whisk together the pumpkin, ¾ cup cream, milk, ¾ cup sugar, spices and rum. Line an 8- or 9-inch square pan with plastic wrap, and pour the mixture into the pan. Wrap the whole pan in plastic, and freeze it for at least four hours; it can keep for as long as two days.

2. Remove the pan from the freezer about 20 minutes before serving.

3. Whip the remaining cream with the 2 tablespoons sugar. Refrigerate while completing the dessert.

4. Cut the frozen pumpkin mixture into small cubes and, a few at a time, puree them in a food processor until they are smooth. In small parfait or wineglasses, layer 2 tablespoons pumpkin mixture, then a rounded tablespoon whipped cream, alternating for six layers. Serve immediately.

Peach Melba

Peach melba was invented in 1894 by Auguste Escoffier at the Savoy Hotel in London in honor of Dame Nellie Melba, an Australian diva who was singing in *Lohengrin* at Covent Garden. Escoffier never heard the opera, but he knew the singer was partial to vanilla ice cream and peaches. He added the raspberry puree. (And he also created Melba toast in the singer's honor.) Kay Rentschler, whose version this is, has contributed recipes to *The New York Times*.

Kay
Rentschler

TIME: 25 minutes, plus cooling   YIELD: 4 servings

3½ cups superfine sugar
1 lemon
1 vanilla bean, split lengthwise
4 ripe peaches, halved

3 cups raspberries
¼ cup confectioners' sugar
1 pint vanilla ice cream (page 446)

1. In a wide saucepan, combine superfine sugar, juice of ½ lemon, vanilla bean and 3 cups water. Place over medium-low heat until sugar dissolves. Increase heat and allow to boil for 5 minutes. Reduce heat until syrup is at a lively simmer. Add peach halves and poach just until lightly softened, 2 to 3 minutes on each side depending on ripeness of fruit. Using a slotted spoon, transfer peaches to a plate, reserving the syrup.

2. Allow peaches to cool. Peel, and discard pits. Peaches may be placed in a container, topped with syrup and refrigerated for up to 24 hours. Gently reheat in syrup before serving. (Syrup may be saved and frozen for future use.)

3. In the bowl of a food processor, combine raspberries, confectioners' sugar and juice of ½ lemon. Process until smooth. Pour through a fine sieve to remove seeds and transfer sauce to a small pitcher.

4. To assemble, place a scoop or two of ice cream on each of four chilled serving plates. Place two peach halves on each plate and drizzle with a small amount of raspberry sauce. Pass remaining sauce at the table.

Baked Alaska ☀

Stacie
Pierce,
Union
Square
Café,
New York

The French call baked Alaska *omelette norvégienne,* or Norwegian omelet. Either way it's a magical combination of ice cream and cake, slathered with meringue, and baked just long enough to set and toast the meringue without melting the ice cream. It's one of those desserts that looks far more impressive than it is to prepare. Union Square Café is the flagship restaurant for Danny Meyer in New York.

TIME: 2 hours   YIELD: 8 servings

4 ounces bittersweet chocolate
16 large eggs
½ cup granulated sugar
2 teaspoons vanilla extract
Salt
1 quart caramel or coffee ice
   cream, or another flavor

4 tablespoons sliced almonds,
   toasted
2 tablespoons cream of tartar
2 cups plus 4 tablespoons
   superfine sugar

1. Preheat oven to 350 degrees, and line a 10-by-15-inch baking sheet with sides with parchment paper. Melt chocolate in a double boiler, and set aside.

2. Separate 4 eggs into two bowls of an electric mixer. To the yolks add ¼ cup granulated sugar and 1 teaspoon vanilla. Using an electric mixer, beat until the mixture is thick and pale yellow. Set aside. Using the mixer, whisk the egg whites and a pinch of salt until they hold soft peaks. Slowly add the remaining ¼ cup granulated sugar until the whites are stiff and shiny.

3. Using a rubber spatula, fold the melted chocolate into the yolk mixture; then, fold the chocolate mixture into the meringue. Do not overmix. Spread the batter in an even layer, about ½ inch thick, on the baking sheet. Bake until the cake is spongy and moist, and slightly crisp on top, 10 to 15 minutes. Remove from oven and cool completely.

4. Using a 3-inch round cutter, cut eight circles of cake. Position circles on a large baking sheet lined with parchment. Place a large scoop of ice cream on each circle. Sprinkle with toasted nuts. Put baking sheet in freezer.

5. Separate the 12 remaining eggs, reserving yolks for another use and placing whites in a large bowl. Add a pinch of salt and cream of tartar. Using an electric mixer, whisk until frothy; then, increase speed to high and mix until soft peaks form. Slowly add superfine sugar, whisking until meringue is very stiff. Add remaining teaspoon of vanilla; whisk until blended.

6. Fit a pastry bag with a large closed-star tip, and fill the bag with meringue. Remove baking sheet from the freezer. Starting at the base of each cake, pipe rosettes in a circular pattern until cake and ice cream are completely covered. Freeze at least 30 minutes.

7. When ready to serve, preheat the broiler. Place baked alaskas under the broiler for 10 to 15 seconds, until meringue is caramelized on the edges. (This may also be done with a kitchen blowtorch.) Transfer to plates, and serve immediately.

Tropical Baked Alaska

Florence
Fabricant

This is a beautiful party dessert that brightens a winter night with a change of pace from the usual chocolate, vanilla and strawberry that often make up the heart of a baked Alaska. I first made it for dessert to serve at a small New Year's Eve dinner.

TIME: 5 hours, including freezing   YIELD: 8 servings

½ pint orange sorbet, softened
1 pint coconut sorbet, softened
½ pint mango sorbet, softened
Yellow cake layer (page 529)
4 large egg whites at room
 temperature

½ cup sugar
2 tablespoons sweetened shredded
 coconut
Tropical fruit sauce (page 543)

1. Line a round metal bowl that is 10 inches in diameter with plastic wrap. Spread the orange sorbet in the bottom. Spread half the coconut sorbet in a layer on top of the orange sorbet. Next spread on the mango sorbet and finish with the remaining coconut sorbet. Place the cake layer into the bowl on top of the sorbet. Cover with foil or plastic wrap and place in the freezer until hard, 3 to 4 hours or overnight.

2. Just before serving, preheat oven to 500 degrees. Cover a round baking sheet at least 12 inches in diameter with foil.

3. Whip the egg whites until softly peaked. Continue beating, gradually adding the sugar, until they are stiff.

4. Remove the bowl with the cake and sorbet from the freezer. Invert onto the baking sheet and lift off the bowl. Peel off the plastic wrap.

5. Thickly frost the dome of sorbet and cake with the egg whites. Be sure that the egg whites have lots of little peaks. Sprinkle with the coconut. Place in the oven and bake until the meringue is browning and the coconut is toasted, 6 to 8 minutes. Watch it carefully so it does not become too brown. While the cake is browning gently warm the sauce on top of the stove.

6. Serve the cake at once, with the warm sauce on the side.

Warm Frozen Lemon Soufflé

This recipe is for frozen lemon soufflés that are then caramelized on top by using a blowtorch. The caramelizing is not essential. Without it, serve the frozen soufflés with raspberry coulis (page 536). This recipe is from Palio, an Italian restaurant that was in the Equitable Building in New York and featured a mural by artist Sandro Chía in the bar.

Palio,
New York

TIME: 45 minutes, plus several hours' freezing   YIELD: 6 servings

2 envelopes unflavored gelatin
5 large eggs, separated
3½ tablespoons cornstarch
1 cup sugar, plus more for
  sprinkling
½ cup plus 1 tablespoon fresh
  lemon juice

½ cup plus 1 tablespoon heavy
  cream
Zest of ½ lemon, grated
6 or 12 strips of lemon zest for
  garnish
Six thin 4-inch circles of sponge
  cake (optional)

1. Cover a large cookie sheet with plastic wrap, and place six 4-inch flan rings on it. Dissolve gelatin in ½ cup cold water. Set aside.

2. Place egg yolks in electric mixer. Stir together the cornstarch and ¼ cup sugar, and then stir into yolks. Beat mixture on high speed until it turns light yellow.

3. In a 1-quart saucepan, bring lemon juice, heavy cream and grated lemon zest just to a boil. Slowly pour lemon mixture into yolk mixture, beating all the time, until lemon mixture is completely incorporated. Return mixture to saucepan. Bring to a boil, whisking constantly, and boil for 3 minutes to thicken. Remove from heat. Stir dissolved gelatin into yolk mixture.

4. Beat egg whites in mixer until they form soft peaks. In a saucepan, stir ¾ cup sugar with ½ cup water, and bring to 250 degrees on a candy thermometer, making sure sugar does not stick to sides of pan. Remove from heat, and with mixer running slowly pour hot sugar mixture into egg whites. Make sure sugar mixture does not get on beaters.

5. Fold meringue into yolk mixture. Spoon some into each flan ring, and with a spatula, make a dome shape. Cover each loosely with plastic wrap, and freeze for several hours or overnight.

6. Remove soufflés from freezer one or two at a time. Unmold by running a knife around edge of flan ring and pushing gently from bottom. Place each on a microwave-safe plate by itself or on a very thin circle of sponge cake, if desired. Sprinkle sugar on top of each soufflé to about ⅛-inch thickness, and with a handheld blowtorch, caramelize sugar. Place the plate in microwave oven on high for 35 to 45 seconds. If you can fit two in the oven at the same time, cook for 90 to 100 seconds. Decorate with strips of lemon zest, and serve.

Frozen Profiteroles au Chocolat

Who does not love this dessert? The cream puffs are simple to prepare, but must be done enough in advance to permit them to cool thoroughly before they are filled. Then they can be refrozen until serving time. You can use your imagination when it comes to the ice cream and sauce flavors to use. Craig Claiborne and Pierre Franey were the star recipe team for *The New York Times* for many years.

TIME: 30 minutes, plus optional freezing   YIELD: 12 servings

36 baked, cooled cream puffs (page 528)

3 pints vanilla or chocolate ice cream, or a mixture, slightly softened

1½ cups fudge sauce (page 537)

1. Split cream puffs in half horizontally. Place a small scoop of ice cream inside each and replace tops. If desired, filled puffs can be frozen until ready to serve, or served at once.

2. To serve, place three puffs on each chilled dessert plate. Spoon chocolate sauce over and around and serve.

Craig
Claiborne
and
Pierre
Franey

Vietnamese Coffee Tapioca Affogato with Condensed Milk Ice Cream ✳

Pichet
Ong

"Bubble tea" made with tapioca pearls has become wildly popular. This is a recipe for condensed milk ice cream served with the tapioca pearls and over which is poured coffee. Coffee sweetened with condensed milk is typically Vietnamese, so this is essentially a deconstructed Vietnamese coffee. A regular Italian *affogato* is made with espresso poured over vanilla gelato or ice cream. Pichet Ong is a New York pastry chef who specializes in Asian-accented desserts.

TIME: 1 hour, plus chilling and freezing   YIELD: 8 servings

2 cups milk
1 can (14 ounces) sweetened
    condensed milk
½ vanilla bean, split lengthwise,
    pulp and seeds scraped out (or
    ½ teaspoon vanilla extract)

5 large egg yolks
1 teaspoon salt
½ cup sugar
½ cup small pearl tapioca
2 cups brewed chicory coffee or
    espresso

1. For the ice cream, set a fine-mesh strainer over a bowl. In a heavy saucepan over medium heat, combine milk, condensed milk, vanilla pod and pulp. Bring to a simmer. In a bowl, whisk egg yolks, then drizzle a little hot milk mixture into yolks, whisking constantly. Reduce heat to low and pour yolk mixture back into pot. Cook, stirring constantly, until thickened enough to coat a wooden spoon. Do not allow to boil. Strain custard into bowl and stir in ½ teaspoon salt and vanilla extract, if using. Let cool, then refrigerate at least 3 hours. Churn in an ice cream maker according to manufacturer's instructions, then transfer to freezer.

2. For the tapioca, combine 6 cups water, the sugar and remaining salt in a saucepan and bring to a boil. Add tapioca and simmer, stirring, until pearls are tender yet not mushy, 20 to 25 minutes. Cool tapioca in liquid for at least 30 minutes, then use, or store in refrigerator up to one day.

3. To serve, strain tapioca pearls, discarding liquid. Divide tapioca among 8 tall glasses. Put 2 scoops of condensed milk ice cream in each glass. Pour about ¼ cup hot or warm coffee or espresso into each glass. Serve.

Frozen White Hot Chocolate

This slushy chocolate confection is a specialty of Serendipity 3, a café that opened in New York in 1959.

Serendipity 3,
New York

TIME: 15 minutes   YIELD: 1 or 2 servings

½ cup heavy cream
6 ounces white chocolate,
    preferably two ounces each of
    different brands, like Lindt,
    Valrhona, Callebaut, or
    Ghirardelli

¾ cup milk
6 fresh mint leaves, plus 1 or 2
    sprigs for garnish
Maraschino cherries, candy canes
    or dark chocolate sprinkles,
    optional

1. Whip cream and refrigerate. Chill 2 10- to 12-ounce goblets, or 1 20-ounce goblet.

2. Break up chocolate, place in a heavy saucepan over very low heat and stir until melted. Remove from heat and whisk in half the milk until well-blended.

3. Place remaining milk in a blender with chocolate mixture, mint leaves and 2 cups ice. Blend at high speed until smooth and frothy and ice is pulverized. Pour into goblets, top with whipped cream, mint sprigs and optional cherries, candy canes or sprinkles. Serve at once.

Ginger Semifreddo

Nigella
Lawson

A semifreddo, meaning half-frozen, is ice cream made simple. The custard is folded into whipped cream, then frozen. Because the whipped cream is already aerated, churning, which incorporates air, is not necessary. Sometimes a sweetened meringue is also folded in, for an even lighter semifreddo. Once frozen, the semifreddo can be unmolded and sliced like a terrine. Nigella Lawson is the author of *Feast* and a number of other cookbooks.

TIME: 20 minutes, plus freezing   YIELD: 6 servings

1 large egg
4 large egg yolks
Scant ½ cup honey, preferably
   acacia or orange blossom
2 tablespoons finely grated fresh
   ginger

1⅓ cups heavy cream
2 to 3 nuggets preserved ginger in
   syrup, finely diced

1. Line an 8½-by-4½-inch loaf pan with plastic wrap, leaving enough overhang to fold over top.

2. Bring an inch or two of water to a simmer in a medium saucepan. In a heatproof mixing bowl that will fit on saucepan, combine egg, egg yolks, honey and ginger. Place bowl over simmering water, and whisk mixture until pale and thick. Do not overheat or mixture will curdle. Remove from heat and set bowl into a larger bowl of ice cubes and water to chill the custard.

3. Using an electric mixer, or by hand, whip cream just until firm peaks form. Fold chilled egg mixture into cream, and pour into loaf pan. Fold plastic so it covers top of pan, and place in freezer until solid, at least 3 hours. Chill a serving platter that will hold loaf. Chill 6 dessert plates.

4. To serve, unmold semifreddo from pan and peel off plastic wrap. Place on chilled platter, and scatter about half the diced ginger over top. Working quickly because semifreddo will melt more quickly than ice cream, slice and serve, scattering each plate with more ginger cubes.

Semifreddo Amaretti with Fresh Peaches

This semifreddo was served at the Venice Economic Summit, June 15, 1987. It was created by Andrea da Merano, who owned Palio restaurant in New York. Note that the recipe is made with uncooked eggs, which can be a problem for some people. Use organic eggs.

Andrea
da Merano

TIME: 30 minutes, plus chilling   YIELD: 8 to 12 servings

6 large egg yolks
½ cup amaretto cookie crumbs
1 tablespoon amaretto liqueur
3 large egg whites
1 cup sifted confectioners' sugar

1½ cups heavy cream
2 pounds ripe peaches
1 tablespoon lemon juice
Lightly crushed amaretto cookies
    for garnish

1. In the bowl of an electric mixer, beat the egg yolks until they thicken. Add the amaretto cookie crumbs and continue beating for 5 minutes, scraping the sides of the bowl periodically, until the mixture becomes quite light in color and very thick. Stir in the liqueur.

2. In a clean, dry bowl beat the egg whites until they foam. With the mixer at high speed, continue beating, gradually adding ½ cup of the confectioners' sugar. Beat until the egg whites hold firm peaks, about 3 minutes longer.

3. In a chilled bowl beat the cream until it holds soft peaks. Fold the egg whites and cream together. Fold one-quarter of the cream and egg white mixture into the egg yolk mixture until well blended. Gently fold in the remaining cream and egg white mixture.

4. Spread the mixture in 12 individual half-cup custard cups or 8 6-ounce custard cups or molds or a 6-cup loaf pan or mold, cover with plastic wrap and freeze for several hours or overnight. The semifreddo will keep at least a week in the freezer.

5. Shortly before serving, plunge the peaches into boiling water for 15 seconds, rinse under cold water, peel, pit and cut into thin slices. Toss with remaining ½ cup of confectioners' sugar and the lemon juice.

6. Dip the mold or molds briefly into hot water and turn out onto individual chilled plates or a serving platter. Surround with peach slices. Sprinkle the semifreddo with the crumbled amaretto cookies and serve.

Raspberry Semifreddo

Florence
Fabricant

This semifreddo is something of a blank slate. Change the eau de vie, the preserves and the fruit and you can offer an entirely new flavor profile: apricot, strawberry or, with white rum, pineapple. The egg whites beaten with hot sugar syrup become what is called an Italian meringue.

TIME: 30 minutes, plus chilling   YIELD: 10 to 12 servings

¾ cup sugar

3 large egg whites

¼ cup raspberry eau de vie

2 cups heavy cream

½ cup seedless raspberry
    preserves, chilled

½ pint fresh raspberries

1. Mix the sugar and ¼ cup water in a small saucepan, bring to a boil and cook until the mixture reaches 237 to 239 degrees, the soft-ball stage, on a candy thermometer. Remove from heat.

2. While the sugar is cooking, begin to beat the egg whites with an electric mixer, beating until soft peaks form.

3. Slowly drizzle the hot sugar syrup into the egg whites, beating constantly. Continue beating for at least five minutes, until the egg whites are stiff and glossy. Add three tablespoons of the raspberry eau de vie, a tablespoon at a time, beating for 30 seconds after each addition. Refrigerate the mixture.

4. Whip the cream until softly peaked. Add the remaining raspberry eau de vie and beat until the cream is stiff. Fold the whipped cream into the egg white mixture. Line a 6-cup mold or loaf pan with plastic wrap or waxed paper and spread the mixture into the pan. Cover with plastic wrap and freeze 6 hours or overnight.

5. Just before serving unmold the semifreddo and peel off the wrapping. Spread the top with the chilled raspberry preserves, then arrange a layer of fresh raspberries on the preserves.

CANDIES

Over the years *The New York Times* has featured a few recipes for candies, especially the flavored truffles included here. The basic chocolate ganache (page 531) can also be used to make truffles. Some, but not all, of these recipes require a candy thermometer.

Hazelnut-Almond Brittle

Florence
Fabricant

Marcella Hazan does not use a rolling pin to spread caramel for brittle. Her trick, which I have adopted, is to cut a raw baking potato in half and use the cut side as a spreader. It protects your hands and the hard surface does an excellent job, its moistness keeping the mixture from sticking.

TIME: 1 hour   YIELD: 3 dozen candies

⅓ cup shelled hazelnuts
⅓ cup sliced almonds
3 tablespoons canola oil or other
   vegetable oil

1 cup sugar, preferably superfine
¼ teaspoon freshly squeezed
   lemon juice

1. Preheat oven or toaster oven to 350 degrees.

2. Place the hazelnuts in a pan and toast for 15 minutes, or until lightly browned. Remove the pan from the oven, allow to cool for 10 minutes. While they are cooling, place the almonds in a pan and toast until lightly browned, about 6 minutes, shaking the pan once during toasting. Rub the cooled hazelnuts between your palms or in a clean kitchen towel to remove most of the skins. Chop the almonds and hazelnuts fairly fine and mix them together.

3. Use the oil to coat a baking sheet, a metal rolling pin or a wooden one wrapped tightly with heavy-duty foil and a pizza-cutter.

4. Heat ¼ cup of the sugar in a heavy saucepan, preferably nonstick, over medium-high heat, stirring constantly with a wooden spoon. The sugar will start to melt and turn gold. When it is completely liquid and light amber, add another tablespoon of the sugar and stir until it melts. Continue adding the sugar a tablespoon at a time, stirring constantly, until it is all liquid.

5. Remove the pan from the heat and quickly stir in the lemon juice and chopped nuts, stirring to coat the nuts with caramel. Quickly turn the mixture out onto the oiled baking sheet and roll it very thin with the rolling pin. Then use the pizza wheel to cut the brittle into 1-inch squares. Allow to cool to room temperature, about 30 minutes.

6. Break the brittle into squares and serve at room temperature or store in an airtight container. It will last up to 3 weeks, but less if it is not under lock and key.

Mexican Peanut-Sesame Brittle

This is an adaptation of a Mexican recipe by Zarela Martinez, a New York–based Mexican chef and cookbook author. Her recipe is made with *piloncillo*, a kind of hard brown sugar, instead of caramel. But by making the caramel with brown sugar instead of white, approximately the same flavor is achieved more simply.

Zarela
Martinez

TIME: 2 hours   YIELD: 40 pieces

½ cup raw peanuts
½ cup sesame seeds

3 tablespoons peanut oil
1½ cups light brown sugar

1. In a heavy skillet over medium heat, toast peanuts, turning them so they do not burn, for about 5 minutes. Immediately transfer to a food processor, or spread them out on a large baking sheet. If using a food processor, pulse gently until nuts are just broken up, about 1 minute. Otherwise, use a rolling pin to crush nuts on the baking sheet.

2. In the same skillet over medium heat, toast sesame seeds, stirring, for about 3 minutes. Mix with peanuts in food processor or baking sheet.

3. Use the oil to coat another baking sheet. Also coat a metal rolling pin or a wooden one wrapped tightly with heavy-duty foil and a pizza-cutter with oil.

4. Mix sugar with 1½ cups water in a heavy saucepan over medium-high heat, stirring constantly with a wooden spoon. When the mixture is completely liquid, continue cooking until it starts to boil. Keep cooking until the sugar just begins to foam up and reaches 280 degrees on a candy thermometer. This will take about 20 minutes.

5. Remove the pan from the heat and quickly stir in the nuts and sesame seeds, stirring to coat the nuts with caramel. Quickly turn the mixture out onto the oiled baking sheet and roll it very thin with the rolling pin. Allow it to cool and harden. Then use the pizza wheel to cut the brittle into 1-inch squares.

6. Store in an airtight container.

All-American Popcorn Balls

Kay
Rentschler

These popcorn balls amount to elaborate Rice Krispie treats. Instead of making them large, roll tiny ones, the size of golf balls, to delight grownups at the end of a dinner party. Kay Rentschler has contributed numerous recipes to *The New York Times*.

TIME: 20 minutes   YIELD: About 14 popcorn balls

1 cup large-flake sweetened
   coconut
1 cup pecan halves
Vegetable oil spray
1 cup sugar
⅓ cup light corn syrup
½ teaspoon salt
4 tablespoons unsalted butter

1 3-ounce bag plain microwave
   popcorn or ⅓ cup regular
   popcorn kernels (enough to
   yield 11½ cups popped corn)
1 teaspoon vanilla extract
1 cup Rice Krispies
½ cup mini-marshmallows

1. Heat oven to 300 degrees. Spread coconut evenly over a baking sheet and toast on lowest oven rack until deep golden brown, 15 to 20 minutes, stirring occasionally. While coconut toasts, halve pecans lengthwise, turn them onto a separate baking sheet and toast on upper rack until fragrant, about 10 minutes. Cool both, combine and set aside.

2. Spray a large mixing bowl or deep stock pot with vegetable spray and set aside. Combine sugar, corn syrup, ⅓ cup water, salt and butter in a small saucepan and bring to a simmer over medium-high heat, stirring frequently. When butter melts and liquid is simmering, stop stirring, place candy thermometer in a pot and cook until syrup registers 230 degrees. At this point, begin popping corn.

4. Cook syrup until temperature is just under 245 degrees. Remove the saucepan from heat, and stir in vanilla. Turn warm popped corn into the prepared bowl or pot and drizzle half the sugar syrup over, stirring vigorously with a rubber spatula to coat kernels evenly. Add remaining syrup, coconut, pecans and Rice Krispies and stir to combine; add marshmallows and continue stirring from bottom of pot until dry ingredients are evenly coated and no syrup remains on bottom.

5. Rinse hands with cold water, and while mixture is still hot, begin forming popcorn balls, 3 to 3½ inches in diameter, placing finished balls on a sheet lined with parchment or waxed paper. Use a light touch, but a little pressure to help balls become round and compact. Popcorn balls are best eaten within 8 hours but will keep nicely in covered containers for three days.

Rum Balls

Windows
on the
World,
New York

These rum balls are American classics, popular as postprandial nibbles or to give at Christmas. The recipe is from Windows on the World, the restaurant on the top of the World Trade Center that was destroyed on September 11.

TIME: 1 hour, plus chilling   YIELD: About 80 rum balls

½ cup dark rum

3 ounces raisins

2 pounds cookie and cake scraps (like meringues, florentines, butter cookies, ladyfingers, shortbreads and brownies, but nothing with butter cream or whipped cream, which spoils)

1 cup chopped pecans or walnuts

6 ounces bittersweet chocolate, melted

1 cup dark chocolate ganache (page 531)

⅓ cup unsweetened cocoa

1. Soak the raisins in the rum for two or three hours or overnight.

2. In a food processor, grind the cookies until they are like fine bread crumbs. Depending on the size of the food processor, this may have to be done in batches. Add water, one tablespoon at a time, to each batch to make a mass that sticks together like firm cookie dough. (How much water, ¼ cup to 1 cup, will depend on the moisture of the cookies.)

3. Stir in chopped nuts and melted chocolate, and mix well by hand. Add rum and raisins, and mix until thoroughly blended. The mixture can be a little sticky; it will harden in the refrigerator. Flatten the mixture on a baking sheet, making it about ½ inch thick, and refrigerate about one hour until mixture hardens.

4. Mix ganache with the firmed dough by hand. Shape into small balls, about 1 tablespoon of dough for each. Roll in cocoa powder, and refrigerate or freeze, well wrapped, for as long as a month. If frozen, defrost to serve. Serve chilled. Recoat with cocoa if needed.

Creole Pralines

Unlike the French mixture of caramel and almonds or hazelnuts, cooked and cooled to a brittle, then crumbled or ground to use in dessert-making, in Louisiana, Creole-style pralines are made with pecans, butter and brown sugar, cooked to emerge at a softer consistency, and are a traditional candy in their own right. This is one of Craig Claiborne's recipes. He was the food editor of *The New York Times,* and was born in Sunshine, Mississippi.

Craig
Claiborne

TIME: 30 minutes, plus cooling   YIELD: About 3 dozen

2 cups granulated sugar
1 cup dark brown sugar
¼ pound unsalted butter

1 cup milk
2 tablespoons dark corn syrup
4 cups pecan halves

1. Spread several sheets of waxed paper over layers of newspaper.

2. Combine all ingredients except pecans in a heavy 3-quart saucepan. Cook 20 minutes, stirring constantly, after the mixture comes to a boil. Add pecans and continue cooking until the mixture reaches 236 degrees on a candy thermometer, the soft-ball stage.

3. Stir mixture well. Drop it by tablespoons onto the sheets of waxed paper. Allow to cool. When cool, peel the candies off the paper and stack in airtight containers, separated by sheets of waxed paper or parchment.

White Chocolate Hazelnut-Apricot Clusters

Florence
Fabricant

The variations on this candy recipe are endless: raisins and peanuts with milk chocolate, dried cranberries and walnuts with dark chocolate, and candied citrus peel with cashews in white chocolate are a few that come to mind. And for a touch of innovation, use salted nuts instead of unsalted.

TIME: 45 minutes   YIELD: 36 clusters

8 ounces good quality white
   chocolate, finely chopped
1 cup toasted skinned hazelnuts,
   roughly chopped and chilled

1 cup roughly chopped dried
   apricots, at room temperature

1. Place the chocolate in the top of a double boiler over hot water, stirring often. When it has melted, remove the double boiler from the heat. Place the top pan with the chocolate in a bowl of cool water and stir gently, taking care not to allow any droplets of water to mix with the chocolate, until the temperature of the chocolate is about 92 degrees. Use an instant-read thermometer or place a dab of chocolate on your lower lip: it should feel neither hot nor cold. When it reaches this temperature place the pot of chocolate back over the lower pot of hot water but not on the stove.

2. Line a baking sheet with waxed paper. Mix the hazelnuts and apricots together in a bowl, then stir them into the chocolate.

3. Using a spoon, form 1-inch-diameter clusters and place them on the baking sheet. Place the baking sheet in the refrigerator for 15 minutes.

4. Place the clusters in paper candy cups and serve at room temperature or place them in an airtight container wrapped with foil in the refrigerator.

506   ·   The New York Times Dessert Cookbook

Chocolate-Port Wine Truffles

These truffles are the traditional kind, rolled in cocoa, a dusting that gives them the "freshly dug" look of black truffles, the fungi that inspired the candy.

Florence
Fabricant

TIME: 4 hours, including chilling   YIELD: About 40 small truffles

6 ounces semisweet or bittersweet chocolate in small pieces
½ cup heavy cream

3 tablespoons ruby port
½ cup unsweetened Dutch-process cocoa

1. Combine the chocolate and the cream in a heavy saucepan and place over low heat, stirring occasionally, until the chocolate has melted.

2. Remove from the heat and transfer to a bowl. Stir in the port. Refrigerate until the mixture is firm, 2 hours or longer.

3. Spread a sheet of waxed paper on a baking sheet. With a spoon or spoons, scoop mounds about ½ inch to an inch in diameter and place them on the paper. Refrigerate until firm, 2 hours or overnight.

4. Spread the cocoa powder onto a chilled plate.

5. Remove the truffles from the refrigerator and roll them in the cocoa. Return them to the pan lined with waxed paper and refrigerate again until firm. The truffles can be frozen for up to a week.

Meyer Lemon Truffles ✳

Bill
Yosses

Meyer lemon, which is sweeter than regular lemon, seasons these truffles. Try making them with other citrus, including orange and kumquat. Bill Yosses was the executive chef for the Citarella stores and Joseph's restaurant in New York.

TIME: About 3 hours   YIELD: About 95 truffles

4 Meyer lemons
3 tablespoons sugar
1 pound plus 12 ounces
   bittersweet chocolate, finely
   chopped

1¾ cups heavy cream
7 tablespoons unsalted butter,
   softened, cut into pieces
Cocoa for dusting (optional)

1. Remove zest from lemons. Juice lemons and strain juice into a small saucepan. Add sugar. Bring to a simmer and cook, stirring, until sugar dissolves. Allow to cool by placing pot in an ice water bath or refrigerating it.

2. Place 12 ounces chocolate in a heatproof bowl. In a saucepan, bring cream to a simmer. Pour cream over chocolate and let rest 3 minutes. Starting in center, whisk together chocolate and cream. Continue to whisk until mixture turns dark and shiny and has the consistency of mayonnaise. Cool until slightly warm.

3. Whisk butter into chocolate mixture until melted, then stir in lemon mixture. Refrigerate until mixture is as thick as icing, 30 minutes to an hour.

4. Transfer mixture to a pastry bag with a large plain tip or to a resealable plastic bag with a corner cut off. Line a baking sheet with parchment or waxed paper and squeeze 1¼-inch chocolate drops (a bit larger than a Hershey's Kiss) onto paper. Refrigerate drops until firm, about 1 hour.

5. Using your hands, roll chocolate drops into balls, then return them to baking sheet and refrigerate for another 15 minutes, until their surfaces are matte.

6. Meanwhile, to make the coating, set aside one-quarter of the remaining chocolate. Place the rest of the chopped chocolate in a microwave-proof bowl. Microwave on high for 3 minutes, stopping every 15 seconds to stir. Chocolate should feel very warm to the touch (115 to 120

degrees). Add reserved chopped chocolate to bowl; stir until mixture is melted and smooth and chocolate has cooled to 82 degrees. Return chocolate to the microwave on high for another 5 seconds. Stir again.

7. Line another baking sheet with waxed or parchment paper. Use a fork to lower chocolate balls one by one into chocolate coating. Turn each one to coat, drain off excess, and place balls on parchment paper. If the melted chocolate cools too much and thickens, return it to the microwave for 3 to 5 seconds, and stir well.

8. Let truffles rest for at least 20 minutes. If desired, roll truffles in cocoa powder before serving. Store in airtight containers in the refrigerator for up to 2 weeks. Bring to room temperature before removing lid.

THE INTENSE PLEASURES OF DARK CHOCOLATE
By Florence Fabricant

First, the aroma beckons. The intense scent drawing you in is unmistakably that of rich chocolate, but you detect exotic hints of clove, coffee, orange peel, even cedar. The bar is dark and shiny, scored into sections. It breaks cleanly, with a definite snap.

At this point, you don't even need to taste it to know you're dealing with extremely fine chocolate. Today fine chocolate like Valrhona from France, Callebaut from Belgium, Lindt from Switzerland and El Rey from Venezuela are increasingly easy to find. And they have been joined by American chocolates like Guittard and Scharffen Berger, which are just as powerful, and often at prices just as high.

What makes all these chocolates superb? It starts with the selection of the cacao beans and how they are fermented, roasted and blended. The finesse with which the chocolate is processed and how much sugar or other ingredients are added all affect the aroma, flavor and texture.

Like winemakers, chocolate-makers start by homing in on the best beans from particular regions and microclimates. Most of the world's chocolate is made from forestaro beans, the equivalent of the cheaper robusta beans that dominate the coffee business. Forestaro is the most disease-resistant, highest-yielding cacao, from trees grown in Brazil and West Africa, but it is certainly not the most flavorful and tends to have a rough, astringent taste.

Trinitario, from Central America, has a more pronounced flavor and is usually blended with forestaro to give it character. Criollo, grown mostly in Venezuela and Central America but also in Indonesia, is the richest and most fragrant, but it is also the most fragile, rarest and costliest. Most chocolate is a blend, and the more trinitario and criollo, the better the flavor.

Once the bumpy football-size cacao pods are harvested, the beans are taken out and left to ferment for a few days in the tropical heat. Fermentation turns them from violet to brown and encourages the characteristic aromas and flavors of chocolate to develop. Next, the beans are dried, then roasted.

The finest European and European-style chocolates are made from beans that have been roasted longer and at lower temperatures than most American manufacturers use, so the chocolate delivers more nuanced flavors. The quicker, higher-heat roasting generally employed in the United States tends to result in more bitterness, which is masked only by adding more sugar and ingredients like vanilla.

After roasting, the beans are cracked open and their husks winnowed away, leaving the essence of chocolate, called the nibs. These are ground, heated and turned into chocolate liquor, a thick, nonalcoholic substance that is about half cocoa butter, which is melted and separated out. The rest of the liquor is finely ground and can be turned into cocoa powder or mixed with cocoa butter, sugar and other ingredients.

At this point, the chocolate goes through a final refining, or pulverizing, process called conching (the ch is pronounced as in *poncho*). The longer the chocolate is conched, the more velvety it will feel. The highest-quality chocolate may be conched for up to three days.

The Food and Drug Administration requires that all semisweet and bittersweet chocolate contain a minimum of 35 percent chocolate, a decidedly low standard. Sweet chocolate must have 15 percent, and milk chocolate only 10 percent. The manufacturers of low-grade chocolate stick to the minimum and bulk up the product with sugar, emulsifiers, vegetable oil and other fats and fillers. (White chocolate is technically not considered chocolate because it contains no chocolate liquor. The cheapest white chocolate may even be made without any cocoa butter.)

The finest semisweet and bittersweet chocolates post percentages ranging from 62 to 72 percent. And there is little or no room for junk in a bar that's 70 percent chocolate—the rest is basically sugar. Top-quality milk chocolate may have only 54 percent chocolate solids.

Once you unwrap chocolate, you can gauge it by eye: the best is flawlessly smooth, with a lustrous sheen. Dull or grayish spots or streaks may be a sign of inferior quality, poor handling or bad storage conditions.

You also judge chocolate by the way it breaks at room temperature. It should not crumble or splinter, but should have what is called "snap," a clean brittleness. The milk solids added to milk chocolate soften the texture and prevent it from having the same snap as dark chocolate.

Because chocolate melts at close to body temperature, it should start to melt in your mouth, with a smooth creaminess and nothing waxy, gritty, gummy or greasy about it.

With great chocolate, even the unsweetened type can provide sensory pleasure. Unsweetened supermarket baking chocolate is inedible. But a few small bites of 99 percent chocolate from a fine maker, for example, with a coffee or Cognac can be thoroughly satisfying, extreme chocolate for those who dare.

Chocolate-Pecan Truffles

Florence
Fabricant

Pecans and bourbon give these truffles a dash of American flavor. Other spirits, including dark rum, brandy and Scotch can be substituted for bourbon. Take care when grinding these relatively soft, high-fat nuts; they can turn into nut butter in a flash. If you have time, place the chopped toasted nuts in the freezer for an hour before grinding them. It will help prevent them from becoming a puree.

TIME: 4 hours, including chilling   YIELD: About 50 truffles

1½ cups finely ground pecans
10 ounces semisweet or
   bittersweet chocolate
¼ pound (1 stick) unsalted butter,
   softened

4 tablespoons bourbon
⅔ cup unsweetened Dutch-
   process cocoa

1. Preheat a broiler. Spread the nuts on a foil-lined baking sheet and place under the broiler for about a minute to toast them lightly and evenly. Do not allow them to burn. Set them aside.

2. Shave the chocolate into a heatproof mixing bowl and place the bowl over a pan of simmering water until the chocolate is nearly all melted. Remove the bowl and stir the chocolate until smooth. Stir in the nuts and allow to cool to room temperature.

3. Stir in the butter and the bourbon. Refrigerate the mixture until it is firm.

4. When firm, remove from the refrigerator and allow to soften for about 15 minutes. Place the cocoa in a shallow dish. Using a spoon, scoop half-tablespoons of the chocolate mixture, form somewhat uneven balls about an inch in diameter and roll them quickly into the cocoa. Refrigerate until ready to serve. The balls can also be frozen without the cocoa for later use, and dusted with cocoa just before serving.

White Chocolate Champagne Truffles

It is critical to use the finest white chocolate you can find. Cheap ones are too waxy. Sweet wines like Muscat de Beaumes-de-Venise can replace the Champagne. Apple cider is another possibility.

Florence
Fabricant

TIME: 6 hours, including chilling   YIELD: About 40 coated truffles

6 ounces semisweet or bittersweet
   chocolate in small pieces
½ cup heavy cream
3 tablespoons demi-sec
   Champagne

½ pound good quality white
   chocolate for coating

1. Combine the chocolate and the cream in a heavy saucepan and place over low heat, stirring occasionally, until the chocolate has melted.

2. Remove from the heat and transfer to a bowl. Stir in the Champagne. Refrigerate until the mixture is firm, 2 hours or longer.

3. Spread a sheet of waxed paper on a baking sheet. With a spoon or spoons, scoop mounds about ½ inch to an inch in diameter and place them on the paper. Refrigerate until firm, 2 hours or overnight.

4. Break the white chocolate in pieces and melt in the top of a double boiler or in a microwave oven. Remove the melted chocolate from the heat or the oven, and allow it to cool to tepid, 90 to 100 degrees, stirring it from time to time.

5. Drop the truffles one at a time into the melted chocolate, then quickly lift them out with a fork or a professional dipping loop, allowing excess chocolate to drip off.

6. Arrange on a sheet of waxed paper on a baking sheet and refrigerate at least 2 hours, until firm and cold.

Jasmine Tea Truffles

Bill
Yosses

Tea and chocolate, as in these truffles, have become a popular combination. Bill Yosses was the pastry chef at Bouley and Bouley Bakery in New York.

TIME: About 3 hours, including chilling   YIELD: About 95 truffles

⅔ cup jasmine tea leaves
2 cups heavy cream,
   approximately
1 pound plus 12 ounces
   bittersweet chocolate, finely
   chopped

7 tablespoons unsalted butter,
   softened, cut into pieces
Unsweetened cocoa for dusting,
   optional

1. Place tea leaves in a bowl. Bring cream to a boil and pour over tea. Stir, and steep 5 minutes. Pour through a mesh strainer into a glass measuring cup, pressing to extract liquid. Pour off or add cream to make 1¾ cups.

2. Pour into a clean saucepan, and bring to a simmer. Place 12 ounces chocolate in a heatproof bowl. In a saucepan, bring tea-scented cream to a simmer. Pour cream over chocolate and let rest 3 minutes. Starting in center, whisk together chocolate and cream. Continue to whisk until mixture turns dark and shiny and has the consistency of mayonnaise. Cool until slightly warm.

3. Whisk butter into chocolate mixture until melted. Refrigerate until mixture is as thick as icing, 30 minutes to an hour.

4. Transfer mixture to a pastry bag with a large plain tip or to a resealable plastic bag with a corner cut off. Line a baking sheet with parchment or waxed paper and squeeze 1¼-inch chocolate drops (a bit larger than a Hershey's Kiss) onto paper. Refrigerate drops until firm, about 1 hour.

5. Using your hands, roll chocolate drops into balls, then return them to baking sheet and refrigerate for another 15 minutes, until their surfaces are matte.

6. Meanwhile, to make the coating, set aside one-quarter of the remaining chocolate. Place the rest of the chopped chocolate in a microwave-proof bowl. Microwave on high for 3 minutes, stopping every 15 seconds to

stir. Chocolate should feel very warm to the touch (115 to 120 degrees). Add reserved chopped chocolate to bowl; stir until mixture is melted and smooth and chocolate has cooled to 82 degrees. Return chocolate to the microwave on high for another 5 seconds. Stir again.

7. Line another baking sheet with waxed or parchment paper. Use a fork to lower chocolate balls one by one into chocolate coating. Turn each one to coat, drain off excess, and place balls on parchment paper. If the melted chocolate cools too much and thickens, return it to the microwave for 3 to 5 seconds, and stir well.

8. Let truffles rest for at least 20 minutes. If desired, roll truffles in cocoa powder before serving. Store in airtight containers in the refrigerator for up to 2 weeks. Bring to room temperature before removing lid.

Raspberry-Rose Truffles

Bill
Yosses

For these truffles the ganache is scented with rose syrup, which is available online and sold in New York at Kalustyan's (see Sources, page 551). Bill Yosses trained in France before returning to New York to work at a number of restaurants, from Perigord Park to Bouley.

TIME: About 3 hours, including chilling   YIELD: About 95 truffles

1½ cups fresh raspberries
1 tablespoon sugar
¼ cup rose syrup (see note)
1 pound plus 12 ounces
    bittersweet chocolate, finely
    chopped

1¾ cups heavy cream
7 tablespoons unsalted butter,
    softened, cut into pieces
Unsweetened cocoa for dusting,
    optional

1. In a food processor or blender, puree raspberries with sugar. Push mixture through a fine-mesh sieve; discard solids. Stir rose syrup into raspberry puree and set aside.

2. Place 12 ounces chocolate in a heatproof bowl. In a saucepan, bring cream to a simmer. Pour cream over chocolate and let rest 3 minutes. Starting in center, whisk together chocolate and cream. Continue to whisk until mixture turns dark and shiny and has the consistency of mayonnaise. Cool until slightly warm.

3. Whisk butter into chocolate mixture until melted, then stir in raspberry mixture. Refrigerate until mixture is as thick as icing, 30 minutes to an hour.

4. Transfer mixture to a pastry bag with a large plain tip or to a resealable plastic bag with a corner cut off. Line a baking sheet with parchment or waxed paper and squeeze 1¼-inch chocolate drops (a bit larger than a Hershey's Kiss) onto paper. Refrigerate drops until firm, about 1 hour.

5. Using your hands, roll chocolate drops into balls, then return them to baking sheet and refrigerate for another 15 minutes, until their surfaces are matte.

6. Meanwhile, to make the coating, set aside one-quarter of the remaining chocolate. Place the rest of the chopped chocolate in a microwave-proof bowl. Microwave on high for 3 minutes, stopping every 15 seconds

to stir. Chocolate should feel very warm to the touch (115 to 120 degrees). Add reserved chopped chocolate to bowl; stir until mixture is melted and smooth and chocolate has cooled to 82 degrees. Return chocolate to the microwave on high for another 5 seconds. Stir again.

7. Line another baking sheet with waxed or parchment paper. Use a fork to lower chocolate balls one by one into chocolate coating. Turn each one to coat, drain off excess, and place balls on parchment paper. If the melted chocolate cools too much and thickens, return it to the microwave for 3 to 5 seconds, and stir well.

8. Let truffles rest for at least 20 minutes. If desired, roll truffles in cocoa powder before serving. Store in airtight containers in the refrigerator for up to 2 weeks. Bring to room temperature before removing lid.

BASICS

The essential building blocks of the dessert repertory include the recipes that, with time and repetition, can become second nature to the cook, accomplished without even opening a cookbook. Like mixing a vinaigrette that will season a salad at dinner, knowing how to stir a custard sauce to embellish a bowl of seasonal fruit or having a pie crust recipe you like literally at the tips of your fingers can simplify dessert-making and menu-planning. The recipes I have selected for this chapter are necessary components in others: a cake layer for a trifle, quick puff pastry to bake with a fruit topping instead of using the commercial frozen kind, sauces for ice creams, candied fruit peel and cream puff batter are just a few of them.

Large Pie or Tart Shell ✳

TIME: 35 minutes   YIELD: Two 12-inch pie or tart shells

Roland
Mesnier,
former
White House
pastry chef

3½ cups cake flour

4 tablespoons sugar

½ teaspoon salt

1½ cups shortening

1. Place all ingredients in a mixing bowl. Using a paddle attachment of an electric mixer, mix until well blended, about 3 minutes. Divide dough in two. Shape each into a ball.

2. To make a pre-baked pastry shell, roll out on floured surface into a round to fit a 12-inch glass pie plate. Trim crust at edge of plate. Prick crust with fork on bottom and sides. Line pastry with parchment or foil and weight with pie weights or dry beans.

3. Bake 15 minutes. Remove liner and weights or beans. Return crust to the oven. Bake another 10 minutes, until crust is brown. Remove it from the oven and fill at once or cool before filling.

Butter Pastry ✳

TIME: 15 minutes, plus chilling   YIELD: Pastry for a double-crust 9-inch pie

Deborah
Tyler,
"The Pie
Lady," Nyack,
New York

8 ounces unsalted butter
   (2 sticks), softened

½ teaspoon salt

3 cups all-purpose flour

1. Combine butter, salt and flour in a bowl. Cut flour into butter, rubbing mixture through fingers until the texture of cornmeal. Lightly stir in 3 to 4 tablespoons ice water, turning mixture so it comes together in a ball. Wrap in plastic.

2. Refrigerate dough for 15 minutes before using.

Rich Butter Pastry

TIME: 45 minutes, plus chilling   YIELD: Pastry for two 9-inch pies or tarts,
or one double-crust 9-inch pie

2½ cups all-purpose flour, plus
   flour for rolling
1 teaspoon salt
6 ounces (1½ sticks) cold butter,
   preferably high-fat European-
   style, diced

2 large egg yolks

Florence
Fabricant

1. Place flour and salt in a food processor and whirl briefly to mix. Open lid, scatter butter in, then pulse until mixture is crumbly.

2. Beat egg yolks with ¼ cup ice water. Open lid, sprinkle egg yolk mixture over flour, then pulse for 20 to 30 seconds, until dough begins to clump together. Add a little more water if needed. Remove dough, divide in two and form into flat disks. Wrap in plastic and chill 30 minutes.

3. To pre-bake pastry shells, preheat oven to 400 degrees. Roll dough out on a floured surface, fit into one or two 9-inch pie or tart pans, prick lightly, line with foil and weight with pastry weights. Bake about 10 minutes, until dry-looking. Remove foil and weights and bake until golden. Alternatively, pastry can be used to line a 9-inch pie pan, then filling added and the remaining dough can be rolled out for the top crust before baking.

Flaky Pastry

TIME: 20 minutes, plus chilling   YIELD: One 9-inch single crust

Charlie
Palmer,
Aureole,
New York

1¼ cups all-purpose flour
1½ teaspoons sugar
½ teaspoon salt, or to taste

½ cup very cold vegetable
shortening, cut into small
pieces

1. Sift flour, sugar and salt into a medium mixing bowl. Add shortening and, using a fork, toss to coat well. Using a pastry blender or two knives, cut shortening into flour mixture until mixture resembles a rather lumpy, coarse meal.

2. Add about 3 tablespoons ice water, a tablespoon at a time, around edge of bowl. Using a fork, mix dough together as water is added; all the water may not be needed. The dough will begin to form solid lumps. When there are more lumps than there is loose flour, and the dough holds together when pressed against the side of the bowl, with floured hands quickly form the dough into a ball. Flatten ball into a large disk and cover with plastic wrap. Refrigerate for at least 30 minutes or up to 3 days.

Sweet Pastry

TIME: 10 minutes, plus chilling   YIELD: Pastry for 8- or 9-inch tart or six 4-inch tartlets

Payard
Pâtisserie
and Bistro,
New York

9 tablespoons (1 stick plus
  1 tablespoon) unsalted butter,
  softened
1 cup all-purpose flour, plus flour
  for rolling

½ cup sifted confectioners' sugar
½ teaspoon salt
1 large egg, lightly beaten

1. Place butter, flour, sugar and salt in the bowl of a food processor, and process until the ingredients are well blended. Scrape down the sides of the bowl, and add egg. Pulse just until the egg is completely incorporated and you have a very soft, creamy dough.

2. Remove the dough, flatten it into a disk, wrap it in plastic and freeze for 1 hour.

3. To pre-bake pastry shell, preheat oven to 400 degrees. Roll out dough on a lightly floured surface and fit into an 8- or 9-inch pie or tart pan. Prick bottom, line with foil and pastry weights and bake about 10 minutes, until pastry looks dry. Remove foil and weights and continue baking until golden, about 15 minutes more.

Cream Cheese Pastry

TIME: 15 minutes, plus chilling   YIELD: Pastry for two 9-inch tarts or 8 tartlets

1 cup plus 1 tablespoon cake flour
¾ cup plus 2 tablespoons all-
    purpose flour
1 teaspoon granulated sugar
¼ teaspoon salt

8 ounces (2 sticks) cold unsalted
    butter, cut into small pieces
8 ounces cold cream cheese, cut
    into small pieces

Aqua at
Bellagio,
Las Vegas
Nevada

1. In a food processor, combine flours, sugar and salt and pulse a few times. Add butter and cream cheese. Process until mixture just comes together.

2. Turn dough onto a piece of plastic wrap, press it into a disk, wrap it well and refrigerate until chilled, at least 2 hours or overnight.

Pie Crust with Lard ✳

TIME: 1 hour   YIELD: Two 9-inch single crusts or pastry
for a double-crust pie

Matt Lee
and
Ted Lee,
food writers

11 tablespoons cold lard
2 tablespoons unsalted butter,
    softened, plus more for pan
2½ cups all-purpose flour, plus
    more for work surface

½ teaspoon salt
3 tablespoons sour cream
Milk, optional

1. In a large bowl, work lard and butter into flour and salt with a fork or pastry blender until evenly distributed. Roll out on a floured surface, then scrape into a ball and roll out again. Return dough to bowl, and place in freezer to chill for 10 minutes.

2. Blend sour cream into dough to moisten, then roll out once more. If dough needs more moisture to hold it together, add a few tablespoons of milk. Work dough into a ball, cover with plastic wrap and refrigerate for 20 minutes.

3. To pre-bake crust, preheat oven to 375 degrees. Divide the dough in two, then roll out again. Lightly butter a pie pan. Fit one crust into pan. Bake for 10 minutes. Repeat with the rest of the dough or use it to make a top for a double-crust pie. For later use, wrap it in plastic wrap and refrigerate for up to three days or freeze it.

Hazelnut Pastry

TIME: 15 minutes, without baking   YIELD: Pastry for a one-crust 10-inch tart

⅞ cups all-purpose flour, plus
   flour for dusting
⅓ cup finely ground hazelnuts
7 tablespoons cold unsalted butter

2 tablespoons sugar
¼ teaspoon salt
½ teaspoon vanilla extract

Florence
Fabricant

1. Combine flour and hazelnuts in bowl of an electric mixer. Cut butter in one-inch pieces and add. Mix at low speed just until ingredients are evenly blended and crumbly.

2. Mix sugar, salt and vanilla with ¼ cup cold water. Add liquid to mixer bowl, mixing at low speed just until ingredients come together to make a soft dough.

3. Gather dough in a ball and flatten slightly on lightly floured surface to make a 6-inch disc. Wrap in plastic and refrigerate until ready to use.

Graham Cracker Crust ✳

TIME: 15 minutes   YIELD: One 9-inch crust

1½ cups graham cracker crumbs
1¼ cups sugar

5⅓ tablespoons unsalted butter,
   melted

Florence
Fabricant

1. Preheat oven to 350 degrees. In a medium bowl, mix graham cracker crumbs, sugar and butter until combined. Press onto bottom and 1 inch up sides of a 9-inch springform or 9-inch pie pan.

2. Bake until set, 6 to 8 minutes. Remove from oven, and cool.

Quick Puff Pastry

Craig
Claiborne,
food editor,
*The New York
Times*

This shortcut puff pastry will not produce as many parchment-thin layers as a traditional method, but it is an excellent substitute. And you know exactly what the ingredients are, including high-quality butter. The dough can be frozen.

TIME: 1 hour   YIELD: 1 pound pastry

½ pound (2 sticks) cold unsalted butter, preferably European-style high-fat, diced

1¾ cups all-purpose flour, plus flour for dusting

½ teaspoon salt

¼ teaspoon cream of tartar

1. Place diced butter on a dish and freeze for 20 minutes. Refrigerate rolling pin.

2. Place frozen butter, flour, salt and cream of tartar in food processor. Sprinkle in 6 to 8 tablespoons ice water and pulse briefly and rapidly just until dough holds together. The butter will not be completely incorporated and bits of it should show. (The dough can be mixed by hand. First combine the flour, salt and cream of tartar in a mound on a cold, flat work surface. Make a well in the center, add the butter, sprinkle on the water and bring the flour up and around the butter to enclose it. Then start working the flour and butter together, lightly kneading, until the dough can be gathered in a ball.)

3. Shape the ball of dough into a flattened disk about 5 inches in diameter. Wrap in plastic and refrigerate 15 minutes.

4. Sprinkle a flat work surface, preferably a cold one, with flour. Place dough on flour and roll into a rectangle about 12 by 18 inches. Turn pastry over once or twice, and keep surface dusted with flour as you roll. Fold one-third of the short side of the rectangle over the center, brush off excess flour and fold the other third over, like folding a business letter. Brush off excess flour.

5. Reroll the dough and repeat the previous step. Lightly flour the dough and place on a lightly floured baking sheet. Cover with a clean cloth and refrigerate 15 to 20 minutes before using.

Cream Puffs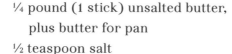

TIME: 1 hour, including baking   YIELD: 36 small puffs

Craig
Claiborne
and
Pierre
Franey,
food editor
and writer,
*The New York
Times*

¼ pound (1 stick) unsalted butter,
  plus butter for pan
½ teaspoon salt
½ teaspoon sugar

1 cup all-purpose flour, plus more
  for pan
4 large eggs at room temperature

1. Place 1 cup water in a heavy saucepan. Add butter, salt and sugar and bring to a boil. Add flour all at once, stirring vigorously and thoroughly with a wooden spoon until the mixture forms a ball that clears the sides of the pan.

2. Add the eggs, one at a time, beating vigorously and rapidly with each addition. Alternatively, the flour mixture can be placed in a food processor. With the machine running, add the eggs through the feed tube one at a time, waiting until each is incorporated before adding the next.

3. Preheat oven to 425 degrees. Lightly butter and flour a baking sheet.

4. Using a #6 pastry tube or two teaspoons dipped in cold water, pipe or form ping-pong ball-size mounds of the paste all over the baking sheet. A wet pastry brush can be used to smooth the pastry rounds.

5. Place in oven and bake 30 minutes, until the puffs are golden brown and firm. Remove from the oven and allow to cool completely. The puffs are ready to fill.

Yellow Cake Layer

TIME: 45 minutes, plus cooling   YIELD: 1 layer

4 ounces (1 stick) unsalted butter,
  plus more for cake pan
1½ cups sifted cake flour plus
  more for cake pan
½ teaspoon baking powder

Pinch of salt
1 cup sugar
2 large eggs
¾ cup milk
1 teaspoon vanilla extract

Florence
Fabricant

1. Preheat oven to 350 degrees. Butter and flour a 9-inch round cake pan.

2. Sift the flour, baking powder and salt together and set aside.

3. Beat the remaining butter and the sugar together until creamy. Beat in the eggs one at a time.

4. Mix the milk and vanilla together and add it alternately in thirds with the flour mixture, mixing just enough to blend the ingredients without overbeating.

5. Pour into the prepared pan, place in the oven and bake about 25 minutes, until the cake is lightly browned and a cake tester comes out clean. Remove from the oven and cool on a rack for 10 minutes.

6. Remove the cake from the pan and allow to cool completely before using.

Chocolate Frosting ✳

TIME: 20 minutes   YIELD: 2 cups

Larry
Forgione,
An American
Place,
New York

10 ounces (2½ sticks) unsalted
   butter
¼ cup unsweetened cocoa
1 cup confectioners' sugar, sifted

1 teaspoon vanilla extract
6 large egg yolks
1¼ pounds semisweet chocolate,
   melted and cooled

1. In a saucepan over medium heat, melt butter with ⅓ cup water and the cocoa, stirring until smooth. Remove from heat, transfer to a mixing bowl and let cool.

2. Add confectioners' sugar and vanilla, and stir until smooth. Stir in egg yolks until smooth, and then chocolate. Use immediately.

Cream Cheese Frosting ✳

TIME: 15 minutes   YIELD: Frosting for top and sides of a 9-inch three-layer cake

Craig
Claiborne,
food editor,
*The New York
Times*

2 cups sifted confectioners' sugar
½ pound cream cheese
4 tablespoons unsalted butter, at
   room temperature

2 teaspoons vanilla extract

1. Sift sugar into the bowl of an electric mixer. Beat in remaining ingredients.

2. Beat until smooth and creamy.

Basic Ganache ❊

TIME: 30 minutes, plus cooling   YIELD: Enough for about 75 small truffles

1 pound bittersweet couverture chocolate, like Valrhona

1 cup heavy cream

Robert
Linxe,
La Maison
du Chocolat,
Paris

1. Chop chocolate with large serrated knife, and place in a 3-quart bowl.

2. Place cream in saucepan, bring to boil and remove from heat. Bring to boil and remove from heat twice more. Wait 20 seconds, then pour cream over chocolate. Use a wooden spoon to mash the chocolate until it is soft. Whisk to combine, starting in center of bowl and gradually working out. Stop whisking as soon as mixture is blended. Ganache can keep in the refrigerator up to two weeks.

Milk Chocolate Ganache ❊

TIME: 15 minutes, plus overnight chilling   YIELD: About 3¾ cups

14 ounces milk chocolate, chopped   3 cups heavy cream

Bill
Yosses,
pastry chef,
New York

1. Place chocolate in a heat-proof bowl. In a small saucepan bring cream to a boil. Pour hot cream over chocolate, and let sit for 3 minutes. Whisk until thoroughly combined and slightly cooled, then cover and refrigerate overnight.

2. Before using ganache, transfer it to the bowl of an electric mixer and whip on medium-low speed, just until it holds soft peaks. Do not overwhip.

Pastry Cream ❊

TIME: 10 minutes, plus cooling   YIELD: About 2 cups

Dorie
Greenspan,
food writer

2 cups whole milk
1 plump, moist vanilla bean, split
   lengthwise, pulp and seeds
   scraped out
6 large egg yolks

½ cup sugar
⅓ cup cornstarch, sifted
3½ tablespoons unsalted butter,
   softened

1. Bring milk, vanilla bean pulp and pod to a boil. Cover pan, turn off heat and let rest for at least 10 minutes or for up to 1 hour.

2. Fill a large bowl with ice cubes, and set aside a smaller bowl that can hold finished cream.

3. Whisk yolks, sugar and cornstarch together in a heavy-bottomed saucepan. Whisking constantly, drizzle in one-quarter of the hot milk. When yolks are warm, add the rest of the liquid in a steadier stream. Remove pod, return pan to medium heat and, whisking vigorously, bring mixture to boil. Boil—still whisking—for 1 to 2 minutes before pressing cream through a sieve into the small bowl. Set bowl into ice bath, add cold water and stir frequently to cool cream to 140 degrees on a candy thermometer. Stir in butter. Keep cream over ice until it is completely cool.

Meringue Topping ❊

TIME: 20 minutes   YIELD: 2½ cups

Claudia
Fleming,
pastry chef,
New York

3 large egg whites
⅓ cup plus 1 tablespoon
   confectioners' sugar

⅓ cup plus 1 tablespoon
   granulated sugar
½ teaspoon orange extract

1. Bring a saucepan of water to a simmer. In a stainless-steel bowl, whisk together egg whites and both sugars. Place over simmering water, and whisk mixture constantly until hot to the touch. Remove from heat.

2. With an electric mixer set on high speed, whip mixture until stiff and shiny. Add orange extract, and whip an additional few seconds. Smooth over surface of cake or tart.

Crème Anglaise ✳

TIME: 10 minutes, plus cooling   YIELD: About 2½ cups

1 cup whole milk
1 cup heavy cream
2 plump, moist vanilla beans, split
   lengthwise, pulp and seeds
   scraped out

6 large egg yolks
½ cup sugar

Dorie
Greenspan,
food writer

1. Bring milk, cream and vanilla bean pulp and pod to a boil. Cover pan, turn off heat and let rest for at least 10 minutes or for up to 1 hour.

2. Fill a large bowl with ice cubes, and set aside a smaller bowl that can hold finished cream.

3. Whisk yolks and sugar together in a heavy-bottomed saucepan. Whisking constantly, drizzle in one-quarter of the hot liquid. When yolks are warm, add the rest of the liquid in a steadier stream. Remove pod, return pan to medium heat and, whisking vigorously, cook cream until it thickens slightly, lightens in color and reaches 180 degrees on a candy thermometer. Alternatively, you can coat a wooden spoon with cream, then draw your finger across it; if cream doesn't run into the track you have created, it's done.

4. Immediately remove pan from heat, and allow cream to rest for a few minutes. Strain cream into the small bowl, set bowl into ice bath, add cold water and, stirring frequently, cool completely. Cover cream and chill, if possible for 24 hours.

Brandied Custard Sauce ✳

TIME: 15 minutes   YIELD: 1¼ cups

Melissa
Clark, food
writer

½ cup heavy cream
½ cup milk
3½ tablespoons sugar
½ vanilla bean, split lengthwise,
   pulp and seeds scraped out

3 large egg yolks
1 tablespoon brandy
Freshly grated nutmeg, for
   garnish

1. In a saucepan over medium heat, whisk together cream and milk with 2 tablespoons sugar, vanilla bean pod and pulp.

2. In a bowl, whisk egg yolks with remaining sugar. When cream heats to just below a simmer, drizzle half of it into egg yolk mixture, whisking constantly. Add yolk mixture back into saucepan, whisking constantly.

3. Cook sauce over low heat, stirring with a wooden spoon, until it is thick enough to coat back of spoon, about 5 minutes. Strain mixture into a bowl and stir in brandy. Serve warm or cold.

Vanilla Mousseline ✳

TIME: 20 minutes, plus chilling   YIELD: About 1½ cups

Dorie
Greenspan,
food writer

1 egg
⅓ cup confectioners' sugar
3 tablespoons melted butter
1 teaspoon vanilla extract

Pinch of salt
1 cup heavy cream, whipped to
   soft peaks

1. Bring a small pot of water to a simmer. In the bowl of an electric mixer, combine egg and sugar. Place bowl over water, and whisk steadily until mixture is hot (about 130 degrees) and foamy, about 5 minutes.

2. Remove bowl from heat, and whip in mixer until mixture is thick and slightly cooled, about 3 minutes. Drizzle in melted butter, vanilla and salt.

Continue whipping until cool and thick. Cover bowl with plastic wrap, and chill for at least one hour. Just before serving, fold cream lightly into mixture.

Lemon Cream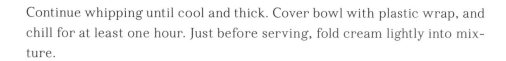

TIME: 30 minutes, plus chilling   YIELD: About 3½ cups

Juice of 3 lemons
½ cup plus 2 tablespoons sugar
2 egg yolks
2 tablespoons unsalted butter

1 vanilla bean, split lengthwise,
    pulp and seeds scraped out
½ teaspoon salt
1 cup heavy cream

Pichet
Ong,
pastry chef,
New York

1. In the top of a double boiler set over simmering water, whisk together all ingredients except cream. Cook, whisking constantly, until thick, about 15 minutes. Remove vanilla bean. Let cool, then refrigerate for at least 1 hour.

2. Whip heavy cream to medium-stiff peaks, then fold it into cold lemon curd. Refrigerate until ready to use.

Praline Powder

TIME: 30 minutes   YIELD: ½ cup

⅓ cup slivered blanched almonds   ½ cup sugar

Michel
Bras, chef,
Laguiole,
France

1. Toast almonds until golden brown. Set aside.

2. Combine the sugar and 3 tablespoons water in a heavy, shallow pan. Cook over medium heat without stirring until the sugar turns a rich honey brown. Stir in the toasted almonds, then immediately pour the mixture out onto a baking sheet or marble slab. Allow to cool 10 to 15 minutes.

3. Pulverize in a food processor and store airtight.

Dulce de Leche ✳

TIME: 1½ hours   YIELD: 2 cups

Rafael
Palomino,
Sonora,
Port Chester,
New York

1 quart whole milk
2 cups sugar

¼ teaspoon baking soda
Pinch of ground cinnamon

1. Combine ingredients in a large heavy saucepan. Place over medium heat and cook without stirring until mixture boils, 15 to 20 minutes. Briefly remove from heat.

2. Reduce heat to low and cook, stirring frequently with a wooden spoon, 45 minutes to one hour. When mixture becomes a caramel color and is thick enough that you can see the bottom of the pan as you stir, remove it from heat. Use at room temperature or cover and refrigerate.

NOTE: For *cajeta,* substitute goat's milk for cow's milk; add 2 teaspoons cornstarch.

Raspberry Coulis ✳

TIME: 5 minutes   YIELD: About 1 cup

Dorie
Greenspan,
food writer

1 pint fresh red raspberries
3 tablespoons sugar,
   approximately, or more to taste

2 tablespoons raspberry eau de
   vie or liqueur, optional

Put berries and sugar in a blender or food processor, and puree. Add sugar if needed. Press coulis through a strainer to eliminate seeds. Add liqueur or eau de vie if using. Use immediately or refrigerate for up to a day.

Fudge Sauce

TIME: 30 minutes   YIELD: 3½ cups

1¼ cups sugar
1 cup heavy cream
¾ cup milk
¾ cup light corn syrup
4 tablespoons (½ stick) unsalted
   butter

½ pound unsweetened chocolate,
   chopped
1 tablespoon vanilla

Village
Restaurant,
New York

1. In a heavy saucepan over medium heat, combine sugar, cream, milk, corn syrup and butter. Cook, stirring frequently, for about 20 minutes, until mixture reaches about 220 degrees on a candy thermometer and becomes a pale caramel.

2. Remove pan from heat, and stir in chocolate until it melts. Stir in ⅓ cup water and vanilla. Use warm or at room temperature.

Hot Fudge Sauce ✳

TIME: 10 minutes   YIELD: 3 cups

Kay
Rentschler,
food writer

2 cups heavy cream
4 tablespoons unsalted butter
½ cup light brown sugar
¾ cup granulated sugar
¼ teaspoon fine sea salt
2 ounces bittersweet chocolate in
   small pieces

1¼ cups sifted high-fat Dutch-
   process cocoa like Valrhona,
   Pernigotti or Droste
½ teaspoon vanilla extract

1. In a medium saucepan, combine cream, butter, sugars and salt. Bring to a simmer over medium-low heat. Simmer 45 seconds. Add chocolate, and whisk to dissolve. Remove from heat, add cocoa and whisk until no lumps remain.

2. Return the pan to low heat, and simmer sauce until glossy, whisking constantly, 20 seconds. Remove from heat, and stir in vanilla. Serve warm. To reheat sauce, warm in a saucepan over low heat, stirring constantly. Do not boil.

Marshmallow Sauce ✳

TIME: 20 minutes   YIELD: 4 cups

Kay
Rentschler,
food writer

1 large egg white
¾ cup sugar
½ cup light corn syrup
1 tablespoon unflavored gelatin

¼ teaspoon fine sea salt
1 teaspoon vanilla extract

1. Place egg white in the bowl of a standing mixer fitted with whisk attachment, and set aside. Measure sugar, and set 3 teaspoons aside.

2. Combine remaining sugar and the corn syrup in a medium saucepan with ¼ cup water, and bring to a boil over medium heat, stirring to com-

bine. Cook syrup without stirring until it reaches 240 degrees on a candy thermometer.

3. As sugar cooks, pour ¾ cup cold water into a small saucepan, and sprinkle gelatin on it. Let stand 5 minutes. Put the pan over burner on very low heat, and stir to dissolve. Do not overheat. Leave the pan on warm burner.

4. Just before sugar syrup reaches 240 degrees, beat the egg white on low speed until foamy. Add 1 teaspoon of reserved sugar and the salt. Increase speed to high, and continue beating, sprinkling with remaining 2 teaspoons sugar, until medium-stiff peaks have formed. With the mixer running, pour syrup into egg white. Beat on high speed 2 minutes. Add dissolved gelatin. Beat until fluffy and cool, about 5 minutes. Add vanilla.

5. The sauce will hold at room temperature for 4 hours. After refrigeration, the sauce may be heated over a double boiler until lukewarm, and beaten in a standing mixer until fluffy.

Caramel Sauce ☀

TIME: ½ hour   YIELD: About 2 cups

1½ cups sugar	Pinch of salt
1 tablespoon light corn syrup	1 tablespoon cold unsalted butter
1½ cups heavy cream	½ teaspoon vanilla extract

Kay
Rentschler,
food writer

1. In a heavy medium-size saucepan, combine half cup water and sugar. Stir briefly to combine. Cover and bring to simmer over medium heat; uncover the pan, and add the corn syrup. Continue boiling until the sugar begins to color, about 10 minutes. Reduce the heat to low.

2. In a small saucepan, bring cream and salt to a simmer over medium heat. Remove from heat and keep warm.

3. When caramel is deep golden brown (about 345 degrees on a candy thermometer), remove from heat. After 30 seconds, add hot cream little by little, whisking to dissolve caramel. Stir in butter and vanilla. Serve at room temperature.

Butterscotch Sauce ✳

TIME: 40 minutes   YIELD: 3 cups

Kay
Rentschler,
food writer

3½ cups heavy cream
4 tablespoons unsalted butter
½ cup dark brown sugar
½ cup light brown sugar

2 teaspoons light corn syrup
¼ teaspoon fine sea salt
1 teaspoon vanilla extract
2 teaspoons dark rum

1. Pour the cream into a large saucepan, and bring to a simmer over low heat. Pull the saucepan almost off burner, and reduce cream until thickened and measures about 2½ cups, whisking frequently, about 30 minutes. Pour hot cream into a glass measuring cup, and set aside.

2. In the same saucepan, melt butter over low heat until foamy. Add sugars and corn syrup, and stir with a wooden spoon until melted and bubbly, about 1 minute. Pour the cream into the saucepan, whisking constantly, until sugars have dissolved completely and sauce is smooth, about 1 minute. Remove the pan from heat. Add salt, vanilla and rum. Serve warm. To reheat sauce, warm in a saucepan over low heat, stirring constantly. Do not boil.

Ginger Butterscotch Sauce ✳

TIME: 25 minutes, plus cooling   YIELD: 3½ cups

Pichet
Ong,
pastry chef,
New York

1 pound dark brown sugar
2½ ounces (about 4 inches) fresh
    ginger root, peeled and sliced
    into coins
1 vanilla bean, split lengthwise,
    pulp and seeds scraped out

10 tablespoons (5 ounces)
    unsalted butter, cubed
2 cups heavy cream
¾ teaspoon salt

1. Place sugar, ginger and vanilla pod and pulp in a heavy saucepan over medium heat. Cook, stirring occasionally, until sugar is molten and fra-

grant with ginger and vanilla, about 8 minutes. (It won't melt entirely but will be somewhat crumbly.) Add butter (stand back, it will foam up). Stir until melted and smooth, about 2 minutes.

2. Pour cream and salt into the pot, stirring, and bring to a simmer. Let sauce bubble until thickened, about 8 minutes. Let cool for at least ½ hour, then strain out ginger and vanilla pod.

3. Warm sauce before serving. This sauce will keep for up to 2 weeks in the refrigerator.

Strawberry Sauce

TIME: 10 minutes   YIELD: 3 cups

2 pounds ripe strawberries,
  hulled
½ to ⅔ cup sugar (depending on
  berries' sweetness)

2 teaspoons cornstarch
Juice of ½ lemon
Pinch of salt

Kay
Rentschler,
food writer

1. Combine ingredients in a medium saucepan over medium-low heat. Stir gently until sugar dissolves and berries are soft, about 10 minutes.

2. Remove from heat, and cool.

Cherry Sauce ✳

TIME: 25 minutes, plus overnight chilling   YIELD: About 7 cups

Village
Restaurant,
New York

1¼ cups sugar
Large pinch of freshly ground
    black pepper
2 pounds Bing cherries, pitted
    (about 5 cups)

¾ cup kirsch
¼ cup crème de cassis
1 tablespoon balsamic vinegar

1. In a saucepan, combine sugar and pepper with 1 cup of water, and bring to a boil.

2. Put cherries in a large bowl, and pour hot syrup over them. Let cool for 1 minute before adding kirsch, crème de cassis and vinegar. Stir to combine, and refrigerate overnight or up to one week.

Passion Fruit Sauce ✳

TIME: 30 minutes, plus chilling   YIELD: 1 cup

Alain
Ducasse
at the
Essex House,
New York

⅓ cup sugar
1 stalk fresh lemongrass, in pieces
⅔ cup passion fruit nectar (sold
    in fancy food shops)

2 tablespoons lemon juice

1. Mix sugar with ¼ cup water in a small saucepan, simmer until sugar dissolves, add lemongrass and set aside to cool 20 minutes.

2. Stir in passion fruit nectar and lemon juice. Refrigerate.

Tropical Fruit Sauce ☀

TIME: 30 minutes   YIELD: About 2 cups

1 ripe mango, peeled, pitted and finely diced

3 ripe kiwis, peeled and finely diced

4 clementines, peeled and divided in segments

2 star fruit (carambolas), diced

½ cup dark rum

¾ cup fresh orange juice

3 tablespoons sugar

Juice of 1 lime

Florence Fabricant

1. Force half the mango through a sieve into a saucepan. Place the rest in a bowl. Add the remaining fruit to the bowl.

2. Mix the rum, orange juice, sugar and lime juice with the mango puree in the saucepan. Bring to a simmer.

3. Add the fruit to the saucepan, remove from heat and set aside until just before serving.

4. Serve sauce cold or warmed.

Orange Confit ☀

TIME: 9 to 16 hours, plus overnight resting   YIELD: 16 servings

4 big navel oranges

2½ pounds sugar

Scott Carsberg, Lampreia, Seattle, Washington

1. Fill a saucepan large enough to hold oranges with water; bring to a boil. Blanch oranges for 30 seconds, then remove, change water and repeat. Carefully quarter oranges vertically. Return them to saucepan with half the sugar and water to cover. Bring to a boil, then cook over lowest possible heat, adding water as necessary to keep them covered. Cook for 8 hours, then remove from heat and let sit overnight.

2. Drain oranges and repeat process with remaining sugar and water to cover. Oranges are done when very tender but not falling apart, from 1 to 8 hours. Remove pot from heat and let cool, then refrigerate oranges with their syrup. Oranges will keep, refrigerated, for several weeks.

NOTE: For sliced confit, there are directions on page 171, step 1.

Candied Grapefruit Rind

Patrick
O'Connell,
The Inn
at Little
Washington,
Washington,
Virginia

4 large pink unblemished
    grapefruit

6 cups sugar

1. Fill 3 4-quart saucepans with water. Place over high heat, and bring to a boil. Cut each grapefruit vertically (through the stem end) into eight wedges. Peel off and reserve rind from each wedge.

2. Trim off pointed ends of rind wedges, and cut each wedge into strips 1½ to 2 inches long and ¼ inch wide. Discard irregular trimmings.

3. When water boils, submerge strips into one pot, keeping them down with a spoon. Return water to a full boil, then boil rind for 2 minutes. Drain rind immediately, then place it in a second pot of boiling water. Return water to a boil, and boil for 2 minutes. Drain. Place rind in third pot of water. Boil 2 minutes. Drain well.

4. In one pot, combine 5 cups of the sugar and 5 cups water. Boil over medium heat until sugar has dissolved. Add rind to sugar syrup, making sure it is submerged. Boil, stirring occasionally, until candy thermometer reads 238 degrees. Rinds should be translucent.

5. Drain rinds, and transfer them to a wire rack placed over a cookie sheet or waxed paper. Allow them to dry in a single layer in a warm, dry place overnight, until barely sticky.

6. In a large bowl, toss rinds with remaining cup of sugar, to coat evenly. Store in a covered container at room temperature. If rinds become moist or sticky, toss them in sugar again.

Caramel Oranges

TIME: 20 minutes   YIELD: About 1½ cups

3 small oranges, preferably a
  mixture of sweet and blood
  oranges

½ cup sugar
Pinch of salt

Claudia
Fleming,
pastry chef,
New York

1. Peel oranges, removing white membranes. Separate into segments.

2. In a small heavy saucepan, combine sugar and salt with ¼ cup water. Stir mixture over medium heat until sugar dissolves, raise heat to medium-high and cook caramel without stirring until it turns medium amber in color, for about 10 minutes. Immediately remove from heat.

3. Very carefully, add another ¼ cup water to pot (caramel may splatter or bubble over). Set saucepan over low heat, and cook, stirring, until caramel dissolves and is smooth, for about 5 minutes. Add orange segments to pan, and stir to combine.

Bittersweet Caramelized Orange Peel and Orange Syrup

TIME: 1 hour   YIELD: About 1½ cups peel and 2½ cups syrup

Scalini
Fedeli,
New York

6 to 8 oranges
3 cups sugar

2 vanilla beans, split lengthwise

1. Using a sharp vegetable peeler, remove 1- to 1½-inch-long strips of peel from oranges, removing only the orange-colored zest. If necessary, use a sharp knife to remove white pith from strips. Trim ends, and cut strips into slices about ⅟₁₆-inch wide.

2. In a 2-quart saucepan, combine orange strips, sugar, vanilla beans and 4 cups water. Place over high heat to bring to boil, and then reduce heat to low. Simmer until peel is tender to the bite and syrup has thickened, 35 to 45 minutes.

3. Allow peel and syrup to cool to room temperature, and then transfer to a covered container. Store refrigerated. If desired, peel, well drained, and syrup can each be used separately.

NOTE: Directions for candied orange zest are given on page 160, step 1.

Cookie Paint ✳

TIME: 15 minutes, plus resting   YIELD: Enough paint to decorate about 4 dozen cookies

Bill
Yosses,
pastry chef,
New York

1 cup all-purpose flour
4 large eggs

2 tablespoons light corn syrup
Food coloring

1. Combine the flour, the eggs and the corn syrup in the bowl of an electric mixer fitted with a whisk attachment. Beat until smooth, then allow the mixture to rest at room temperature for 1 hour.

2. Divide the mixture among containers, using one container for each color planned. Stir drops of food coloring into the containers for the desired colors.

MENU SUGGESTIONS

Many of the recipes in this book were developed for special occasions or are suitable for holidays and other celebrations. Here is a selection of them, for parties throughout the year.

New Year's Day Brunch:
Raisin Cake with Port (p. 89), Tropical Fruit Trifle (p. 382), Holiday Trifle (p. 385), Morning Bread Pudding (p. 421), Spice Drops (p. 152)

Epiphany:
Galette des Rois (p. 310), Rum Balls (p. 504)

Super Bowl Sunday:
Banana Turnovers (p. 320), Winter Fruit Salad (p. 340), Caramelized Chocolate Bread Pudding (p. 424), Cornmeal Biscotti (p. 156), Brownies (p. 159)

Asian New Year:
Chinese Walnut Cookies (p. 145), Thai Coffee Crème Caramel (p. 393), Green Tea Rice Pudding with Candied Ginger (p. 407), Jasmine Tea Truffles (p. 514)

Valentine's Day:
Molten Chocolate Cakes (p. 35), Crème Brûleé (p. 394), Baked Chocolate Pudding for Two (p. 403), Coeur à la Crème (p. 442), Chocolate–Port Wine Truffles (p. 507)

Mardi Gras:

Praline Cookies (p. 146), Lane Cake (p. 53), Creole Pralines (p. 505)

Birthdays, Anniversaries—for Children, for Adults:

Granny's Chocolate Cake (p. 26), Angel Food Cake (p. 75), Chocolate Tartlets (p. 295), Baked Alaska (p. 486)

St. Patrick's Day:

Sticky Toffee Pudding (p. 416), Mint Chocolate Chip Ice Cream (p. 449)

Easter:

Ricotta Tart (p. 104), Kulich (p. 114), Limoncello Babas with Lemon Cream (p. 124), Raspberry Semifreddo (p. 496), Strawberry Tiramisu (p. 324)

Passover:

Orange-Date-Walnut Passover Cake (p. 94), Intense Chocolate Mousse Cake (p. 30)

Cinco de Mayo:

Dulce de Leche Cheesecake (p. 106)

Mother's Day:

Strawberry Cream Sponge Roulade (p. 48), Warm Vanilla Cakes (p. 76)

Memorial Day Cookout:

All-in-One Chocolate Cake (p. 28), Bing Cherry Doughnuts (p. 126), Cherry Amaretto Folded Tart (p. 282), Chocolate Chip Cookies (p. 138)

Father's Day:

Double Crust Peach Pie (p. 248), Chocolate Cheesecake (p. 98), Summer Pudding (p. 384), Cherry Ice Cream (p. 450)

Fourth of July:

Rhubarb-Berry Cobbler (p. 220), Strawberry-Sour Cream Shortcake (p. 226), Blueberry Chiffon Pie (p. 242), Classic Strawberry Tart (p. 271), Old-Fashioned Peach-Raspberry Duff (p. 195)

Bastille Day:

Brioche Peach Tarts (p. 118), Red Raspberry Napoleons (p. 314)

Labor Day Picnic:

Original Plum Torte (p. 39), Bolzano Apple Cake (p. 40), Lemon Pound Cake (p. 57), Big Apple Pie (p. 233), Sweet-Corn Ice Cream (p. 459)

Rosh Hashanah:

Rustic Apple Tart with Cider Sorbet (p. 265), Jam-Filled Mandelbrot (p. 158), Sugar-Dipped, Pan-Seared Apples with Warm Apple Butter (p. 366)

Columbus Day:

Almond, Apple and Vin Cotto Cake (p. 41), Orange and Olive Oil Cake (p. 69)

Halloween:

Somerset Cider Cake (p. 62), Two-Crust Pumpkin Pie (p. 257), Pumpkin Mousse (p. 432)

Thanksgiving:

Cranberry Upside-Down Cake (p. 83), Sauteed Apple Pie (p. 236), Bourbon-Pecan Pie (p. 238), Pumpkin Pie with Ginger (p. 256), Maple Bourbon Sweet Potato Pie (p. 260), Cider-Pecan Tart (p. 293)

Hanukkah:

Quince Beignets with Orange Flower Crème Anglaise (p. 172), Loukoumades (p. 174)

Christmas:

Chestnut Cake with Chocolate Ganache and Single-Malt Scotch Syrup (p. 42), Castagnaccio (p. 74), Postmodern Fruitcake (p. 84), Spicy Gingerbread (p. 88), Muscadine Yule Log (p. 90), One-Pan Christmas Cake (p. 92), Painted Christmas Cookies (p. 148), Cocoa Christmas Cookies (p. 150)

New Year's Eve:

Magie Noire (p. 31), Glazed Mango with Sour Cream Sherbet and Black Pepper (p. 375), Pear and Rum-Raisin Charlotte (p. 379), Eggnog Bread Pudding (p. 427), Tropical Baked Alaska (p. 488)

SOURCES FOR INGREDIENTS
AND EQUIPMENT

Adriana's Caravan
800-316-0820
www.adrianascaravan.com
Excellent spices, dried herbs,
seasonings and ethnic
ingredients

A. L. Bazzini Co.
212-334-1280
800-228-0172
www.bazzininuts.com
Nuts, dried fruit

www.Amazon.com
Good source for equipment and
many basic ingredients

The Baker's Catalogue
King Arthur Flour
800-827-6836
www.bakerscatalogue.com
The best all-around source
for equipment and baking ingredients,
especially flours, sugars, spices,
chocolate, nuts and nut flours

Bridge Kitchenware
800-274-3435
www.bridgekitchenware.com
Equipment, especially French molds and
baking pans

Broadway Panhandler
866-266-5927
www.broadwaypanhandler.com
Equipment

Chef's Warehouse
www.chefswarehouse.com
For ingredients, including fruit purees
and other items used by chefs, but
available in consumer-size quantities

Chocolate.com
www.chocolate.com
Chocolate from a huge array of
producers

Cooking.com
www.cooking.com
Equipment

Dean & DeLuca
800-221-7714
www.deandeluca.com
Ingredients, including flours,
chocolate, seasonings, sugars; some
equipment

Eli Zabar's Eli's Manhattan, Vinegar
Factory
212-987-0885
212-717-8100
www.elizabar.com
Ingredients, including nuts, flour,
seasonings, candied fruit peels,
especially grapefruit; some
equipment

Ethnic Grocer
www.ethnicgrocer.com
Ethnic ingredients sorted by category,
organic and kosher ingredients

Kalustyan's
800-352-3451
www.kalustyans.com
Exotic ingredients, grains, fruit pastes,
candied fruit, dried fruit, nuts

New York Cake and Baking Distributor
800-942-2539
www.nycake.com
Baking equipment, some ingredients

Sur La Table
800-243-0852
www.surlatable.com
Equipment

Sweet Celebrations
800-328-6722
www.sweetc.com
Source for bakeware and ingredients,
especially for cake-decorating; this
company now owns Maid of Scandinavia

Williams-Sonoma
877-812-6235
www.williams-sonoma.com
Equipment, some ingredients

Zabar's
212-787-2000; 800-697-6301 (outside
New York City)
www.zabars.com
Equipment, ingredients

ACKNOWLEDGMENTS

Over the years, the food pages of *The New York Times* have always saved room for dessert. I am extremely grateful for the rich resource of recipes that has resulted from the newspaper's sweet tooth. It made assembling this book both daunting and delightful.

Starting with Craig Claiborne, who could deliver a recipe for some outrageously rich home-style specialty of the Deep South, where he was born, as easily as he could a French chef's magnificent tour de force, and continuing with the same ecumenical tastes to the present, I must thank all the dedicated writers, reporters and chefs who contributed recipes to the Living and then the Dining sections. And I am proud to be among them.

Editors, a meticulous copy desk, art directors, food stylists, recipe testers and photographers all deserve my thanks, too. Their talents made the presentation of an honest chocolate cake, a silken cream pie, an elaborate dacquoise, a jewel-like fruit terrine and refreshing sorbets seasoned with cutting-edge herbs or spices both smart and alluring. And they made trends in desserts in New York, the United States and the world stand out in sharp focus.

The book department of *The New York Times*, especially Mike Levitas, Alex Ward and Tomi Murata, provided the needed encouragement and assistance to help sort through all the material. Without them this book would not have been possible. Deborah Leiderman, who was a copy editor at the *Times,* was extremely helpful, too. My deepest gratitude goes to all of them.

I was lucky to have Elizabeth Beier as my editor at St. Martin's Press. Her confidence in this project never wavered and was immensely encouraging to me. Her followthrough, along with the efforts of Amelie Littell, Steve Snider, Cheryl Mamaril, Kathryn Parise and Michelle Richter have resulted in a book that is handsome and mouthwatering, and has made me proud.

As always, because my expertise with technology is less advanced than my ability to handle a wire whisk or a rolling pin, Bruce Stark was there when I needed him to make sense of formats and to unravel glitches.

And kisses go to Richard Fabricant, a man who will not hesitate to eat dessert first, who still dotes on milk and cookies, and who, as always, was my best, most invaluable champion.

INDEX